Student Assessment Learning Guide

for use with

UNDERSTANDING BUSINESS

Fifth Edition

William G. Nickels
University of Maryland

James M. McHugh
St. Louis Community College at Forest Park

Susan M. McHugh
Applied Learning Systems

Prepared by
Barbara Barrett
St. Louis Community College - Meramec

Boston   Burr Ridge, IL   Dubuque, IA   Madison, WI   New York   San Francisco   St. Louis
Bangkok   Bogotá   Caracas   Lisbon   London   Madrid
Mexico City   Milan   New Delhi   Seoul   Singapore   Sydney   Taipei   Toronto

Irwin/McGraw-Hill

*A Division of The **McGraw·Hill** Companies*

Student Assessment and Learning Guide for use with
UNDERSTANDING BUSINESS

Copyright ©1999 by The McGraw-Hill Companies, Inc. All rights reserved.
Previous editions copyright 1987, 1990, 1993, and 1996 by Richard D. Irwin, Inc.
Printed in the United States of America.
The contents of, or parts thereof, may be reproduced for use with
UNDERSTANDING BUSINESS
William G. Nickels, James M. McHugh and Susan M. McHugh
provided such reproductions bear copyright notice and may not be reproduced in
any form for any other purpose without permission of the publisher.

1 2 3 4 5 6 7 8 9 0 QPD/QPD 9 3 2 1 0 9 8

ISBN 0-07-289215-3

http://www.mhhe.com

TO OUR STUDENTS

This study guide is designed to give you, the Introduction to Business student, every advantage in mastering the concepts presented in the fifth edition of *Understanding Business,* fifth edition, by Bill Nickels, Jim McHugh and Susan McHugh.

Using this study guide will give you an edge; you will go beyond just memorizing terms, to developing and using the critical thinking and creative problem solving skills that are so important in today's dynamic business environment.

Using The Study Guide

There are many different ways to learn, so I can only make suggestions about how to use this guide more effectively. You may find a different way, which suits you better.

First, this study guide is not designed to replace reading the text! In fact, reading the text is an integral part of using this study guide. You can use the guide to help point out places where you need more work, or need to review. The guide is very detailed, and requires you not only to remember facts, but also to apply concepts in a way that will help you to develop a better understanding of today's business environment.

You will find that there is a lot of writing in completing these exercises. Writing the answers to the questions, rather than just choosing a number or matching a term with a letter, will help to reinforce the material. You will also be better prepared to answer essay or short answer questions when you have studied by writing out answers in your own words.

Finally, to make effective use of this study guide, I suggest that you:

- Read the text before each class period, and outline important concepts. You will probably have a syllabus that outlines the reading assignments for each class.
- Attend class and take good, detailed notes. Ask questions in class; get involved!
- Do the exercises in the study guide *after* you have completed the first two steps. . I would suggest that you do the exercises in stages, and not try to do the whole chapter at one sitting. For example, if there are 6 learning goals, do the exercises pertaining to the first three learning goals on one day, then complete the remaining exercises the next day. Or, do the factual based exercises one day, the critical thinking exercises the next, and so on.
- Do *all* the exercises in the guide, not just the ones that take less time!
- Review your answers, and mark the questions you had problems answering. Then, reread the section of the text that deals with those areas.
- Before a test, review your class notes, the text and the study guide material.
- Remember, your instructor may add material in class which is not in the text, and the study guide won't cover that material. That takes us back to the first suggestions: read the book before class, attend every class, take notes, and get involved!

Design Of This Study Guide

Each chapter in this guide contains the following sections to help you be successful in this Introduction to Business course.

- *Learning goals:* Each learning goal is listed in the order in which it appears in the text. This is to help you focus on what is important throughout the chapter. The appropriate learning goal for each exercise is also noted in the side margin as you go through the chapter.

- *Learning the Language:* This section identifies the key terms and definitions from the chapter. This is a matching section, in which you read the definition then choose the appropriate term. Many of the definitions will be direct quotes from the chapter, or a slight variation.

- *Retention Check:* These exercises help you to learn the facts of the material from the text. You will be writing answers to factually based questions from the chapter, organized by learning goals. This section is designed to develop your knowledge of the text material. I suggest you keep the book nearby while doing these exercises, but do as much as you can without opening the book. This will help you to determine the areas where you need to review.

- *Critical Thinking Exercises:* Business people need a variety of skills. Among the most important skills you can bring to a job is the ability to think for yourself, analyze problems, develop solutions based upon your analysis, and present the solutions in written form. There are many opportunities to hone these skills with this text. In this section of the study guide, the questions will require you to think and apply the material from the chapter to come up with a solution to the situation presented. These application questions are designed to provide you with the opportunity to enhance your decision-making skills, and understanding of the material. In some cases, there are no definitive answers, only suggested answers.

- *Practice Test:* In all likelihood, you will be required to take some objective exams. The practice test is divided into two sections, multiple choice, and true false. Keep in mind this is only a sample of the types of questions you could see on an exam, and these are not the actual questions you will see on a classroom test! The practice exam will give you the chance to find out what areas of the chapters you need to take some extra time with before your classroom exam.

- *Answers:* The answers to all the Retention Check, Critical Thinking Exercises and Practice Tests are at the end of each chapter.

There is no substitute for just plain hard work. To be successful in tomorrow's work world, you will need to work hard today to develop the skills employers are looking for. The text, *Understanding Business,* and this study guide are designed to help you to be successful by starting you on the road to developing those skills. The rest is up to you. Good Luck!

Acknowledgements

Many thanks are due, and I will be brief. First, thanks to Bill Nickels, Susan McHugh and Jim McHugh, and to Irwin/McGraw-Hill for allowing me to continue my involvement with this wonderful text. Laura Spell, thanks for your patience! To David, Ryan and Chad, thank you for your support, understanding, and computer consultation! And to all my colleagues at the Meramec campus of St. Louis Community College, thanks for your support and encouragement.

Barbara Barrett

CONTENTS

Chapter 1: Finding opportunities in Today's Business Environment 1-1
Appendix: Driver's Ed for the Information Superhighway A1-1
Chapter 2: Economics: The Creation And Distribution Of Wealth 2-1
Chapter 3: Competing in Global Markets 3-1
Chapter 4: Demonstrating Ethical Behavior and Social Responsibility 4-1
Appendix: Working within the Legal Environment of Business A4-1
Chapter 5: Forms of Business Ownership 5-1
Chapter 6: Entrepreneurship and Starting a Small Business 6-1
Chapter 7: Management, Leadership, and Employee Empowerment 7-1
Chapter 8: Organizing a Customer-Driven Business 8-1
Chapter 9: Using the Latest Technology to Produce World-Class Products and Services 9-1
Chapter 10: Motivating Employees and Building Self-Managed Teams 10-1
Chapter 11: Human Resource Management 11-1
Chapter 12: Employee-Management Issues: Unions, Executive Compensation, and Other Issues 12-1
Chapter 13: Marketing: Building Customer and Stakeholder Relationships 13-1
Chapter 14: Developing and Pricing Quality Products and Services 14-1
Chapter 15: Distribution, Wholesaling, and Retailing 15-1
Chapter 16: Promoting Products Using Integrated and Interactive Marketing Communication 16-1
Chapter 17: Using Technology to Manage Information 17-1
Chapter 18: Understanding Financial Information and Accounting 18-1
Chapter 19: Financial Management 19-1
Chapter 20: Securities Markets: Financing and Investing 20-1
Chapter 21: Understanding Money and Financial Institutions 21-1
Chapter 22: Managing Personal Finances: The Road to Entrepreneurship 22-1
Appendix: Managing Risk A22-1

CHAPTER 1
FINDING OPPORTUNITIES IN TODAY'S BUSINESS ENVIRONMENT

LEARNING GOALS

After you have read and studied this chapter, you should be able to:

1. Describe how businesses and nonprofit organizations add to the standard of living and quality of life.

2. Explain the importance of entrepreneurship to the wealth of an economy and show the relationship of profit to risk assumption.

3. Examine how the economic environment and taxes affect businesses.

4. Illustrate how the technological environment has affected businesses.

5. Identify various ways that businesses can meet and beat competition.

6. Demonstrate how the social environment has changed and what the reaction of business has been.

7. Analyze what businesses must do to meet the global challenge.

8. Compare the new quality standards and identify what businesses are doing to meet those standards.

9. Review how trends from the past are being repeated in the present and what that will mean for the service sector.

LEARNING THE LANGUAGE

Listed below are important terms found in the chapter. Choose the correct term for each definition and write it in the space provided.

Business	ISO 14000	Quality of life
Databank	Loss	Risk
Demography	Multiculturalism	Services
Entrepreneur	Nonprofit organization	Stakeholders
Factors of production	Productivity	Standard of living
Goods	Profit	Telecommuting
ISO 9000	Quality	

1. The resources businesses used to create wealth are called _____.

2. _____ is the total output of goods and services in a given period of time divided by work hours.

3. The quality and management assurance standards known as _____ are published by the International Organization for Standardization.

4. _____ refers to the general well-being of a society.

5. An _____ is the person who takes the risk of starting and managing a business.

6. Products, which are intangible, such as heath care and education, are known as _____.

7. A _____ is any activity, which seeks profit by providing goods and services to others.

8. When a business's costs and expenses are more than its revenues a _____ has occurred.

9. You take a _____ when you take a chance that you will lose time and money on a business that may not prove to be profitable.

10. A society's _____ is the general level of ability to buy goods and services.

11. A _____ is an organization whose goals do not include making a personal profit for its owners.

12. An electronic storage file where information is kept is known as a(n) _____.

13. When we study _____, we are looking at a statistical study of the human population to learn its size, density and characteristics.

14. In today's firms, _____ is defined as providing customers with goods and services that go beyond the expected.

15. Houses, food, clothing and TV sets are tangible products known as _____.

16. _____ is the money a business earns above and beyond what it spends for salaries, expenses and other costs.

17. An organization's _____ are the people who stand to gain or lose by its policies and activities.

18. Today, _____ allows workers to stay home and send in their work by telecommunications.

19. The process of optimizing the contribution of people from different cultures is commonly known as _____.

20. Known as _____, this is a collection of the best practices for managing an organization's environmental impacts.

RETENTION CHECK

Learning Goal 1   **What is a Business?**

1. Contrast "standard of living" with "quality of life".

2. Explain how businesses, nonprofit organizations and volunteer groups work to accomplish the same objectives.

Learning Goal 2 **Opportunities for Entrepreneurs**

3. How have entrepreneurs benefited from corporate downsizing?

4. What is the difference between revenue and profit?

5. When does a company experience a loss?

6. What is the relationship between risk and profit?

7. What are the 5 factors of production?

    a. _____   d. _____

    b. _____   e. _____

    c. _____

8. Which two factors of production are considered the key ingredients to making countries rich?

    a. _____   b. _____

9. What factors contribute to keeping poor countries poor?

    a. _____   b. _____   c. _____

Learning Goal 3   **The Business Environment**

10. What are the 5 key environmental factors critical to the success of business?

    a. _____

    b. _____

    c. _____

    d. _____

    e. _____

11. Why is a healthy business environment important?

Learning Goal 3　　**The Economic Environment**

12.　　According to the text, what are four actions governments must take to foster entrepreneurial growth?

　　　　a. _____

　　　　b. _____

　　　　c. _____

　　　　d. _____

Learning Goal 4　　**The Technological Environment**

13.　　What is the Internet?

14.　　What is a CIO and what is the role of the CIO in business?

15.　　What is the most important role for an information manager?

16. What information does a bar code provide?

17. How or where is that information stored?

18. What technology makes it possible for you to receive the right ads about the right products at the right time for you to purchase?

Learning Goal 5 **The Competitive Environment**

19. What are the three elements U.S. companies have found they must offer in order to stay competitive in today's world markets?

   a. _____ b. _____ c. _____

20. Companies compete by:

   a. _____

   b. _____

   c. _____

   d. _____

21. Who or what is "driving" business today?

22. Who are a company's stakeholders?

23. What impact has downsizing had on lower-level workers?

24. How will managers' jobs change?

25. Businesses are finding that in order to be competitive in today's marketplace, they must: a. exceed customer expectations, b. meet the needs of the community, c. meet the needs of employees, and d. have concern for the environment. Briefly discuss the important elements of each of these areas.

   a. _____

   b. _____

   c. _____

   d. _____

Learning Goal 6   **The Social Environment**

26. What are 2 demographic trends which are affecting how we live and providing opportunities for U.S. firms?

    a. _____   b. _____

27. In what ways can a multiculturally diverse population benefit U.S. businesses?

28. The desire for a more comfortable lifestyle combined with an interest in careers outside the home have created a surge in the number of two income families. These families have different needs than workers of the past. How have companies responded to the needs of two career families?

Learning Goal 7   **The Global Environment**

29. What is considered to be the number one global environmental change?

30. What have U.S. firms done in order to become world-class competitors?

31. What does NAFTA stand for and what three countries are parts of the agreement?

32. What impact has NAFTA had in the United States?

33. How do companies (and countries) benefit from free trade?

34. What are three ways in which changes in the global market will affect you?

   a. _____

   b. _____

   c. _____

Learning Goal 8   **The Quality Imperative**

35. In order to qualify for the Baldrige Awards, a company has to show quality as measured in what three ways?

    a. _____

    b. _____

    c. _____

36. What three things are companies required to do by the Baldrige Awards?

    a. _____

    b. _____

    c. _____

37. Name 2 major criteria for the Baldrige award.

    a. _____

    b. _____

38. What is the difference between ISO 9000, ISO 14000 and the Baldrige Awards?

    Why is ISO certification considered to be so important for U.S. firms?

Learning Goal 10 **The Evolution of American Business**

39. Describe the changes in the agricultural and manufacturing industries since the early 1900s.

40. Which industry has generated almost all of our economy's employment increases since the mid-1980s?

41. Briefly describe how the service sector is expected to change in the future.

CRITICAL THINKING EXERCISES

Learning Goal 1

1. Monika lives in Germany, works for the Mercedes plant in her hometown and makes the equivalent of 55 American dollars an hour. Her cousin Joe lives in the United States and works for the Chrysler plant in his hometown. When Monika visits Joe she is amazed at how big his house is compared to hers, his expensive stereo equipment and how well he seems to live. "Boy" says Monika, "I sure can't live like this at home. Why not?"

Learning Goals 1, 2

2. Revelle Industries is a small company located in an area of the country where unemployment has been very high for the last 5 years. In 1990, Revelle was struggling. There were only 20 employees, and profits were low. With new management things began to turn around, and now Revelle employs almost 75 people. This year they sold 120,000 units of their only product line, a component part used in the manufacture of automobiles. The price of their product is $20/unit. The costs of salaries, expenses and other items were $2,050,000. Sales forecasts look good for the next several years, as Revelle has customers world wide and will be expanding their product line in the next 18 months.

   a. What are Revelle's revenues?

   b. What are Revelle's profits?

   c. How has the company generated wealth and created a higher standard of living?

Learning Goal 3

3. "If you were to analyze rich countries versus poor countries to see what caused the differences, you would have to look at the factors of production..."

   Eastern Europe experienced dramatic changes during the 1990's, with changes in both government and economic policies. The newly formed countries are struggling with questions about how to move successfully into the next century. What will be the key to developing the economies of these newly formed countries?

Learning Goal 4

4. Schnucks is a large grocery retailer located in the St. Louis, Missouri area. The company is expanding, and continually improving the technology in their stores. How can scanners and a databank help Schnucks better serve its customers?

Learning Goal 5

5. Consider your college or university:

   a. Who are its competitors?

   b. How does the school "delight" its customers" (HEY! It's <u>not</u> a silly question!)

   c. Who are the school's stakeholders? Does it meet the needs of the stakeholders? Why or why not?

   d. How does it meet the needs of its employees?

   e. How do the answers to these questions affect the school's competitive situation?

   f. Do you see a concern for the environment?

Learning Goal 4, 5, 6

6. Take a look at a company with which you are familiar, for example where you or one of your family is currently employed. How important is technology to the business? What are some of the applications used? What kinds of programs has the company implemented to meet the needs of two career families and other employees? Does the company appear to be competing in the areas described by your text (customers, community, employees and the environment)? Does the company do business internationally?

Learning Goal 6

7. How do the changes and programs companies have implemented to meet the needs of two career families help these companies to be more competitive?

Learning Goals 7, 8

8. How has increased global competition forced U.S. firms to "re-think" quality?

Learning Goal 9

9. How do the changes in the agricultural industry in the early 1900's parallel the changes we have seen in the industrial sector recently?

PRACTICE TEST

Multiple Choice: Circle the best answer.

1. Taxes would not be used to support which of the following activities?

    a. Build a new school
    b. Support people in need
    c. Keep a clean environment
    d. Help run a privately owned day care center

2. A clean environment, safety, free time and health care are elements which contribute to our:

    a. standard of living.
    b. quality of life.
    c. economic environment.
    d. factors of production.

3. Which of the following would be considered a non-profit organization?

    a. Microsoft
    b. UPS
    c. The University of Michigan
    d. Chrysler

4. Businesses owned by _____ grew at a rate faster than all other businesses in the early 1990s.

    a. Asians
    b. Latinos
    c. American Indians
    d. Pacific Islanders

5. Downsizing refers to:

   a. going after a smaller share of a particular market.
   b. building smaller factories.
   c. lowering profit expectations.
   d. eliminating workers or managers to become more efficient.

6. In general, the _____ the risk, the _____ the profit.

   a. higher/higher
   b. lower/higher
   c. 65/lower
   d. faster/quicker

7. Which of the following is (are) not considered a factor of production?

   a. Information
   b. Capital
   c. Labor
   d. Taxes

8. The two factors of production which contribute most to making countries rich are:

   a. land and labor.
   b. capital and land.
   c. entrepreneurship and use of knowledge.
   d. use of knowledge and taxes.

9. All of the following would create an environment that would foster entrepreneurial growth except:

   a. raising taxes and increasing regulations.
   b. passing laws which allow businesses to write enforceable contracts.
   c. establishing a currency that is tradable in world markets.
   d. developing governmental policies eliminating corruption.

10. Information management today is:

    a. becoming less important as computers manage information for us.
    b. only important for large companies such as Toyota and Chase Manhattan.
    c. done primarily at colleges and universities.
    d. becoming increasingly important for businesses and for individuals.

11. Businesses are being driven today by:

    a. the expectations of the owners of the business.
    b. the wants and needs of the customers.
    c. the demands of employees.
    d. management.

12. In today's environment, businesses have found they must do all but which of the following in order to remain competitive?

    a. Meet the needs of all stakeholders of the business.
    b. Meet the needs of employees by supervising them more closely.
    c. Delight customers by exceeding their expectations.
    d. Be aware of potential damage and hazards to the environment.

13. The trend toward two-income families has led to:

    a. businesses paying lower wages and hiring fewer workers.
    b. policies allowing only one family member to work for the same company.
    c. programs such as flexible work schedules, child care and cafeteria benefits.
    d. fewer opportunities in the area of human resource management.

14. The process of maximizing the business contributions of a diverse workforce is known as:

    a. multiculturalism.
    b. ethnocentrism.
    c. globalism.
    d. nationalism.

15. The number one global environmental change is considered to be:

    a. the increase in the number of large companies.
    b. the loss of jobs in the U.S. as a result of competition from Japan.
    c. the increase of U.S. worker productivity.
    d. the growth of international business and free trade.

16. The agreement to increase trade between Canada, the United States and Mexico is known as:

    a. NAFTA.
    b. the E.U.
    c. ASEAN.
    d. NATO.

17. As businesses increasingly serve global markets and exports continue to increase, it is likely that:

    a. fewer jobs will be created in the United States.
    b. students who expect to prosper will have to compete in a changing environment, and continually update their skills.
    c. trade agreements will lose their importance.
    d. cooperation among firms will become less likely.

18. The U.S. award that recognizes firms, which meet customer needs, produce high quality products and have high quality internal operations, is known as:

    a. ISO 9000 Standards.
    b. The Customer Excellence Award.
    c. The Malcolm Baldrige National Quality Award.
    d. ISO 14000 Standards.

19. One reason ISO 9000 standards are so important is that:

    a. they must be met in order to win any quality awards.
    b. most free trade agreements require that these standards be met.
    c. meeting these standards will automatically increase worker productivity.
    d. companies that want to do business with the EU must be certified by ISO standards.

20. Since the mid-1980s, the _____ has generated most of the increases in employment in the United States.

    a. manufacturing sector
    b. agricultural sector
    c. service sector
    d. goods producing

21. Cars and machine tools are a part of the _____.

    a. goods producing sector
    b. services sector
    c. agricultural sector
    d. intangible services sector

TRUE/FALSE

1. _____ Mariko, who lives in Tokyo, makes the equivalent of approximately $35,000 per year, while Donada, living in the United States makes only $25,000. From this you can assume Mariko has a higher standard of living than Donada.

2. _____ Business skills are useful and necessary in non-profit institutions.

3. _____ Businesses, nonprofit organizations and volunteer organizations often work for similar objectives.

4. _____ An entrepreneur is an individual who has worked for a nonprofit organization for his or her entire career.

5. _____ Profit refers to the difference between risk and revenue.

6. _____ A loss occurs when revenues exceed expenses.

7. _____ High taxes and increased government regulations can actually drive entrepreneurs out of a particular country, state or city.

8. _____ Electronic data interchange has allowed for a smoother flow of information and goods between manufacturers and retailers.

9. _____ As businesses move toward self-managed teams, employees will need less education than they have in the past.

10. _____ The Bureau of the Census predicts that the U.S. population will remain essentially the same throughout the next century.

11. _____ Telecommuting has increased opportunities for men and women to raise families and increase their standard of living.

12. _____ A more diverse, multicultural population will give U.S. workers an advantage when working and competing in a global marketplace.

13. _____ Cooperation among international firms could lead to the downfall of many economies as people are laid off due to increased competition.

14. _____ Most U.S. companies have not met ISO certification standards.

15. _____ When workers in the industrial sector were laid off, many of them went back to work in the agricultural sector.

ANSWERS

LEARNING THE LANGUAGE

1. Factors of production	8. Loss	15. Goods
2. Productivity	9. Risk	16. Profit
3. ISO 9000	10. Standard of living	17. Stakeholders
4. Quality of life	11. Non profit	18 Telecommuting
5. Entrepreneur	12. Databank	19. Multiculturalism
6. Service	13. Demography	20. ISO 14000
7. Business	14. Quality	

RETENTION CHECK

Learning Goal 1   **What is a Business?**

1. Standard of living refers to the amount of goods and services people can buy with the money they have to spend. Quality of life refers to our general well being, such things as freedom, a clean environment, schools, access to health care, safety, free time, and other things that lead to a sense of satisfaction

2. Businesses and nonprofit organizations, as well as other volunteer groups can help to feed people, provide them with clothing and housing, clean up the environment and keep it clean, and improve the standard of living and quality of life for everyone.

Learning Goal 2   **Opportunities for Entrepreneurs**

3. Corporate downsizing has created many new opportunities for entrepreneurs who provide the services business need, in fields like advertising, building maintenance, computer related services and security services.

4. Revenue is money generated by selling goods, while profit is the money left over after a business has paid its expenses.

5. A company will have a loss when expenses of doing business are greater than the revenues generated.

6. In general, the companies that take the most risk can make the most profit.

7. The five factors of production are:
   a. land and other natural resources.
   b. labor.
   c. capital, such as money, machines tools, and buildings.
   d. entrepreneurship.
   e. knowledge.

8. The key ingredients to making countries rich are considered to be:
   a. entrepreneurship.
   b. information.

9. The factors which contribute to keeping poor countries poor are:
   a. lack of entrepreneurship.
   b. absence of knowledge workers.
   c. lack of freedom.

Learning Goal 3   **The Business Environment**

10. The five key environmental factors critical to the success of business are:
    a. the economic environment.
    b. the technological environment.
    c. the competitive environment.
    d. the social environment.
    e. the global business environment.

11. A healthy business environment helps businesses to grow and prosper. Job growth and wealth make it possible to have a high standard of living and a high quality of life. The wrong environmental conditions lead to job loss, business failures and a low standard of living and quality of life.

12. To foster entrepreneurial growth a government can
    a. Reduce the risk of being an entrepreneur by passing laws which allow for enforceable contracts.
    b. Take economic steps to ensure that the country's currency is tradable on world markets.
    c. Create policies eliminating corruption in business and government. This allows for freer competition and helps businesses to flourish.
    d. Keep taxes and government regulations to a minimum. High federal, state and local taxes are disincentives for entrepreneurs, who are looking for a high return on their investments of time and money.

Learning Goal 4   **The Technological Environment**

13. The Internet is a "superhighway" network of computer and telecommunications equipment that links people all over the world. Through the Internet, information on almost any topic is available, if you know how to use the necessary computer and telecommunications equipment.

14. A CIO is the chief information officer, who is responsible for disseminating the information workers and managers need to make their companies competitive in a global marketplace.

15. The most important role for an information manager is to establish information flows between businesses and their customers.

16. A bar code gives retailers such information as what size product you bought, what color and at what price.

17. That information is put into a databank where it is stored until it is needed.

18. Electronic data interchange sends sales data from bar codes directly to manufacturers, and makes the flow of goods from manufacturers to retailers much smoother. This technology is making it possible for businesses to save time and money, and for you to receive the right ad, about the right products at the right time for you purchase.

Learning Goal 5   **The Competitive Environment**

19. For U.S. companies to stay competitive in today's global market, they must offer:
    a. quality products.
    b. outstanding service.
    c. competitive prices.

20. Companies compete by:
    a. exceeding customer expectations.
    b. meeting the needs of the community.
    c. meeting the needs of employees by restructuring.
    d. demonstrating concern for the natural environment.

21. Businesses today are being "driven" by the wants and needs of customers.

22. A company's stakeholders are all the people who stand to gain or lose by the policies and activities of an organization, including customers, stockholders, suppliers, dealers, people in the local community, environmentalists and elected officials.

23. Downsizing has eliminated managers, and as a result lower-level workers have learned to work in self-managed teams. Because of the self-managed teams, employers will expect a lot more from lower-level workers than in the past. These workers will need more education, and will need to receive higher pay and be treated more as partners in the firm.

24. Managers' jobs will become to train, support, coach and motivate lower-level employees.

25. a. Companies are exceeding customer expectations by listening to customers to determine their needs, and making high quality products at low prices to meet those needs. Products and services in the future will be designed to "fascinate, bewitch and delight" customers, thus exceeding customer expectations.

    b. The needs of the community are being met by being sensitive to the needs of not only the firm's customers, but of all the company's stakeholders.

    c. Companies are restructuring and grouping employees into self-managed teams, with less management oversight. Workers are being treated more as partners in a firm, with greater responsibilities and higher compensation.

    d. Environmentalism and concern for the natural environment will become a major focus of businesses in the years to come.

Learning Goal 6   **The Social Environment**

26. The two major demographic trends discussed in the text are:
    a. multiculturalism.
    b. two-income families.

    These trends are affecting how we live, and are expected to provide many opportunities for businesses in the next century.

27. A multicultural population gives U.S. citizens the opportunity to live and work with people from many different cultures and backgrounds. That should give us an advantage when it comes to working with people in global markets. Further, a diverse population provides businesses with ideas and concepts that will enhance and enrich the business community and culture.

28. A number of programs have been implemented to help two-income families. Pregnancy benefits, parental leave programs, flexible work schedules and eldercare programs are some examples. Many companies either offer day care on site or offer some type of child-care benefits. Others offer cafeteria style benefits packages, enabling families to choose from a "menu" of benefits. Many companies have increased the number of part-time workers they employ, while others allow workers to stay home and work by telecommuting.

Learning Goal 7 **The Global Environment**

29. The number one global environmental change is the growth of international competition and the increase of free trade among nations.

30. In order to become world-class competitors, U.S. manufacturers have been analyzing the best practices from around the world, and many have implemented the most advanced quality methods. U.S. firms are changing the way they operate by going beyond competition, and have learned to cooperate with international firms. That cooperation has the potential to create rapidly growing world markets.

31. NAFTA stand for the North American Free Trade Agreement. The three countries, which are part of NAFTA, are the United States, Canada and Mexico.

32. Since NAFTA was passed, the U.S. has created two and a half million jobs a year. Unemployment has dropped, and many of the new jobs pay high wages, because export industries pay more than manufacturing generally.

33. Open borders can lead to better economies for the countries participating in free trade agreements. People in the U.S. have prospered as a result of free trade between the states. Free trade forces companies to become innovative and competitive. It keeps them from becoming stagnant and thus less globally competitive. Companies are learning to cooperate with firms in other nations to meet the needs of growing world markets.

34.   a. New jobs will be created in the United States and abroad.
      b. It will be important to be prepared for a rapidly changing environment by studying technology, telecommunications and foreign languages.
      c. Continuous learning will be required.

Learning Goal 8   **The Quality Imperative**

35.   To qualify for the Baldrige Awards, a company has to show quality:
      a. by customer satisfaction.
      b. by product service and quality.
      c. by quality of internal operations.

36.   The Baldrige Award requires companies to:
      a. increase employee involvement.
      b. measure themselves against industry leaders.
      c. shorten the time it takes to introduce products.

37.   The two major criteria for the Baldrige Award are:
      a. customer needs and wants are being met.
      b. customer satisfaction ratings are better than those of competitors.

      The Baldrige Award is presented to U.S. firms. To qualify, firms have to show quality as measured by customer satisfaction, product and service quality and by the quality of internal operations. A major criterion for the award is that customer needs and wants are being met and customer satisfaction ratings are better than those of competitors. ISO 9000 and ISO 14000 are not awards, but rather global standards. ISO 9000 is a global standard for quality, which must be met in order to do business with the European Union. ISO 14000 is standard for managing an organization's environmental impact. Companies that qualify for the Baldrige Award will have little trouble being ISO certified. Most U.S. companies have a long way to go to qualify.

38.   ISO 9000 is important because the EU is demanding that firms be ISO certified to do business in Europe. That business is crucial to the success of almost any business in today's global economy.

Learning 9   **The Evolution of American Business**

39.   The agricultural industry led the way for economic development in the U.S. in the early part of this century. That industry became so efficient through the use of technology that the number of farmers dropped dramatically. Small farms were replaced by much larger farms, but agriculture is still a major industry in the U.S. Many of the farmers that lost

jobs in agriculture went to work in factories. Like agriculture, the manufacturing industry used technology to become more productive. This meant fewer jobs in manufacturing, but by increasing productivity new jobs have been created, and many of those displaced manufacturing workers have found employment in the service sector.

40. Almost all of our economy's employment increases have been in service industries. Service sector growth is expected to slow in the coming years. Some will grow rapidly, such as telecommunications, and other will have much slower growth.

CRITICAL THINKING EXERCISES

1. Monika is surprised at the standard of living Joe seems to have attained compared to hers, while working at a similar job. While Monika makes more per hour (equivalent U.S. dollars) than Joe, the cost of food, housing and other services is probably much higher for her. Therefore she can't buy as much with her money as Joe can - it simply costs too much. A similar situation exists in the United States when you compare one region to another. Compare average housing prices for example in San Francisco, California to those in St. Louis, Missouri. When you compare per capita income for those areas, you will also find a difference.

2. a. $2,400,000 in revenue.
   b. Profit is $350,000 after taking expenses of $2,050,000.
   c. Companies like Revelle generate wealth and create a higher standard of living in many ways. Workers pay taxes that federal and local governments use to build hospitals, schools, roads and playgrounds. Tax money is also used to keep the environment clean. Businesses also pay taxes to the federal government and the local community.

   Standards of living go up because people can buy goods and services with the money they earn from being employed. When businesses start, grow and prosper, and generate wealth, our quality of life improves as the taxes the workers and the business pay provide for good schools, good health care, a clean environment and so on.

3. In the analysis of the factors of production, the most important factor is not capital, natural resources, or labor. Countries in Eastern Europe have land and labor, but are still poor. Capital is available, thus countries have money for machinery and tools. The key to developing an economy appears to be entrepreneurship and the effective use of information. In many of these countries businesses have been owned by the government, and there has been little incentive to work hard or create profit.

A government interested in developing its economy must encourage business and entrepreneurship and provide the information necessary to help people to move ahead.

Many of these countries do not have laws which enable companies to write enforceable contracts, necessary to do business. This makes the risk of starting a business much higher. Further, these countries are still attempting to stabilize the value of their currency. The governments are corrupt in many cases, making it impossible to get permits without expensive bribes. Lastly, taxes in many developing countries are high, minimizing a business's return on investment.

4. The new retailing technology allows a retailer to determine what kind of products customers purchase, in what amount, in what size and at what price. That information, plus information such as the name, address and family information about a customer will go into a databank. With that information Schnucks can send direct mail pieces to customers offering exactly what they want. It will allow Schnucks to carry inventory specifically for a customer base in different areas around the city. For example, if there is an area with a large Italian population, the Schnucks store in that area will carry more of the type of products those customers might buy. If there is a large Jewish population in another area of the city, the store serving that area may carry fewer of the Italian products, and more for the dietary needs of the Jewish customer, and so on. These stores will also be able to replace the items quickly through contact with the suppliers, who also have the bar code information. If Schnucks is interested in developing direct mail pieces or other types of services, this technology will help decision makers to know exactly what to feature, and mailing lists will be readily available.

5. a. Competitors for some schools will be the other colleges and universities in the local community. For others it may be other schools in the region or the nation.
b. A college or university may "delight" its customer (students) by offering classes at convenient times (many schools offer weekend college programs for example), in convenient locations (off site locations), encouraging faculty to be accessible to students through designated office hours or mentoring programs, offering a variety of programs, and of course having winning sports teams!
c. The stakeholders are students, parents of students, employees, taxpayers, the community in which the school is located, and alumni for example. How schools meet variety of course offerings, tuition and rate of tuition increases, level of community involvement by the school's administrators, responsiveness to student organizations, cooperation with alumni groups, and so on defines how it meets the needs of its customers.
d. Students may have difficulty answering how the school meets the needs of employees. You may find out if there is a structure for faculty and staff to communicate openly with their manager, for example, or how employees view the administration and the school's policies.

e. By being responsive to students, parents, employees and the community, and working together, any organization can create a better "product". A college or university is more than just the courses it offers. For example, the quality of student life on campus can directly affect enrollment.

f. There may be courses on your campus in Environmental Management, Recycling Management and so on. There may be paper or can recycling programs, or student sponsored clubs or activities relating to the environment.

6. Answers to this question will vary. Most companies make use of computers for everything from inventory management to payroll. Students will find that companies are using technology in hundreds of different ways. Many companies today are offering benefits such as time off to work as a volunteer, day care centers and more. Most will also find that the company is involved in some way in the international area, even if it is just selling a few products imported from overseas.

7. By developing programs such as those mentioned, companies better meet employee needs. This can make a company more competitive by fostering a positive environment with satisfied workers who may then be more productive. Further, these programs can be used to attract the kinds of skilled workers companies will need in the future to remain competitive.

8. If U.S. firms want to be competitive in today's global environment, they must focus on quality issues in the same way that countries like China, India, South Korea and Mexico have done. These countries are often able to produce high quality goods at low prices. U.S. manufacturers have lost much of the market for televisions, videocassette recorders and other products because they were not competitive with Japanese manufacturers. U.S. manufacturers have taken ideas from around the world, and implemented the most advanced quality methods to make U.S. workers among the most productive in the world. Further, U.S. firms have begun to realize that in order to be competitive, they must cooperate with other international firms to continue to serve the growing global markets with the highest quality products and services at the lowest possible prices.

9. As the agricultural industry became more productive through advances in technology, fewer people were needed to produce the same or greater volume. So, agricultural workers had to find jobs elsewhere, in other industries, and learn new skills. Many of these people went to work in manufacturing, helping to make the United States a world manufacturing power in the first half of this century.

The same trend has occurred today in the industrial, or manufacturing sector. As factories have been able to improve productivity through technology, fewer workers are needed to produce the same or greater volume of high quality products. Factory workers today have been laid off and have had to re-train to find new employment. These workers are often finding jobs in the service sector, which has generated almost all of the employment growth increases since the mid-1980s.

PRACTICE TEST

Multiple Choice

1.	d	12.	b
2.	b	13.	c
3.	c	14.	a
4.	b	15.	d
5.	d	16.	a
6.	a	17.	b
7.	d	18.	c
8.	c	19.	d
9.	a	20.	c
10.	d	21.	a
11.	b		

True/False

1.	F	9.	F
2.	T	10.	F
3.	T	11.	T
4.	F	12.	T
5.	F	13.	F
6.	F	14.	T
7.	T	15.	F
8.	T		

APPENDIX
DRIVER'S ED FOR THE INFORMATION SUPERHIGHWAY

RETENTION CHECK

What is the Internet?

1. What is the Internet?

2. What is the World Wide Web?

3. What are two basic difficulties in navigating the Internet without the Web?

    a. _____

    b. _____

4. What did the Web add to the Internet?

5. What does hypertext allow for?

What Do I Need to Be Able to Get on the Web?

6. What two devices do you need to cruise the information highway?

7. What are some ways that you can have access to the Net?

8. Describe a Web browser.

9. What were the two most popular Web browsers at the time the text was written?

Why Would I Want to Cruise the Internet?

10. What are six uses for the Internet?

    a. _____ d. _____

    b. _____ e. _____

    c. _____ f. _____

How Do I Cruise the Web?

11. What are the four things you need to know about to navigate the Web?

    a. _____

    b. _____

    c. _____

    d. _____

12. What does URL stand for, and what is a URL?

13. What are the most popular search engines?

14. How do you move around a site?

15. How do you get back to a previous site after having left?

16. What determines the speed with which you reach Internet sites?

17. What are newsgroups?

18. What are some things you should do before joining a newsgroup?

19. What are the two parts of an e-mail address?

20. List the steps to compose an e-mail message.

   a. _____   d. _____

   b. _____   e. _____

   c. _____   f. _____

21. How do you check for new e-mail messages?

22. What are listservs?

23. How do you join a chat room (i.e., have a real-time conversation with other people)?

    a. _____

    b. _____

    c. _____

24. What are the best ways to use a search engine?

    a. _____

    b. _____

    c. _____

CRITICAL THINKING EXERCISES

1. Describe the development of the Internet.

2. What impact do you think the Internet has had, or will have, on the global marketplace?

PRACTICE TEST

Multiple Choice: Circle the best answer.

1. Workers at the Acquatech Corp. send and receive hundreds of e-mail messages every day. They collaborate with scientists at labs around the world, and keep abreast of the latest developments in their field by accessing various news and discussion groups. This is pssible because Acquatech's workers have access to millions of interconnected networks known as the

    a. Compunet
    b. Electronic village
    c. World wide web
    d. Internet

2. _____ owns the Internet.

    a. The government
    b. A consortium of multinational corporations
    c. A group of researchers and scientists
    d. No one

3. One of the basic difficulties of navigating the Internet is:

    a. There are too many computers on it.
    b. It is difficult to retrieve information without some kind of tool.
    c. There isn't enough information on the Internet to make it worth the effort at this point.
    d. There are no addresses.

4. The _____ is a means of accessing, organizing and moving through the information on the Internet.

    a. modem
    b. search engine Excite
    c. World Wide Web
    d. Internet manager

5. The earliest users of the Internet were:

   a. researchers and scientists.
   b. corporations as a way of selling and advertising.
   c. computer manufacturers.
   d. members of the media.

6. Which of the following would not be considered a use of the Internet?

   a. Communicate on-line
   b. Electronic mail
   c. Shopping
   d. Word processing

7. A URL is:

   a. a type of software needed to cruise the Net.
   b. an Internet address.
   c. a piece of hardware needed to access the Net.
   d. a Web browser.

8. The speed with which you reach an Internet site depends upon:

   a. the type of Web browser you are using.
   b. the speed and size of your phone line and computer.
   c. the area of the country in which you are located.
   d. which Internet you are using.

9. Which of the following steps is not a step in sending e-mail?

   a. Enter the e-mail address of the person to whom you are writing
   b. Type in the message
   c. Alert the person to whom you are sending a message that a message is coming in
   d. Click on the send button

10. Which of the following is not included in suggestions on using a search engine more effectively?

    a. adding more terms from your search string
    b. subtracting terms from the search string
    c. put the search term in quotes
    d. delete spaces between words to make the string shorter

TRUE/FALSE

1. _____ The Internet is relatively new, and has only been around since the early 1990s.

2. _____ There is a central computer which controls all the activities on the Internet.

3. _____ The World Wide Web is a way of navigating the Internet

4. _____ The first thing you need in order to cruise the information highway is a computer with a modem.

5. _____ Once you are on a Web site, you have to go to a home page before going to another site.

6. _____ Credit card security is not a major concern for shoppers on the Internet.

7. _____ Before you can join a newsgroup you need to fill out an application.

8. _____ One way to narrow a search is by inserting an "and" between the words you are using to search.

ANSWERS

RETENTION CHECK

What Is the Internet?

1. The Internet is a network of networks. It involves thousands of interconnected computer networks that include millions of host computers.

2. The World Wide Web is a means of accessing, organizing, and moving through the information in the Internet. Therefore, the Web is part of the Internet.

3. a. The traffic signs on the Internet are written in Unix.
   b. There is no defined structure for organizing information.

4. The Web added graphics and sound to the Internet. It also made navigating parts of the Internet easier.

5. Hypertext allows any part of any document to be linked to any other document, no matter where it is. This allows you to jump around from place to place on the Internet with only a click of the mouse.

What Do I Need to Be Able to Get on the Web?

6. In order to cruise the information superhighway, you need a computer with a modem and a Web browser.

7. You can access the Net through schools, or with an Internet service provider.

8. A Web browser is a program or application that provides you with a way to access the World Wide Web.

9. The two most popular Web browsers are (were) Netscape Navigator and Microsoft Internet Explorer.

Why Would I Want to Cruise the Internet?

10. a. Communicate on-line
    b. News groups
    c. Electronic mail (e-mail)
    d. Internet relay chat (IRC)
    e. Shop
    f. Play games

How Do I Cruise the Web?

11. a. Web addresses
    b. directories and search engines
    c. links
    d. Back Page button

12. URL stands for uniform resource locator. It is the address for a web site.

13. The most popular search engines are Yahoo!, Infoseek, Lycos, Alta Vista, Excite and WebCrawler.

14. Once you're at a site, the two main ways to cruise around are by clicking on an icon button link or on a text link.

15. If you want to go back to a site you have recently left, you can just click on the Back Page button in your browser, or you can enter the desired site's URL.

16. The speed with which you reach other Internet sites depends not only on the speed and size of your phone line and computer but also on the speed and size of phone lines and computers at the other site.

17. Newsgroups are collections of messages from people all over the world on any subject you can imagine. Newsgroups are divided into categories indicated by the first letters of their name.

18. Before joining a newsgroup you should take time to read the frequently asked questions list for that group first. After you read the FAQs, you should read at least a week's worth of postings to get a feel for the group and what kinds of discussions its members have.

19. The two parts of an e-mail address are the user name and the name of the computer on which that user has an account.

20. To compose an e-mail message:
    a. Click on the Mail button.
    b. Enter the e-mail address of the person to whom you are writing.
    c. Enter the subject of your message in the subject field.
    d. Enter the addresses of others you want to receive the message in the cc field.
    e. Enter the body of the message.
    f. When you have completed the message, click on the send button.

21. To check for new e-mail messages, click on the Get Mail button.

22. Listservs, are mailing lists that are similar to Usenet newsgroups. However, listserv discussions are delivered to your in-box as e-mail.

23. To join a chat room, or IRC you need to:
    a. Connect to a server.
    b. Choose a nickname.
    c. Join a room (or channel).

24. To use a search engine effectively:
    a. Add words appropriate to what you are searching for linked with an "and".
    b. Subtract words from your search by using "not".
    c. Put your search term in quotes.

CRITICAL THINKING EXERCISES

1. The Pentagon began a network in 1969 when the world feared that a nuclear war would paralyze communications. The computer network was developed to reach far-flung terminals even if some connections were broken. The system began to change as scientists and academics used it to share data and electronic mail. No one owns the Internet, and there is no central computer. There is no Internet manager.

2. The Internet allows for a fast, economical and efficient method of communicating. Companies around the world can keep track of operations and keep in touch with employees anywhere with the ease of a mouse click. The Internet also enables companies to reach customers around the world, through advertising and sales.

PRACTICE TEST

Multiple Choice				True/False			
1.	d	6.	d	1.	F	5.	F
2.	d	7.	b	2.	F	6.	F
3.	b	8.	b	3.	T	7.	F
4.	c	9.	c	4.	T	8.	T
5.	a	10.	d				

CHAPTER 2
ECONOMICS: THE CREATION AND DISTRIBUTION OF WEALTH

LEARNING GOALS

After you have read and studied this chapter you should be able to:

1. Explain how wealth is created in an economy.
2. Discuss the major differences between capitalism, socialism, and a mixed economy.
3. Describe how the free market system works.
4. Use key terms (e.g. GDP and productivity) to explain the U.S. economic condition.
5. Describe monetary policy and its importance to the economy.
6. Discuss fiscal policy and its importance to the economy.

LEARNING THE LANGUAGE

Listed below are important terms found in this chapter. Choose the correct term for each definition below and write it in the space provided.

Capitalism	Fiscal policy	National debt
Command economy	Free market economies	Oligopoly
Consumer price index	Gross Domestic Product (GDP)	Perfect competition
Deflation	Inflation	Productivity
Demand	Invisible hand	Recession
Depression	Mixed economy	Socialism
Disinflation	Monetary policy	Supply
Economics	Monopoly	Unemployment rate
Federal deficit		

1. The quantity of products that manufacturers or owners are willing to sell at different prices at a specific time is known as _____.

2. _____ is the difference between federal revenue and federal spending in any given year.

3. The country is in a _____ when GDP has declined for two consecutive quarters.

4. The economic system known as _____ is one in which all or most of the means of production and distribution are privately owned and operated for profit.

5. _____ is the quantity of products that people are willing to buy at different prices at a specific time.

6. We define the _____ as the number of civilians who are unemployed and tried to find a job within the prior four weeks.

7. Buyers and sellers negotiating prices for goods and services are working within _____, in which decisions about what to produce and in what quantities are decided by the market.

8. The _____ consists of monthly statistics that measure changes in the prices of about 400 goods and services that consumers buy.

9. The sum of all the federal deficits over time is called the _____.

10. A course in _____ will teach us how society chooses to employ resources to produce various goods and services and to distribute them for consumption among various competing groups and individuals.

11. Government economists keep a close watch on _____, which is the general rise in the price level of goods and services over time.

12. One key economic indicator is _____, the total value of goods and services in a given year.

13. Countries such as Cuba operate under a _____ where the government largely decides what goods and services will be produced, who will get them, and how the economy will grow.

14. In developing _____ the government is managing the amount of money placed into the economy and managing interest rates.

15. _____ is a condition where price increases are slowing.

16. A severe recession is known as a(n) _____.

17. _____ is an economic system based on the premise that businesses should be owned by the people (workers).

18. When the government makes an effort to keep the economy stable, it may use _____, by increasing or decreasing taxes and/or government spending.

19. _____ is defined as the total output of goods and services one worker can produce in a given period of time.

20. A _____ exists where some allocation of resources is made by the market and some by the government.

21. The economy is experiencing _____ when prices are actually declining.

22. A _____ is a market in which there is only one seller.

23. The market situation known as _____ is where there are many sellers of nearly identical products and no seller is large enough to dictate the price of the product.

24. Adam Smith coined the term _____ to describe the mechanism for creating wealth and jobs.

25. A form of competition where the market is dominated by just a few sellers is called a(n) _____.

RETENTION CHECK

Learning Goal 1   **The Importance of Capitalism**

1. Who is known as the "father of capitalism"?

2. In a capitalist system, who/what owns the businesses and decides what to produce, how much to produce, how much to pay workers and how much to charge for goods?

3. What is the foundation of capitalism?

4. What did Adam Smith believe was vital to the survival of any economy?

5. How does the economy benefit if workers can keep the profits from working?

6. What is Adam Smith's theory of the invisible hand?

Learning Goal 2   **The History of Business and Economics**

7. According to the text, why does free market capitalism lead to inequality of wealth?

8. Who is known as the father of communism?

In a communist system, who/what make economic decisions?

10. Why have communist systems been a problem, and what has been the result?

11. What is the basic premise of a socialist system?

12. In a socialist system, what is the government expected to provide?

13. What could be the "motto" of socialism?

14. Why did people who earned high incomes choose to leave socialist countries such as Sweden?

15. What are the two major economic systems vying for dominance in the world?

   a. _____   b. _____

16. What is the major principle of each?

   a. _____

   _____

   b. _____

   _____

17. Experience has shown that neither capitalism nor socialism has had optimal results in terms of the economy. What are the problems with:

   a. A free market system

   b. Socialism/communism

   c. What has been the result of those problems?

18. What is considered a "mixed economy"?

19. What kind of economic system do we have in the United States?

Learning Goal 3 **The Foundations of Capitalism**

20. What are the four basic rights of a free market (capitalist) system?

   a. _____   c. _____

   b. _____   d. _____

21. In general, how do consumers in the U.S. and other free market systems send signals to producers – in other words, what tells producers what and how much to produce?

22. What is "supply"?

23. What happens to quantity supplied as price goes up?

24. What is demand?

2-8

25. What happens to demand as price goes up?

26. Label the graph

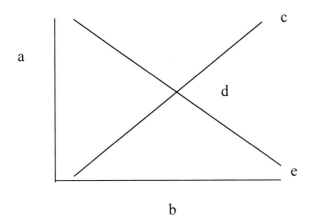

27. What does the equilibrium point represent?

28. Describe:

   a. perfect competition

   b. monopolistic competition

   c. oligopoly

   d. monopoly

29. What has happened in Poland and China since capitalist principles have been introduced?

30. Why have governments intervened in the free market system?

31. What are the questions to be debated in evaluating the amount of total output taken by the government?

Learning Goal 4 **Understanding the Economic System of the United States**

32. What are three major indicators of economic health?

   a. _____

   b. _____

   c. _____

33. Why is the level of GDP actually larger than what the figures show?

34. What are four types of unemployment?

    a. _____   b. _____

    c. _____   d. _____

35. List two measures of price changes over time.

    a. _____   b. _____

36. What is the difference between inflation and deflation?

37. Why is the CPI an important figure?

38. What are three other indicators of the country's economic health?

    a. _____   b. _____

    c. _____

39. The income earned from producing goods and services goes to:

    a. _____

    b. _____

40. What is productivity?

41. What is the benefit of an increase in productivity?

42. What is the difficulty in measuring productivity in the service sector?

43. Two ways to describe inflation are:

   a. _____

   b. _____

44. What does the CPI measure?

45. What is the difference between inflation and disinflation?

46. What is a recession?

47. What three things happen when a recession occurs?

   a. _____

   b. _____

   c. _____

48. What are three consequences of a recession?

   a. _____

   b. _____

   c. _____

49. What is the difference between a recession and a depression?

Learning Goal 5   **The Issue of Monetary Policy**

50.   What are two areas managed by monetary policy?

   a. _____

   b. _____

51.   What does the Fed do when there is too much money in the economy?

52.   What is the effect of rising interest rates?

53.   What will the Fed do when unemployment gets too high?

54.   What is the effect of lowering interest rates?

55. What is the Fed doing when it is "loosening up" on the money supply?

56. Why does the Fed implement a "tight monetary policy"?

Learning Goal 6   **The Issue of Fiscal Policy**

57. What are 2 areas managed by fiscal policy?

   a. _____   b. _____

58. What effect do higher taxes have on investment?

59. What is the difference between the federal deficit and the national debt?

60. How high is the national debt?

61. What are 2 questions surrounding the national debt?

    a. _____

    b. _____

62. How did the national debt get so large?

63. What are 3 issues being discussed in deciding how to solve the problem of the national debt?

    a. _____

    b. _____

    c. _____

64. Why is it clear that taxing the rich is not the answer to the government's problems?

CRITICAL THINKING EXERCISES

Learning Goal 1

1. They're everywhere! McDonald's hamburgers can be purchased in cities and suburbs, on riverfronts, in college football stadiums and in discount stores. There are fast food restaurants at most major road intersections, and billions of dollars are spent annually to advertise everything from fast food frozen yogurt to kid's meals. Grocery stores have gotten into the act with their own versions of fast food restaurants.

   Families with sick children can stay in Ronald McDonald houses located close to the hospital where the children are receiving treatment, and grocery stores in the Midwest and California, along with many other businesses came to the aid of flood victims in the mid and late 1990's.

   How does the story of the founding and growth of McDonald's and the resulting growth in other, similar businesses illustrate Adam Smith's invisible hand theory?

Learning Goal 2

2. Julie Marshall is a business student at a university in the United States. In her business history class the professor discussed the development of capitalism and the subsequent emergence of socialism. What did Julie learn about capitalism and why socialism was seen as an alternative?

3. The three key economic systems are:

   a. Capitalism.

   b. Mixed Economy.

   c. Socialism.

Read the following examples and using the table on page _50_ of the text to determine which system is most likely being described:

a. _____ John works for a local television station in the country in which he lives. He is considered to be a government employee, but his brother owns his own small printing business.

b. _____ Because the market is "ruled " by supply and demand with little government involvement, Maria has a wide variety of goods and services available for purchase where she lives.

c. _____ Many of the products Maria purchases have been made or assembled outside her country. These products are available because the government of her country does not control or interfere with trade with other countries.

d. _____ In his country, Devon has been reading a number of articles regarding prayer in school. The courts in his country have declared prayer in school to be illegal.

e. _____ Hong's uncle works for a large corporation where promotions and raises are given to those who work hard and do a good job. The only problem is, the tax rate is so high there is little incentive for anyone to work that hard. Hong is a teacher in a public school, and his wages are controlled by the government.

f. _____ Sam is a farmer in his country, and has been paid by the government for the last 3 years not to plant and harvest his land.

g. _____ Ramon works hard at his job because where he lives and works, profits are kept by the owners of the company, and he is one of the owners. Workers are well rewarded for high productivity, and they work hard.

h. _____ Vladimir would like to go to college, but he isn't sure he will be allowed to go by his government. He first has to make adequate grades and pass a test to determine his ability to perform in any college. His government may also tell him which college he will be able to attend.

Learning Goal 3

4. There are four basic rights under the capitalist economic system:

   a. Private property.   c. Competition.

   b. Profit.   d. Freedom of choice.

   Read the situations below and determine which of these is being demonstrated.

   a. The owners of Pro Performance, Inc. make a profit for the owners for the first time in their history and decide to pay themselves a dividend. _____

   b. The owners of Pro Performance, Inc. bought a piece of land for investment purposes. _____

   c. Procter & Gamble spends over $1 billion a year on advertising. _____

   d. Tom Oswalt decided not to join the union at the shop where he is employed for the summer. _____

   e. Arthur Tower receives a patent for a new method he devised to make metal springs. _____

   f. Alfred Rockwood, after he retired, decided to move to northern Michigan and start his own fly-tying business. _____

   g. Coleco adds accessories to its line of dolls, in an attempt to grab a greater share of the toy market. _____

   h. The Andersens, a young couple, draw up a will, making their children their beneficiaries.

5. Plot a supply curve using the information below:

Unit price (dollars)	Amount supplied (units)
$125	500
100	400
75	300
50	200
25	100

    Now, plot the demand curve using the information listed below.

Unit price (dollars)	Amount demanded (units)
$125	100
100	200
75	300
50	400
25	500

    a. What is the equilibrium price? _____

    b. How many units will be supplied and purchased? _____

6. Indicate whether the price of a product will most likely go up or down in the following situations:

    a. There is a drought in the Midwest (bushel of wheat). _____

    b. Strawberries are in season with a bumper crop. _____

    c. It's the ski season (price of motel rooms). _____

    d. A nutrition study indicates that red meat should be eaten only in moderation, if at all (price of red meat). _____

    e. A major corporation announces that it has to borrow money from the government in order to stay in business (price of its stock). _____

7. There are four degrees of competition:

   a. perfect competition. c. oligopoly.

   b. monopolistic competition. d. monopoly.

   Match the type of competition to the situation described below:

   a. Murray Barnard takes his soybean crop to the grain elevator in Decatur, Illinois. He found that because of government price supports he would make a nice profit this year. _____

   b. Because it is the only provider of electrical service in the area, Ameren UE is carefully regulated by the Missouri Public Service Commission. _____

   c. Cheer cleans in all temperatures. Ivory Snow is gentle enough to launder a baby's clothes and Tide cleans the dirtiest clothes. Procter & Gamble makes these brands, as well as several others, which all appear to be different. Procter & Gamble competes with many other manufacturers and retains control over advertising, branding and packaging.

   d. The purchasing agent for Missouri Rolling Mills says that he buys the steel the company uses to make their sign posts primarily on the basis of the best delivery date and the highest quality, rather than price, since all of his suppliers charge the same dollar amount per ton.

Learning Goal 4

8. Discuss the relationship between productivity and price levels. What is the relationship between productivity and Gross Domestic Product?

9. There are four types of unemployment:

   a. frictional.   c. cyclical.

   b. structural.   d. seasonal.

   Match the situation being described to the type of unemployment

   a. As sales of new homes decline, the construction industry lays off thousands of workers. _____

   b. A migrant worker, finished with his job in the potato fields in Idaho, travels to Michigan to look for a job harvesting fruit. _____

   c. A middle manager is laid off. His job has been eliminated with the installation of high tech information processing equipment. _____

   d. A businessman quits his job over a major disagreement with company policy. _____

10. Bob Sloan is concerned. He is up for promotion at General Dynamo where he has worked for several years. For the last three years, Bob was the general manager of the G.D. service division. His counterpart, Gerry Franz, is also in line for the job Bob wants. Gerry is the general manager of a manufacturing division. Bob's concern is that while he has completely automated his division and has received recognition for high quality work, productivity in his division is only up one percent. Gerry's division, through automation, has increased productivity by over six percent. Bob is afraid he won't look as good as Gerry in performance reviews. What's the problem?

11. We often hear about the Federal Reserve's attempts to implement a tight or a loose monetary policy. Read the following situations and determine which policy the Fed may implement.

   a. Full employment (i.e. a very low rate of unemployment) _____

   b. High unemployment _____

   c. Declining productivity _____

   d. Extremely high levels of consumer borrowing _____

   e. High rate of inflation _____

   f. Low levels of business investment in growth programs _____

12. During the mid-1990s, as the United States was emerging from a prolonged recession, the Federal Reserve raised interest rates 6 times in a one year period. Why did the Fed take this action, and what do you think was the effect?

Learning Goal 5, 6

13. Determine whether fiscal policy or monetary policy is being discussed:

   a. Congress debates a major income tax revision. _____

   b. The Federal Reserve raises interest rates to its member banks. _____

   c. A candidate for major political office promises to cut spending for social programs to reduce the national debt. _____

   d. Major government programs lose federal funding. _____

e. In an attempt to ease unemployment, the Fed increases the money supply. _____

f. A proposal is made to cut defense spending, but to raise taxes to fund defense spending. _____

g. American taxpayers express concern over tax loopholes for the rich. _____

h. A debate centers around whether to lower the national debt through an increase in the tax rate, less spending, or both. _____

14. Political campaigns often revolve around the issue of taxes and how an increase or a decrease will affect government spending and revenues. Since government revenues come from collecting taxes, discuss how a tax *decrease* could have the effect of *raising* government revenues.

PRACTICE TEST

Multiple Choice: Circle the best answer.

1. Bill Ding started his own construction company to support his family. The going was slow at first but after some time, Bill got so busy he had to hire 3 workers. Bill and his workers do high quality work, and now, there is quite a demand for their services. Bill is considering hiring 2 more people. He also has an exclusive deal with a local lumber yard. Because of Bill's business, the yard has added another employee. This is an example of the _____ in action.

   a. marketing concept
   b. invisible hand
   c. benefits of communism
   d. resources development theory

2. One of the problems with _____ is that it naturally leads to unequal distribution of wealth.

   a. communism
   b. socialism
   c. a command economy
   d. capitalism

3. Karl Marx believed that:

   a. businesses should be owned by workers and decisions should be made by the government.
   b. business and government should not mix, and so all businesses should be privately owned by stockholders.
   c. capitalism was not the kind of system where wealth could be created.
   d. eventually all of the countries in the world would operate under capitalist beliefs.

4. Citizens of socialist nations can rely on the government to provide all of the following except:

   a. education.
   b. health care.
   c. unemployment and retirement benefits.
   d. money to start a business.

5. What kind of a system exists when the marketplace largely determines what goods and services get produced, who gets them and how the economy grows?

   a. command economy
   b. socialist economy
   c. free market economy
   d. communist economy

6. <u>Most</u> countries in the world have a _____ economy.

   a. capitalist
   b. socialist
   c. mixed
   d. communist

7. Which of the following is not one of the four basic rights of a capitalist system?

   a. The right to have a job
   b. The right to private property
   c. The right to compete
   d. The right to freedom of choice

8. Typically, the quantity of products that manufacturers are willing to supply will _____ when prices _____

   a. increase/increase
   b. decrease/increase
   c. stay the same/increase
   d. increase/stay the same

9. A(n) _____ shows the amount people are willing to buy at the prices at which sellers are willing to sell.

   a. supply curve
   b. demand curve
   c. marginal revenue point
   d. equilibrium point

10. One holiday season a few years ago, there was a toy called Tickle My Elbow that was all the rage. Demand for this toy was so high, that stores couldn't keep them on the shelves! There was quite a shortage of Tickle My Elbow that year. When a shortage such as this exists, what generally happens?

   a. The price goes up.
   b. The price stays the same, and mothers everywhere fight for the last toy.
   c. The government intervenes, and forces the manufacturer to make more of the toy.
   d. When customers realize they can't get the toy, they give up, and the price goes down.

11. What's going on here? As soon as Dewey Cheatum and Howe Motors increases the prices on their sport utility vehicle, then so does their only competitor, You Betcha Motors! Their prices are basically the same for similar vehicles, although their advertising says their products are really very different. What kind of competition exists here?

   a. perfect competition
   b. monopoly
   c. oligopoly
   d. monopolistic competition

12. Which of the following would not be considered a key economic indicator?

   a. GDP
   b. The unemployment rate
   c. The tax rate
   d. The price indexes

13. Juan Valdez was laid off from his job at the coffee factory, because the demand for coffee has weakened. The kind of unemployment Juan is experiencing would be:

   a. frictional.
   b. seasonal.
   c. structural.
   d. cyclical.

14. Measures to increase productivity:

   a. are failing in manufacturing, as productivity is slowly decreasing.
   b. can improve quality of service providers, but not always improve worker output.
   c. are always successful in manufacturing and services industries.
   d. are becoming unimportant in today's competitive market.

15. Which of the following probably won't occur during a recession?

    a. high unemployment
    b. increase in business failures
    c. drop in the standard of living
    d. increase in interest rates

16. Monetary policy involves:

    a. raising and/or lowering interest rates and inflation.
    b. raising and/or lowering government spending.
    c. raising and/or lowering interest rates and the money supply.
    d. raising and /or lowering government spending and the money supply.

17. When the Federal Reserve tightens monetary policy:

    a. interest rates go down and businesses begin to borrow money.
    b. production slows because businesses cut back borrowing due to high interest rates.
    c. inflation will begin to slowly creep up, and businesses step up production in anticipation of higher profits.
    d. businesses borrow more money, because interest rates are increasing and companies want to get the money they need before the rates go too high.

18. Fiscal policy is at issue when:

    a. The Federal Reserve raises interest rates to its member banks.
    b. The Federal Reserve debates combating inflation by cutting the money supply.
    c. Congress debates a proposal to cut defense spending, but raise taxes to support spending for education.
    d. Unemployment goes up as the country slides into a recession.

19. The sum of all the federal deficits over time is known as the:

    a. fiscal policy.
    b. gross national debt.
    c. national debt.
    d. aggregate demand for money.

20. All of the following is true regarding government spending except:

    a. government programs have built in spending increases.
    b. government expenditures are growing faster than the economy's ability to support the programs.
    c. deficits can be reduced only by raising taxes.
    d. a major portion of federal income goes for social security payments.

TRUE/FALSE

1. ____ Adam Smith believed that as long as workers, or entrepreneurs, had the freedom to own property (or business), and could see economic reward for their efforts, they would work long hours.

2. ____ One of the consequences of a socialist system is a high tax rate on those who do work, in order to pay for services for those that don't, or can't work.

3. ____ The United States is a purely free market economy.

4. ____ In a free market system, price is determined through negotiation between buyers and sellers.

5. ____ When there is a surplus of products, manufacturers will tend to raise the price so that they will make a profit from those products they are able to sell.

6. ____ As capitalist systems evolved in the United States and other parts of the world, wealth became more equally distributed.

7. ____ A communist system is based upon the premise that all economic decisions are made by the state and the state owns all major forms of production.

8. ____ Socialism and communism are popular terms used to describe free market economies.

9. ____ Mixed economies exist where some allocation of resources is made by the marketplace, and some by the government.

10. ____ Monopolistic competition exists when there is only one supplier of a good or service.

11. ____ Total gross domestic product in the United States in 1997 was just under $6 trillion.

12. ____ Betty Bixler worked for Chrysler for 20 years before being laid off when her job was eliminated because updated technology made her job obsolete. Betty is structurally unemployed.

13. ____ The CPI is important because some government benefits, wages and salaries, rents and leases, tax brackets and interest rates are all based upon this figure.

14. ____ Part of the income from producing goods and services goes to the government in the form of taxes.

15. ____ An increase in productivity means the same worker produces more in the same amount of time.

16. _____ During a recession, we could experience an overall drop in our standard of living, high unemployment and increased business failures.

17. _____ If inflation is a problem, the Federal Reserve System will lower interest rates to stimulate the economy.

18. _____ Discussions regarding reduction of the national debt must include a discussion of what our national priorities should be.

19. _____ The major portion of our federal spending goes toward our national defense.

20. _____ It is common knowledge that if we raise taxes on the rich, we could easily pay off our national debt.

ANSWERS

LEARNING THE LANGUAGE

1. Supply	10. Economics	19. Productivity
2. Federal deficit	11. Inflation	20. Mixed economy
3. Recession	12. Gross Domestic Product	21. Deflation
4. Capitalism	13. Command economy	22 Monopoly
5. Demand	14. Monetary policy	23. Perfect competition
6. Unemployment rate	15. Disinflation	24. Invisible hand
7. Free market economies	16. Depression	25. Oligopoly
8. Consumer price index	17. Socialism	
9. National debt	18. Fiscal policy	

RETENTION CHECK

Learning Goal 1   **The Importance of Capitalism**

1. Adam Smith is known as the father of capitalism.

2. Business people decide for their own businesses what to produce, how much to produce and how much to charge in capital systems.

3. Competition is the foundation of capitalism.

4. Adam Smith believed that the freedom to own your own property and to keep the profits from working were vital to the survival of any economy.

5. Smith believed that people would work hard if they knew they would be rewarded for work. As a result, the economy would prosper with plenty of food and available goods.

6. The "invisible hand" is what Smith believed was the mechanism for creating wealth. The idea is that people working for their own benefit will provide goods and services, which are needed by others. As a business grows and prospers, jobs are created and people are hired to work for the business. As a consequence, people will have food and goods available, and many people will have jobs. So, anyone who is willing and able to work will have a job and access to homes and so forth.

Learning Goal 2 **The History of Business and Economics**

7. A free market economy leads to inequality of wealth because business owners and managers will make more money and have more wealth than workers. Further, there will be people who are unable or unwilling to work.

8. The father of communism is Karl Marx.

9. In a communist system all economic decisions are made by the state and the state owns all the major forms of production.

10. The problem with a communist system is that a government doesn't always know what is the right amount to produce. As a result, there can be shortages of many goods, even basics such as food.

11. The basic premise of a socialist system is that some businesses should be owned by the government and that the government should decide what gets produced, how much workers should be paid and how much trade should take place between nations.

12. In a socialist system, the government is expected to provide education, health care, retirement benefits, unemployment benefits and care for everyone not able to work.

13. The motto of socialism could be "From each according to ability, to each according to need." In other words, those who work hard must share with those who don't work as hard, or those whose jobs don't pay as well.

14. Many professionals chose to leave Sweden, a socialist country, because tax rates were so high on those with high incomes.

15. The two major economic systems vying for dominance in the world are:

    a. Free market economies.   b. Command economies.

16. a. Free market economies exist when the marketplace largely determines what goods and services get produced, who gets them and how the economy grows. The popular term for this system is capitalism.
    b. Command economies exist when the government largely decides what goods and services to produce, who'll get them and how the economy will grow. Socialism and communism are terms used to describe this type of system.

17. a. Many believe that a free market system is not responsive enough to the needs of the old, the disabled, the elderly and the environment.
    b. Socialism and communism have not created enough jobs or wealth to keep economies growing fast enough.
    c. Voters in free market countries have elected officials who adopted the social programs needed to solve the problems created by a free market system. Communist governments are disappearing and socialist governments have been cutting back on social programs and lowering taxes. The result has been a trend for "capitalist" countries, such as the United States, to move toward more socialism, and for "socialist" countries to move toward capitalism.

18. Mixed economies exist where some allocation of resources is made by the market and some by the government.

19. The United States is a mixed economy.

Learning Goal 3 **The Foundations of Capitalism**

20. a. The right to private property   c. The right to freedom of competition
    b. The right to profits after taxes   d. The right to freedom of choice

21. The consumers in a free market economy send signals to producers which tell them what and how much to make. We do so by buying products and services, at the price we are charged in the store. As long as we are willing to pay the price, the supplier will continue to make that supply available.

22. Supply refers to the quantity of products that manufacturers or owners are willing to sell at different prices at a specific time.

23. As price goes up, the quantity supplied will go up.

24. Demand refers to the quantity of products that people are willing to buy at different prices at a specific time.

25. In general, as price goes up, quantity demanded will go down.

26.   a. Price   c. Supply curve   e. Demand curve
        b. Quantity   d. Equilibrium point

27. The equilibrium point is the point on a graph where the quantity supplied is equal to the quantity demanded. This will tend to be the market price.

28. a. Perfect competition exists when there are many sellers in a market and products appear to be identical. No one producer is big enough to dictate the price of a product. An example would be agricultural products.

    b. Monopolistic competition exists when a large number of sellers produce products that appear similar, but are perceived as being different by the buyers. Product differentiation is the key to success in this type of competitive situation.

    c. In an oligopoly, just a few sellers dominate the market, as is the case in the automotive, cereal and soft drink markets for example. The initial investment to enter an oligopoly is very high, and prices are similar. Product differentiation is usually the main factor in market success.

    d. A monopoly exists where there is only one seller for a product or service. One seller controls supply, and so could raise prices dramatically. For this reason laws in the United States prohibit monopolies, except for approved monopolies such as utility service.

29. In countries such as Poland and China capitalist principles created inequality. New entrepreneurs became wealthy while the average worker did not.

30. Governments have intervened in free market systems to create more social fairness and a more equal distribution of wealth.

31. The questions to be debated in evaluating the amount of total output taken by the government include: How much money should be available to the government for national defense and social welfare? What is the proper blend of government and free markets?

Learning Goal 4   **Understanding the Economic System of the United States**

32. a. the gross domestic product
    b. the unemployment rate
    c. the price index

33. The GDP is actually larger than what the figures show because they don't take illegal activities into account.

34. a. frictional unemployment   c. cyclical unemployment
    b. structural unemployment   d. seasonal unemployment

35. a. consumer price index
    b. producer price index

36. Inflation means that consumer prices are going up and deflation means that consumer prices are going down.

37. The CPI is an important figure because some government benefits, wages and salaries, rents and leases, tax brackets and interest rates are all based on the CPI.

38. a. housing starts   c. changes in personal income
    b. retail sales

39. Income earned from producing goods and services goes to:
    a. the people who own businesses in the form of dividends.
    b. the government in the form of taxes.

40. Productivity is the total volume of goods and services one worker produces in a given period of time.

2-36

41. An increase in productivity means that a worker can produce more goods and services than before. Higher productivity means lower costs in producing goods and services and lower prices. This can help to make a firm more competitive.

42. Productivity is an issue in the service industry because service firms are labor intensive. In manufacturing, machines can increase labor productivity, but in the service area, machines may add to the quality of the service provided, but not to the output per worker.

43. Inflation can be described as:
    a. general rise in the price level of goods and services over time.
    b. too many dollars chasing too few goods.

44. The CPI measures the price of an average market basket of goods for an average family over time. Items included in the basket are food, automobiles, clothing, homes, furniture, drugs, and medical and legal fees.

45. Inflation is a rise in prices, and disinflation is a condition where the rise in prices is slowing, or in other words, the inflation rate is declining.

46. A recession is two or more consecutive quarters of a decline in the GDP.

47. When a recession occurs:
    a. prices fall.
    b. people purchase fewer products.
    c. more businesses fail.

48.
    a. high unemployment
    b. increased business failures
    c. an overall drop in living standards

49. A depression is a severe recession.

Learning Goal 5 **The Issue of Monetary Policy**

50. a. money supply
    b. interest rates

51. When there is too much money in the economy, the Fed will cut the money supply and increase interest rates.

52. The effect of raising interest rates discourages businesses and consumers from borrowing money. When businesses find it hard to borrow money they may cut back on production and lay off workers, or cut workers hours. This slows the economy and lowers inflation.

53. When unemployment gets too high the Fed may put more money into the economy and lower interest rates.

54. Lower interest rates stimulate spending and encourage business growth which leads to hiring.

55. When the Fed is loosening up on the money supply, it means that the Fed is trying to stimulate the economy by increasing spending and business investment.

56. The Fed will implement a tight monetary policy to lower inflation.

Learning Goal 6 **The Issue of Fiscal Policy**

57. Two areas managed by fiscal policy are:
    a. taxes.
    b. government spending.

58. Higher taxes will have the result of lower investment, and increase the amount the government receives.

59. The federal deficit is the difference between federal revenue and federal spending, while the debt is the sum of the federal deficits over time.

60. The national debt is about $6 trillion.

61. Two questions surrounding the national debt are:
    a. How did the debt get so large?
    b. What can be done about it?

62. The national debt is so large because most government programs have automatic increases built in, so spending goes up automatically every year. Consequently, government expenditures are going up faster that the economy's ability to support its programs.

63. a. What are our national priorities, i.e. do we want a strong military system, or can money be shifted to other programs?

    b. Should the government reduce social security benefits?

    c. What is the national priority regarding such payments as Medicare, school lunches, food stamps, housing subsidies, student loans, and other government paid assistance?

64. The problem with taxing the rich is that there aren't enough wealthy people making enough money so that by increasing their taxes the government would be able to pay for all its programs. Further, wealthy people make money from investing in business. If the government increases taxes on the wealthy, less money would be available for investment and the economy would slow.

CRITICAL THINKING EXERCISES

Learning Goal 1

1. Adam Smith believed that an economy would prosper when people were allowed to produce needed goods and services and keep the profit in an attempt to improve their own standard of living. When people saw the potential gain from working hard and hiring others to help work, Smith argued that new businesses would be created, fueled by a desire for wealth. The invisible hand turned self-directed gain into social and economic

benefits. Ray Kroc saw a need for fast food in the marketplace. He took an idea and developed it into a multibillion dollar corporation. He became the quintessential self-made millionaire, and spawned several companies along the way.

These companies have provided jobs for thousands of people, from high school kids working the counter after school to the franchisee who owns twenty restaurants to the advertising executive in charge of the McDonald's account. The companies benefiting from McDonalds' success are providing a service U.S. consumers need and want, while providing goods and services and giving people jobs. McDonald's also goes beyond jobs and other tangible economic benefits, with Ronald McDonald Houses providing a social benefit beyond economic measure.

Learning Goal 2

2. Julie learned that Adam Smith's invisible hand created jobs and benefited society. It was assumed that as people became wealthier in a capitalist society, they would help out the less fortunate. Instead, great disparities in wealth began to appear. Business owners and managers made more money and had more wealth than the workers, and lived in luxury. People who were either unable or unwilling to start businesses were living in much poorer conditions.

Karl Marx noted the disparity of wealth between the business owners and the workers. He believed that wealth should be more evenly distributed. Marx thus became the father of communism, and wrote *The Communist Manifesto*, in which he proposed that workers should take over ownership of businesses and share in the wealth. This would create a more equal distribution of resources, and avoid the problems inherent in a capitalist system.

3.
   a. Socialism
   b. Capitalism
   c. Capitalism
   d. Mixed economy
   e. Socialism
   f. Mixed economy
   g. Could be either capitalism or mixed economy
   h. Socialism

Learning Goal 3

4.
   a. Profit
   b. Private property
   c. Competition
   d. Freedom of choice
   e. Private property
   f. Freedom of choice
   g. Competition
   h. Private property

5.

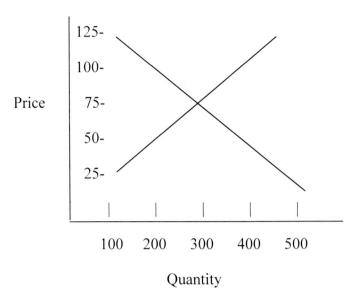

   a. $75
   b. 300 units

6. a. up   d. down
   b. down   e. down
   c. up

7. a. perfect competition   c. monopolistic competition
   b. monopoly   d. oligopoly

Learning Goal 4

8. Increases in productivity mean that the same amount of labor is able to produce a greater output. Costs are thus lower in producing goods and services, so prices can be lower. So, efficiency in both manufacturing and the service sector can help to hold down inflation. If productivity slows, GDP growth could also slow. This would have a negative effect on the economy.

9. a. cyclical   c. structural
   b. seasonal   d. frictional

10. Bob's concern stems from how productivity gains are measured. Productivity increases measure the increase in output using the same amount of labor, thus reducing costs. Service productivity, which is the area Bob is concerned with, is difficult to measure because services are labor intensive, and increases often come not in the form of higher quantity, but higher quality, which is much more difficult to measure. This type of measurement system will favor Bob's friend Gerry, who works in manufacturing.

11.
   a. Tight
   b. Loose
   c. Loose
   d. Tight
   e. Tight
   f. Loose

12. In the early 1990s the economy was coming out of a recession more rapidly than the Fed liked, and the chairman of the Fed feared inflation would begin to creep up to unacceptable levels. The Fed therefore raised its lending rates to banks, which had the effect of raising interest to both consumers and businesses. As a result, consumers didn't borrow as freely and businesses did not borrow as easily and thus didn't expand as rapidly. The threat of inflation then eased.

Learning Goals 5, 6

13.
   a. Fiscal policy
   b. Monetary policy
   c. Fiscal policy
   d. Fiscal policy
   e. Monetary policy
   f. Fiscal policy
   g. Fiscal policy
   h. fiscal policy

14. Small business owners, who create many of the jobs and much of the wealth for the economy, are often severely affected by changes in the tax rates. These business owners may add jobs and hire more people when they know their tax liability will be lower as a result of a tax reduction. Consequently, while tax rates may be lower, a greater number of people will be paying into the system, and this could have the effect of increasing government tax revenues.

PRACTICE TEST

Multiple Choice

1.	b	11.	c
2.	d	12.	c
3.	a	13.	d
4.	d	14.	b
5.	c	15.	d
6.	c	16.	c
7.	a	17.	b
8.	a	18.	c
9.	d	19.	c
10.	a	20.	c

True/False

1.	T	11.	F
2.	T	12.	T
3.	F	13.	T
4.	T	14.	T
5.	F	15.	T
6.	F	16.	T
7.	T	17.	F
8.	F	18.	T
9.	T	19.	F
10.	F	20.	F

CHAPTER 3
COMPETING IN GLOBAL MARKETS

LEARNING GOALS

After you have read and studied this chapter, you should be able to:

1. Discuss the increasing importance of the global market and the roles of comparative advantage and absolute advantage in international trade.

2. Explain how the marketing motto "Find a need and fill it" applies to global markets and define the terms used in international business.

3. Describe the current status of the United States in global business.

4. Illustrate the strategies used in reaching global markets.

5. Discuss the hurdles of trading in world markets.

6. Debate the advantages and disadvantages of trade protectionism.

7. Discuss the future of global trade.

8. Discuss the role of multinational corporations in global markets.

LEARNING THE LANGUAGE

Listed here are important terms found in this chapter. Choose the correct term for each definition and write it in the space provided.

Absolute advantage	Export Assistance Centers (EACs)	Licensing
Balance of payment	Export trading company	Mercantilism
Balance of trade	Exporting	Multinational corporation
Bartering	Floating exchange rate	North American Free Trade Agreement (NAFTA)
Common market	Foreign Corrupt Practices Act of 1978	Protective tariff
Comparative advantage theory	Foreign direct investment	Revenue tariff
Contract manufacturing	Global marketing	Trade deficit
Countertrading	Foreign subsidiary	Trade protectionism
Debtor nation	Free trade	
Devaluation	Free trade area	World Trade Organization (WTO)

Dumping	General Agreement on Tariffs and Trade (GATT)	
Embargo	Import quota	
Ethnocentricity	Importing	
Exchange rate	Joint venture	

1. A(n) _____ is an import tax designed to raise money for the government.

2. The term _____ is used to describe selling the same product in essentially the same way everywhere in the world.

3. The practice of selling products in foreign countries for less than you charge for the same products in your own country is known as _____.

4. There is a(n) _____ when a country has a monopoly on the production of a specific product or is able to produce it more efficiently than all other nations.

5. The difference between money coming into a country and money leaving the country plus money-flows from other factors such as tourism, foreign aid, military expenditures and foreign investment is the _____.

6. A(n) _____ is a complete ban on the import or export of certain products.

7. When there is a limit on the number of products in certain categories that can be imported, a(n) _____ has been established.

8. When a country has a _____ it is buying more goods from other nations than are sold to them.

9. The relationship of exports to imports is called the _____.

10. The _____ is the value of one currency relative to the currencies of other countries.

11. A country is involved in _____ when it is buying products from another country.

12. In a _____, a partnership is formed in which companies often from two different countries, join to undertake a major project.

13. _____ is the exchange of goods or services for goods or services.

14. An organization that attempts to match buyers and sellers from different countries is called a(n) _____.

15. A company is involved in _____ when it signs an agreement in which a producer allows a foreign company to produce its product in exchange for royalties.

16. The economic principle of _____ advocates the selling of more goods to other nations than a country purchases.

17. The European Union is an example of a _____, a regional group of countries that have no internal tariffs, a common external tariff and the coordination of laws to facilitate exchange between countries.

18. A company is involved in _____ when it is selling products to another country.

19. In a _____ there exists a market in which nations can trade freely with each other without tariffs or other trade barriers.

20. An organization that manufactures and markets in many different countries and has multinational stock ownership and multinational management is considered a _____.

21. A theory that states that a country should produce and sell to other countries those products that it produces most efficiently is the _____.

22. The _____ is a law, which specifically prohibits "questionable" or "dubious" payments to foreign officials to secure business contracts.

23. An import tax designed to raise the price of imported products so that domestic products will be more competitive is called a(n) _____.

24. A company is involved in _____ when it produces private-label goods to which another company attaches its brand name or trademark.

25. Lowering the value of a nation's currency relative to other currencies is known as _____.

26. There is _____ when the movement of goods and services among nations occurs without political or economic obstruction.

27. The use of government regulations to limit the import of goods and services is considered to be _____, which is based on the theory that domestic producers can survive and grow, producing more jobs.

28. American business people have been accused of _____ which is a feeling that one's own culture is superior to all others.

29. Poorer countries will use a form of bartering among several countries, which is known as _____.

30. Many countries today are involved in _____, which is the buying of permanent property and businesses in foreign nations.

31. A _____ is a company that is owned by another company in a foreign country.

32. The United States has been called a _____ which is a country that owes more money to other nations than they owe it.

33. The _____ was an agreement among 23 countries which provided a forum for negotiating mutual reductions in trade restrictions.

34. These organizations known as _____ were created to provide hands-on exporting assistance and trade finance support for small and medium-sized businesses.

35. This organization, known as the _____ replaced the GATT agreement, and was assigned the duty to mediate trade disputes.

36. The value of currencies that fluctuate according to the supply and demand in the market for the currency is called the _____.

37. Canada, the United States and Mexico formed a free trade area through an agreement known as the _____.

RETENTION CHECK

Learning Goal 1   **The Dynamic Global Market**

1. What are some statistics that indicate the importance of international business for U.S. firms?

    a. _____

    b. _____

    c. _____

    d. _____

2. What are three reasons why countries trade with each other?

   a. _____

   b. _____

   c. _____

3. Describe the basic theory of comparative advantage.

Learning Goal 2 **Getting Involved in Global Trade**

4. What's the difference between comparative advantage and absolute advantage?

5. What is a favorable balance of trade?

6. Why do countries prefer to have a favorable balance of trade?

7. Why have some countries used the tactic of "dumping"?

Learning Goal 3   **Trading in Global Markets: The U.S. Experience**

8. What factors led to American businesses going global in the late 1980s and early 1990s?

9. Does the U.S. have a trade surplus or trade deficit?

10. Why was the U.S. called a "debtor nation?"

Learning Goal 4   **Strategies for Reaching Global Markets**

11. List seven strategies for reaching global markets.

    a._____   e._____

    b._____   f._____

    c._____   g._____

    d._____

12. What are the advantages of:

    a. Licensing

    b. Creating subsidiaries

    c. Contract manufacturing

    d. International joint ventures

    e. Countertrading

13. What are the disadvantages of:

    a. Licensing

b. International joint ventures

a. Creating subsidiaries

Learning Goal 5   **Hurdles of Trading in Global Markets**

14. What are four hurdles to trading in global markets?

    a. _____

    b. _____

    c. _____

    d. _____

15. What is "ethnocentricity?"

16. What is "global marketing?"

17. a. What is the Foreign Corrupt Practices Act?

  b. What is the impact of this Act on American firms?

18. What is meant by a "high value of the dollar?"

19. What impact does a "high value of the dollar" have on U.S. businesses?

20. What is a floating exchange rate?

21. How is supply and demand for currencies created?

Learning Goal 6   **Trade Protectionism**

22. List five forms of trade protectionism.

   a._____   d._____

   b._____   e._____

   c._____

23. Why do countries use trade protection measures?

24. What is the difference between a revenue tariff and a protective tariff?

25. What is the difference between an import quota and an embargo?

26. What is a form of non-tariff barrier used by the Japanese?

27. What are three trade agreements negotiated in the early 1990s?

   a. _____

   b. _____

   c. _____

28. What are two areas covered by the new GATT, passed in 1994?

   a. _____

   b. _____

29. What organization replaced the GATT in 1995?

30. What is a common market?

31. What is the EU?

32. What are 5 elements of the European Union agreement that are "scary" to the countries, which are part of the EU?

   a. _____

   b. _____

   c. _____

   d. _____

   e. _____

33. What does NAFTA stand for?

34. What three countries are part of the NAFTA agreement?

   a. _____   b. _____   c. _____

35. What were the three primary questions surrounding the NAFTA debate?

   a. _____

   b. _____

   c. _____

Learning Goal 7   **Multinational Corporations and the Future of Global Trade**

36. What are three characteristics of a multinational corporation?

   a. _____

   b. _____

   c. _____

37. What three countries are mentioned in the text as having tremendous market potential?

   a. _____   b. _____   c. _____

CRITICAL THINKING EXERCISES

Learning Goal 1

1. Using the theory of comparative advantage, explain Figure 3-1 in your text.

Learning Goal 2

2. Re-read the example of the ice factory in Africa, and the other examples of opportunities found in international markets. How do they illustrate the importance of entrepreneurship, capitalism and Adam Smith's "invisible hand" theory in the international market? How can you take advantage of the opportunities?

Learning Goal 3

3. Find the most recent trade statistics for

    a. The United States   Exports / Imports /   Balance of Trade (deficit) (surplus)

                                                                                                              _____

    b. Your state   Exports / Imports   _____

What are the top ten countries with which your state trades?

What is the largest category of foreign sales?

These statistics can be found on the Internet, with just a bit of looking around. A good place to start for the information regarding the U.S Trade Statistics is www.census.gov. For the state data, you may be able to start with www.ecodev.state.(state abbreviation).us, or, using a search engine, use the key words "exports" and the name of your state.

4. The United States is the world's largest exporter, yet the text indicates that the U.S. "in general has never been very active in exporting." How can you explain these seemingly contradictory statements?

5. How can direct foreign investment in the United States, (for example, the purchase of Pebble Beach Golf Club by the Japanese) be considered a sign of strength for the American economy?

Learning Goal 4

6. There are several ways to become involved in world trade:

    Exporting   Franchising

    Licensing   Joint ventures

    Creating subsidiaries   Countertrading

    Contract manufacturing

    Match the term with the situations below:

    a. This kind of an agreement with a Japanese food concern will give Campbell Soup a chance to increase its market share in Japan's soup market, which is very difficult to enter._____

    b. In this kind of agreement, also known as outsourcing, Nike's name is placed on shoes manufactured overseas and distributed here._____

    c. McDonald's, Ramada Inns, and KFC have successfully used this form of operation in foreign markets, after changing their product to suit local tastes._____

    d. Chrysler traded its vehicles in Jamaica for bauxite in this form of international trade._____

    e. In 1995, Grand Metropolitan, a corporation headquartered in Great Britain, acquired Pet, Inc. of St. Louis._____

f. GE has a number of bilingual workers with advanced degrees in its trading department to help the corporation with this kind of international trade, selling their product to foreign markets._____

g. Coke and Pepsi often enter foreign markets by allowing a foreign manufacturer to use its trademark and pay them (Coke and Pepsi) a royalty for that right._____

Learning Goal 5

7. Discuss the issues of the value of the dollar relative to other currencies. What impact does lowering the value of the dollar have? How would American businesses be affected if the dollar were devalued, as the Mexican peso was a few years ago?

8. The everyday difficulties of doing business at home are compounded by a variety of differences between U.S. and foreign markets. Difficulties can stem from cultural and social differences, economic problems, legal and political regulations and problems with currencies. Keep those ideas in mind in completing the following.

You have a successful ice cream/frozen yogurt business in the United States, and are especially interested in opening a store in the Middle East, probably Saudi Arabia. You market your product through free-standing buildings in the U.S., but are unsure of how to start up in Saudi Arabia. You have begun to seriously think about the possibility, but are concerned about some of the problems you may encounter. What are the things you need to consider before going ahead with your plan?

Learning Goal 6

9. Governments have developed a number of ways to protect their domestic industries from what they would consider the potentially negative impact of foreign trade:

    Protective tariffs   Embargoes

    Revenue tariffs   Non-tariff barriers

    Import quotas

Match the correct type of trade protectionism to each of the following:

a. The amount of Argentine beef brought into the United States is limited by this form of agreement._____

b. Mexico has several of this type of tariff, designed to raise money for its government._____

c. In early 1995, the U.S. imposed this type of "restriction" on Chinese-made goods, in retaliation for the pirating of U.S.-made products by Chinese manufacturers. The effect of this "restriction" was a 100% increase in the cost of Chinese-made goods sold in the United States._____

d. The U.S. has refused to allow the products of Cuba and some other countries to be sold in the U.S. under one of these programs._____

e. Belgium requires margarine to be sold in cubes, cutting off those companies, which manufacture margarine in tubs.
_____

Learning Goal 7

10. What is the underlying principle of mercantilism?

11. What distinguishes an MNC from a company less involved in global business?

PRACTICE TEST

Multiple Choice: circle the best answer.

1. Selling products to another country is known as:

    a. importing
    b. trade protectionism
    c. comparative advantage
    d. exporting

2. All of the following are reasons for countries to participate in foreign trade except:

    a. countries need to make a profit from foreign trade, because the market in the U.S. has slowed.
    b. no nation can produce all of the product its people want and need.
    c. even if a country were self-sufficient, other nations would demand to trade with that country.
    d. some nations have resources, but not technological know-how, others have know-how, but lack resources.

3. Producing and selling goods that we produce most effectively and efficiently, and buying goods that other countries produce most effectively and efficiently is known as:

    a. absolute advantage.
    b. free trade.
    c. international marketing.
    d. comparative advantage.

4. When the value of exports from a country exceeds the value of imports into that country, there is a _____.

    a. trade deficit
    b. balance of payments
    c. unfavorable balance of trade
    d. favorable balance of trade

5. The difference between money coming into a country from exports and money leaving a country due to imports, plus money flows from other factors, is known as the:

   a. balance of trade.
   b. dumping effect.
   c. balance of payments.
   d. trade deficit.

6. A basic formula for success in exporting to the global marketplace would be:

   a. buy here, sell there.
   b. find a need and fill it.
   c. always sell a product for less than what you charge at home.
   d. focus only on countries where incomes are the highest.

7. The United States exports:

   a. less volume, but a greater percentage of our products than other countries.
   b. greater volume than other countries, and a greater percentage of our products.
   c. about the same volume as other countries, but a lower percentage of our products.
   d. a greater volume than other countries, but a lower percentage of our products.

8. In the 1990s Grand Metropolitan acquired several U.S. firms, such as Pillsbury, and itself owned Pet, Inc. Pet and Pillsbury now operate in the U.S. as:

   a. exporters.
   b. subsidiaries.
   c. licensing agent.
   d. franchise.

9. Coke and Pepsi often enter foreign markets by allowing a foreign manufacturer to use their trademark and pay them (Coke or Pepsi) a royalty for that right. This is an example of:

   a. joint venture.
   b. exporting.
   c. licensing.
   d. creating a subsidiary.

10. Nike uses this type of global strategy when Nike distributes products which have been manufactured by a foreign company, but which have the Nike brand name.

    a. international joint venture
    b. franchising
    c. exporting
    d. contract manufacturing

11. In franchising to foreign markets, companies such as McDonald's and KFC have had to:

    a. be careful to adapt to the countries they are attempting to enter.
    b. find franchisees with money they can afford to lose if the franchise fails.
    c. be sure not to alter their products for foreign markets, so that consumers know exactly what they are getting.
    d. find opportunities for joint ventures, as franchising doesn't seem to work in foreign markets.

12. Americans are often called ethnocentric. This means that:

    a. Americans feel their culture is superior to others.
    b. Americans welcome diversity in their workforce.
    c. U.S. firms are actively seeking international markets.
    d. U.S. businesses are pursuing a policy of multiculturalism.

13. Guillermo Martinez was concerned that his new boss, Donald Darr didn't know his job very well. Donald is continually asking Guillermo and the other workers in this plant in Mexico City, to give him their opinions before he makes a final decision. Guillermo's concern stems from _____ differences between him and Donald.

    a. economic
    b. cultural
    c. language
    d. regulatory

14. The makers of Whirlpool washers and other electrical appliance manufacturers need to be concerned about the kind and availability of electricity in the global marketplace. If there were a compatibility problem, it would be the result of a _____ difference.

    a. cultural
    b. technological
    c. economic
    d. societal

15. The law that specifically prohibits "questionable" or "dubious" payments to foreign officials in an effort to secure business contracts is called the:

    a. North American Free Trade Agreement.
    b. General Agreement on Tariffs and Trade.
    c. Securities and Exchange Act.
    d. Foreign Corrupt Practices Act.

16. A high value of the dollar would mean:

    a. your money is worth more at the stores where you shop.
    b. a dollar could be traded for more foreign currency than normal.
    c. you could trade in your money for gold.
    d. costs of foreign manufacturing would be higher.

17. When Mexico devalued the peso, the peso became _____ valuable relative to other currencies.

    a. more
    b. less
    c. equally
    d. significantly more

18. Using government regulations to limit the import of goods and services in order to protect domestic industries against dumping and foreign competition is called:

    a. mercantilism.
    b. regulating the balance of trade.
    c. global marketing.
    d. trade protectionism.

19. When the U.S. government imposes a tax on imported textiles, to protect the American textile industry, a(n) _____ is being levied.

    a. protective tariff
    b. import quota
    c. embargo
    d. revenue tariff

20. Which of the following would not be considered a non-tariff barrier?

    a. A requirement that all products sold in a country be packaged in a certain way.
    b. A tradition of semi-permanent ties between domestic firms, which have the effect of shutting out foreign manufacturers.
    c. Signing a trade agreement such as the GATT.
    d. A set of quality standards that must be met by all companies wishing to do business within a country.

21. This agreement was established in 1948, and is designed to facilitate the exchange of goods, services, ideas and cultural programs.

    a. General Agreement on Tariffs and Trade (GATT)
    b. World Trade Organization (WTO)
    c. North American Free Trade Agreement (NAFTA)
    d. The European Union (EU)

22. The _____ replaced the _____ in 1995, and is assigned the task of mediating trade disputes.

    a. NAFTA/WTO
    b. GATT/ EU
    c. WTO/GATT
    d. GATT/NAFTA

23. An organization that does manufacturing and marketing in many different countries, has multinational stock ownership and multinational management is considered a:

    a. common market.
    b. free trade area.
    c. global marketer.
    d. multinational corporation.

24. Which of the following is not considered to be a concern when evaluating trade with China?

    a. The one-party political system
    b. Human rights policies
    c. A shrinking market
    d. A growing trade imbalance

25. Since the fall of communism, Russia:

    a. is considered to be too great a risk for foreign investment.
    b. is considered to have a great deal of potential for the future.
    c. is not an especially attractive market.
    d. still is basically closed to Western investment.

TRUE/FALSE

1. ____ It is expected that the amount of international trade will level off or decline in the next millenium.

2. ____ Trade relations enable a nation to produce what it's most capable of and to buy what it needs but cannot produce.

3. ____ An example of exporting is the Meridian Group, based in the United States, selling sand to customers in the Middle East.

4. ____ When the country of Monrovia is buying more from the United States than it is selling to the United States, a favorable balance of trade exists for Monrovia.

5. ____ The goal of global trade is always to have more money flowing into the country than flowing out of the country.

6. ____ The tactic of dumping is used to gain a foothold in a foreign market.

7. ____ The purchase of the Pebble Beach Golf Club by the Japanese is an example of foreign direct investment.

8. ____ While the U.S. is considered to be a debtor nation, that is not necessarily a bad sign.

9. ____ Export Assistance Centers serve the role of matching buyers and sellers from different countries and of providing other services to ease the process of exporting.

10. ____ One disadvantage of licensing is the cost to the company licensing its product or trademark (the licensor) to the foreign firm. (the licensee)

11. ____ An international joint venture is helpful to companies wishing to enter countries with planned economies, such as China, or in markets which for some reason are difficult to enter.

12. ____ Countertrading, or bartering is not a particularly important part of international trade, and few countries participate.

13. ____ Religion is an important element of a society's culture, and should be considered in making many business decisions.

14. ____ Economic differences between countries can affect purchasing patterns, such as quantity purchased at a given time.

15. ____ A sound global philosophy is " always assume that what works in one country will work in another.

16. _____ Trade protectionism is based upon the idea that barriers will help domestic producers grow, and create more jobs.

17. _____ Non-tariff barriers can be just as detrimental to free trade as tariffs.

18. _____ The World Trade Organization was replaced by the GATT.

19. _____ It is possible that there will be a new currency in the European Union, called the "euro."

20. _____ Investment in China is still considered to be too risky to invest a great deal of money.

ANSWERS

LEARNING THE LANGUAGE

1. Revenue tariff	14. Export trading company	27. Trade protectionism
2. Global marketing	15. Licensing	28. Ethnocentricity
3. Dumping	16. Mercantilism	29. Countertrading
4. Absolute advantage	17. Common market	30. Foreign direct investment
5. Balance of payments	18. Exporting	31. Foreign subsidiary
6. Embargo	19. Free trade area	32. Debtor nation
7. Import quota	20. Multinational corporation	33. General Agreement on Tariffs and Trade (GATT)
8. Trade deficit	21. Comparative advantage theory	34. Export Assistance Centers(EACs)
9. Balance of trade	22. Foreign Corrupt Practices Act	35. World Trade Organization(WTO)
10. Exchange rate	23. Protective tariff	36. floating exchange rate
11. Importing	24. Contract manufacturing	37. North American Free Trade Agreement (NAFTA)
12. Joint venture	25. Devaluation	
13. Bartering	26. Free trade	

RETENTION CHECK

Learning Goal 1   **The Dynamic Global Market**

1.
   a. There are 6 billion people in the world, and 95% of them live outside the U.S.
   b. We are currently buying approximately $100 billion worth of goods from Japan alone.
   c. Sales of U.S. made goods sold outside the U.S. are growing.
   d. We are the largest importer in the world

2.
   a. No nation can produce all of the products its people need and want.
   b. Even if a given country were self-sufficient, other nations would want to trade with that country to meet the needs of its people.
   c. Trade allows nations to produce what they are capable of producing and to buy from other nations what they need.

3. The theory of comparative advantage states that a country should produce and sell to other countries those products that it produces most effectively and efficiently, and should buy from other countries those products it cannot produce as effectively or efficiently.

Learning Goal 2   **Getting Involved in Global Trade**

4. As stated in the last answer, comparative advantage states that a country should produce and sell the products it produces most effectively and efficiently, and should buy those products other countries are better at producing and selling. A country has an absolute advantage when it has a monopoly on production of a good, or can produce it more cheaply that any other country.

5. A favorable balance of trade exists when the value of exports exceeds the value of imports.

6. Countries prefer to export more than they import, or have a favorable balance of trade, because the country will retain more of its money to buy other goods and services. As the example in the text illustrates, if I sell you $200 worth of goods, and only buy $100, I have an extra $100 available to buy other things.

7. The tactic of dumping is used to unload surplus products in foreign markets or to gain a foothold in a new market by offering products cheaper than domestic competitors.

Learning Goal 3   **Trading in Global Markets: The U.S. Experience**

8. Slow economic growth in the U.S. lured more businesses to global markts in the late 1980s and early 1990s.

9. As of this writing, the U.S. has an overall trade deficit.

10. A debtor nation is a country that owes more money to other nations than they owe to it. In the 1980s it was reported that the U.S. was a debtor nation because it owed more money than was owed to it.

Learning Goal 4   **Strategies for Reaching Global Markets**

11. a. Exporting
    b. Licensing
    c. Creating subsidiaries
    d. Contract manufacturing
    e. Franchising

3-29

    f. International joint ventures
    g. Countertrading (bartering)

12. a. The advantages of licensing are several: additional revenue from a product that would not have generated domestic revenues; start-up supplies, materials and consulting services must be purchased from the licensing firm, which generates even more revenue and reduces costs of entering a foreign market. Most costs are borne by the licensee.

  b. The primary advantage of creating a subsidiary is that the company maintains complete control over any technology or expertise it possesses.

  c. Through contract manufacturing a company can experiment in a new market without heavy start-up costs, which reduces risk.

  d. The advantages of an international joint venture are easier for some countries to enter difficult markets, shared markets, shared marketing expertise, and shared risk.

  e. Countertrading or bartering is especially important to poorer countries, which have little cash available for trade. It allows these countries to get what their people need by using the advantages the country may have.

13. a. One problem with licensing is that a firm often must grant licensing rights to its product for as long as 20 years. Revenue from an especially successful product would then go to the licensee. Further, if a foreign licensee learns the technology, it could break its agreement and begin to produce the product on its own. The licensing company loses trade secrets and royalties.

  b. An important disadvantage of an international joint venture is that the partner can learn your technology and go off on its own as a competitor. Over time technology may become obsolete, or the partnership may become too large to be flexible.

  c. The major drawback of creating a subsidiary is the heavy investment in a foreign country. If relations with the host country sour, the firm's assets could be taken over by the foreign government.

Learning Goal 5 **Hurdles of Trading in Global Markets**

14. Hurdles of trading in global markets are:
  a. Cultural differences.
  b. Societal and economic differences.
  c. Legal and regulatory differences.
  d. Problems with currency shifts.

15. Ethnocentricity is the feeling that one's own culture is superior to all others. Many American businesspeople have been accused of this.

16. Global marketing is selling the same product in essentially the same way everywhere in the world.

17. a. The Foreign Corrupt Practices Act specifically prohibits "questionable" or "dubious" payments to foreign officials to secure business contracts.

    b. This type of legislation can create hardships for American businesses in competing with foreign competitors, because in some countries actions such as corporate bribery are acceptable, and sometimes the only way to secure a lucrative contract.

18. A high value of the dollar means that the dollar will buy, or can be traded for, more foreign currency than normal.

19. When the dollar is high the products of foreign producers become cheaper, because it takes fewer dollars to buy them. The costs of U.S.-produced goods on the other hand, become more expensive to foreign buyers, because of the dollar's high value.

20. The floating exchange rate is a system in which currencies "float" according to the supply and demand in the market for the currency.

21. Supply and demand for currencies is created by global currency traders, who create a market for a nation's currency based upon the perceived trade and investment potential of the country.

Learning Goal 6 **Trade Protectionism**

22. Forms of trade protectionism are:
    a. Protective tariffs.
    b. Revenue tariffs.
    c. Import quotas.
    d. Embargoes.
    e. Non-tariff barriers.

23. Countries use trade protection measures to protect their industries against dumping and foreign competition that hurts domestic industry. It is based upon the theory that such practices will help domestic producers survive and grow, which will produce more jobs.

24. A protective tariff is designed to raise the retail price of an imported good so the domestic product will be more competitive. The revenue tariff is designed to raise money for the government.

25. An import quota limits the number of products in certain categories that can be imported into a nation. An embargo is a complete ban on the import or export of products into a certain country.

26. The Japanese use non-tariff barriers in the form of semi-permanent ties with suppliers, customers and distributors, making it difficult for foreigners to enter their markets.

27. a. General Agreement on Tariffs and Trade (GATT).
    b. European Union (EU).
    c. North American Free Trade Agreement (NAFTA).

28. The new GATT
    a. lowers tariffs by 38 percent worldwide.
    b. extends GATT rules to new areas such as agriculture, services and the protection of patents.

29. In 1995 the World Trade Organization (WTO) replaced the GATT.

30. A common market is a regional group of countries that have no internal tariffs, a common external tariff and have coordinated laws to facilitate exchange between countries.

31. The EU is a group of nations in Western Europe that dissolved their economic borders and formed a common market in the early 1990s.

32. The member countries of the EU have been slow to unify, because they fear:
    a. movement of labor.
    b. shared social programs.
    c. new and strange tax systems.
    d. a new currency.
    e. shared professional standards.

33. The North American Free Trade Agreement

34. The NAFTA consists of an agreement between:
    a. The United States.
    b. Canada.
    c. Mexico.

35. The questions surrounding the NAFTA were:
    a. U.S. employment.
    b. Exports.
    c. The environment.

Learning Goal 7 **Multinational Corporations and the Future of Global Trade**

36. A multinational corporation, or MNC:
    a. does manufacturing in many different countries.
    b. has multinational stock ownership.
    c. has multinational management.

37. Three countries with tremendous market potential are:

a. China.
b. Russia.
c. Japan.

CRITICAL THINKING EXERCISES

Learning Goal 1

1. The theory of comparative advantage states that a country should produce and sell to other countries those products that it produces most effectively and efficiently and should buy from other countries those products it cannot produce as effectively or efficiently. Figure 3-1 shows that the United States would seem to have a comparative advantage in areas such as high technology (Intel, Sun Microsystems, Hewlett-Packard) and in aerospace or aviation technology (Boeing, and McDonnell-Douglas which has been acquired by Boeing). We import products that are more expensive to produce here in the United States, such as shoes, coffee, and videotape recorders.

Learning Goal 2

2. It was stated in Chapter 2 that developing countries (particularly Eastern Europe) must allow entrepreneurship to flourish, so to speak, if their economies are to develop and become active participants in the global market. The same can be said for any part of the world. Adam Smith's idea of the invisible hand was simply that when an individual is allowed the incentive to work hard by being allowed to keep the profits from his business, society will benefit by getting needed goods or services. The story of the ice factory illustrates the invisible hand theory – the entrepreneur who started the factory "is indeed wealthy" and the country has a needed resource.

   The way to take advantage of these ideas is by doing research, travelling, finding a need either in the United States for a product that can be imported, or overseas for a product that can be exported. The key is to <u>be creative</u>.

Learning Goal 3

3. Information about U.S. trade statistics will vary, depending upon the year for which you are able to find information. These statistics will also be different from one state to another. However, by comparison, the state of Missouri had $ 8.1 billion of sales to foreign markets in 1997, and ranked 28th in foreign sales. Missouri products were sold in 179 countries, with the top five being Canada, Mexico, Finland, Belgium and Japan. The largest industrial category of foreign sales was chemicals, which was followed by agricultural products, transportation equipment, industrial machinery and computers, and electronic equipment and components.

4. While a majority of large businesses are involved in global trade, we export a much lower percentage of our products than other countries. Therefore, by comparison, we are not as active as many other nations in the global marketplace. Further, the United States does not depend upon exporting as much as other industrialized nations, as indicated by the percentage of GDP exported by the U.S.

5. Many see direct foreign investment as a positive sign. They believe that the level of foreign investment has increased because the American economy has been so strong and we have been perceived worldwide as an economic leader. Property, building and stock have been a more attractive investment in the United States than elsewhere. The time to worry is when the level of investment begins to drop off, and other countries become more attractive.

Learning Goal 4

6.
   a. Joint venture
   b. Contract manufacturing
   c. Franchising
   d. Countertrading
   e. Creating a subsidiary
   f. Exporting
   g. Licensing

Learning Goal 5

7. Lowering the value of the dollar means that a dollar is traded for less foreign currency than normal. Foreign goods would become more expensive because it would take more dollars to buy them. It also makes American goods cheaper to foreign buyers because it would take less foreign currency to buy them. In the long run, this could benefit U.S. firms in foreign markets. Devaluing a currency means lowering the value of a nation's currency relative to other currencies. This can cause problems with changes in labor costs, material costs and financing.

American businesses would find their products less expensive in foreign countries, which could be beneficial for sales, but their cost of doing business in foreign countries could be negatively affected by devaluation.

8. One of the first things to consider is how the Saudis feel about ice cream/frozen yogurt as a product. How it's eaten, their views on dairy products (some religions have different views on dairy products and how they should be handled), where it can be marketed (do they have the same kind of grocery stores? Do you open a free standing store?), even their familiarity with the product are all issues that must be addressed. There is a possibility that this may be a totally new product concept and you, as a seller of the product, will need to be aware of how to convince the Saudi people that this is a viable and acceptable product.

Social and economic differences from the American market must also be considered. In the U.S. frozen yogurt and ice cream may be purchased on a trip to the grocery store, and stored at home in the refrigerator. Is that a similar life style to the Saudis? Is the type of equipment available, which is needed to store the product before it is purchased? Does a typical Saudi home have the type of storage needed, i.e., a freezer? American families may go to an ice cream or frozen yogurt stand as a family outing. Would that be true of a typical Saudi family? We eat ice cream or frozen yogurt as a dessert or sometimes as a snack. How would the Saudi population view the product? When might they choose to eat it?

Although Saudi Arabia as a nation may be wealthy, does the average Saudi have the money to buy a nonessential item like this?

Further questions to be answered revolve around legal and regulatory differences. The way of doing business in the Middle East is quite different from that of the U.S. Laws and regulations will vary, and practices will be different there than at home. The manner of entering business in the Middle East will be different from the U.S.

Additionally, will it be economically feasible to invest in the Middle East? How is the American dollar against the Saudi's currency? That may affect the ability and willingness of the Saudis to try your product should you decide to export your product to the country. Should you decide to attempt to produce and sell your product in Saudi Arabia, the value of the U.S. dollar will take on even more significance in light of the greater investment.

Learning Goal 6

9. a. Import quota
    b. Revenue tariffs
    c. Protective tariffs
    d. Embargo
    e. Non-tariff barriers

Learning Goal 7

10. The underlying principle of mercantilism is to sell more goods to other nations than you buy from them. In other words, the goal is to have a favorable balance of trade. Mercantilism is the foundation for trade protectionism, and the various kinds of trade barriers discussed in the text.

11. A company is only considered a multinational if it does manufacturing and marketing in more than one foreign nation. An MNC will manufacture and market in several countries, has multinational stock ownership and multinational management. The more multinational a company is, the more it will attempt to operate without being influenced

by restrictions from various governments. Typically, multinationals are very large corporations.

PRACTICE TEST

Multiple Choice

1.	d	14.	b
2.	a	15.	d
3.	d	16.	b
4.	d	17.	b
5.	c	18.	d
6.	b	19.	a
7.	d	20.	c
8.	b	21.	a
9.	c	22.	c
10.	d	23.	d
11.	a	24.	c
12.	a	25.	b
13.	b		

True/False

1.	F	11.	T
2.	T	12.	F
3.	T	13.	T
4.	F	14.	T
5.	T	15.	F
6.	T	16.	T
7.	T	17.	T
8.	T	18.	F
9.	F	19.	T
10.	F	20.	F

CHAPTER 4
DEMONSTRATING ETHICAL BEHAVIOR AND SOCIAL RESPONSIBILITY

LEARNING GOALS

After you have read and studied this chapter, you should be able to:

1. Explain why legality is only the first step in behaving ethically.

2. Ask the three questions one should answer when faced with a potentially unethical action.

3. Describe management's role in setting ethical standards.

4. Distinguish between compliance-based and integrity-based ethics codes and list the six steps in setting up a corporate ethics code.

5. Define social responsibility and examine corporate responsibility to various stakeholders.

6. Analyze the role of American businesses in influencing ethical and social responsibility in global markets.

LEARNING THE LANGUAGE

Listed here are important terms found in this chapter. Choose the correct term for each definition and write it in the space provided.

Compliance-based ethics codes	Ethics
Corporate philanthropy	Integrity-based ethics codes
Corporate policy	Social audit
Corporate responsibility	Social responsibility

1. Known as _____, these ethical standards emphasize preventing unlawful behavior by increasing control and by penalizing wrongdoers.

2. When a corporation performs a _____ it is conducting a systematic evaluation of an organization's progress toward implementing programs that are socially responsible and responsive.

3. _____ is the position a firm takes on issues that affect the firm and society, including political issues.

4. Standards of moral behavior, or _____ is behavior that is accepted by society as right or wrong.

5. _____ are ethical standards that define the organization's guiding values, create an environment that supports ethically sound behavior, and stress a shared accountability among employees.

6. The dimension of social responsibility that includes charitable donations to nonprofit groups is called _____.

7. When a business shows concern for welfare of a society as a whole, it is demonstrating _____.

8. A dimension of social responsibility known as _____ includes everything from minority hiring practices to making safe products.

RETENTION CHECK

Learning Goal 1   **Managing Business Ethically and Responsibly**

1. What is the difference between being "ethical" and being "legal"?

2. Where does a sense of personal ethics begin?

3. How do many Americans decide what is ethical?

Learning Goal 2

4. What are three questions to ask yourself when faced with an ethical dilemma?

    a. _____

    b. _____

    c. _____

Learning Goal 3   Ethics is More Than an Individual Concern

5. Where does a sense of organizational ethics begin?

6. How do people learn standards and values?

7. What are six reasons to manage ethically?

    a. _____

    b. _____

    c. _____

    d. _____

    e. _____

    f. _____

Learning Goal 4   **Setting Corporate Ethical Standards**

8. What are two types of ethics codes?

   a. _____

   b. _____

9. What is the difference between them?

10. What are six steps to follow for a long-term improvement of America's business ethics?

    a. _____

    b. _____

    c. _____

    d. _____

    e. _____

    f. _____

Learning Goal 5   **Corporate Social Responsibility**

11. What is corporate social responsibility?

12. What are three dimensions of corporate social responsibility?

   a. _____

   b. _____

   c. _____

13. What are four groups which comprise the stakeholders to whom businesses are responsible?

   a. _____

   b. _____

   c. _____

   d. _____

14. What are three responsibilities businesses have toward employees?

   a. _____

   b. _____

   c. _____

15. What are three areas of responsibility to society?

   a. _____

   b. _____

   c. _____

16. What is a social audit?

17. What is a major problem in conducting a social audit?

18. What are some examples of socially responsible business activities?

    a. _____

    b. _____

    c. _____

    d. _____

    e. _____

19. What are four types of "watch-dog" groups which monitor how well companies enforce ethical and social responsibility policies?

    a. _____

    b. _____

    c. _____

    d. _____

Learning Goal 6   **International Ethics and Social Responsibility**

20. What are questions regarding American standards of ethics being imposed on international suppliers?

CRITICAL THINKING EXERCISES

Learning Goal 1

1. "...people learn their standards and values from observing what others do, not what they say."

    The following situation is typical of those in which businesspersons may find themselves at some time. Refer to the ethics check questions in your text and determine what you would do.

    Daryl, the general supervisor of a marketing department of a mid-sized Midwestern corporation, is an ambitious young man. He is writing a book that he hopes will make a name for himself in the business community. Because the word processing for the actual text is very time-consuming Daryl is using the secretary he shares with 2 other managers, as well as some of his market research interns to type the book while they're at work. Because they are often busy doing his book, people from the other departments are finding they can't get their work-related business done. The secretary and interns feel they have to do what Daryl says because he is their direct supervisor.

    You are Daryl's peer in another department, and you also have some outside work you need to have typed. You're annoyed at Daryl's actions, but would rather not inform your boss (who is also Daryl's boss) about what's going on because you want to maintain a friendly working relationship with Daryl, and besides, you never know how "the boss" is going to react. Sometimes you begin to think that if Daryl can get away with using company equipment, personnel and time for his personal projects, why can't you?

Learning Goals 2, 3

2. You work for a major car manufacturer as a district manager, calling on car dealerships as a representative of the manufacturer. It is three days before the end of a sales incentive contest, and one of your dealers is close to winning a trip to Hawaii. If your dealer wins the contest for your area, you get a lot of recognition and a good chance for a promotion, which will enable you to stop traveling so much during the week. The dealer wants you to report as "sold" eight cars that he has not yet sold but will have deals on next week, several days after the end of the contest. Those eight cars will put him over the top and enable him to win the contest. Your just received a directive from the corporate headquarters on this practice of pre-reporting sales, indicating that the company would take strong action against anyone discovered taking such steps. Your boss and his superior have taken you aside and encouraged you to take whatever action is necessary to win the contest. You think you could get by with it and not get caught. An added problem is that the customer warranty starts the day the car is reported sold, so whoever purchases the car would lose several days of warranty service. What would you do?

Learning Goal 4

3. Ethics codes can be classified into two major categories:

    Compliance-based

    Integrity-based

    Read the following examples of corporate behavior, and determine which kind of ethical code the company may be operating under.

    a. At Mary's Flowers, employees are encouraged to be active in community affairs, and to be aware of their obligation to society. The company stresses honesty, provides seminars on making ethical choices and has a commitment to hire an ethnically diverse workforce. _____

b. At Pro-Tec, management has developed and distributed a code of ethics for employees. It defines what is acceptable behavior, and states that "behavior deemed to be unethical will not be tolerated." The policy does not define behavior that would be considered unethical, but does say that if there is a question a manager should be consulted. _____

Learning Goal 5

4. "...corporate social responsibility is the concern businesses have for the welfare of society."

    Read the situation described below and answer the questions that follow:

    MUMC is a successful medium-sized firm that supplies parts for electric motors. Dan Furlong, the president, was being interviewed by the business features writer of the local newspaper. The reporter asked Dan his views on social responsibility, and how MUMC reflected a socially responsive position. Dan replied that although he had never done a so-called social audit ("as the textbooks call it") he did figure that the firm was a good corporate citizen. He said, "We pay our employees a good salary, and the guys in the shop are getting paid above hourly for this area. We make a profit, and give everyone a bonus at the holidays. We take a lot or precautions in the shop, and no one has had an accident to speak of in several years. A few cuts or bruises, but that's part of that kind of job. Whenever we have customer complaints I make sure someone handles them right away. We charge what I think is a fair price for our product, which I think is of a higher quality than most of my competitors. I pay my bills on time and don't cheat on my taxes. I guess you could say that we are a pretty socially responsible company."

    a. In keeping with the idea of social audits and socially responsible business activities, is Mr. Furlong running the business in a socially responsible manner?

    b. Who are Mr. Furlong's stakeholders?

    c. What suggestions can you make to improve MUMC's position?

Learning Goal 6

5. How does the increasingly global nature of U.S. business impact the issue of social responsibility and ethics?

PRACTICE TEST

Multiple Choice: Circle the best answer.

1. The difference between ethics and legality is that:

    a. Legality reflects how people should treat each other, while ethics is more limiting.
    b. Ethics refers to ways available to us to protect ourselves from theft, violence and fraud.
    c. Legality is more limiting than ethics and applies to written laws.
    d. Ethics refers to a narrower range of behavior than legality.

2. _____ is behavior that is accepted by society as right and wrong.

    a. Ethics
    b. Legality
    c. Integrity
    d. Social responsibility

3. In the book <u>The Day America Told the Truth,</u> it was revealed that:

    a. many Americans decide what's ethical behavior based upon the situation in which they find themselves.
    b. most Americans give a considerable amount of time to their communities.
    c. employees rarely violate safety standards or "goof off" at work.
    d. most Americans have an absolute sense of what is moral.

4. Which of the following is not included as one of the questions we must ask when faced with an ethical dilemma?

    a. Is it legal?
    b. Is it balanced?
    c. How will it make me feel about myself?
    d. Is it okay if everyone else is doing it?

5. Sometimes an obvious choice from an ethical standpoint has personal or professional drawbacks. An example might be when a supervisor asks you to do something unethical, and you face negative consequences if you refuse. When you are in such a situation you are faced with:

   a. two lousy choices.
   b. an ethical dilemma.
   c. deciding the legality of your choice.
   d. a social responsibility issue.

6. The most basic step in an ethics based management system is asking the question:

   a. Is it legal?
   b. Who will know?
   c. Is it balanced?
   d. Has it been done before?

7. An ethics based manager has all of the following in mind when attempting to make an ethical decision except:

   a. creating a win-win situation for all parties.
   b. avoiding major imbalances whenever possible.
   c. making sure his/her department wins over another department.
   d. making a decision that benefits all parties involved.

8. Many people now believe that ethics has _____ to do with management.

   a. little
   b. nothing
   c. something
   d. everything

9. Organizational ethics begin:

   a. at the top levels of management.
   b. only with employees.
   c. with the unions.
   d. with mid level managers.

10. People learn standards from:

    a. observing what others do.
    b. listening to what people say.
    c. making their own decisions.
    d. following corporate goals and standards.

11. Which of the following is not a part of an integrity-based ethics code?

    a. stresses shared accountability
    b. emphasizes penalizing of wrong-doers
    c. supports ethically sound behavior
    d. defines an organization's guiding principles

12. The first step to improving corporate America's business ethics is:

    a. Managers must be trained to consider ethical implications of decisions.
    b. An ethics office should be set up.
    c. Outsiders should be told about the ethics program.
    d. Top management must adopt a code of conduct.

13. A(n) _____ based ethics code stresses preventing unlawful behavior by increasing controls and penalizing wrongdoers.

    a. compliance   c. integrity
    b. socially   d. legally

14. Which of the following would not be considered as a dimension of the social performance of a corporation?

    a. corporate philanthropy   c. corporate policy
    b. corporate legal standards   d. corporate responsibility

15. Being energy conscious, ensuring that employees have a safe working environment and monitoring corporate hiring policies to prevent discrimination is part of:

    a. corporate philanthropy.   c. corporate policy.
    b. corporate responsibility.   d. corporate legal standards.

16. Who are the stakeholders to whom a business is responsible?

    a. employees   c. investors
    b. customers   d. all of the above

17. In terms of social responsibility, many people believe that:

    a. it makes good financial sense when companies are not "up front" about potential product problems.
    b. it makes financial and moral sense to invest in companies whose goods and services benefit the community and the environment.
    c. businesses have no responsibility to create jobs.
    d. businesses have no responsibility to social causes.

18. Which of the following would not be included in a social audit?

    a. Support for higher education, the arts and nonprofit social agencies
    b. Community related activities such as fund raising
    c. Employee-related activities
    d. Ability to compete with other major firms

19. All of the following contribute to the difficulty of conducting a social audit except:

    a. establishing procedures for measuring a firm's activities.
    b. determining what to measure.
    c. deciding whether or not positive actions should be added and then negative effects subtracted.
    d. comparing charitable donations from one firm to another.

20. Which of the following is not one of the watchdog groups which evaluate how well companies enforce their ethical and social responsibility policies?

    a. Socially conscious investors and consumers
    b. Environmentalists
    c. Union officials
    d. Employees

21. Government and business leaders are being held to:

    a. lower ethical standards than in the past.
    b. ethical standards in the United States, but foreign leaders are not being subjected to ethical scrutiny.
    c. higher ethical standards than in the past.
    d. ethical standards that cannot be met by most leaders.

22. American businesses are:

    a. demanding socially responsible behavior from international suppliers, particularly in the areas of environmental standards and human rights issues.
    b. holding international suppliers to different standards than American companies must adhere to in the United States.
    c. not concerned with the ethical or socially responsible behavior of their international suppliers.
    d. are demanding that international suppliers adhere to higher standards than their American counterparts.

TRUE/FALSE

1. _____ The first step in ethical behavior is following the law.

2. _____ According to the text, ethical behavior begins with observing religious leaders.

3. _____ The most basic step in an ethics-based management system is to think of the legal implications of what you do.

4. _____ An ethics-based manager will always try to do whatever will benefit his or her department over all others.

5. _____ There are usually easy solutions to ethical problems.

6. _____ With strong ethical leadership, employees feel part of a corporate mission that is socially beneficial.

7. _____ Integrity-based ethics codes define an organization's guiding values, create an environment that supports ethical behavior and stresses shared accountability.

8. _____ The first step to improving America's business ethics is for top management to adopt and unconditionally support explicit codes of conduct.

9. _____ The best way to communicate to all employees that an ethics code is serious and cannot be broken is to back the program with timely action if rules are broken.

10. _____ Corporate social responsibility is the concern businesses have for their profitability.

11. _____ Corporate policy refers to the position a firm takes on issues that affect it and society.

12. _____ In reality, it appears that people want to be socially responsible, but they can't define what being socially responsible means.

13. _____ One of the best ways to please customers is to hide product defects from them.

14. _____ Businesses have a responsibility to employees to create jobs.

15. _____ Businesses owe it to employees to maintain job security, or warn employees if layoffs are inevitable.

16. _____ One of businesses' major responsibilities to the environment is not to pollute.

17. _____ One element of a business's social responsibility programs includes such activities as local fund raising campaigns and donating executive time to nonprofit organizations.

18. _____ One social responsibility watchdog group are customers, who can take their business elsewhere if a company demonstrates unethical and socially irresponsible practices.

19. _____ Ethical problems and issues of social responsibility are unique to the United States.

20. _____ Many American businesses are demanding socially responsible behavior from international suppliers.

ANSWERS

LEARNING THE LANGUAGE

1. Compliance-based ethics codes	5. Integrity-based ethics codes
2. Social audit	6. Corporate philanthropy
3. Corporate policy	7. Social responsibility
4. Ethics	8. Corporate responsibility

RETENTION CHECK

Learning Goal 1 **Managing Business Ethically and Responsibly**

1. As the text states, many immoral and unethical acts are legal. Being legal means following the laws written to protect ourselves from fraud, theft and violent acts. Ethical behavior requires more than simply following the law, and looks at behavior in terms of people's relations with one another.

2. A sense of personal ethics begins at home.

Learning Goal 2

3. Many Americans decide situationally whether it's all right to steal, lie, or drink and drive. In other words, it's the situation that determines what's ethical.

4. Three questions to ask are:
   a. Is it legal?
   b. Is it balanced? (Am I acting fairly?)
   c. How will it make me feel about myself?

Learning Goal 3 **Ethics is More Than an Individual Concern**

5. A sense of organizational ethics is instilled by the leadership and example of strong top managers.

6. People learn their standards and values from observing what others do.

7. Six reasons to manage ethically are:
   a. to maintain a good reputation.
   b. to keep existing customers.
   c. to attract new customers.
   d. to avoid lawsuits.
   e. to reduce turnover.
   d. to avoid government intervention.
   e. to please customers, employees and society.
   f. it's the right thing to do!

Learning Goal 4   **Setting Corporate Ethical Standards**

8. Two types of ethics codes are:
   a. Compliance-based
   b. Integrity-based

9. Compliance-based ethics codes emphasize preventing unlawful behavior by increasing control and by penalizing wrongdoers. This type of ethics code is based on avoiding legal punishment. Integrity-based ethics codes define the organization's guiding values, create an environment that supports ethically sound behavior and stress a shared accountability among employees.

10. a. Top management must adopt and support an explicit code of conduct.
    b. Employees must understand that top management expects ethical behavior.
    c. Managers and employees must be trained to consider ethical implications of business decisions.
    d. Companies must set up an ethics office for employees to inquire about ethical matters.
    d. Outsiders must be told about the ethics program.
    f. The ethics code must be enforced.

Learning Goal 5   **Corporate Social Responsibility**

11. Corporate social responsibility is the concern businesses have for the welfare of society.

12. a. Corporate philanthropy—charitable donations
    b. Corporate responsibility—in all business decisions
    c. Corporate policy—the position taken on issues affecting the firm and society

13. Four stakeholder groups are:
    a. Customers.
    b. Investors.
    c. Employees.
    d. Society.

14. Business's responsibility to employees include:
    a. a responsibility to create jobs.
    b. an obligation to fairly reward hard work and talent.
    c. a responsibility to maintain job security, or if layoffs are impossible to avoid, businesses have a responsibility to give employees warning.

15. Three areas of responsibility to society are:
    a. to create wealth
    b. to promote social justice
    c. to make a contribution toward making the environment a better place

16. A social audit is a systematic evaluation of an organization's progress toward implementing programs that are socially responsible and responsive.

17. A major problem of conducting a social audit is establishing procedures for measuring a firm's activities and their effects on society. The question is: What should be measured?

18. Examples of socially responsible business activities include:
    a. Community related activities such as fund raising for local causes.
    b. Programs designed to benefit employees such as flextime, improved benefits, equal opportunity programs, and others.
    c. Taking a stand on such political issues as gun control, pollution control and nuclear safety.
    d. Support higher education, the arts and non-profit agencies.
    e. Consumer education programs, honest advertising, prompt complaint handling and honest pricing policies.

19. Four watchdog groups are:
   a. Socially conscious investors, who insist that companies extend the company's high standards to all their suppliers.
   b. Environmentalists, who apply pressure by naming companies that don't abide by environmentalists' standards.
   c. Union officials, who force companies to comply with standards to avoid negative publicity.
   d. Customers who take their business elsewhere if a company demonstrates unethical and socially irresponsible practices.

Learning Goal 5 **International Ethics and Social Responsibility**

20. Examples of the questions surrounding the issues of international ethics are:
   a. Is it always ethical for American companies to demand compliance with our moral standards?
   b. What about countries where child labor is an accepted part of society?
   c. What about foreign companies doing business in the U.S.?
   d. Should foreign companies expect American companies to comply with their ethical standards?

CRITICAL THINKING EXERCISES

Learning Goal 1

1. This is a difficult problem, but ethically it's not really too hard to figure out what to do. The decision about going to the boss is an individual one, but using the secretary and the interns for personal business, particularly to the extent that Daryl is doing, is unethical.

Learning Goal 2, 3

2. There is no "correct" answer to this question although there is probably a "most appropriate" mode of behavior. In this era of customer service and quality products in a competitive marketplace, these kinds of decisions are likely to come up frequently. Now is the time to think about how you would act. A helpful guide would be to ask yourself the questions the text proposes: a. Is it legal? b. Is it balanced? Would I want to be treated this way? Do I win at the expense of someone else? c. How will it make me feel about myself?

Learning Goal 4

3. a. Integrity-based ethics code
    b. Compliance-based ethics code

Learning Goal 5

4. a. Social responsibility includes providing a safer work environment, good benefits, a safe, high quality product line, prompt complaint handling and honest pricing policies. The result of a social audit would indicate that Mr. Furlong is running his business in a socially responsible manner, as far as he goes.
    b. Mr. Furlong's stakeholders would be his boss, the stockholders, employees, customers, competitors, suppliers and the general public.
    c. Although he would get fairly high scores from his employees in the area of social responsibility, Mr. Furlong doesn't appear to have any involvement with the community in which he operates. Of the three dimensions of corporate social performance, he addresses only the corporate responsibility issue; those of corporate philanthropy and corporate policy appear to be ignored. He could improve community relations (and even increase his customer base) by encouraging his employees to get involved in community related projects, donating time and/or money to local charities, developing a stand on local issues, improving employee-related benefits with job enrichment and employee development and making opportunities for members of ethnic and minority groups.

Learning Goal 6

5. In the past, officials of foreign firms have been judged by standards that were less harsh than those used in the United States. More recently, it seems that top leaders in some parts of the world are being judged by stricter standards. This could stem from the fact that American businesses have begun to demand more socially responsible behavior from international suppliers. As the business sector becomes increasingly globalized, international suppliers will be expected to conform to U.S. standards concerning ethics, human rights codes and the environment.

PRACTICE TEST

Multiple Choice

1.	c	12.	d
2.	a	13.	a
3.	a	14.	b
4.	d	15.	c
5.	b	16.	d
6.	a	17.	b
7.	c	18.	d
8.	d	19.	d
9.	a	20.	d
10.	a	21.	c
11.	b	22.	a

True/False

1.	T	11.	T
2.	F	12.	T
3.	T	13.	F
4.	F	14.	T
5.	F	15.	T
6.	T	16.	T
7.	T	17.	T
8.	T	18.	T
9.	T	19.	F
10.	F	20.	T

APPENDIX
WORKING WITHIN THE LEGAL ENVIRONMENT OF BUSINESS

LEARNING THE LANGUAGE

Listed here are important terms found in this chapter. Choose the correct term for each definition below and write it in the space provided.

Administrative agencies	Implied warranties
Bankruptcy	Involuntary bankruptcy
Breach of contract	Judiciary
Business law	Negotiable instruments
Common law	Patent
Consideration	Product liability
Consumerism	Statutory law
Contract	Taxes
Contract law	Tort
Copyright	Trademark
Damages	Uniform Commercial code
Deregulation	Voluntary bankruptcy
Express warranties	

1. Something of value, one of the requirements of a legal contract is _____.

2. Government withdrawal of certain laws and regulations that seem to hinder competition is known as _____.

3. Forms of commercial paper known as _____ are transferable among businesses and individuals and represent a promise to pay a certain amount.

4. Rules, statutes, codes, and regulations called _____ are established to provide a legal framework within which business may be conducted that is enforceable in court.

5. The _____ covers sales laws and other commercial law and has been adopted by every state in the United States.

6. Specific representations by the seller regarding its goods are called _____.

7. A _____ is a wrongful conduct that causes injury to another person's body, property, or reputation.

8. The legal process of _____ is one by which a person or business, unable to meet financial obligations, is relieved of those obligations by having the court divide any assets among creditors, freeing the debtor to begin anew.

9. A _____ protects an individual's rights to materials such as books, articles, photos, and cartoons.

10. State and federal constitutions, legislative enactment, treaties, and ordinances (written laws) are known as _____.

11. _____ are guarantees legally imposed on the seller.

12. A social movement known as _____ tries to increase the rights and powers of buyers in relation to sellers.

13. A _____ means that one party fails to follow the terms of a contract.

14. A legally enforceable agreement between two or more parties is a _____.

15. A document called a _____ gives inventors exclusive rights to their inventions for 20 years.

16. The body of law known as _____ comes from judges' decisions; also known as "unwritten law."

17. Laws called _____ specify what constitutes a legally enforceable agreement.

18. Legal procedures called _____ are initiated by a debtor.

19. The part of tort law known as_____ holds businesses liable for negligence in the production, design, sale, or use of products they market.

20. Institutions created by Congress with delegated power to pass rules and regulations within their mandated area of authority are _____.

21. The branch of the government called the _____ oversees the legal system.

22. A _____ is a legally protected name, symbol, or design that identifies the goods or services of one seller.

23. Bankruptcy procedures filed by a debtor's creditors are _____.

24. The government raises money through _____.

25. The monetary settlement awarded to a person who is injured by a breach of contract is known as _____.

RETENTION CHECK

The Need for Laws

1. Why has government expanded its control of business law?

Business Law

2. What is the difference between statutory and common law?

3. What is "precedent" in law?

4. Name seven federal regulatory agencies.

   a. _____

   b. _____

   c. _____

   d. _____

   e. _____

   f. _____

   g. _____

Tort Law

5. What is the difference between an intentional tort and negligence?

6. What is the rule of "strict liability?"

Laws Protecting Ideas

7. What is required to file a patent?

8. What is a submarine patent?

9. How long does a patent last compared to a copyright?

10. How long does a trademark last?

11. What are two specific areas of sales law covered by the Uniform Commercial Code?

12. What is the difference between express and implied warranties?

13. What is the difference between a full and a limited warranty?

14. What are four conditions that must be met by a negotiable instrument?

   a. _____

   b. _____

   c. _____

   d. _____

Contract Law

15. List six conditions that must be met to make a contract legally binding.

    a. _____

    b. _____

    c. _____

    d. _____

    e. _____

    f. _____

16. When does an offer become legally binding?

17. What is the principle of mutual acceptance?

18. How is competency determined?

19. What kind of contracts must be put in writing?

20. Identify three results of a breach of contract.

    a. _____

    b. _____

    c. _____

21. What are three elements that <u>must</u> be present in a contract?

    a. _____

    b. _____

    c. _____

Laws to Promote Fair and Competitive Practices

22. What are six important pieces of pro-competitive federal legislation?

    a. _____

    b. _____

    c. _____

    d. _____

    e. _____

    f. _____

23. Why was the Interstate Commerce Act passed?

24. What did the act stipulate?

25. What two things does the Sherman Act forbid?

26. What four "anticompetitive practices" does the Clayton Act prohibit?

27. What is:

    a. an exclusive dealing?

    b. a tying contract?

    c. an interlocking directorate?

28. What does the FTC Act prohibit?

29. What does Robinson Patman prohibit?

30. What did the Wheeler-Lea Amendment do?

31. List four basic rights of consumers proposed by John F. Kennedy.

   a. _____

   b. _____

   c. _____

   d. _____

Tax Laws

32. What are taxes used for?

33. What is the purpose of a sin tax?

34. What are four basic types of taxes?

Bankruptcy Laws

35. Why did the number of bankruptcies increase in the 1990s?

36. Distinguish between the 2 kinds of bankruptcy.

37. List the three most often used sections of the Bankruptcy Law.

   a. _____

   b. _____

   c. _____

38. In what order are assets distributed among creditors in a bankruptcy case under Chapter 7?

39. What does Chapter 11 bankruptcy allow for?

Deregulation

40. What prompted the move toward deregulation?

41. How has deregulation affected certain businesses in the United States?

CRITICAL THINKING EXERCISES

1. The types of laws governing business are varied. They include:

Contract law.	Bankruptcy law.
Sales law (Uniform Commercial Code).	Tort law.
Patent law.	

Match the correct type of business law to each of the following situations.

    a.   TWA is being sued by the families of those people who perished in the crash of Flight 800when an explosion occurred apparently from a faulty part.

    b.   A Sears Kenmore washer comes with a 12-month warranty.

    c.   Venture Corporation declared itself unable to meet its debt obligations, and filed for Chapter 11 reorganization.

    d.   The formula for a woman's facial moisturizer is advertised as being protected from duplication until the year 2001.

    e.   Bob and Dee Slone sue for damages when a building contractor fails to complete the building of their new home.

2. How has the definition of product liability changed and how has that affected manufacturers?

3. Match the correct federal administrative agency to each of the statements listed below.

    FTC   FCC
    FDA   EPA
    ICC   FPC

Consumer Product Safety Commission

a. Regulates rates and sales of natural gas and electricity _____.

b. Regulates rates, finance and franchises of interstate transportation _____.

c. Enforces laws regarding unfair business practices and acts to stop false and deceptive advertising and labeling _____.

d. Enforces laws and regulations regarding distribution of adulterated or misbranded food, drugs, and cosmetics _____.

e. Seeks to protect the public from unreasonable risk of injury from consumer products not covered by other agencies _____.

f. Develops and enforces environmental protection standards and researches the effects of pollution _____.

g. Regulates wire, radio, and television communication. _____.

4. A contract will be legally binding if it meets the following conditions:

   a. An offer is made.
   b. There is voluntary acceptance of the offer.
   c. Both parties give consideration.
   d. Both parties are competent.
   e. The contract is legal.
   f. The contract is in proper form.

   Given the information below, determine whether each contract is legally binding (assuming other conditions are met) and why or why not t meets legal standards.

   a. A resident of Tennessee signs an IOU to a casino in Las Vegas.

   b. You see a newspaper ad for a used car, and after looking the car over, you agree to pay the owner $800 on the spot, with an oral contract.

   c. A 17-year-old puts a down payment on a new motorcycle.

   d. A student offers to buy your well-used *Understanding Business* textbook for $10, and you agree.

5. Three actions that can be taken when a breach of contract occurs are:

   a. Specific performance.

   b. Payment of damages.

   c. Discharge of obligation.

   Indicate which action might be taken in each of the following breach of contract situations.

   a. An actor fails to show up for a scheduled theater performance, without prior warning.

   b. A typist working for an author finds that she doesn't have time to finish the manuscript, and quits.

   c. An art dealer fails to deliver a piece of sculpture when promised for an art show.

6. Which of the following major pieces of federal legislation would be associated with each of the situations below?

   a. Sherman Act　　　　　d. Robinson—Patman Act
   b. Clayton Act　　　　　 e. Federal Trade Commission Act
   c. Wheeler-Lea Act　　　f. Interstate Commerce Act

   a. Prohibits conspiracies in restraint of trade and attempts to monopolize.

   b. A greeting card company unsuccessfully attempted to coerce its independently owned distributors into carrying only the products it manufactures.

   c. The agency created by this act has conducted three times as many investigations and brought twice as many cases in the 1990s as it did in the 1980s. The legislation prohibits unfair methods of competition in commerce.

   d. Prohibits several forms of price discrimination and applies to buyers as well as sellers.

e. Created the Interstate Commerce Commission and stipulated that railroad rates must be "reasonable" and prohibited favoritism.

f. This act gives the FTC even more power to prevent false and misleading advertising.

7. Using the list of consumer protection laws in your text, identify the law associated with each of the following statements.

a. A coat label indicates that the coat is made from "various" wool products.

b. Baby cribs are required to have slats close enough together to prevent an infant's head from getting caught.

c. Fisher-Price was forced to recall a toy that had caused several injuries to young infants.

d. A car has a sticker price of $16,999.

e. The FDA has "food filth" allowances for such products as peanut butter and chocolate.

f. "Surgeon General's Warning: Cigarette Smoke Contains Carbon Monoxide."

g. Hot dogs are labeled as "all meat" or "all beef," but must contain only meat products.

h. The monthly statement on a Shell credit card indicates a periodic rate per month of 1.5% and an annual percentage rate of 18%.

i. The warranty for a Fisher-Price camera discloses that there is a three-year express warranty, and describes the conditions.

j. A bankruptcy filed several years ago will not show up on a credit report needed for aloan approval.

k. A tee-shirt label indicates that the shirt is 50% cotton and 50% polyester, and provides care instructions.

l. Marti Gilchrist purchases a fur coat that is part rabbit and part pine martin.

m. Apple Jacks cereal contains sugar, corn, wheat and oat flour, salt, dried apples, apple juice concentrate, and cinnamon. These ingredients must be accurately labeled.

n. A toy with a mechanical arm is packaged with a warning that it is intended only for children 8 years and older.

o. Indicates that flammable fabrics and wearing apparel can't be transported interstate.

p. Anheuser-Busch brought out Catalina Blond in 1998. The cans and bottles had to have a warning label in a visible place on the container. This is especially important as women are the target markets.

q. When Judith Durham buys a box of Snack-Wells cookies, she knows exactly what ingredients are in the cookies and how much fat they contain.

8. When persons or businesses file for bankruptcy, they are relieved of their financial obligations by the courts.

Most bankruptcies are filed under one of the following three sections of the act:

Chapter 7   Chapter 11   Chapter 13

Which section of the bankruptcy law is being invoked in each of the following situations?

a. LTV Corporation filed for reorganization, and continued operations after declaring bankruptcy.

b. When the fast-food restaurant Jim S. owned failed, he filed for bankruptcy and sold all the assets to pay off his creditors, including his SBA loan.

c. Because of recent revisions in the bankruptcy law, a small dry cleaner was enabled to declare bankruptcy and set up a three year schedule for repayment to his creditors.

PRACTICE TEST

Multiple Choice: Circle the best answer.

1. In Missouri, a law was passed to allow riverboat gambling. The law has been challenged in the legislature several times by different groups. This kind of law is an example of:

   a. common law.
   b. statutory law.
   c. tort law.
   d. liability law.

2. The fact that a company can be held liable for damages or injuries caused by a product with a defect even if the company did not know of the defect at the time of the sale is referred to as:

   a. business law.
   b. negligence.
   c. strict product liability.
   d. implied warranty.

3. A _____ is a document that gives inventors exclusive rights to their inventions for 20 years.

   a. trademark
   b. copyright
   c. express warranty
   d. patent

4. The Uniform Commercial Code covers:

   a. sales law.
   b. bankruptcy law.
   c. product negligence.
   d. contract law.

5. Which of the following is not a requirement for a contract to be legally enforceable?

    a. Both parties must be competent
    b. An offer must be made
    c. There must be voluntary acceptance
    d. Both parties must receive money

6. When John Pegg decided he wanted to buy a car, he went looking in the used car ads, and found one in his price range, $400, from a private seller. John, who is 16, drove the car, and decided he wanted to buy it. What needs to happen to make John's purchase an enforceable contract?

    a. The contract needs to be written up.
    b. John needs to find a person older than he, like a parent, to make the contract for him.
    c. The seller must wait for 3 days before he can sell it to John.
    d. all of the above

7. The _____ prohibits exclusive dealing, tying contracts and interlocking directorates.

    a. Clayton Act
    b. Federal Trade Commission Act
    c. Robinson-Patman Act
    d. Interstate Commerce Act

8. Which of the following is not one of the rights of consumers outlined by President John F. Kennedy?

    a. the right to safety
    b. the right to be informed
    c. the right to be heard
    d. the right to fair prices

9. Chapter _____ of the bankruptcy code allows businesses to continue operations while paying a limited portion of their debts.

    a. 7
    b. 11
    c. 13
    d. 22

10. How has deregulation affected business in the U.S.?

    a. Some industries have become more competitive.
    b. Some companies must follow a stricter code of ethics.
    c. Many businesses are raising prices because the government is not controlling them anymore.
    d. Companies are becoming less ethical.

TRUE/FALSE

1. _____ Government has reduced its control and enforcement procedures over the years.

2. _____ Common law is often referred to as unwritten law.

3. _____ A submarine patent is one that has not yet been granted.

4. _____ An express warranty is a specific representation by the seller that is relied upon by the buyer regarding the goods.

5. _____ Any contract for the sale of real property must be written.

6. _____ If a breach of contract occurs, the individual who breached the contract will always be required to live up to the contract eventually.

7. _____ The Sherman Act prohibits price discrimination.

8. _____ In a bankruptcy case, the first thing to be paid will be federal and state taxes.

ANSWERS

LEARNING THE LANGUAGE

1. Consideration	13. Breach of contract
2. Deregulation	14. Contract
3. Negotiable instruments	15. Patent
4. Business law	16. Common law
5. Uniform commercial code	17. Contract law
6. Express warranties	18. Voluntary bankruptcy
7. Tort	19. Product liability
8. Bankruptcy	20. Administrative agencies
9. Copyright	21. Judiciary
10. Statutory law	22. Trademark
11. Implied warranties	23. Involuntary bankruptcy
12. Consumerism	24. Taxes
25. Damages	

RETENTION CHECK

The Need for Laws

1. Business has not been perceived as implementing acceptable practices of doing business, and standards of behavior fast enough. Therefore, the government has expanded its control and enforcement procedures to hasten the process.

Business Law

2. Statutory law is written law, and includes state and federal constitutions, legislative enactments and so forth. Common law is the body of law that comes from decisions handed down by judges. It is often referred to as unwritten law.

3. Precedent is what judges have decided in previous cases. Precedent guides judges in the handling of new cases.

4.   a. Federal Trade commission (FTC)
   b. Food and Drug Administration (FDA)
   c. Consumer Product Safety Commission
   d. Securities and Exchange Commission
   e. Federal Communications Commission (FCC)
   f. Environmental Protection Agency (EPA)
   g. Federal Power Commission (FPC)

Tort Law

5. An intentional tort is a willful act that results in injury. Negligence deals with *unintentional* behavior that causes harm or injury.

6. The rule of "strict liability" refers to product liability. It is the idea that a company can be liable for damages caused by placing a product on the market with a defect even if the company did not know of the defect at the time of the sale.

Laws Protecting Ideas

7. Filing a patent with the U.S. Patent office requires a search to make sure the patent is unique, followed by the filing of forms. The advice of a lawyer is usually recommended.

8. Some inventors have been accused of intentionally delaying or dragging out a patent application, then waiting for others to develop the technology. The inventor surfaces to claim the patent, and demands large fees, after others have developed the technology. This is a submarine patent.

9. A patent lasts for 20 years. A copyright protects an individual's right to materials for the lifetime of the author or artist plus 50 years.

10. A trademark belongs to the owner forever, so long as it is properly registered and renewed every 20 years.

11. Article 2, which contains laws regarding warranties, and Article 3, which covers negotiable instruments.

12. An express warranty is often enclosed with the product when purchased. It spells out the seller's warranty agreement. An implied warranty is legally imposed on the seller. It is implied that the product will conform to the customary standards of the trade or industry in which it competes.

13. A full warranty requires a seller to replace or repair a product at no charge if the product is defective. Limited warranties typically limit the defects or mechanical problems that are covered.

14. Negotiable instruments must be:
    a. Signed by the maker.
    b. Made payable on demand at a certain time.
    c. Made payable to the bearer or to order.
    d. Contain an unconditional promise to pay a specific amount of money.

Contract Law

15. a. An offer is made.
    b. There is voluntary acceptance.
    c. Both parties give consideration.
    d. Both parties are competent.
    e. The contract is legal.
    f. The contract is in proper form.

16. An offer is legally binding only when other conditions of a contract have been met.

17. The principle of mutual acceptance means that both parties to a contract must agree on the terms of the contract.

18. In order to be judged competent to enter into a contract, a person must not be under the influence of drugs or alcohol, be of sound mind and be of legal age.

19. An agreement for the sale of goods worth $500 or more must be in writing. Contracts that cannot be fulfilled within one year and contracts regarding real property must also be in writing.

20. a. Specific performance, i.e., the person may be required to live up to the agreement.
    b. Payment of damages
    c. Discharge of obligation

21. A contract does not have to be complicated, but should have the following three elements:
    a. It should be in writing.
    b. Mutual consideration is specified.
    c. There is a clear offer and agreement.

Laws to Promote Fair and Competitive Practices

22. a. Interstate Commerce Act
    b. Sherman Act (1890)
    c. Clayton Act (1914)
    d. Federal Trade Commission Act (1914)
    e. Robinson–Patman Act (1936)
    f. Wheeler-Lea Act

23. The Interstate Commerce Act was passed when railroads began to grow, and the railroads began to agree among themselves to fix prices.

24. Congress passed the Interstate Commerce Act in 1887, and it stipulated that railroad rates must be "reasonable," prohibited discriminatory rates, and other forms of favoritism, and outlawed price fixing.

25. The Sherman Act forbids contracts, combinations or conspiracies in restraint of trade, and actual monopolies or attempts to monopolize any part of trade or commerce.

26. The Clayton Act prohibits exclusive dealing, tying contracts, interlocking directorates and buying large amounts of stock in competing corporations.

27. a. Exclusive dealing is selling goods with the condition that the buyer will not buy goods from a competitor.
    b. A tying contract requires a buyer to purchase unwanted items in order to purchase the desired items.
    c. An interlocking directorate occurs when a board of directors includes members of the board of competing corporations.

28. The FTC Act prohibits unfair methods of competition in commerce.

29. The Robinson-Patman Act prohibits price discrimination. It applies to both sellers and buyers who knowingly induce or receive an unlawful discrimination in price.

30. The Wheeler-Lea Amendment gave the FTC additional jurisdiction over false or misleading advertising.

31. a. The right to safety
    b. The right to be informed
    c. The right to choose
    d. The right to be heard

Tax Laws

32. Taxes have traditionally been used as a source of funding for government operations and programs. They have also been used as a method of encouraging or discouraging taxpayers from doing something.

33. If the government wants to reduce the use of certain types of products, it will pass a "sin tax." This is what has happened in the cigarette and alcohol industry.

34. Four basic types of taxes are income taxes, property taxes, sales taxes and excise taxes.

Bankruptcy Laws

35. The number of bankruptcies increased in the 1990s primarily due to a lessening of the stigma of bankruptcy, the changing economy, an increase in understanding of bankruptcy law and the protection it offers, increased advertising by attorneys, and the ease with which consumers can get credit.

36. In voluntary bankruptcy cases, the debtor applies for bankruptcy, whereas in involuntary bankruptcy cases the creditors start legal procedures against the debtors.

37.
    a. Chapter 7
    b. Chapter 11
    c. Chapter 13

38. Unsecured claims are paid in this order:
    a. Costs involved in the bankruptcy case.
    b. Any business costs incurred after bankruptcy was filed.
    c. Wages, salaries, or commissions.
    d. Employee benefit plan contributions.
    e. Refunds to consumers who paid for undelivered products.
    f. Federal and state taxes.

39. Chapter 11 allows a company to reorganize operations while paying only a limited portion of its debts. Under certain conditions, the company can sell assets, borrow money, and change officers to strengthen its market position. A company will continue to operate but has court protection against creditor's lawsuits while it tries to work out a plan for paying off its debts.

Deregulation

40. The move toward deregulation stemmed from a concern that there were too many laws and regulations governing business and that these laws and regulations were costing the public money.

41. The most publicized examples of deregulation have been in the airlines and the telecommunications industry. When restrictions were lifted in the airline industry, the airlines began competing for different routes and charging lower prices. New airlines were created to take advantage of new opportunities. In the telecommunications industry, deregulation gave consumers many more options in the telephone service market.

CRITICAL THINKING EXERCISES

1.   a.   Tort law
   b.   Sales law (UCC)
   b.   Bankruptcy law
   d.   Patent law
   e.   Contract law

2.   At one time, the legal standard for measuring product liability was if a producer knowingly placed a hazardous product on the market. Today, many states have extended product liability to the level of strict liability. Legally this means without regard to fault. Therefore, a company could be liable for damages caused by placing a product on the market with a defect even if the company did not know of the defect at the time of the sale. This has subjected manufacturers to expensive lawsuits.

3.   a.   FPC
   b.   ICC
   c.   FTC
   d.   FDA
   e.   Consumer Product Safety Commission
   f.   EPA
   g.   FCC

4.   a   Yes, this is a binding contract. Although the signer is a resident of Tennessee, he is in Nevada, where gambling is legal.
   b.   No, this is not binding. Oral contracts are binding only when the value of the goods is less than $500. It's usually best to get a written contract for the protection of both parties.
   c.   No, this is not a binding contract because a minor isn't legally competent to make a contract.
   d.   Yes this is a binding contract. The offer was voluntary, so was the acceptance and both parties received consideration.

5.   a.   Payment of damages
   b.   Discharge of obligation
   c.   Specific performance

6. a. Sherman Act (1890)
   b. Clayton Act (1914)
   c. Federal Trade Commission Act (1914)
   d. Robinson-Patman Act (1936)
   e. The Interstate Commerce Act
   f. Wheeler-Lea Act

7. a. Wool Products Labeling Act
   b. Consumer Product Safety Act
   c. Child Protection Act
   d. Automobile Information Disclosure Act
   e. Food, Drug and Cosmetic Act
   f. Cigarette Labeling Act
   g. Pure Food and Drug Act
   h. Truth-in-Lending Act
   i. Magnuson-Moss Warranty-Federal Trade Commission Improvement Act
   j. Fair Credit Reporting Act
   k. Textile Fiber Products Identification Act
   l. Fur Products Labeling Act
   m. Fair Packaging and Labeling Act
   n. Child Protection and Toy Safety Act
   o. Flammable Fabrics Act (1953)
   p. Alcohol Labeling Legislation
   q. Nutrition Labeling and Education Act

8. a. Chapter—11
   b. Chapter—7
   c. Chapter—13

PRACTICE TEST

Multiple Choice				True/False			
1.	b	6.	b	1.	F	5.	T
2.	c	7.	a	2.	T	6.	F
3.	d	8.	d	3.	F	7.	F
4.	a	9.	b	4.	T	8.	F
5.	d	10.	a				

CHAPTER 5
FORMS OF BUSINESS OWNERSHIP

LEARNING GOALS

After you have read and studied this chapter, you should be able to:

1. Compare the advantages and disadvantages of sole proprietorships.

2. Describe the differences between general and limited partnerships and compare the advantages and disadvantages of partnerships.

3. Compare the advantages and disadvantages of corporations and summarize the differences between C corporations, S corporations, and limited liability companies.

4. Define and give examples of three types of corporate mergers and explain the role of leveraged buyouts and taking a firm private.

5. Outline the advantages and disadvantages of franchises and discuss the opportunities for diversity in franchising and the challenges of international franchising.

6. Explain the role of cooperatives.

LEARNING THE LANGUAGE

Listed below are important terms found in this chapter. Choose the correct term for each definition and write it in the space provided.

Acquisition	Leveraged buyout
Conglomerate merger	Limited liability
Cooperative	Limited liability company
Corporation	Limited partner
Franchise	Limited partnership
Franchise agreement	Master limited partnership
Franchisee	Merger
Franchisor	Partnership
General partner	S corporation
General partnership	Sole proprietorship
Horizontal merger	Unlimited liability
	Vertical merger

1. The business proposition known as a _____ joins two firms in the same industry.

2. A company formed when two or more people legally agree to become co-owners of a business is called a _____.

3. A _____ is an arrangement whereby someone with a good idea for a business sells the rights to use the business name and to sell a product or service to others in a given territory.

4. In a(n) _____ one company buys the property and obligations of another company.

5. This means that limited partners are not responsible for the debts of a business beyond the amount they invest; so, limited partners and shareholders have _____.

6. This unique government creation called a(n) _____ looks like a corporation but is taxed like sole proprietorships and partnerships.

7. A _____ is a company that develops a product concept and sells others the rights to make and sell the products.

8. A business proposition that joins firms in completely unrelated industries is called a(n) _____.

9. An agreement such as a(n) _____ is a partnership with one or more general partners and one or more limited partners.

10. A (n) _____ looks much like a corporation in that it acts like a corporation and is traded on the stock exchange like a corporation, but is taxed like a partnership and thus avoids the corporate income tax.

11. A legal entity with authority to act, a(n) _____ has liability separate from its owners.

12. The result of two firms forming one company is a _____.

13. A _____ is a person who buys a franchise.

14. An individual is called a _____ when he has invested money in a business but does not have any management responsibility or liability for losses beyond the investment.

15. A new business entity which is similar to an S corporation, but without the special eligibility requirements is called a(n) _____.

16. An partner who has unlimited liability is called a _____ and is active in managing the firm.

17. A _____ is an organization that is owned by the people who use it – producers, consumers or workers with similar needs who pool their resources for mutual gain.

18. A partnership is called a(n) _____ when all owners share in operating the business and in assuming liability for the business's debts.

19. An attempt by employees, management or a group of investors to purchase an organization primarily through borrowing is called a(n) _____.

20. A _____ is the right to use a business name and to sell a product or service in a given territory.

21. In the business venture known as a(n) _____, two companies join which are involved in different stages of related industries.

22. A business that is owned, and usually managed, by one person is a _____.

23. Sole proprietorships and general partnerships have _____, because the responsibility of the owners for all of the debts falls on them, making their personal assets vulnerable to claims against the business.

RETENTION CHECK

Learning Goal 1 **Forms of Business Ownership**

1. What are three general forms of business ownership?

   a. _____

   b. _____

   c. _____

2. Which form of ownership is separate from its owners?

3. Which is the most common form of business ownership?

4. What are the advantages of a sole proprietorship?

   a. _____

   b. _____

   c. _____

   d. _____

   e. _____

5. What are the disadvantages of sole proprietorships

   a. _____

   b. _____

   c. _____

   d. _____

   e. _____

   f. _____

   g. _____

Learning Goal 2 **Partnerships**

6. The Uniform Partnership Act (UPA) identifies what three key elements of a general partnership?

   a. _____

   b. _____

   c. _____

7. What are 2 kinds of partnerships?

   a. _____   b. _____

8. What is the difference between a limited partner and a general partner?

9. What are the advantages of a partnership?

   a. _____

   b. _____

   c. _____

10. What are the disadvantages of a partnership?

   a. _____

   b. _____

   c. _____

   d. _____

Learning Goal 3   **Corporations**

11. What is a "C" corporation?

12. What are the advantages of conventional "C" corporations?

   a. _____

   b. _____

   c. _____

   d. _____

   e. _____

   f. _____

   g. _____

13. What are the disadvantages of conventional "C" corporations?

   a. _____

   b. _____

   c. _____

   d. _____

   e. _____

   f. _____

   g. _____

14. List the items included in the articles of incorporation.

   a. _____

   b. _____

   c. _____

   d. _____

   e. _____

   f. _____

   g. _____

   h. _____

   i. _____

   j. _____

15. What is an "S" corporation?

16. What criteria must be met in order to qualify as an "S" corporation?

    a. _____

    b. _____

    c. _____

    d. _____

17. What are the types of corporations, other than an "S"?

    a. _____ e. _____ i. _____

    b. _____ f. _____

    c. _____ g. _____

    d. _____ h. _____

18. What major changes were made in the Small Business Jobs Protection Act of 1996 laws governing "S" corporations?

    a. _____

    b. _____

    c. _____

19. What is a limited liability corporation?

20. What are the advantages of limited liability corporations?

   a. _____

   b. _____

   c. _____

Learning Goal 4   **Corporate Expansion: Mergers and Acquisitions**

21. What is a merger?

22. What is the difference between a merger and an acquisition?

23. What are three types of corporate mergers?

   a. _____

   b. _____

   c. _____

24. What does it mean to "take a firm private"?

25. What happens in a leveraged buyout?

26. What are four reasons to explain the recent "buying binge" we have seen here and overseas?

   a. _____

   b. _____

   c. _____

   d. _____

Learning Goal 5 **Special Forms of Business Ownership**

27. What is the difference between a franchisor and a franchisee?

28. What are four statistics that indicate the importance of franchising to the U.S. economy?

   a. _____

   b. _____

   c. _____

   d. _____

29. List the advantages of owning a franchise.

   a. _____

   b. _____

   c. _____

   d. _____

   e. _____

30. Why does a franchisee have a greater chance of succeeding in business?

   a. _____

   b. _____

   c. _____

   d. _____

31. List the disadvantages of owning a franchise.

   a. _____

   b. _____

   c. _____

   d. _____

   e. _____

   f. _____

32. What is a recent change in franchising regarding management regulation?

33. How has women and minority involvement in franchising changed?

34. What are four advantages of home franchising?

   a. _____

   b. _____

   c. _____

   d. _____

35. What are some of the considerations of franchising in international markets?

Learning Goal 6   **Cooperatives**

36. What are two kinds of cooperatives?

    a. _____   b. _____

37. What kinds of needs do non-farm cooperatives meet for their members?

38. What kind of involvement do members of cooperatives have?

CRITICAL THINKING EXERCISES

Learning Goal 1

1. As the owner of a tanning salon in his hometown, Jeff Baker has his own business. He is talking with a good friend, Bill Jacobs, who is interested in going into business for himself. "After I had purchased the necessary equipment, all I had to do was fill out a form for the county and open my doors, easy as that" Jeff mentioned, over lunch one day. "The only problem is, now I owe a lot of money for this tanning equipment. I'll be in rough shape if we go under!" "You know", said Bill, "I have company paid life and health insurance where I work now. I'm a little concerned about losing that." "Yeah, that's a concern," replied Jeff," but I can try things with this business that my old bosses would never have let me try. I can be really creative. I think we earned enough this year to open a second facility after we pay off the loans we have now. We're at our limit at the bank. But at least I can do what I want to with the money, and not share it with anyone

else." "What about the amount of time you spend at work? Any problem?" asked Bill. "Well... I usually get to the salon at 8 a.m. and don't leave until 10 or 11 p.m., if that's what you're asking," answered Jeff, "but you know, I don't mind, because this business is all mine, and it has been worth the hard work. Right now, though, I am having some problem finding a good person to help me out." "Listen," he continued, "I have to go. I've got an appointment with the tax accountant in 20 minutes. He saved me a lot of money last year, and I didn't owe anything. Great guy! My lawyer needs some information from him too. I'm making a will to make sure the kids will get the business if anything happens to me. Hey Bill, good luck!"

What advantages and disadvantages did Jeff mention about owning a sole proprietorship?

Learning Goal 2

2. There are three basic types of partnerships:

    general partnership.   limited partnership.   master limited partnership.

Using the information below, distinguish between each type of partnership

a. Burger King is a type of partnership that is traded on a stock exchange. _____

b. When Joe Allen invested in his friend Jose's business, he didn't want to have any management responsibilities. _____

c. Dave Pardo and his partner Bettina Gregory both stand to lose a lot of money if their business goes under, as they are both responsible for the debt the business has undertaken. _____

d. Even though any of us could buy stock in Perkins Family Restaurant, the company is taxed like a partnership. _____

e. When Terry Esser invested in Dave and Bettina's company, she figured it was a minimal risk, because she (Terry) would only stand to lose what she invested if the company didn't make it. _____

f. Randy Ford and Marty Dietrich have agreed to spend all their time managing the business they have just started. _____

3. After thinking about it for a few days, Bill Jacobs decided he would ask Jeff Baker if he could become a partner in Jeff's business. "After all" Bill said to himself, "I've got some money, and Jeff does want to expand, and he's looking for someone to work for him. I'll just work with him, give him some free time. I'm a little nervous about taking on the debt, but the statistics say we're more likely to stay in business than a sole proprietorship is, so it shouldn't be too bad."

Bill went to Jeff and began to discuss becoming a partner in the business.

"Whoa.. wait a minute," interrupted Jeff when he heard Bill's offer. "I have to think about this. I like making my own decisions and I like keeping my profits! How do I know you'll work as hard as I do? Who will work when? What happens when I want to borrow money for some new equipment and you don't want to?" Bill had to admit these were things he hadn't thought of. "Well...if it doesn't work out, we can just split up, can't we? " said Bill. "It's just not that simple, Bill..."

What advantages and disadvantages of partnerships did Bill and Jeff discuss?

Learning Goal 3

4. Bill and Jeff eventually did form a partnership. Business has been very good. They have expanded their facility, rented some space to several hair stylists, and added several product lines that complement the tanning and hair salon area. They now have a total of three facilities and are wondering if they should incorporate their business, as they would like to expand even further, perhaps one day franchising their idea. What can you tell them about the advantages and disadvantages of incorporation, and what would you suggest for them?

5. What benefit does a corporation have over partnerships and sole proprietorships?

6. Types of Corporations

   There are several terms used to describe different types of corporations:

alien	closed	professional
domestic	open	nonprofit
foreign	quasi-public	multinational

   Match the type of corporation to each of the following:

   a. The stock of United Parcel Service, Inc. is held by a small number of people and is not listed on a stock exchange. _____

   b. Ralston-Purina has sold more than 200 million shares of stock. _____

   c. General Motors is incorporated in Delaware, but has its headquarters in Detroit, Michigan. _____

   d. You can have a Big Mac and fries in Three Rivers, Michigan; Paris, France; Sydney, Australia; and Moscow. _____

   e. Toyota is incorporated in Japan, but has corporate offices located in the United States. _____

   f. Mainini Home Improvement is incorporated in Missouri, has its headquarters in Ellisville, Missouri and only does business in Missouri. _____

   g. The Red Cross sponsors a classic car show and auction every year to raise funds for disaster relief. _____

   h. Ameren U.E., an electrical service provider, must apply to a government agency when it wants to raise rates to its customers. _____

   i. The City of Ann Arbor, Michigan sponsors a carnival each year and the city's recreation department runs a pool and baseball leagues for its residents. _____

7. Two forms of business ownership have received some attention recently are, "S" corporations and limited liability companies. Which one is being described in the following?

   a. This offers flexible ownership rules, and personal asset protection. _____

   b. This type can tell the IRS how it wants to be taxed. _____

   c. Looks like a corporation but is taxed like sole proprietorships and partnerships. _____

   d. New legislation will allow this type to own subsidiaries. _____

   e. This business may have no more than 75 shareholders. _____

   f. This is a very new type of ownership. _____

Learning Goal 4

8. There are several types of corporate mergers and buyouts. Match the situation being described to the correct term:

   Acquisition   Conglomerate merger

   Vertical merger   Leveraged buyout

   Horizontal merger   Taking a firm private

   a. Tommy Hilfiger bought its Canadian distributor, and its American licensee, Pepe Jeans USA in order to own manufacturing and distribution rights. _____

   b. When K.K.R. bought out RJR Nabisco, they borrowed close to $25 billion. _____

   c. In the late 1990s, Boeing bought McDonnell Douglas. _____

d. Two drug companies, Glaxo Wellcome PLC and SmithKline Beecham PLC began talks to merge their companies in the late 1990s. _____

e. In 1997, Berkshire-Hathaway, which owns Samsonite Luggage and the Sara Lee corporation, also bought Helzberg Diamonds, a jewelry store chain in the Midwest. _____

f. When the management of Levi Strauss wanted to avoid a hostile takeover attempt, they formed a group to buy all the outstanding stock. _____

Learning Goal 5

9. Kentucky Fried Chicken (KFC) is a nationwide fast-food franchise. All prospective KFC franchise owners must go through an evaluation process, during which they must submit an application and site proposal for approval and submit to a personal interview in Louisville, KY, KFC's headquarters. Upon approval, KFC offers the franchisee a training program covering management functions such as accounting, sales, advertising and purchasing. KFC pays a portion of this training program. KFC makes available to the franchisee an advertising and promotion kit, opening assistance, equipment layout plans and a choice of interior decor from a list they provide. In addition to standard menu items, a franchisee may offer other items upon approval from KFC management. KFC outlines the estimated cash requirements for opening for such things as equipment, insurance payments, utility down payments, as well as for the facility itself to give franchisees an idea of their cash needs. The franchise fee and the costs of the building and land are the responsibility of the franchisee. There is a royalty rate based on a percentage of gross sales which is paid on a regular basis to KFC for continuing franchises.

    KFC advertises on nationwide television on behalf of its franchisees, so local owners do not have to develop their own television advertising. The local owners do pay a percentage of their gross sales to KFC as a national advertising fee, and each franchisee is required to spend an additional percentage for local advertising.

    Based on this description, identify some of the benefits and drawbacks of owning a franchise.

10. How has technology helped franchises?

Learning Goals 1,2,3,4

11. There are many choices for business ownership. What would be the best choices for these types of businesses? Why?

   a. Landscape/lawn care service

   b. Small manufacturer of component parts for automobiles

   c. Fast food restaurant

   d. Construction/remodeling firm

PRACTICE TEST

Multiple Choice: Circle the best answer.

1. Which of the following is not considered to be an advantage of sole proprietorships?

    a. It's easy to start and end.
    b. You don't have to share the profits with anyone.
    c. You get to be your own boss.
    d. You have limited liability for debts and damages.

2. One of the problems with a _____ is that there is no one to share the burden of management with.

    a. sole proprietorship
    b. limited partnership
    c. S corporation
    d. limited liability company

3. If you are interested in starting your own business, you want to minimize the hassle, and you don't want to have anyone tell you what to do, you should organize your business as a:

    a. S corporation.
    b. limited partnership.
    c. sole proprietorship.
    d. closed corporation.

4. At Sound Off!, a store that buys and sells used CD's, there is only one owner, Sonia. She spends all her time running the business, and makes all the decisions. Sonia's mother and brother put up money for her to buy the store, but they work full time at other jobs and have no management say in the running of Sound Off! This is an example of a:

    a. general partnership.
    b. master limited partnership.
    c. S corporation.
    d. limited partnership.

5. When going into a partnership, you should always:

   a. put all terms of the partnership into writing, in a partnership agreement.
   b. make sure that you have limited liability while you are in charge.
   c. make sure all the profits are reinvested into the company.
   d. divide the profits equally.

6. One of the benefits a general partnership has over a sole proprietorship is:

   a. limited liability.
   b. more financial resources.
   c. easy to start.
   d. a board of directors to help with decisions.

7. The owners of a corporation are called:

   a. general partners.
   b. stockholders.
   c. limited partners.
   d. proprietors.

8. A _____ is one whose stock is not available to the general public through a stock exchange.

   a. alien corporation
   b. domestic corporation
   c. public corporation
   d. closed corporation

9. All of the following are advantages of a corporation except:

   a. unlimited liability.
   b. the amount of money for investment.
   c. the ease of changing ownership.
   d. ability to raise money from investors without getting them involved in management.

10. A form of ownership which can have only 75 shareholders who must be permanent residents of the United States is called a:

    a. limited liability company.
    b. closed corporation.
    c. domestic corporation.
    d. S corporation.

11. Which of the following is not considered an advantage of a limited liability company?

    a. limited number of shareholders
    b. personal asset protection
    c. choice of how to be taxed
    d. flexible ownership rules

12. When Jean-Marie Delacourt was born, her American grandmother bought her 10 shares of Disney stock. As Jean-Marie grows, so will her investment. However, if Disney should happen to go out of business:

    a. Jean-Marie will be responsible for some of the debt of Disney.
    b. Jean-Marie will have to go to court to show she has no involvement in the firm.
    c. Jean-Marie will only lose the value of her shares.
    d. Jean-Marie will have to borrow money from her grandmother to pay for the value of her shares.

13. Which of the following is not a form of corporate mergers?

    a. vertical merger
    b. horizontal merger
    c. conglomerate merger
    d. cooperative merger

14. When the May Company, which owns several department store chains, bought Lord & Taylor, another department store chain, so May could expand their product offerings, it was a:

    a. vertical merger.
    b. horizontal merger.
    c. conglomerate merger.
    d. cooperative merger.

15. The main reason for a conglomerate merger is that:

    a. the investors want more for their money.
    b. it ensures a constant supply of materials needed by other companies.
    c. it allows for a firm to offer a variety of related products.
    d. the business can diversify its business operations and investments.

16. When a major national bakery bought out a smaller more regional bakery in the east, it took over all their assets and their debt. This is an example of a(n):

    a. acquisition.
    b. merger.
    c. nationalization.
    d. appropriation.

17. In order to avoid a hostile takeover by a Kollmorgaen, managers at Pacific Scientific considered making a bid for all the company's stock themselves and taking it off the open market. This would be:

    a. a leveraged buyout.
    b. a conglomerate merger.
    c. taking the firm private.
    d. forming a master limited partnership.

18. When Pat Sloane bought a Tidy Maid franchise, she became a:

    a. franchisor.
    b. stockholder.
    c. venture capitalist.
    d. franchisee.

19. One of the advantages of a franchise is:

    a. receiving management and marketing expertise from the franchisor.
    b. fewer restrictions on selling than in other forms of businesses.
    c. lower start up costs than other businesses.
    d. you get to keep all the profits after taxes.

20. International franchising is:

    a. a successful area for both small and large franchises.
    b. costs about the same as domestic franchising.
    c. becoming increasingly difficult, and so is not growing.
    d. easy, because you really do not have to adapt your product at all.

21. In a _____, members democratically control the business by electing a board of directors that hires professional management.

    a. corporation
    b. cooperative
    c. franchise
    d. master limited partnership

TRUE/FALSE

1. ____ One of the benefits of a sole proprietorship is that you have easy availability of funds from a variety of sources.

2. ____ It is relatively easy to get in and out of business when you are a sole proprietor.

3. ____ A common complaint among sole proprietors is that good people to work for you are hard to find.

4. ____ It is best to form a limited partnership, because then there is no one individual who takes on the unlimited liability.

5. ____ In a partnership, one of the major disadvantages is the potential for conflict.

6. ____ A master limited partnership is much like a corporation because its stock is traded on a stock exchange.

7. ____ The owner of a corporation is called a director.

8. ____ One advantage of a corporation is the ability to sell stock to raise money.

9. ____ An S corporation avoids the double taxation of a conventional C corporation.

10. ____ An individual may not incorporate.

11. ____ A limited liability company can choose to be taxed either as a corporation or as a partnership.

12. ____ An example of a vertical merger is MCI Communications and WorldCom, another communications company.

13. ____ A conglomerate merger is the merger of two very large companies in related industries.

14. ____ A leveraged buyout is when the managers of a company buy all of the stock of a firm and take it off the open market.

15. ____ A franchise can be formed as a sole proprietorship, a partnership or a corporation.

16. ____ As a franchisee, you are entitled to financial advice and assistance from the franchisor.

17. ____ One of the disadvantages of a franchise is that if you want to sell, the franchisor must approve of the new owner.

18. _____ It is likely that women and minorities will not participate in franchising in the future.

19. _____ One of the advantages that a home based franchisee has over a business owner based at home is that the franchisee feels less isolated.

20. _____ One element of some cooperatives is for members to work a few hours a month as part of their duties.

ANSWERS

LEARNING THE LANGUAGE

1. Horizontal merger	9. Limited partnership	17. Cooperative
2. Partnership	10. Master limited partnership	18. General partnership
3. Franchise agreement	11. Corporation	19. Leveraged buyout
4. Acquisition	12. Merger	20. Franchise
5. Limited liability	13. Franchisee	21. Vertical merger
6. S Corporation	14. Limited partner	22. Sole proprietorship
7. Franchisor	15. Limited liability company	23. Unlimited liability
8. Conglomerate merger	16. General partner	

RETENTION CHECK

Learning Goal 1 **Forms of Business Ownership**

1. a. sole proprietorship   b. partnership   c. corporation

2. A corporation is the only form of ownership where the business is separate from the owners.

3. The most common form of ownership is the sole proprietorship.

4.
   a. Ease of starting and ending business
   b. Being your own boss
   c. Pride of ownership
   d. Retention of profit
   d. No special taxes

5.
   a. Unlimited liability and the risk of losses
   b. Limited financial resources
   c. Difficulty in management'
   d. Overwhelming time commitment
   e. Few fringe benefits
   f. Limited growth
   g. Limited life span

Learning Goal 2 **Partnerships**

6. a. Common ownership
    b. Shared profits and losses
    c. The right to participate in managing the operations of the business

7. Two forms of partnership agreements are:
    a. general partnership.   b. limited partnership.

8. In a general partnership agreement, the partners agree to share in the operation of the business and assume unlimited liability for the company's debts. In a limited partnership, the limited partners do not have an active role in managing the business, and have liability only up to the amount invested in the firm.

9. a. More financial resources
    b. Shared management/pooled knowledge
    c. Longer survival

10. a. Division of profits
    b. Disagreements between partners
    c. Difficult to terminate
    d. Unlimited liability

Learning Goal 3 **Corporations**

11. A conventional 'C' corporation is a state-chartered entity with authority to act and have liability separate from its owners.

12. The advantages of a "C" corporation include:
    a. More money for investment.
    b. Limited liability.
    c. Size.
    d. Perpetual life.
    e. Ease of ownership change.
    f. Ease of drawing talented employees.
    g. Separation of ownership from management.

13. The disadvantages of a "C" corporation include:
    a. Initial cost.
    b. Paperwork.
    c. Two tax returns.
    d. Size.
    e. Difficulty of termination.
    f. Double taxation.
    g. Possible conflict with board of directors.

14. The information included in the articles of incorporation includes:
    a. The corporation's name.
    b. Names of people incorporating.
    c. Its purpose.
    d. Its duration.
    e. The number of shares, voting rights, and other rights.
    f. The corporation's capital.
    g. Address of corporate office.
    h. Name and address of corporation's lawyer.
    i. Names and addresses of the first directors.
    j. Any other public information.

15. An S corporation is a unique government creation that looks like a corporation but is taxed like sole proprietorships and partnerships.

16. An "S" Corporation must:
    a. have no more than 75 shareholders.
    b. have shareholders that are individuals or estates and are citizens or permanent residents of the United States.
    c. have only one class of outstanding stock.
    d. not have more than 25% of income derived from passive sources such as rents, royalties, interest etc.

17.
    a. Alien
    b. Domestic
    c. Foreign
    d. Closed (private)
    e. Open (public)
    f. Quasi-public
    g. Professional
    h. Nonprofit
    i. Multinational

18. Changes in the Small Business Jobs Protection Act include:
    a. an increase in the maximum number of shareholders to 75.
    b. allows tax-exempt organizations such as charities to own shares in S corporations.
    c. allows S corporations to own subsidiaries.

19. A limited liability company is similar to an S corporation without the special eligibility requirements.

20. The advantages of a limited liability company are:
    a. personal asset protection.
    b. choice to be taxed as a partnership or corporation.
    c. flexible ownership rules.

Learning Goal 4   **Corporate Expansion: Mergers and Acquisitions**

21. A merger is the result of two companies forming one company.

22. An acquisition is one company buying the property and obligations of another company, while a merger is when two companies join and create one company. It's like the difference between a marriage (merger) and buying a house (acquisition).

23. a. Vertical mergers
    b. Horizontal mergers
    c. Conglomerate mergers

24. When taking a firm private, a group of stockholders or management obtains all a firm's stock for themselves.

25. A leveraged buyout is an attempt by employees, management or a group of investors to purchase an organization primarily through borrowing.

26. The recent "buying binge" can be attributed to:
    a. the slumping dollar.
    b. depressed stock prices.
    c. sluggish U.S. spending.
    d. increased globalization.

Learning Goal 5   **Special Forms of Business Ownership**

27. A franchisor is someone with a good idea for a business who sells the right to use the business name to someone else, the franchisee.

28. Statistics that indicate franchising is important are:
    a. eight million people work in a franchise in the U.S.
    b. franchising accounts for 40 percent of the national retail sales.
    c. one out of twelve American businesses is a franchise.
    d. a new franchise opens every eight minutes each business day.

29. The advantages of a franchise are:
    a. Management assistance.
    b. Personal ownership.
    c. Nationally recognized name.
    d. Financial assistance.
    e. Lower failure rate.

30. A franchisee has a greater chance of succeeding because franchises generally:
    a. have an established product.
    b. help with choosing a location.
    c. help with promotion.
    d. assist in all phases of operation.

31. The disadvantages of franchising are:
    a. High start up cost
    b. Shared profit.
    c. Management regulation.
    d. Coattail effects.
    e. Restrictions on selling.
    f. Fraudulent franchisors.

32. One of the biggest changes in franchising in recent years is the banding together of many franchisees to resolve their grievances with franchisors rather than fighting their battles alone.

33. Indications are that women and minorities will play a much larger role in franchising in the future than in previous years. Women have often turned to franchising to expand their businesses when financing was difficult, and so are participating in franchising as both franchisee and franchisor. The government is encouraging minorities to become involved in franchising through the Commerce Department's Federal Minority Business Development Agency.

34. Four advantages of home franchising are:
    a. relief from the time and stress of commuting.
    b. extra time for family activities.
    c. low overhead expenses.
    d. home-based franchisees feel less isolated than home-based entrepreneurs.

35. One of the considerations of franchising in international markets is the cost, which can be high. Less competition and a fast growing market may counterbalance these high costs. Another consideration is the need to adapt products and services to the region into which the franchisor wants to expand.

Learning Goal 6   **Cooperatives**

36. Two kinds of cooperatives are:
    a. food cooperatives.
    b. farm cooperatives.

37. Non-farm cooperatives meet members needs for things such as electricity, childcare, housing, health care, food and financial services.

38. Some cooperatives ask members to work in the organization as part of their duties. Also, members democratically control these businesses by electing a board of directors that hires professional management.

CRITICAL THINKING EXERCISES

Learning Goal 1

1. Jeff and Bill covered most of the advantages and disadvantages of owning a sole proprietorship. Jeff mentioned the ease of starting the business, the fact that you are your own boss and how proud he seemed to be of what he had accomplished with his hard work. He also mentioned that his tax liability was reasonable (in other words, he didn't have to pay any special taxes), and that he was making a profit that was his to keep and do with as he pleased. Some of the disadvantages Jeff mentioned were that he worked long hours, and had some difficulty in finding financial sources beyond the bank. He was nervous about the unlimited financial liability, and agreed that few fringe benefits was a concern. He also noted that he's having a problem finding a good person to work for him as is common with sole proprietorships. Lastly, he noted one final disadvantage of sole proprietorship, the limited life span. He is making arrangements for his children to inherit the business and continue with it if something happens to him.

Learning Goal 2

2. a. Master Limited Partnership (MLP)
   b. Limited partnership
   c. General partnership
   d. MLP
   e. Limited partnership
   f. General partnership

3. It appears that Bill thought of most of the advantages and Jeff could only find disadvantages! Bill realized that he could give Jeff the financial resources he needed, and could relieve Bill of the long hours he was spending at the business. He also recognized that statistics indicate that partnerships have a longer survival rate than sole proprietorships. The one disadvantage Bill mentioned was the unlimited liability taken on by a general partner. Jeff was quick to point out the disadvantages of shared profits, potential disagreements, and the difficulty of terminating a partnership.

Learning Goal 3

4. There are a number of things to consider before Bill and Jeff decide to incorporate. If they are interested in expanding even further, incorporating would give them a wider source of funds for investment, because they could sell stock and keep the investors out of management for the most part. However, their business is small, and there is a question of how "marketable" their stock would be. A major advantage for them both is the aspect of limited liability. Expansion may require going into debt, and if they incorporate, Bill and Jeff would not be liable should something happen to the business. Another advantage for both of the partners is the perpetual life of a corporation. If something should happen to either Bill or Jeff, the remaining owners could still continue

with the business. Further, if one of them decided to get out of the business, it is relatively easy, as they would simply have to sell their stock to the remaining owners.

One major disadvantage of incorporating is the initial cost, which can be very high. It also requires a lot of additional paperwork, particularly regarding the accounting records. Bill and Jeff would have to file more tax returns, and they would be taxed twice, once on their earned income and additionally on the income they received from dividends.

My advice to Bill and Jeff would be to incorporate, as it looks like the advantages may outweigh the disadvantages. Because they are a small company, they will become a <u>closed</u> corporation. That will eliminate the problem of having a market for their stock. They may also want to consider becoming an "S" corporation.

5. One of the primary advantages of a corporation over proprietorships and partnerships is limited liability for the owners. There are additional sources of revenue for a corporation and many times it is easier to attract talented employees because a corporation may be able to offer better benefits. Some corporations are very large, and so size becomes a distinct advantage in terms of facilities and the ability to hire specialists.

6.
- a. Closed
- b. Open
- c. Foreign
- d. Multinational
- e. Alien
- f. Domestic
- g. Nonprofit
- h. Quasi public
- i. Public

7.
- a. Limited liability
- b. Limited liability
- c. "S" corporation
- d. "S" corporation
- e. "S" corporation
- f. Limited liability

Learning Goal 4

8.
- a. vertical merger
- b. leveraged buyout
- c. acquisition
- d. horizontal merger
- e. conglomerate merger
- f. taking a firm private

Learning Goal 5

9. This description identifies several of the benefits of owning a franchise. One of the first in this case is the fact that KFC is a nationally recognized name, which almost guarantees an established customer base. That helps to reduce the risk of failing. KFC provides management training and pays for part of it. They offer advice with opening the store, for such things as advertising, layout, and interior decor. They offer financial advice also and give the franchisee a feel for what the initial costs are going to be. The franchisee can take advantage of a national advertising campaign, while still advertising on a local basis so they are able to meet local needs.

   The drawbacks stem from the franchise fee which could be relatively high for a nationally recognized franchise, and so adds to the initial cost of opening. Further, a royalty rate must be paid on a regular basis to KFC, and the franchisee must contribute to a national advertising fund which takes away part of your profits. Your menu items are limited to what the franchisor tells you, and you must get permission to offer anything different, so you are closely regulated in terms of the menu, as well as interior decor.

10. Franchisors are using the Internet to meet the needs of both customers and their franchisees. Franchisors have set up Web sites to streamline effective communication for employees, customers and vendors. Intranets are also being built to help franchisees communicate with one another, which has reduced paperwork. Using Web sites, franchisees have immediate access to every subject that involves franchise operations, including forms.

11. a. The landscape/lawn care firm could start out as a sole proprietorship or partnership. There may be no great need for capital to start out with, so there would be no need to incorporate. A partnership may be an advantage because of the amount of labor involved, to build the business, and do more than one job in a day. Another possibility would be to be a sole proprietor and hire workers to help.
    b. A small manufacturer of component parts would likely do best as a corporation, primarily due to the capital investment required and the need for a variety of skills such as marketing, manufacturing, engineering and so on. There is also the potential for liability in a manufacturing setting, and a corporate structure would protect the owners. This may initially be a closed corporation or even an "S" corporation.
    c. If you want to get into the fast food business, one of the easiest ways would be to investigate owning a franchise. Some fast food franchises are among the fastest growing franchises in the country, and the industry is very competitive. A "guaranteed" market would be a definite plus! The drawback, of course, is the initial expense, but if you can come up with the money a franchise may be the best way to go.

d. The construction/remodeling business again could be a sole proprietorship or partnership. There is a definite need for several people to be working, so you could either hire workers to work for you, or find a partner who can help in the business. The investment in tools may be substantial which may be another indication of the need for a partner.

PRACTICE TEST

Multiple Choice				**True/False**			
1.	d	12.	c	1.	F	11.	T
2.	a	13.	d	2.	T	12.	F
3.	c	14.	b	3.	T	13.	F
4.	a	15.	d	4.	F	14.	F
5.	a	16.	a	5.	T	15.	T
6.	b	17.	c	6.	T	16.	T
7.	b	18.	d	7.	F	17.	T
8.	d	19.	a	8.	T	18.	F
9.	a	20.	a	9.	T	19.	T
10.	d	21.	b	10.	F	20.	T
11.	a						

CHAPTER 6
ENTREPRENEURSHIP AND STARTING A SMALL BUSINESS

LEARNING GOALS

After you have read and studied this chapter, you should be able to:

1. Explain why people are willing to take the risks of entrepreneurship; list the attributes of successful entrepreneurs and describe the benefits of entrepreneurial teams and intrapreneurs.

2. Discuss the importance of small business to the American economy and summarize the major causes of small-business failures.

3. Summarize ways to learn about how small businesses operate.

4. Analyze what it takes to start and run a small business.

5. Outline the advantages and disadvantages of small businesses entering global markets.

LEARNING THE LANGUAGE

Listed here are important terms found in this chapter. Choose the correct term for each definition and write it in the space provided.

Active Corps of Executives (ACE)	Market
Business plan	Micropreneur
Entrepreneurial team	Service Corps of Retired Executives (SCORE)
Entrepreneurship	Small Business
Incubators	Small Business Investment Company (SBIC)
Intrapreneurs	Venture capitalists

1. A _____ consists of people with unsatisfied wants and needs who have both the resources and willingness to buy.

2. Volunteers from industry, trade associations and education who counsel small business make up a group known as _____.

3. A group of experienced people from different areas of business who join together as a _____ with the skills needed to develop, make and market a new product.

4. A _____ is independently owned and operated, not dominant in its field of operation, and meets certain standards of size in terms of employees or annual receipts.

5. Investors who ask for a hefty stake in your company in exchange for the cash to start your business are called _____.

6. Created by states to provide low-cost offices, _____ give small businesses basic business services such as accounting, legal advice and secretarial help.

7. This SBA office known as the _____ has 13,000 volunteers who provide consulting services for small businesses free.

8. _____ is accepting the risk of starting and running a business.

9. Creative people known as _____ work as entrepreneurs within corporations.

10. A _____ is a detailed written statement that describes the nature of the business, the target market, the advantages the business will have in relation to competition, and the resources and qualifications of the owners.

11. A private investment company which the Small Business Administration licenses to lend money to small businesses is called the _____.

12. A _____ is interested in enjoying a better lifestyle and in having the opportunity of making a living doing the kind of work he/she wants to do.

RETENTION CHECK

Learning Goal 1   **The Age of the Entrepreneur**

1. What are four reasons why people become entrepreneurs?

   a. _____

   b. _____

   c. _____

   d. _____

2. What are five desirable attributes for entrepreneurs?

   a. _____

   b. _____

   c. _____

   d. _____

   e. _____

3. What is an entrepreneurial team?

4. What are 2 advantages of entrepreneurial teams?

   a. _____

   b. _____

5. What is the difference between an entrepreneur and a micropreneur?

6. Identify five points of advice for home-based business owners.

   a. _____

   b. _____

   c. _____

   d. _____

   e. _____

7. What are two ways countries can encourage entrepreneurship?

   a. _____

   b. _____

8. What is an intrapreneur?

9. What is the difference between an entrepreneur and an intrapreneur?

Learning Goal 2 **Getting Started In Small Business**

10. What are three criteria used to classify a business as "small?"

   a. _____

   b. _____

   c. _____

11. What is meant by "small is relative"?

12. How are women-owned and minority-owned businesses doing?

13. How "big" is small business?

14. What three areas reported the biggest employment increases?

    a. _____ b. _____ c. _____

15. Why do small businesses have an advantage over big businesses?

    a. _____

    b. _____

    c. _____

16. What are two general reasons for small business failure?

    a. _____

    b. _____

17. In general the easiest businesses to start are:

18. In general the easiest businesses to keep going are:

Learning Goal 3 **Learning About Small-Business Operations**

19. What are three ways to learn about small business?

    a. _____

    b. _____

    c. _____

20. What is the "rule of thumb" about getting experience in small business?

21. Where do many new entrepreneurs come from?

22. What are three factors used to determine the value of a business?

    a. _____

    b. _____

    c. _____

Learning Goal 4 **Managing a Small Business**

23. What two management functions are of primary concern when you are first starting your business?

   a. _____

   b. _____

24. What three functions are of concern after the start-up, when managing the business?

   a. _____

   b. _____

   c. _____

25. What are the tips for small business owners who want to borrow money?

   a. _____

   b. _____

   c. _____

   d. _____

   e. _____

   f. _____

   g. _____

26. List the information that generally should be included in a business plan.

   a. _____
   b. _____
   c. _____
   d. _____
   e. _____
   f. _____
   g. _____
   h. _____
   i. _____
   j. _____

27. What are several sources of small business funding?

   a. _____
   b. _____
   c. _____
   d. _____
   e. _____
   f. _____
   g. _____

h. _____

i. _____

j. _____

28. How are states beginning to support entrepreneurs?

29. Other than personal savings, what is the primary source of capital for entrepreneurs?

30. What is one potential drawback with using venture capital?

31. What are seven types of financial assistance provided by the Small Business Administration?

   a. _____

   b. _____

   c. _____

   d. _____

   e. _____

f. _____

g. _____

32. How does the microloan program award loans?

33. What are Small Business Development Centers?

34. What are the two most important elements of small-business success regarding a market?

a. _____

b. _____

35. What three criteria are critical for a small business owner with regard to managing employees?

a. _____ b. _____ c. _____

36. In what area do most small business owners feel they need assistance the most?

37. How can an accountant help in managing a small business?

38. What are five areas in which you may need assistance as a small business owner?

   a. _____   d. _____

   b. _____   e. _____

   c. _____

39. In what ways can a lawyer help?

40. How can marketing research help?

41. What government-sponsored agencies are helping small business owners?

   a. _____   b. _____   c. _____

Learning Goal 5   **Going International: Small-Business Prospects**

42. What are four hurdles small businesses face in the international market?

   a. _____

   b. _____

   c. _____

   d. _____

43. Identify five reasons for going international.

   a. _____

   b. _____

   c. _____

   d. _____

   e. _____

44. List the advantages small businesses have over large business in the international market.

   a. _____

   b. _____

   c. _____

   d. _____

CRITICAL THINKING EXERCISES

Learning Goal 1

1. You have read in earlier chapters that many parts of Eastern Europe and developing countries in other parts of the world are trying to move to a free market system. How can these developing countries encourage entrepreneurship, and why is it important that entrepreneurship be supported and encouraged?

2. How did Compaq use an entrepreneurial teams to become successful?

3. Eric is a young man with a vision. He sees himself as heading up a large corporation someday, that he has started and helped to grow. He has basically supported himself since he was fifteen, and has, at the age of 20, already started and sold 2 successful small businesses. Right now he is going to college full time because he feels that getting an education will be beneficial to him in the long run. He is supporting himself partially with the money he received from the sale of his last business. He intends to start yet another business as soon as he graduates.

    Eric's most recent business was in a fairly competitive market in the area in which he lives, St. Louis. He says that while he received some encouragement from a few friends, for the most part they all said he was crazy to work as hard as he was working. But Eric says he just felt that he "had to do things my own way." the built his business into the second largest of its type in the St. Louis area.

    How does Eric portray the entrepreneurial attributes your text identifies?

Learning Goals 2, 3

4. Eric seems to have beaten the odds already. What do you think Eric would tell you about success (or failure) and how to learn to be a successful small business owner?

Learning Goal 4

5. Eric has graduated from school, and is ready to start his new business. He has never applied for a bank loan, and has come to you for advice on how to get the loan. What will you tell him?

6. Distinguish between the following types of SBA loans:

    Direct loan   Women's Financing Section

    Guaranteed loans   Women's Prequalification Pilot Loan

    Participation loans   Microloans

    MESBICs

    a. _____ Maria Araruiz received this loan for $100,000 because she owns 60% of the business she runs with her brother.

    b. _____ Terry Krull got a loan for his construction company directly from the SBA and partly from his bank. The SBA will guarantee repayment of the bank loan.

    c. _____ Dennis Franks is a painter, who was disabled several years ago. The SBA gave him a loan when Dennis had difficulty obtaining a conventional loan.

d. _____ John Hoffman got a loan for his home automation business from his local bank, but the SBA will repay the loan if John stops making the payments.

e. _____ Jack Peterson, who lives in an urban housing project, started his own accounting business with this SBA loan for $5,000.

f. _____ John Rattler is an African-American who started a business writing software for small business application.

g. _____ Danielle Frontiere took out a loan for $35,000 to start her home business of importing lace from Germany.

Learning Goals 3, 4

7. After planning and financing, the functions necessary to be successful in running your small business include:

   Knowing your market   Keeping efficient records

   Managing employees   Looking for help

Read the following situation, keeping in mind what you have learned about successful small businesses. Do you think this small business will "beat the odds?"

Dave and Kevin worked together as sales representatives for a clothing manufacturer in Michigan. They were successful, but were interested in working on their own, and started to develop a plan for a partnership as manufacturer's representatives selling clothing and hats to their current customers, using a supplier network they would develop. While they were working full time, Dave and Kevin spent 6 months finding backers and lining up suppliers, and got a feel for which of their current customers they could count on later. They casually consulted with an accountant and a lawyer.

Finally they decided they were ready, and opened up under the name of Premium Incentives, Inc. Here is the situation on the day Premium Incentives opened:

* They each worked at home.
* They had promises, but no written contract from two suppliers to lend them a total of $100,000 over a one year period in return for all their business.
* They decided not to do a business plan, as they already had financing.

* Dave's wife agreed to do the bookkeeping as a favor. She had a degree in business, but not in accounting, had a full time job and a three-year-old child and was expecting another child in 5 months.
* They hired sales representatives to help with sales outside their home state, and planned to pay them on commission.
* They set up a price schedule designed to under-cut their competitors by a significant amount.

After two months in business, Dave and Kevin were still hopeful, but disappointed. They had made $5000 in sales, but hadn't yet been paid, as the product hadn't been delivered to the customers, and they had over $3,000 in start-up expenses. This would not have been a problem had the suppliers come through on their promises to finance Premium Incentives. However, one of the suppliers, after reconsidering, decided not to lend them any money, and the second dropped his offer down to $5000 a month for six months, with repayment beginning in the seventh month. Since Premium Incentives, Inc. did not have a written contract, they had no legal recourse. Dave and Kevin didn't worry too much about repaying the $60,000 loan, as they figured they still had four months to build up the business. The problem was, their customers weren't buying as much as Dave and Kevin had anticipated, and they weren't sure what to do to find new customers.

Dave's wife was having problems keeping up with the books, so Dave began spending several days a week working on that, in addition to trying to sell. His wife suggested they develop some way of billing a customer, then re-billing if they hadn't paid within 15 days. Dave and Kevin disagreed about what to do, and eventually did nothing. They did finally hire a bookkeeper after several months of doing the books themselves. They continued to struggle with not knowing when a customer was going to pay, and therefore had no idea how much income they were going to have each month.

What do you think? What did Dave & Kevin do right? What did they do wrong? What are their chances of success?

8. "Small business people have learned, sometimes the hard way, that they need outside consulting advice early in the process."

   A. Draw up a list of the types of consultants whose services you may need in starting and managing your small business.

   a. _____

   b. _____

c. _____

d. _____

e. _____

f. _____

B. What are other sources of information available?

a. _____ d. _____

b. _____ e. _____

c. _____ f. _____

Learning Goal 5

9. Chad Lane is the owner of a small software business based in California. Because there is so much competition in the U.S. he has begun to look for opportunities in global markets. What would you tell him as his advisor?

PRACTICE TEST

Multiple Choice: Circle the best answer

1. Entrepreneurs take the risk of starting a business for all of the following reasons except:

    a. they want independence.
    b. they like the challenge and the risk.
    c. they want to make money for themselves.
    d. they want to work less.

2. An entrepreneurial team is:

    a. a group of people who work within a corporation to expand the market for the company's products.
    b. a group of experienced people who join together to develop and market a new product.
    c. a group from the Small Business Administration which consults with small business owners.
    d. a group of managers who get together to find creative solutions to problems.

3. Federiko Romero is a business owner who works from home as a freelance video producer. He really enjoys his work, but isn't looking to "set the world on fire" with his company. He just wants to make a good living and spend time with his family when he can. Federiko would be classified as a(n):

    a. entrepreneur.
    b. intrapreneur.
    c. micropreneur.
    d. venture capitalist.

4. Which of the following is a false statement about small business?

    a. The number of women owning small businesses is increasing.
    b. The vast majority of non-farm businesses in the U.S. are considered small.
    c. The first job for most Americans will probably not be in a small business.
    d. The majority of the country's new jobs are in small business.

5. A small business:

   a. must have fewer than 100 employees to be considered small.
   b. is considered small relative to other businesses in its industry.
   c. cannot be a corporation.
   d. should be an S corporation.

6. In general:

   a. the easier to start the business, the more likely it is to succeed.
   b. businesses that are more difficult to start are most likely to fail.
   c. the easier a business is to start the higher the growth rate.
   d. businesses that are difficult to start, are the easiest ones to keep going.

7. Miriam Njunge wants to start a small business importing some products from her native Kenya. Before she starts, some good advice to Miriam would be:

   a. talk to others who have been or are in the import business.
   b. get a loan right away.
   c. find a business to buy as soon as possible.
   d. incorporate immediately.

8. In measuring the value of a small firm, which of the following would not be included?

   a. What the business owns
   b. What the business earns
   c. What makes the business unique
   d. What products the business makes

9. The primary concerns when first starting your business are:

   a. marketing and accounting.
   b. planning and human resources.
   c. financing and planning.
   d. financing and marketing.

10. A business plan for a new business does not need to include:

    a. a marketing plan.
    b. a discussion of the purpose of the business.
    c. a description of the company background.
    d. the name of the lending bank.

11. What are the primary sources of funding for entrepreneurs?

    a. personal savings and individual investors
    b. finance companies and banks
    c. the Small Business Administration and banks
    d. former employers and the Economic Development Authority

12. This program awards loans on the basis of belief in the borrower's integrity and the soundness of their business ideas.

    a. SBIC loan   c. Direct loan
    b. Guaranteed loan   d. Microloan

13. For a market to exist, there must be potential buyers:

    a. and a product that is safe and inexpensive.
    b. who have a willingness and the resources to buy.
    c. and stores which are willing to carry the product.
    d. who are looking for a bargain.

14. Employees in small businesses generally:

    a. are more satisfied with their jobs than counterparts in big business.
    b. are less satisfied with their jobs because there is less room for advancement.
    c. are generally only using the job as a springboard to get into a larger company.
    d. are most likely going to quit to find a company that accepts their ideas.

15. Small business owners often say that the most important assistance they need is in:

    a. marketing.   c. planning.
    b. accounting.   d. manufacturing.

16. The Small Business Administration sponsors groups of volunteers who consult with small businesses for free or for a small fee. These groups are:

    a. venture capitalists and entrepreneurs.
    b. retired executives and people currently in business.
    c. stockholders and investors.
    d. franchisors and bankers.

17. There are many reasons why small business owners don't go international. Which is not considered to be one of the reasons?

    a. They don't know how to get started.
    b. Financing is often difficult to find.
    c. Paperwork is often overwhelming.
    d. The market doesn't have great potential.

18. Small businesses have an advantage over large business in international trade in all these ways except:

    a. They can begin shipping faster.
    b. They can provide a wide variety of suppliers.
    c. Overseas buyers like dealing with individuals rather than large bureaucracies.
    d. Their prices are usually lower.

19. Small business owners who want to explore the opportunities in international business will find that:

    a. There is not much information about exporting.
    b. Most small businesses still don't think internationally.
    c. There is usually no need to adapt products to foreign markets.
    d. It is more difficult for small businesses to enter international markets than for large businesses.

TRUE/FALSE

1. ____ It is important for an entrepreneur to be self-directed and self-nurturing.

2. ____ An intrapreneur is an individual who is a member of an entrepreneurial team.

3. ____ The Immigration Act of 1990 created investor visas which allow 10,000 people to come to the U.S. if they invest $1 million in an enterprise that creates 10 jobs.

4. ____ Taxes have little effect on entrepreneurship.

5. ____ The majority of new jobs in the private sector are created by small business.

6. ____ Many of the businesses with the lowest failure rates require advanced training to start.

7. ____ One of the ways to get information about starting a small business is by attending classes at a local college.

8. ____ A substantial percentage of small-business owners got the idea for their businesses from their prior jobs.

9. ____ An effective business plan should catch the reader's interest right away.

10. ____ The most important source of funds for a small business owner is bank loans.

11. ____ States have not been especially supportive of small business.

12. ____ The SBA offers a lot of advice, but no financial assistance to small business owners.

13. ____ Finding funding for a small business is probably the easiest thing about starting a small business.

14. ____ A market is basically anyone who wants to buy your product.

15. ____ Employees of small businesses are often more satisfied with their jobs than counterparts in big business.

16. ____ Most small businesses can't afford to hire experts as employees, so they need to turn to outside assistance for help.

17. ____ It is best to stay away from other small business owners for counsel, as they are likely to use your ideas before you can get started.

18. ____ A relatively small number of firms accounts for over 80 percent of U.S. exports.

ANSWERS

Learning the Language

1. Market	7. Service Corps of Retired Executives (SCORE)
2. Active Corps of Executives (ACE)	8. Entrepreneurship
3. Entrepreneurial team	9. Intrapreneurs
4. Small business	10. Business plan
5. Venture capitalist	11. Small Business Investment Company (SBIC)
6. Incubators	12. Micropreneur

RETENTION CHECK

Learning Goal 1   **The Age of the Entrepreneur**

1. Four reasons people become entrepreneurs are:
   a. Opportunity.
   b. Profit.
   c. Independence.
   d. Challenge.

2.
   a. Self-directed
   b. Self-nurturing
   c. Action-oriented
   d. Highly energetic
   e. Tolerant of uncertainty

3. An entrepreneurial team is a group of experienced people from different areas of business who join together to form a managerial team with the skills needed to develop, make and market a new product.

4. a. A team combines skills from several areas of the business, to create a synergistic effect. Creative areas (such as design) are combined with production and marketing from the beginning.
   b. A team can ensure coordination between functions of a business, and better cooperation.

5. An entrepreneur is not all that different from a micropreneur. Actually, a micropreneur is a "kind "of entrepreneur who is interested in simply enjoying a better lifestyle and in having the opportunity of making a living doing the kind of work they want to do. Therefore a micropreneur may be quite happy to keep the business small. An entrepreneur may be interested in "growing" the business.

6. Home-based business owners should focus on:
   a. opportunity instead of security.
   b. getting results instead of following a routine.
   c. earning a profit instead of a paycheck.
   d. trying new ideas instead of avoiding mistakes.
   e. long-term vision instead of a short-term payoff.

7. Countries can encourage entrepreneurship by:
   a. offering investment tax credits and tax breaks.
   b. investing to build the nation's infrastructure to support business.

8. Intrapreneurs are creative people who work as entrpreneurs within a corporation.

9. Entrepreneurs are risk takers who have started their own businesses. Intrapreneurs work as entrepreneurs within corporations. They use existing human, financial and physical resources to launch new products and generate new profits.

Learning Goal 2 **Getting Started in Small Business**

10. A small business is one that is:
    a. independently owned and operated.
    b. not dominant in its field of operation.
    c. meets certain standards of size in terms of employees or annual receipts.

11. A small business is considered small relative to the industry it is in. If it meets the criteria listed above, a $22 million business would still be considered small.

12. The number of women- and minority-owned businesses has increased considerably. The number of small businesses owned by minority women has grown 153% in nine years.

13. Small business is very "big". Small businesses account for over 40% of GDP, produce 90% of new jobs, and employ more than the populations of Australia and Canada combined. In the 1980's small businesses created almost a million jobs, while big businesses lost 4.1 million jobs. There are about 24.5 million full and part-time home-based businesses in the United States.

14. The areas which have reported the biggest employment increases are:
    a. services.   b. manufacturing.   c. construction.

15. Small businesses' advantages over large businesses are:
    a. providing employment opportunities.
    b. more personal customer service.
    c. their ability to respond quickly to opportunities.

16. Two general reasons for small business failure are:
    a. managerial incompetence.   b. inadequate financial planning.

17. In general the easiest businesses to start are the ones that tend to have the least growth and the greatest failure rate.

18. In general the easiest businesses to keep going are the difficult ones to get started.

Learning Goal 3   **Learning About Small Business Operations**

19. Three ways to learn about small business are:
    a. learn from others.   b. get some experience.   c. take over a successful firm.

20. The rule of thumb is: Have three years' experience in a comparable business.

21. Many new entrepreneurs come from corporate management.

22. Value is based on:
    a. what the business owns.   b. what it earns.   c. what makes it unique.

Learning Goal 4   **Managing a Small Business**

23. The two management functions of primary concern are:
    a. Planning.   b. Financing.

24. The three important functions after the startup are:
    a. Knowing your customers (marketing).
    b. Managing your employees (human resource development.)
    c. Keeping records (accounting).

25. Tips for small business owners wanting to borrow money are:
    a. Pick a bank that serves small businesses.
    b. Have a good accountant prepare a complete set of financial statements and personal balance sheet.
    c. Go to the bank with an accountant and all the necessary financial information.
    d. Make an appointment before going to the bank.
    e. Demonstrate good character.
    f. Ask for all the money you need.
    g. Be prepared to personally guarantee the loan.

26. a. Cover letter
    b. Executive summary of proposed venture
    c. Company background
    d. Management team
    e. Financial plan
    f. Capital required
    g. Marketing plan
    h. Location analysis
    i. Manufacturing plan
    j. Appendix which includes marketing research and other information about the product

27. Sources of small business funding include:
    a. Personal savings.
    b. Relatives.
    c. Former employers.
    d. Banks.
    e. Finance companies
    f. Small Business Administration.
    g. Farmers Home Administration.
    h. Economic Development Authority.
    i. Potential suppliers.
    j. SBIC (Small Business Investment Company).

28. States are supporting entrepreneurs by creating programs that invest directly in new businesses. Some states are also creating incubators and technology centers to reduce start up costs. These incubators provide low cost offices with basic business services.

29. Other than personal savings the primary source of capital for entrepreneurs are individual investors.

30. The potential drawback with venture capitalists is that they will often ask for as much as 60% ownership in your business.

31. The types of financial assistance from the Small Business Administration are:
    a. Direct loans.
    b. Guaranteed loans.
    c. Participation loans.
    d. Loans from Minority Enterprise Small Business Investment Companies (MESBICs).
    e. Loans from the Women's Financing Section.
    f. The Women's Prequalification Pilot Loan Program.
    g. Microloans.

32. Microloans are awarded on the basis of belief in the borrowers' integrity and the soundness of their business deals.

33. Small Business Development Centers are funded jointly by the federal government and individual states and are usually associated with state universities. SBDCs can help a small business owner evaluate the feasibility of the idea, develop the business plan and complete the funding application, all of which is free of charge.

34. A market must have:
    a. people with unsatisfied wants and needs.
    b. people who have the resources and the willingness to buy.

    Further, once you have identified the market and its needs, you must set out to fill those needs.

35. Three criteria critical for a small business owner regarding managing employees are:
    a. hiring.   b. training.   c. motivating employees.

36. Most small business owners say they need the most assistance in accounting.

37. A good accountant can help in setting up computer systems for record keeping such as inventory control, customer records and payroll. He/she can also help make decisions such as whether to buy or lease equipment and whether to own or rent a building. Further, an accountant can help with tax planning, financial forecasting, choosing sources of financing and writing requests for funds.

38. Small business owners have learned they need help with:
    a. legal advice.   b. tax advice.   c. accounting advice.
    d. marketing.   e. finance.

39. Lawyers can help with such areas as leases, contracts and protection against liabilities.

40. Marketing research can help you determine where to locate, whom to select as your target market and what would be an effective strategy for reaching those people.

41. Government agencies helping small business owners are:
    a. SBA.   b. SCORE.   c. ACE.

Learning Goal 5   **Going International : Small Business Prospects**

42. Four hurdles in the international market are:
    a. Financing is difficult to find.
    b. Many would-be exporters don't know how to get started.
    c. Potential global business people do not understand cultural differences.
    d. The bureaucratic paperwork can be overwhelming.

43. Good reasons for going international are:
    a. Most of the world's markets lie outside the U.S.
    b. Exporting can absorb excess inventory.
    c. Exporting softens downturns in the domestic market.
    d. Exporting extends product lives.
    e. Exporting can spice up dull routines.

44. Small businesses have advantages over big businesses such as:
    a. Overseas buyers enjoy dealing with individuals rather than large corporate bureaucracies.
    b. Small companies can begin shipping faster.
    c. Small companies provide a wide variety of suppliers.
    d. Small companies can give more personal service and more undivided attention.

CRITICAL THINKING EXERCISES

1. Developing (and developed) countries have several options available to support entrepreneurship. Creating a system which makes it easy for investors to come into the country is an important step. The United States, for example, passed the Immigration Act of 1990 which created a special category of visa designed to lure entrepreneurs to the U.S.

    Many developing countries do not have the infrastructure to support a rapidly growing economy. Governments need to prioritize building the kind of infrastructure businesses need. Providing tax credits and tax breaks to businesses is another way to encourage entrepreneurship.

    Entrepreneurship creates jobs, and when people are working, and spending, that creates more jobs, and so the economy grows. Developing countries need the kind of programs that will encourage investments which create jobs. Encouraging and supporting entrepreneurship is one way these countries can help their economies to grow, become self-sufficient and be participants in the emerging global economy.

2. Compaq's team was comprised of experienced managers who wanted to combine the discipline of a big company with an environment where people could participate in a successful venture. They recruited seasoned managers, and everyone worked as a team. The company's treasurer and top engineer contributed to production and marketing decisions. Everyone worked together to create, develop and market products.

3. The text mentions that desirable entrepreneurial attributes include being self-directed, self-nurturing, action-oriented, highly energetic and tolerant of uncertainty. Eric demonstrates these characteristics in several ways. He is self-directed in that he had the discipline not only to build 2 businesses, but to leave those businesses when he decided that he wanted to go on to college. He has been self-supporting for a number of years, and most likely is quite tolerant of uncertainty, and probably felt quite comfortable with that element of risk in starting his own businesses. He continued to work while his friends told him he was "crazy for working that hard" so it seems that he doesn't depend on other people's approval, i.e., he's self-nurturing, and appears to be pretty energetic. He must be action-oriented, able to build his "dream into a reality" by taking an idea and creating a successful business.

4. Eric seems to lend validity to the questionable failure statistics the text refers to. He has beaten the odds twice, and it would seem that the odds of failure may have been lower than traditionally reported.

   Eric may tell you that you need to talk to people who have already started their own businesses and get their advice. They can give you valuable information about the importance of location, finding good workers and having enough capital to keep you going.

   He may also suggest that you work for a successful entrepreneur and get some experience in the fields in which you're interested.

   Another idea is to take over a firm that has already been successful. (That's what the buyers of Eric's most recent firm decided to do!) A strategy may be to work for the owner for a few years, then offer to buy the business through profit sharing, or an outright purchase.

5. I would tell Eric to be prepared. First, have a business plan already prepared. Pick a bank that serves small businesses, have an accountant prepare complete financial statements, including a personal balance sheet and take all the financial information with you to the bank, along with the business plan. Make an appointment with the loan officer, and ask for exactly what you need. Be prepared to personally guarantee the loan.

6.
   a. Women's Prequalification Pilot Loan
   b. Participation loan
   c. Direct loan
   d. Guaranteed loan
   e. Microloan
   f. MESBIC
   g. Women's Financing Section

7. Dave and Kevin followed one of the suggestions in the text for successfully starting a business, as they worked for someone else in the same field before starting out on their own. They knew their customers, and by all indications the market was there with the resources to buy what Dave and Kevin were selling. Other than Dave's wife they had no employees to manage, as they were using independent sales representatives. As is typical in some small business partnerships, Dave and Kevin couldn't agree on some issues.

   Keeping efficient records seems to be a real weakness. Dave's wife didn't really have the skill or time to do the books. Hiring a bookkeeper was a good idea. Perhaps the bookkeeper can suggest an effective billing method.

Although Dave and Kevin had funding, it appears to have been very "casual", and not very well thought out. They made no plan to repay the supplier's loan which was to come due in 4 months. They didn't look for any help, and so ran the risk of running into legal as well as financial problems. Since they decided not to do a business plan, they don't seem to have been very well organized. They had no marketing plan, and no effective strategy for reaching customers other than those they started out with. They appear to have made many of the mistakes the text mentions as being causes for small business failure, i.e. poor planning and inadequate financial management.

The company "limped along" for about three years before Dave and Kevin began to disagree on how to proceed. They were sued by the supplier for nonpayment of the loan, and eventually the business dissolved. Each partner went out on his own. Neither is still in business.

8. A. There are a number of outside consultants that a small business owner can go to for help in starting and managing their businesses, for example:
   a. Accountant.
   b. Lawyer.
   c. Marketing research service.
   d. Commercial loan officer.
   e. Insurance agent.
   f. Other business owners.
   g. Business professors.

   B. Other sources of information include:
   a. Chambers of Commerce.
   b. Better Business Bureau.
   c. National and local trade associations.
   d. Library business sections.
   e. The Internet.
   f. Computer bulletin boards.

Learning Goal 5

9. The international market can be very lucrative, and Chad is in a good business for that market, according to Figure 6-2. It may be a good idea for Chad if he has extra inventory, or sees a softening in the domestic market. As a small business owner he has several advantages over larger businesses because he can deal with his customers personally and he can start providing his product immediately.

   There are several hurdles to overcome in the international market, especially if Chad is inexperienced. Cultural differences for the product may not be a problem, but sales techniques will vary from those in the United States. In addition the paperwork in developing an international market can be overwhelming. Chad has several places available to him to find information, including the SBA, the Commerce Department, export management companies and export trading companies.

PRACTICE TEST

Multiple Choice				True/False			
1.	d	11.	a	1.	T	11.	F
2.	b	12.	d	2.	F	12.	F
3.	c	13.	b	3.	T	13.	F
4.	c	14.	a	4.	F	14.	F
5.	b	15.	b	5.	T	15.	T
6.	d	16.	b	6.	T	16.	T
7.	a	17.	d	7.	T	17.	F
8.	d	18.	d	8.	T	18.	T
9.	c	19.	b	9.	T		
10.	d			10.	F		

CHAPTER 7
MANAGEMENT, LEADERSHIP, AND EMPLOYEE EMPOWERMENT

LEARNING GOALS

After you have read and studied this chapter, you should be able to:

1. Explain the four functions of management and why the role of managers is changing.

2. Relate the planning process to the accomplishment of corporate goals

3. Describe the organizing function of management and illustrate how the function differs at various management levels.

4. Summarize the five steps of the control function of management

5. Explain the differences between managers and leaders, and compare the characteristics and uses of the various leadership styles.

6. Describe the three general categories of skills needed by top, middle, and first-line managers.

7. Illustrate the skills you will need to develop your managerial potential and outline activities you could use to develop these skills.

LEARNING THE LANGUAGE

Listed below are important terms found in the chapter. Choose the correct term for the definition and write it in the space provided.

Autocratic leadership	Goals	Organizing
Conceptual skills	Human relations skills	Planning
Contingency planning	Internal customers	Strategic planning
Controlling	Laissez-faire leadership	Supervisory management
Decision making	Leadership	SWOT
Delegating	Management	Tactical planning
Democratic leadership (participative)	Managing diversity	Technical skills
Empowerment	Middle management	Top management
Enabling	Mission Statement Objectives	Vision
External customers	Operational planning	

1. Assigning authority and accountability to others while retaining responsibility for results is called _____.

2. Units within the firm, called _____, receive services from other units.

3. _____ are specific short-term statements detailing how to achieve goals.

4. The process of _____ involves developing specific, short-term statements about what is to be done, who is to do it, and how it is to be done.

5. Communication and motivation skills that enable managers to work through and with people are _____.

6. The level of management which includes plant managers and department heads who are responsible for tactical plans is called _____.

7. The process of _____ means choosing among two or more alternatives.

8. An individual who uses _____ makes managerial decisions without consulting others and implies that he or she has power over others.

9. The management function of _____ involves designing the organization structure, attracting people to the organization, and creating conditions that ensure everyone and everything works together to achieve the goals and objectives of the organization.

10. A _____ is a sense of why the organization exists and where it is heading.

11. When an individual uses _____, managers and employees work together to make decisions.

12. _____ is the process of determining the major goals of the organization and the policies and strategies for obtaining and using resources to achieve those goals.

13. A manager's ability to picture the organization as a whole and the relationship of various parts is known as a _____.

14. When a manager is involved in _____, he or she is building systems and a culture that unites different people in a common pursuit without undermining their diversity.

15. The management function of _____ includes anticipating future trends and determining the best strategies and tactics to achieve organizational objectives.

16. The highest level of management consisting of the president and other key company executives who develop strategic plans is called _____.

17. When a manager does _____, he or she is in the process of preparing alternative courses of action that may be used if the primary plans do not achieve the objectives of the organization.

18. When using _____, managers set objectives and allow employees to be relatively free to do whatever it takes to accomplish those objectives.

19. These _____ demonstrate the ability to perform tasks of a specific department such as selling or bookkeeping.

20. _____ is the process used to accomplish organizational goals through planning organizing, directing and controlling people and other organizational resources.

21. A term that means giving employees the authority and responsibility to respond quickly to customer requests is _____.

22. The management function of _____ involves checking to determine whether or not an organization is progressing toward its goals and objectives, and taking corrective action if it is not.

23. Creating a vision for others to follow, establishing corporate values and ethics, and transforming the way the organization does business so that it is more effective and efficient is called _____.

24. The level of management known as _____ includes people directly responsible for assigning specific jobs to workers and evaluating their daily performance.

25. The broad, long-term statements known as _____ are accomplishments an organization wishes to attain.

26. An analysis of strengths, weaknesses, opportunities and threats is called a _____.

27. _____ means giving workers the education and tools needed to assume their new decision-making powers.

28. When a manager is doing _____, he or she is setting work standards and schedules necessary to implement the tactical objectives.

29. Dealers who buy to sell to others, and ultimate customers such as you and me, who buy products for our own personal use are called _____.

30. The _____ outlines the fundamental purposes of the organization.

RETENTION CHECK

Learning Goal 1   **The New Approach to Corporate Management**

1. List three reasons why changes to corporate management are necessary.

    a. _____

    b. _____

    c. _____

2. How has technological change affected management?

3. How are today's managers different from "traditional" managers?

4. What are the four functions of management?

    a. _____   c. _____

    b. _____   d. _____

5. Identify the activities performed in each of the management functions.

Function

a. _____

b. _____

c. _____

d. _____

Activities

a. _____
b. _____
c. _____
d. _____

a. _____
b. _____
c. _____
d. _____

a. _____
b. _____
c. _____
d. _____
e. _____

a. _____
b. _____
c. _____

Learning Goal 2   **Planning: Creating a Vision for the Organization**

6. Distinguish between a "vision" and a goal.

7. What are three fundamental questions answered by planning?

   a. _____

   b. _____

   c. _____

8. What are four types of planning?

   a. _____   c. _____

   b. _____   d. _____

9. What is decided at the strategic planning stage?

10. Describe tactical planning.

11. What is operational planning?

12. Why is contingency planning important?

Learning Goal 3 **Organizing: Creating a Unified System Out of Multiple Organizations**

13. What are the three levels of management?

    a. _____   b. _____   c. _____

14. What positions will be found in top management?

15. List some positions found in middle management.

16. What is supervisory management?

17. What has been the dominating question regarding organizing?

18. According to the text, how are companies organizing today?

19. What has made the organizing task more complex today?

20. In traditional organizations, what does the directing function involve?

21. How will this process change in the future?

22. What is the purpose of self-managed teams?

Learning Goal 4   **Controlling**

23.   List the five steps in the control process

   a. _____

   b. _____

   c. _____

   d. _____

   e. _____

24.   Standards must be:

   a. _____   b. _____   c. _____

25.   What are the criteria for measuring success in a customer-oriented firm?

26.   What is a corporate scorecard?

Learning Goal 5   **Leadership: Vision and Values**

27.   What is the difference between management and leadership?

28. What are four things leaders do?

   a. _____

   b. _____

   c. _____

   d. _____

29. What is a learning organization?

30. Leaders who create winning organizations:

   a. _____

   b. _____

   c. _____

31. Identify three leadership styles.

   a. _____

   b. _____

   c. _____

32. When is autocratic leadership effective?

33. What is participative leadership?

34. When is laissez-faire leadership the most effective?

35. What leadership style is best?

36. What is the trend in leadership styles for the future?

Learning Goal 6   **Tasks and Skills at Different Levels of Management**

37. List three categories of skills managers should have.

   a. _____

   b. _____

   c. _____

38. What is meant by technical skills?

39. What are human relations skills?

40. Describe conceptual skills.

41. What four steps must be taken in order to delegate effectively?

   a. _____

   b. _____

   c. _____

   d. _____

42. What things will a manager of the 21st century do?

   a. _____

   b. _____

   c. _____

   d. _____

43. What are the steps of the decision-making process?

   a. _____

   b. _____

   c. _____

   d. _____

   e. _____

   f. _____

   g. _____

Learning Goal 7 **Learning Management Skills**

44. What are seven specific skills managers must have?

   a. _____   e. _____

   b. _____   f. _____

   c. _____   g. _____

   d. _____

45. How do managers use verbal skills?

46. How can you develop writing skills?

47. How can you develop human relations skills?

48. Why is managing diversity an important skill today?

49. How will time management skills help you?

CRITICAL THINKING EXERCISES

Learning Goal 1

1. The introduction to this chapter describes the new "breed" of worker as being more educated with a higher level of skill. This type of worker demands more freedom and a "different managerial style." How does the changing role of managers, described also in the introductory portion of this chapter, meet the needs of the new "breed" of workers?

Learning Goal 2

2. There is a difference between goals and objectives. In essence, objectives are short-term statements that indicate how we will reach our goals. Read each of the following and determine if a "goal" or an "objective" is being described.

   a. "I want to be the CEO of a major corporation someday!" _____

   b. "I am going to take 15 hours toward a bachelor's degree in business this semester, and 16 next semester." _____

   c. In its attempt to expand beyond the increasingly competitive music video market, MTV wants to create a Beavis & Butthead amusement park ride.
   _____

   d. MTV wants to expand beyond the music video market. _____

3. <u>Strategic</u> and <u>Tactical</u> planning provide the framework for the planning process. <u>Contingency</u> planning provides alternative plans of action.

   Look back to Chapter 5, where we introduced Eric, the young man who wants to start his own business. Eric has decided to start a small manufacturing business, making a product he invented for the automotive industry. It's a component part, designed as a "built-in" carrier for tapes and CD's which can be removed and taken with you when you get out of the car. The product is called "Music-stor". He wants to sell it to both auto manufacturers and auto parts stores. Can you outline a strategic plan, tactical plan and a contingency plan for Eric?

   a. Strategic plan _____

   _____

   b. Tactical plan _____

   _____

   c. Contingency plan _____

   _____

Learning Goal 3

4. When organizing, a manger develops a framework called the organization structure. This is called an organization chart. Identify two individuals at your college or university at each level of management.

   a. Top managers   _____

                            _____

   b. Middle   _____

                            _____

   c. Supervisory   _____

                            _____

5. We have read about changes occurring in business and in the marketplace in previous chapters. In this chapter we read about the changes in the <u>structure</u> of business, which is becoming customer-oriented and is taking on the perspective of a "system" of interfirm relationships. Given what you know from previous chapters, why do you think this type of organizational structure begun to evolve?

6. Eric has hired you to be the supervisor in the "Music-stor" plant where they are going to make the tape/CD storage cases. Your workers are well educated and highly skilled. How do you intend to "direct" and organize these employees of the 1990s?

7. How will your "directing" differ from Eric's, the top manager?

Learning Goal 4

8. "The control system's weakest link tends to be the setting of standards." Standards must be: specific, attainable and measurable.

   Improve the way the following vague standards are written:
   1. Increase sales. _____

   2. Get a degree. _____

   3. Be a better manager. _____

Learning Goal 5

9. You have been in your supervisory position for several months, and have found your boss to be a great person to work with. She speaks often about the kind of division she wants to create, one where all the employees feel a sense of loyalty to a team. She stresses customer service, high product quality and fair treatment of her employees. If she makes a mistake, she is always up front about it. She insists on honesty from her employees, and you notice that all her employees are treated fairly and with respect. She expects a lot from you and her other subordinates, but is sure to let you make your own decisions (as well as your own mistakes)! She encourages employee problem solving and is quick to implement changes, which will make the division more effective and efficient. How does your boss differ from the old style "manager," and demonstrate the leadership of today?

10. Effective leadership styles range along a continuum based upon the amount of employee involvement in setting objectives and making decisions. The three leadership styles are called:

    Autocratic   *Democratic (participative)*   *Laissez-faire*

Which of those styles are being illustrated in the following situations?

A. Production workers complain about having to punch a time clock each day.

   a. "Too bad, I'm not getting rid of it!" _____

   b. "Let's get a committee together and see if we can come up with some alternatives to using the time clock." _____

B. A university sees a need for some action to be taken to reverse declining enrollment trends.

   a. "Let's form a committee of faculty and administrators to study the problem and give recommendations on how to solve the problem." _____

   b. "The objective for each division is to increase enrollment by 10% for the next school year." Each division is free to take whatever action is appropriate for their area in order to reach the objective. _____

C. A manager notices that an employee consistently turns in work past the deadline.

   a. "Bob, your work has been late three times this month. This is a problem. How can we work together to solve it?" _____

   b. "Bob, your work has been late three times this month. One more time and you will be disciplined. Two times and you're fired. Got it?" _____

11. What is meant by the statement "There is no one best leadership style"?

12. "Music-Stor" has been in business for several months and you have just been assigned to reorganize the production department. Eric knows that he will need inventory if things go as planned, production is very slow right now and there are already some orders to fill. Money, however, is tight. All the production workers are peers (none are supervisors), but there is one member of the group who appears to be the informal leader. The workers are paid by the hour, and they are well paid by normal standards.

    You have some ideas about how to increase production without increasing costs. One idea, for example, is to change the method of paying workers from hourly to by how much they produce. The way you have it figured, the workers would have to produce more to make the same income. Another way is to set up individual workstations to cut down on the amount of socializing you have seen going on.

    While you are confident these ideas, and others you have thought of, are the best solutions, you aren't sure how to implement the changes. You do know that this will be a test of your management and leadership skills.

    a. How would you go about developing alternatives and implementing changes you believe are necessary to increase productivity and save money?
    b. What leadership style do you think you used in developing your solution? Why?
    c. Which of the twelve "golden" rules of leadership does your solution illustrate? Which of the seven "sins" of leadership?

13. Why is it important that a manager delegate effectively in today's new workplace with today's new workers?

Learning Goals 6, 7

14. Managers of the 21st century must be able to write clearly and precisely.

    a. Rewrite the following paragraph to be clear and precise.

    Due to unforeseen and uncertain economic conditions, which we can't predict, it is quite possible that there may be a layoff of unknown proportions in some of the production departments. As you know this is our slow time of year and even though it is winter we are making it possible for those of you who would be eligible for vacations next summer to take your vacation during the layoff if you want to. Express your honest wishes and desires to your supervisor.

b. Can you make a presentation clearer through a picture? The following is an excerpt of a sales report presented at a recent sales meeting.

"Our sales are up 7.8 million dollars over 1996, which was up 6 million over 1995; and 1995, 1994 and 1993 were $4 million over the previous year. Sales of $30 million were virtually the same for the previous two years."

Take the figures and the years mentioned and in the space provided, graphically sketch the above statement If your graph is correct, sales representatives should more easily understand what was meant.

15. Do you have an idea of what you want to be doing in 5 years? How about in a year? Write out one of your long-range (strategic) goals, one tactical objective which will help you to reach your long-range goal, and one thing you could do within the next week or month which will get you one step closer to your goals.

Next, keep a time log for the next 48 hours. How did you spend your time? Did you spend some time doing the things that will help you reach those long-term goals?

Strategic:

Tactical:

Operational:

Sample Tally of Time Spent
Hours spent:
Working
Studying
In class
Sleeping
Recreation
Commuting

SAMPLE TIME LOG

Day 1	Day 2
Out of bed – noon	
Noon - 6:00 p.m.	
6:00 p.m. to bed	

16. There are seven specific skills needed by various levels of management:

Verbal skills   Human relations skills

Writing skills   Time management skills

Computer skills   Technical skills

Managing diversity

For each of the following situations, indicate the management level and the skills being used or described.

A. Alice Burling is concerned about Bob Mailing's sales performance. In their meeting, Alice and Bob agree there's a problem. Alice listens carefully to Bob while he explains the situation in his territory, and after asking some questions, Alice shows Bob how to handle things differently. After the meeting, Alice completes a schedule assigning new accounts to various salesmen in her department.

   a. Management level

   _____

   b. Skills

   _____

B. In a typical week in her office, Hong Ngu composes a newsletter to be distributed to all employees, works on a long range forecast for a new product the company is considering and decides to implement a new program to encourage communication and idea exchange between division heads. She appoints several division heads to formulate a plan for implementation. She includes someone from human resources who is in charge of the company's cultural diversity sensitivity training program. She schedules most meetings, but leaves time open for interruptions and unplanned meetings with subordinates.

   a. Management level

   _____

   b. Skills

   _____

C. In reviewing weekly production reports, Joel Hodes notices a drop in overall production from last month. He works for several days on an incentive plan he thinks will push production back up to the company's objectives and still maintain high morale. He then calls a meeting with the line supervisors. After getting their responses and suggestions, Joel revises and implements the plan in his plant.

   a. Management level

   _____

   b. Skills

   _____

D. Don Lui begins each day by writing a "to do" list of what he wants to accomplish, then prioritizes the items on the list. He then generally looks through his electronic mail, and responds to those memos needing immediate response. Later in the day, he works on a project for a class he is taking in management, and composes a speech he has to give as the President of the local Chamber of Commerce.

   a. Management level

   _____

   b. Skills

   _____

PRACTICE TEST

Multiple choice: Circle the best answer.

1. Workers in the future:

   a. will be more closely supervised and highly skilled.
   b. will require managers that will give them direction and give precise orders.
   c. will be more educated, highly skilled and self-directed.
   d. will work more individually rather than in teams.

2. Which of the following would not be included in a discussion of the four functions of management?

   a. producing
   b. organizing
   c. leading
   d. controlling

3. Managers of the future

   a. will closely supervise highly skilled workers who would like to "do their own thing."
   b. will emphasize teamwork and cooperation, and will act as coaches, rather than "bosses."
   c. will have to become specialists in one or two functional areas.
   d. will have to function as intermediaries between workers and unions.

4. Antoine Gaudette is doing a performance evaluation for one of his employees. Antoine is looking at the employee's performance for the past year, and identifying areas where his employees could improve their performance. Antoine is performing the management function of:

   a. planning
   b. organizing
   c. controlling
   d. directing

5. A(n) _____ is a specific short-term statement detailing how to achieve _____.

   a. mission statement/goals
   b. goal/objectives
   c. goal/the mission statement
   d. objective/goals

6. Maria Mainini is in the middle of setting her plan for the next year. She knows the company wants more market share in the Northeast, so she has developed a plan for increasing the advertising budget for the next year, and adding at least one more sales person to cover the larger territories. Maria is involved in:

   a. Contingency planning
   b. Operational planning
   c. Strategic planning
   d. Tactical planning

7. Which of the following employees of the local hardware store, Hammerhead, would most likely be involved in strategic planning?

   a. Joe Hartley – department head
   b. Annelise Oswalt – advertising manager
   c. Elliot Nessy – President and CEO
   d. Manny Martinez – chief accountant

8. General managers, division managers, plant managers and college deans are all a part of

   a. supervisory management
   b. middle management
   c. top management
   d. first-line management

9. Which of the following is a false statement?

   a. Companies are looking at the best way to organize to respond to the needs of customers.
   b. General consensus is that larger companies are more responsive to customer needs than smaller companies.
   c. Most large firms are being restructured into smaller, customer-focused units.
   d. Companies are organizing so that customers have more influence, not managers.

10. In the future

    a. Workers are more likely to be empowered to make decisions on their own.
    b. Firms will be less likely to establish close relationships with suppliers.
    c. Top managers will be allocating more of their time to giving more detailed instructions to workers.
    d. Small firms will stay away from each other as competition gets fierce.

11. Measuring performance relative to objectives and standards is part of _____.

    a. planning
    b. organizing
    c. directing
    d. controlling

12. Which step in the control process is considered to be the weakest?

    a. Setting clear standards
    b. Monitoring and recording results
    c. Communicating results to employees
    d. Taking corrective action

13. Which of the following statements is stated most effectively as a control standard?

    a. Cut the number of finished product rejects.
    b. Empower employees to make more decisions next year
    c. Praise employees more often this month
    d. Increase sales of our top end product from 2000 in the first quarter to 3000 during the same period.

14. In measuring success in today's firms:

    a. companies must focus primarily on satisfying the external customers.
    b. traditional measures of success should be considered most important.
    c. firms must go beyond financial measures, and look at how to please all stakeholders.
    d. companies must focus on satisfying employees who deal most with customers.

15. Which of the following is not characteristic of a leader?

    a. A leader has a vision and rallies others around the vision.
    b. A leader will establish corporate values.
    c. A leader will emphasize corporate ethics.
    d. A leader will always attempt to keep things from changing.

16. Pixel Electronics is a young company, run by some enthusiastic managers. These managers are very skilled at acquiring information, and at using the information they get to change and modify the way they do things. The managers at Pixel make especially sure that employees learn from the mistakes they make! Pixel would be considered a:

    a. multinational corporation
    b. multicultural organization
    c. learning organization
    d. bureaucratic corporation

17. When a manager uses democratic leadership, he or she will

    a. make managerial decisions without consulting employees.
    b. set objectives and allow employees to be relatively free to do what it takes to accomplish them.
    c. give employees direction, and be sure that they are doing their job the way the manager wants them to.
    d. work with employees to make decisions together.

18. As the trend toward self-managed teams continues, managers will

    a. find their jobs will remain essentially the same.
    b. delegate more planning, organizing, and controlling to lower levels.
    c. use more autocratic styles of leadership.
    d. be empowering more individuals than teams.

19. The basic categories of skills managers must have include all except:

    a. technical skills
    b. mechanical skills
    c. human relations skills
    d. conceptual skills

20. The level of management most likely to need conceptual skills is:

    a. supervisory management.
    b. first–line management.
    c. middle management.
    d. top management.

21. In the Schwinn example in the text, managers of the various new departments were told "go out and shape the department the way you want. You have total freedom." That is an example of:

    a. effective delegating.
    b. participative leadership.
    c. decision making.
    d. technical skills.

22. The bulk of the duties of a manager will involve:

    a. writing clearly.
    b. communicating with others through such things as meetings, and presentations.
    c. using computers to send e-mail and surf the Internet.
    d. helping team members to learn how to work with people from different cultures.

TRUE/FALSE

1. ____ Accelerating change in business has increased the need for workers who are more highly educated and have higher skill levels.

2. ____ Today progressive managers are being educated to tell people what to do and to watch over these new type of workers.

3. ____ Organizing involves determining the best strategies and tactics to achieve the organization's objectives.

4. ____ A mission statement outlines a company's fundamental purpose.

5. ____ Planning answers the questions, "What is the situation now and Where do we want to go?"

6. ____ The consensus is that smaller organizations are more responsive to stakeholder needs than larger organizations.

7. ____ In today's organizations it is necessary to establish close relationships with suppliers and with retailers who sell our products.

8. ____ The planning function of management is the heart of the management system because it provides the feedback that enables managers and workers to make adjustments.

9. ____ The criteria for measuring success in a customer-oriented firm is customer satisfaction of both internal and external customers.

10. ____ The difference between managers and leaders is that a leader creates the vision, the manager carries it out.

11. ____ Generally, there is one best leadership style to which all leaders should adhere.

12. ____ Autocratic leadership will be effective in emergencies or when absolute followership is needed.

13. ____ The trend in the United States is toward placing more workers on teams, which are often self-managed.

14. ____ The skills needed by managers are different at different levels.

15. ____ To delegate effectively a manager must make the people to whom a task has been assigned responsible for getting it completed on time.

16. ____ Most progressive managers of the 21st century will be team leaders.

17. ____ Managers of the future will not need to be computer literate, as their workers will be empowered, and will have decision-making responsibility anyway.

18. ____ Research has shown that homogeneous (similar) groups are more effective than heterogeneous (mixed) groups in the workplace.

ANSWERS

LEARNING THE LANGUAGE

1. Delegating	16. Top management
2. Internal customers	17. Contingency planning
3. Objectives	18. Laissez-faire leadership
4. Tactical planning	19. Technical skills
5. Human relations skills	20. Management
6. Middle management	21. Empowerment
7. Decision making	22. Controlling
8. Autocratic leadership	23. Leadership
9. Organizing	24. Supervisory management
10. Vision	25. Goals
11. Democratic leadership	26. SWOT
12. Strategic planning	27. enabling
13. Conceptual skills	28. operational planing
14. Managing diversity	29. external customers
15. Planning	30. mission statement

RETENTION CHECK

Learning Goal 1 **The New Approach to Corporate Management**

1. Three reasons why changes to corporate management are necessary are:
   a. global competition
   b. technological change
   c. the importance of pleasing customers

2. Technological change has increased the need for a new type of worker, who is more educated and has higher skill levels. These workers demand more freedom and different managerial styles.

3. Traditional managers were called "bosses", and their job was to tell people what to do and watch over them to be sure the employees did what they were told. Today's managers are being educated to guide, train, support, motivate and coach employees rather than to boss them around. Modern managers will emphasize teamwork and cooperation. In many companies, managers are dressing more casually, are more friendly than bosses were in the past, and treat employees as partners rather than workers who have to be disciplined and watched over.

4. The four functions of management are:
   a. planning.   c. leading.
   b. organizing.   d. controlling.

5. | Function | Activities |
   |---|---|
   | a. Planning | a. Set goals. |
   | | b. Develop strategies to reach goals. |
   | | c. Determine resources needed. |
   | | d. Set standards. |
   | b. Organizing | a. Allocate resources, assign tasks, establish procedures. |
   | | b. Create structure. |
   | | c. Recruit, select, train, develop employees. |
   | | d. Effective placement of employees. |
   | c. Directing | a. Lead employees to work effectively. |
   | | b. Give assignments. |
   | | c. Explain routines. |
   | | d. Clarify policies. |
   | | e. Provide performance feedback. |
   | d. Controlling | a. Measure results against objectives. |
   | | b. Monitor performance relative to standards. |
   | | c. Take corrective action. |

Learning Goal 2 **Creating a Vision for the Organization**

6. Goals are broad, long-term accomplishments which an organization wants to reach. A vision is greater than a goal; it's the larger explanation of why the organization exists and where it's trying to head.

7. a. What is the situation now?
    b. Where do we want to go?
    c. How can we get there from here?

8. Four types of planning are:
    a. Strategic.   b. Tactical.   c. Operational.   d. Contingency.

9. Strategic planning determines the major goals of the organization, as well as the policies and strategies for obtaining and using resources to achieve the goals.

10. Tactical planning is the process of developing detailed, short-term strategies about what has to be done, who will do it and how it is to be done.

11. Operational planning is the setting of work standards and schedules necessary to implement the tactical objectives.

12. Contingency planning is important to do in the event that the primary plans don't achieve the organization's goals. The environment changes so rapidly that contingency plans are needed in anticipation of those changes. The idea is to stay flexible, and to take opportunities when they present themselves, whether they were planned or not.

Learning Goal 3 **Organizing: Creating a Unified System Out of Multiple Organizations**

13. The three levels of management are:
    a. supervisory or first-line.   b. middle.   c. top.

14. Top management consists of the president and other key executives who develop strategic plans, such as the CEO (chief executive officer), COO (chief operating officer) and CFO (chief financial officer).

15. Middle management positions include general managers, divisional mangers, branch managers, plant managers, and at a college, deans.

16. Supervisory or first-line management includes people directly responsible for supervising workers and evaluating their daily performance.

17. The dominating question of organizing in recent years has been how to best organize the firm to respond to the needs of customers and other stakeholders.

18. Companies today are organizing so that customers have influence. Many large firms are being restructured into smaller, more customer-focused units.

19. Today the organizing task is more complex because firms are forming partnerships and joint ventures, so the job becomes an effort to organize the whole system, not just one firm.

20. In traditional organizations, directing involves giving assignments, explaining routines, clarifying policies and providing feedback on performance. In this type of company, all managers, from top to supervisory, direct employees, but the process is different at the various levels of the organization.

21. In the future, managers are less likely to be giving specific instructions to employees. Instead, they are more likely to empower employees to make decisions on their own. This means giving employees the authority and responsibility to respond quickly to customer requests. The manager's role will be less of a "boss" and more of a coach, assistant, counselor and team member.

22. The purpose of self-managed teams, or smart teams, is to respond quickly to customer needs and market changes. Another purpose is to empower employees who know the most about products and what makes them good, to do what needs to be done to make world-class products.

Learning Goal 4 **Controlling**

23. The five steps in the control process are:
    a. Setting clear performance standards.
    b. Monitoring and recording actual performance.
    c. Comparing results against plans and standards.

    d. Communicating results and deviations to the employees involved.
    e. Taking corrective action when needed.

24. Standards must be:
    a. specific.   b. attainable.   c. measurable.

25. The criteria for measuring success in customer-oriented firms is customer satisfaction of both internal and external customers. Further, while traditional financial control measures are still important, others have been added which measure the success of the firm in pleasing customers, employees and other stakeholders. Other criteria may include the contribution the firm is making to society or improvements in the quality of the environment.

26. A corporate scorecard is a broad measurement tool that measures customer satisfaction, financial progress, return on investment and everything else that needs to be managed for a firm to be profitable.

Learning Goal 5   **Leadership: Vision and Values**

27. The difference between leadership and management is that leadership is creating a vision for others to follow, while management is the carrying out of the vision.

28. Four things leaders do are:
    a. Have a vision and rally others around the vision.
    b. Establish corporate values.
    c. Emphasize corporate ethics.
    d. Embrace and create change.

29. A learning organization is one skilled at creating, acquiring, interpreting, retaining and transferring knowledge, and at modifying its actions based upon new knowledge and insights.

30. Leaders who create winning organizations:
    a. stress continuous improvement.
    b. set up cross-functional teams.
    c. reward people for innovation and risk taking.

31. Three leadership styles are:
    a. Autocratic.
    b. Democratic or participative.
    c. Laissez-faire or free rein.

32. Autocratic leadership is effective when absolute followership is needed, and with new, unskilled workers who need more direction and guidance.

33. Participative leadership consists of managers and employees working together to make decisions.

34. Laissez-faire leadership is effective in professional organizations, where managers deal with doctors, engineers or other professionals.

35. Research indicates that successful leadership depends on who is being led and in what situation. Different leadership styles, ranging from autocratic to laissez-faire, may be successful depending on the people and the situation.

36. The trend in leadership will continue away from autocratic leadership toward laissez-faire leadership. More managers will be empowering teams, rather than individuals.

Learning Goal 6 **Tasks and Skills at Different Levels of Management**

37. Three skills managers must have are:
    a. technical skills.   b. human relations skills.   c. conceptual skills.

38. Technical skills involve the ability to perform tasks of a specific discipline or department.

39. Human relations skills include skills such as communication and motivation, leadership, coaching, morale building, training and development, help and being supportive.

40. Conceptual skills refer to a manger's ability to picture the organization as a whole and the relationship of various parts to perform tasks such as planning, organizing, controlling, decision making, problem analysis, coordinating and delegating.

41. To delegate effectively a manager must:
    a. select the appropriate people to do the job.
    b. assign the task.
    c. give the authority to complete the job.
    d. make those people who assume the task responsible for getting it completed on time.

42. Progressive managers of the 21st century will be team leaders. They will:
    a. set specific goals in cooperation with a team of workers.
    b. set up feedback and communication procedures.
    c. minimize the tendency to look over the team's shoulder.
    d. empower employees to decide how and when specific tasks will be completed, as long as the goals are accomplished on time.

43. The steps in the decision-making process are:
    a. Define the problem.
    b. Describe and collect needed information.
    c. Develop alternatives.
    d. Decide which alternative is best.
    e. Develop agreement among those involved.
    f. Do what is indicated (implement solution).
    g. Determine whether the decision was a good one and follow up.

Learning Goal 7   **Learning Management Skills**

44. Skills managers must have are:
    a. Verbal skills.
    b. Writing skills.
    c. Computer skills.
    d. Human Relations skills.
    e. Managing diversity.
    f. Time management skills.
    g. Technical skills.

45. Managers have to give talks, conduct meetings, make presentations and generally communicate their ideas to others. Half of communication is skilled listening. A good manager mixes with other managers, workers, clients and others and listens to recommendations or complaints and acts on them.

46. To develop good writing skills a student can take courses in grammar, composition and keyboarding. To learn to write, you must practice! It helps to write something every day.

47. You can develop human relations skills by joining student groups, volunteering, and getting involved in political organizations. Try to assume leadership positions where you are responsible for contacting people, assigning work and motivating.

48. Managing diversity is important today because we are working on teams with people who have different personalities, different priorities, and different lifestyles. The issue of diversity, then, goes beyond dealing with questions of race, gender, and ethnicity.

49. Time management skills will help because there are so many demands on a manager's time. With time management skills you will learn to develop such skills as setting priorities, delegating work, choosing activities that will produce the most results, doing work when you are at your best and dealing with interruptions.

CRITICAL THINKING EXERCISES

Learning Goal 1

1. As the book describes, at one time managers were "bosses" who directed the activities of their subordinates and generally kept a close watch over them. People who made mistakes or didn't perform according to the bosses' expectations were reprimanded, sometimes very sternly. This tends to be the "old school" of managing and certainly doesn't fit the new type of worker who is better educated and skilled in areas such as communication, teamwork and information technology. This type of worker is probably self-motivated and self-directed, and needs little or no supervision or direction from a "boss." The new kind of manager is trained to guide and train, support and motivate the new type of worker, emphasizing teamwork and cooperation. In other words, managers are working side by side with workers, rather than "above" them.

    This makes better sense for workers who no longer need the kind of "boss" we used to know.

Learning Goal 2

2.   a. Goal   c. Objective
            b. Objective   d. Goal

3. Eric has a big job ahead of him. There are many possible responses to this question, but some suggestions are:
   a. Strategic plan - Become the major supplier of tape and CD storage cases for automobiles within the next 5 years.
   b. Tactical - Contact the production and/or engineering managers of the major automobile manufacturers and sell them on the product within the next 12 months. Continue to look for other markets.
   c. Contingency plan - If the auto makers are not interested right now, begin focusing on the automotive after-market, to sell the product as an add-on.

Learning Goal 3

4. There are many variations for answering this question, depending upon your school. Some possibilities are:
   a. Top Managers - Chancellor, President, Provost.
   b. Middle - Dean of Instruction, Executive Dean, Associate Dean.
   c. Supervisory - Lab supervisor, Department chair, Business manager.

5. In earlier chapters we have learned about the changing nature of U.S. business, increasing global competition, and the continuing push for quality and increased productivity. These new structures are reflective of the need to focus on productivity, quality and the needs of the consumer in an increasingly competitive marketplace. For example, to be more productive we must cut costs, which interfirm relationships help to make possible. Further, to be more competitive, we must respond to customer demands by creating a "Customer-Oriented organization" with smaller, more customer-focused units.

6. As a manager of the new "breed" of workers, you are less likely to be giving specific instructions to your employees. Instead, you may give them the authority to make decisions which will allow them to respond quickly to any customer requests. In all likelihood, you will set up a team approach for the plant, using self-managed work teams if possible. Your job will be more that of a coach and team member, allowing for more participation in decision making and more flexibility for the workers.

7. Eric, as the top manager of the company, will be concerned with a broader view of where he wants the company to go. As a first line manager, your job will be more specific, and your goals and objectives more specific than those Eric has outlined for the entire company. So your directions to subordinates, to the extent you will give them direction, will be more specific.

Learning Goal 4

8. a. Increase sales of Product X by 10% in the next 6 months.
    b. Get a Bachelor's Degree in Business in 4 years.
    c. Spend 3 hours a week reading management articles or books. Praise employees twice a week.

Learning Goal 5

9. Leaders differ from managers is several ways. Effective leaders look at the four functions of management, planning, organizing, leading and controlling, from a much broader perspective. Planning is more global, the focus of organizing is on structuring the company to be more competitive in a global market, their leading involves creating a vision, and control means empowering people and holding them responsible.

    Your boss appears to have those qualities. She has a vision of how she wants the division to operate. She trusts employees to make their own decisions, thus empowering them with control over their jobs. Her sense of corporate values is demonstrated by her concern for quality, customer service, and in her fair treatment of her employees.

10. A. a. Autocratic   C. a. Democratic
        b. Democratic   b. Autocratic
    B. a. Democratic
        b. Laissez-faire

11. It is generally believed that there is no one leadership style which would be best in all situations. The most effective or successful manager will use a variety of leadership styles depending upon who is being led and upon the situation.

12. Your answers will vary, as each of you will have your own individual style. However, review the material in this section of the chapter. Is there any opportunity to organize a self-managed team? Earlier in the study guide, the workers were described as the "new" breed of worker. Would a team-based approach be appropriate for this group? Could you use a participative management style? Did you consider getting opinions from the workers about what they see as a method to increase production without raising costs? In terms of the "Rules" and "Sins" of leadership, review them. Did you ask for advice? Did your solution inform them of the need for changing? Did you ask for new ideas?

13. As is noted throughout this chapter, the leaders and managers of the next century will be team leaders who are empowering their workers, giving them the freedom to decide how and when specific tasks will be done, as long as the goals of the company are accomplished. That is, by definition, delegating. Today's new "breed" of workers are more educated and trained, and will have the ability to work more within a team structure and with less direction from their manager. The manager will minimize the tendency to look over the team's shoulder to make sure things are being done correctly.

14. a. To avoid the possibility of layoffs, we are making it possible for employees eligible for vacations next summer to take them now. Let your supervisor know if you are interested.
    b. The graph could look like this:

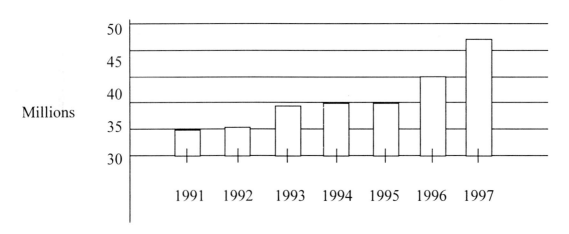

15. Obviously, your answers will vary, depending upon your goals. An example might be:

    Strategic: Get a bachelor's degree in business in the next 4 years.
    Tactical: Take 12 hours next semester, 12 hours the following, and take at least one business course each semester.
    Operational: Go to the registrar's office and get a catalog for next semester, or decide which courses you need to take, or if the timing is right, register.

    The time log will be different for each one of you. The big question will be whether or not you spent any time on the activities that will help you to reach the long-term goal you said you wanted to reach.

16.
- A. a. Supervisory level
  b. Human relations, verbal skills
- B. a. Top management
  b. Writing skills, managing diversity, time management
- C. a. Middle management
  b. Human relations skills, technical skills
- D. a. There is no real way of knowing what management level is being described! Managers at all levels will perform these activities.
  b. Technical skills, time management skills, computer skills, writing skills

PRACTICE TEST

Multiple Choice				True/False			
1.	c	12.	a	1.	T	10.	T
2.	a	13.	d	2.	F	11.	F
3.	b	14.	c	3.	F	12.	T
4.	c	15.	d	4.	T	13.	T
5.	d	16.	c	5.	T	14.	T
6.	d	17.	d	6.	T	15.	T
7.	c	18.	b	7.	T	16.	T
8.	b	19.	b	8.	F	17.	F
9.	b	20.	d	9.	T	18.	F
10.	a	21.	a				
11.	d	22.	b				

CHAPTER 8
ORGANIZING A CUSTOMER-DRIVEN BUSINESS

LEARNING GOALS

After you have read and studied this chapter, you should be able to:

1. Describe the traditional hierarchical, bureaucratic organization structure and how it is being restructured.

2. List the organizational theories of Fayol and Weber.

3. Discuss the various issues connected with organizational design.

4. Describe the differences between line, line and staff, matrix and cross-functional organizations.

5. Explain the benefits of turning organizations upside down and inside out.

6. Give examples to show how organizational culture and the informal organization can hinder or assist organizational change.

LEARNING THE LANGUAGE

Listed below are important terms found in the chapter. Choose the correct term for each definition and write it in the space provided.

Bureaucracy	Line personnel
Centralized authority	Matrix organization
Competitive benchmarking	Networking
Continuous improvement	Organizational culture
Core competencies	Organizational design
Cross-functional teams	Outsourcing
Decentralized authority	Reengineering
Departmentalization	Restructuring
Formal organization	Span of control
Hierarchy	Staff personnel
Informal organization	Total quality management (TQM)
Inverted organizations	

1. Groups of employees from different departments who work together on a semi-permanent basis are called _____.

2. A _____ is an organization with several layers of management.

3. Linking of organizations with communications technology, or _____ is done in order for them to work together on common objectives.

4. Redesigning organizations to make them more productive is known as _____.

5. Widely shared values within an organization, or the _____ provides coherence and cooperation to achieve common goals.

6. The _____ is the system of relationships that develop spontaneously as employees meet and form power centers.

7. Those functions that the organization can do better than anyone else in the world are called _____.

8. A _____ is an organization with three layers of authority: top managers who make decisions, middle managers who develop procedures for implementing decisions, and workers and supervisors who do the work.

9. When decision-making authority is maintained with the top level of management there is _____.

10. In an _____ contact people are at the top and the chief executive officer is at the bottom of the organization chart.

11. The _____ refers to the optimum number of subordinates a manager should supervise.

12. The process of _____ is the establishment of manageable groups of people who have clear responsibilities and who know how to accomplish the objectives of the organization and the group.

13. Employees known as _____ perform functions that contribute directly to the primary goals of the organization.

14. When a company is using _____, it is rating an organization's practices, processes and products against the world's best.

15. When decision-making authority is delegated to lower-level managers and employees who are more familiar with local conditions, a company is said to have _____.

16. When a company uses _____ it is assigning various functions, such as accounting and legal work, to outside organizations.

17. A company is implementing _____ when it satisfies customers by building in and ensuring quality from all departments in the organization.

18. In a system known as _____ procedures are designed to ensure and inspire constant creative interaction and problem solving.

19. Dividing organizational functions into separate units is called _____.

20. In the _____, the structure that details lines of responsibility, authority and position are shown on the organizational chart.

21. When a company is in the process of _____, it is rethinking and radically redesigning organizational processes to achieve dramatic improvements in critical measures of performance.

22. A _____ is an organization in which specialists from different parts of the organization are brought together to work on specific projects but still remain part of a traditional line and staff structure.

23. These employees, known as _____, perform functions that advise and assist line personnel in performing their goals.

RETENTION CHECK

Learning Goal 1 **Changing the Organizational Hierarchy**

1. How were organizations designed in the past?

2. What is a hierarchy?

3. What impact did a traditional hierarchy have on decision making?

4. What are organizations doing about the layers of management? What is the term used to describe that trend?

5. What are the characteristics of a bureaucratic organization?

   a. _____

   b. _____

   c. _____

   d. _____

6. What is a problem with a typical bureaucratic structure?

7. What have firms done to resolve the problems created by a bureaucratic structure?

Learning Goal 2 **How Organizations Have Evolved**

8. Identify 10 of Fayol's "principles" of organizing

   a. _____   f. _____

   b. _____   g. _____

   c. _____   h. _____

   d. _____   I _____

   e. _____   j. _____

9. How were organizations designed in the past, using Fayol's principles?

10. What was the result of that design?

11. What are the three layers of management, according to Weber's bureaucracy?

   a. _____   b. _____   c. _____

12. Identify four characteristics of Max Weber's bureaucracy.

   a. _____

   b. _____

   c. _____

   d. _____

Learning Goal 3 **Designing More Responsive Organizations**

13. What are four organizational issues that have led to design changes?

   a. _____   c. _____

   b. _____   d. _____

14. What is a "tall" organization?

15. What was the net effect of tall organizational structures?

16. What is the trend in organizations today regarding management layers?

17. How does span of control vary in the organization?

18. List eight factors used to determine the optimum span of control

   a. _____   e. _____

   b. _____   f. _____

   c. _____   g. _____

   d. _____   h. _____

19. What is the trend in span of control?

20. What are the advantages and disadvantages of the traditional functional structure?

Advantages	Disadvantages
_____	_____
_____	_____
_____	_____
_____	_____

21. What are five methods of grouping, or departmentalizing, workers.

   a. _____   d. _____

   b. _____   e. _____

   c. _____

22. What determines the decision about which way to departmentalize?

23. What is the difference between centralized authority and decentralized authority?

Learning Goal 4 **Organization Models**

24. Name four types of organizational structures.

   a. _____   c. _____

   b. _____   d. _____

25. What are the advantages and disadvantages of these forms of organizing?

   Line

   Advantages

   a. _____

   b. _____

   c. _____

Disadvantages

a. _____

b. _____

c. _____

d. _____

e. _____

Line and Staff

Advantages

a. _____

b. _____

c. _____

Disadvantages

a. _____

b. _____

c. _____

d. _____

Matrix

Advantages

a. _____

b. _____

c. _____

d. _____

Disadvantages

a. _____

b. _____

c. _____

d. _____

26. What areas of a business are considered "staff?"

27. What disadvantage is common to both line and line and staff organizational structures?

28. What benefits do both types of organizations have in common?

29. How does a matrix system work?

30. What kinds of industries benefit from a matrix structure?

31. Describe cross-functional teams.

32. What are the advantages and disadvantages of cross-functional, self-managed teams?

    Advantages

    a. _____

    b. _____

    c. _____

Disadvantages

a. _____

b. _____

c. _____

d. _____

33. What are five kinds of teams?

a. _____ d. _____

b. _____ e. _____

c. _____

34. What is an extranet?

35. What is an intranet?

Learning Goal 5 **The Restructuring Process and Total Quality**

36. What is the difference between continuous improvement and reengineering?

37. What happens in the reengineering process?

38. Illustrate an "upside-down" organization.

39. How does turning the organization "inside-out" help it to become customer service oriented?

40. How does a company set up an "internal customer?"

41. When will a company choose to go with outsourcing?

Learning Goal 6   **Establishing a Service-Oriented Culture**

42. What kind of organizational cultures do the best organizations have?

43. What are two organizational systems that all companies have?

    a. _____   b. _____

44. Describe the difference between the formal and the informal organization.

45. What are the benefits of the formal organization?

46. What are the drawbacks of the formal organization?

47. What is the benefit of the informal organization?

48. What is the drawback?

49. What is at the center of the informal organization?

CRITICAL THINKING EXERCISES

Learning Goal 1

1. Think about the organizational design of the school you are attending, or an organization with which you are familiar, like where you work. Can you identify the "hierarchy?" Identify how many layers of management come between the front-line workers and the highest level of management. Are there separate departments for various functions (instruction, bookstore, and so on)? (Hint - perhaps your instructor will have a copy of the organizational chart for your school, or your manager may have one for the company for which you work.)

2. Can you find any evidence of restructuring, or changes that have helped the school or the company to "more effectively and efficiently serve customers"? (Who are the customers of a college or university?)

Learning Goal 2

3. Many organizations today have been organized around principles developed earlier in this century by Henri Fayol and Max Weber. Read the following and determine whose ideas are being described.

    a. Introduced several "principles" of organizing. _____

    b. Believed workers should think of themselves as coordinated teams, and the goal of the team is more important than individual goals. _____

    c. Promoted a bureaucratic organization. _____

    d. Believed that large organizations demanded clearly established rules and guidelines which were to be precisely followed. _____

    e. Wrote that each worker should report to only one boss. _____

    f. Said that managers should treat employees and peers with respect.
_____

    g. Wrote that functions are to be divided into areas of specialization such as production, marketing and so on. _____

    h. Believed in written rules, decision guidelines and detailed records.
_____

    i. Said that staffing and promotions should be based solely on qualifications.
_____

    j. Proposed that an organization should consist of three layers of authority: top managers, middle managers, and supervisors. _____

    k. Believed the less decision-making employees had to do, the better.
_____

    l. Believed that managers have the right to give orders and expect obedience.
_____

Learning Goal 3

4. The factors to be considered in determining a span of control are:

Capabilities of the manager.	Functional similarity.
Capabilities of the subordinates.	Need for coordination.
Complexity of the job.	Planning demands.
Geographical closeness.	Functional complexity.

Read the following descriptions. Draw a simple organizational chart and indicate the span of control at each level and the reasons for your design.

A. A research lab, where a total of 10 chemists and doctors are working on several different types of research. All experiments are related to one particular disease. Often one experiment must be completed before another can be started, so coordination among the researchers is very important.

ORGANIZATION CHART:

REASONS:

B. An assembly plant, consisting of fifteen groups of six workers each. Each group has the responsibility of completing several stages of the assembly of the product before it moves on to the next group. In the plant, there are a total of three sections, all of which are working on the same product simultaneously. The finished product from the groups of all three sections goes to a separate and final quality control group, led by the plant supervisor who checks out all products assembled in the plant.

ORGANIZATION CHART:

REASONS:

5. There are a number of ways companies have tried to departmentalize to better serve customers:

Function.   Process.   Geographic location.

Customer group.   Product.

Match each of the following to the correct form:

A. General Motors has the Saturn, Chevrolet and Pontiac divisions, and the Buick, Oldsmobile divisions, each employing separate staffs for design, engineering, product development and so on. _____

B. At the highest corporate levels, G.E. has a corporate strategic planning staff, production staff, human resources staff, technical resources staff and finance staff. _____

C. Apple Computer, in manufacturing the Macintosh Computer System, begins with an assembly line that makes the logic board; another line makes the analog board. Once assembled, the boards go through diagnostic tests before being assembled into a computer unit. _____

D. When Wendy's made the decision to expand into the European market, the company created a separate European division. _____

E. Most banks have commercial loan officers who deal only with business customers and consumer loan specialists for personal loans. _____

6. Re-read the advantages and disadvantages of the traditional functional method of departmentalizing organizations. Apply what you know about changes in the global marketplace and in businesses to explain why companies are redesigning their structures, away from the traditional methods.

7. As companies are moving away from traditional methods of organizing, and taking different perspectives regarding span of control, how are companies changing in the area of centralization vs decentralization?

Learning Goal 4

8. There are 4 types of organizational structures:

   Line.   Matrix.

   Line and Staff.   Cross-functional.

Read below brief descriptions of several companies and decide which form of organizational structure would be most suitable for each.

A. A small company, Dynalink is in the biotechnology industry. Competition is fierce, and new product development is of highest importance. The field is changing and growing so rapidly that new product ideas must come fast and furious. The firm employs highly skilled, very creative people.
_____

B. Another small firm is Cleanem Up, a dry cleaning establishment, with one owner and one store. They are located in a suburban area and have a loyal clientele. The store is known for its quality and courteous service. _____

C. Wells Industries is a medium-sized firm employing about 1500 people. Wells makes a variety of business-related products such as stationary, forms and so forth. They have a good sales force, which knows the product very well. While this is a fairly competitive industry, new product development happens as the need arises, such as when firms went from sophisticated word processing machines to even more sophisticated computerized office management.
_____

D. Chrysler wants to develop a new luxury car to compete with Lexus, Infiniti and others. Time is important, as they want to enter the market within 18 months.
_____

9. How will cross-functional teams impact organizational designs of the future?

10. What problems are sometimes associated with cross-functional teams?

Learning Goal 5

11. How does the upside down (inverted) organizational structure relate to the other kinds of changes we have read about in this chapter, such as wider spans of control, decentralization, cross-functional self-managed teams and so on?

12. Why does Gallo Winery, known for its wines, choose not to grow grapes?

13. How does the "internal" customer concept help a business become more competitive?

Learning Goal 6

14. What is the relationship among leadership style, the organizational structure (such as tall vs flat organizations, span of control, delegation, teams) and the creation of an organizational culture?

15. How does the informal organization help to create the corporate culture?

Learning Goal 4, 5, 6

16. Music-stor is in a growth state, and Eric, the founder, wants to be sure to build on a good foundation. You are already familiar with the product, and have re-engineered the production area. Eric is now interested in the organizational design of the entire company. What suggestions can you give him, knowing what you already know about the company and its employees?

PRACTICE TEST

Multiple Choice: Circle the best answer.

1. In general, organizations today are:

    a. eliminating managers and giving power to lower-level employees.
    b. getting bigger, more international, and so are adding management layers.
    c. becoming more bureaucratic.
    d. managing employees more closely as they reduce the layers of management.

2. Which of the following does not fit in when describing a bureaucratic organization?

    a. many rules and regulations that everyone is expected to follow
    b. people tend to specialize in many functions
    c. communication is minimal
    d. the organization is set up by function, with separate departments for marketing, engineering and so on

3. When IBM changed its organizational design, the company gave more authority to lower-level employees, to become more flexible in responding to customer needs. The company broke down barriers between functions, and ended top-down management. This process is known as:

    a. downsizing.
    b. changing span of control.
    c. restructuring.
    d. becoming more bureaucratic.

4. According to Henry Fayol, the principle of _____ means that each person should know to whom they report, and that managers should have the right to give orders and expect others to follow.

    a. unity of command
    b. division of labor
    c. order
    d. hierarchy of authority

5. Max Weber believed that:

   a. large organizations demanded clearly established rules and guidelines.
   b. workers and supervisors should make decisions together.
   c. rules were to be considered only as guidelines, and employees should be flexible.
   d. there was no need for job descriptions.

6. Robin Banks is a supervisor for a large, bureaucratic organization on the West Coast. According to the views of a bureaucratic organization held by Max Weber, this means that Robin should:

   a. be included on decision making when decisions affect her workers.
   b. have a wide span of control.
   c. try to get her workers organized into cross-functional teams.
   d. do her work and let middle and upper-level managers do the decision making.

7. The process of reorganizing firms into smaller, less complex units is the result of:

   a. new technologies and international competition.
   b. employees rebelling against too many rules.
   c. upper-level managers who were not good decision makers.
   d. bureaucrats changing their way of thinking.

8. Who Dunnit is a new firm which makes murder mystery games for sale in retail stores and through catalogs. The company is run by very few people, and most everybody pitches in when they need to, to get the job done. It is really a "team" effort, with very few layers of management. Who Dunnit is an example of a:

   a. tall organization.
   b. bureaucratic organization.
   c. centralized organization.
   d. flat organization.

9. A manager's span of control:

   a. can narrow as subordinates need less supervision.
   b. will narrow as the manager gets to higher levels in the organization and work becomes less standardized.
   c. will broaden as work is less geographically concentrated.
   d. will broaden as functions become more complex.

10. Dewey, Cheatum and Howe is a car company that makes four models, a sport utility, a sports car, a four door sedan and a compact car. Workers at Dewey basically work on only one type of vehicle, and separate marketing and product development processes are designed for each type of vehicle, to better serve the customers for each type of vehicle. Dewey Cheatum and Howe is departmentalized by:

    a. customer.
    b. function.
    c. process.
    d. product.

11. The form of organizational structure that is most flexible, and allows the organization to take on new projects without adding to the organizational structure is the:

    a. Line.
    b. Line and staff.
    c. Matrix.
    d. Cross-functional self managed team.

12. The line structure has the disadvantage of:

    a. being too inflexible.
    b. being costly and complex.
    c. perceived loss of control for a manager.
    d. requiring self-motivated, highly trained employees.

13. Banana Computers is restructuring, and intends to implement cross-functional teams. All of the following are likely to serve on a cross-functional team except:

    a. a Banana engineer.
    b. an employee of Peelit, Inc. one of Banana's competitors.
    c. an employee of Monkeyshine, one of Banana's suppliers.
    d. a Banana salesperson.

14. Ima Doogooder works for Banana Computers and is very good at her job. However, Ima believes that there is always something she can do better, and she is constantly looking for better ways to satisfy customer needs. Ima is apparently a practitioner of:

    a. Reengineering.
    b. Restructuring.
    c. Continuous improvement.
    d. Benchmarking.

15. In an inverted, or "upside down" organization, the managers' job is to:

    a. maintain direct contact with customers.
    b. direct and closely monitor employee performance.
    c. look for the best ways to outsource functions.
    d. assist and support sales personnel and other employees who work directly with customers.

16. When a firm is rating its processes and products against the best in the world, the firm is practicing:

    a. total quality management.
    b. outsourcing.
    c. their core competencies.
    d. competitive benchmarking.

17. Companies based on an inverted pyramid:

    a. support front-line personnel with data, communication and professional assistance.
    b. need employees who are unskilled, so they can be trained in the new ways.
    c. insist that managers keep close watch on those employees who have direct contact with customers.
    d. have difficulty with slow decision making and with meeting customer needs.

18. Which of the following would not be used to describe a company with a positive corporate culture?

    a. emphasizes service to others, especially customers
    b. people enjoy working together to provide good products at reasonable prices
    c. less need for policy manuals, formal rules and procedures
    d. closer supervision of employees

19. The corporate structure shown on the organizational chart, which details lines of responsibility is known as the:

    a. informal structure.
    b. bureaucratic structure.
    c. formal structure.
    d. grapevine.

20. Sgt. Bilko is the one to see in the company when there is something you need. He will obtain what you need quickly, and can avoid the red tape that often delays action. Bilko is the one to see if you need advice or help. Bilko is an important member of the firm's:

a. purchasing department.

b. informal structure.

c. formal structure.

d. bureaucratic structure.

TRUE/FALSE

1. ____ A typical hierarchy will consist of top management, middle managers and supervisory, or first line managers.

2. ____ A bureaucratic organizational system is a good when workers are relatively well educated and trained to make decisions.

3. ____ Henri Fayol and MaxWeber are best known for such organizational concepts as division of labor, unity of command and strict rules, guidelines and policies.

4. ____ An organization with many layers of management, such as the U.S. army, or a large corporation is a good example of a flat organization.

5. ____ Companies that cut management layers are tending to create cross-functional and self-managed teams.

6. ____ The more experienced a manager is, the broader the span of control can be.

7. ____ One of the advantages of a functional structure is an ability to respond quickly to external changes.

8. ____ Today's rapidly changing markets tend to favor centralization of authority, so decisions can be made quickly.

9. ____ Safety, quality control and human resource management are examples of staff positions in a manufacturing firm.

10. ____ An extranet is a communication link within a specific company that travels over the Internet.

11. ____ Total quality management calls for continuous improvement of processes to deal with both internal and external customers.

12. ____ When a company can't perform a certain function as well as the best, the company may outsource that function, in order to concentrate on the functions at which they are the best.

13. ____ To improve internal services, some companies will set up a buy-sell relationship between teams and business units in the company, thus creating internal customers.

14. ____ In general, an organizational culture cannot be negative.

15. ____ The informal organization in most organizations is not particularly powerful.

ANSWERS

KEY TERMS AND DEFINITIONS

1. Cross-functional teams	13. Line personnel
2. Hierarchy	14. Competitive benchmarking
3. Networking	15. Decentralized authority
4. Restructuring	16. Outsourcing
5. Organizational culture	17. Total quality management (TQM)
6. Informal organization	18. Continuous improvement
7. Core competencies	19. Departmentalization
8. Bureaucracy	20. Formal organization
9. Centralized authority	21. Reengineering
10. Inverted organization	22. Matrix organization
11. Span of control	23. Staff personnel
12. Organizational design	

RETENTION CHECK

Learning Goal 1   **Changing the Organizational Hierarchy**

1. In the past, many organizations were designed so that managers could control workers. Everything was set up in a hierarchy.

2. A hierarchy means that there is one person at the top of the organization. There are many levels of managers who are responsible to that one person. Since one person can't keep track of thousands of workers, the top manager needs many lower-level managers to help.

3. In a traditional hierarchy, when an employee wanted to introduce a change, the employee would ask their manager. That manager would, in turn, ask his or her manager, and so on. Eventually a decision would be passed down. This type of decision making could take days, weeks or months.

4. Organizations are eliminating managers and giving more power to lower-level employees. This process is called downsizing, because the organization is able to operate with fewer employees.

5. The characteristics of a bureaucratic organization are:
   a. many rules and regulations which everyone is expected to follow.
   b. the organization is set up by function.
   c. people tend to specialize in one function.
   d. communication among departments is minimal.

6. The problem today with bureaucratic organizations is that such organizations are not very responsive to customers. Employees tend to follow the rules and aren't very flexible in responding to customer needs and wants.

7. Slow response to consumer demands cuts into sales. Companies have responded by restructuring, or redesigning the organization so it can more effectively and efficiently service customers. Often that will mean breaking down barriers between functions, and giving more authority to lower-level employees.

Learning Goal 2 **How Organizations Have Evolved**

8. Fayol's principles of organizing include:
   a. Unity of command.
   b. Hierarchy of authority.
   c. Division of labor.
   d. Subordination of individual interests to the general interest.
   e. Authority.
   f. Degree of centralization.
   g. Clear communication channels.
   h. Order.
   i. Equity.
   j. Esprit de corps.

9. Organizations in the past were designed so that no person had more than one boss, lines of authority were clear, and everyone knew to whom they were to report.

10. These principles tended to become rules and procedures as organizations became larger. This led to rigid organizations and a feeling among workers that they belonged to an inflexible system.

11. The layers of management, according to Weber are:
    a. top.   b. middle.   c. supervisory.

12. Four characteristics of Weber's bureaucracy are:
    a. Job descriptions.
    b. Written rules, decision guidelines and detailed records.
    c. Consistent procedures, regulations and policies.
    d. Staffing and promotions based on qualifications.

Learning Goal 3   **Designing More Responsive Organizations**

13. Organizational issues leading to design changes include:
    a. tall versus flat structures.
    b. span of control.
    c. departmentalization.
    d. centralization versus decentralization.

14. Tall organizational structures have many layers of management.

15. The net effect of tall structures was a huge complex of managers, management assistants, secretaries, assistant secretaries, supervisors, and trainers. Costs of keeping all these managers is very high, the amount of paperwork was high, and communication and decision making were inefficient.

16. The trend is to eliminate several layers of management. Throughout the 1990s, companies fired managers in an attempt to become more efficient. Companies that cut management are tending to create teams.

17. Span of control narrows gradually at higher levels of the organization. Because work is standardized at lower levels, it is possible to implement a wider span of control.

18. Factors that determine the optimum span of control are:
    a. Capabilities of the manager.   e. Functional similarity.
    b. Capabilities of the subordinates.   f. Need for coordination.
    c. Complexity of the job.   g. Planning demands.
    d. Geographical closeness.   h. Functional complexity.

19. The trend is to expand span of control as organizations get rid of middle managers. This will be possible as employees become more professional, information technology makes it possible for managers to handle more information, and employees take on more responsibility for self-management.

20.
Advantages	Disadvantages
Skills can be developed	Lack of communication
Coordination with the function	Employees don't identify with the corporation as a whole
Economies of scale	Response to change is slow
	People trained too narrowly

21. The methods of departmentalizing are:
    a. Geographic location.
    b. Function.
    c. Customer group.
    d. Process.
    e. Product.

22. The decision about which way to departmentalize depends upon the nature of the product and the customers served.

23. Centralized authority means that decision-making authority is maintained at the top level of management at headquarters. Decentralized authority means that decision-making authority is delegated to lower-level managers and employees.

Learning Goal 4: **Organization Models**

24. a. Line organizations
    b. Line and staff organizations
    c. Matrix-style organizations
    d. Cross-functional, self-managed teams

25. Line - Advantages
    a. Clearly defined responsibility and authority
    b. Easy to understand
    c. One supervisor for each person

Disadvantages
a. Too inflexible
b. Few specialists to advise
c. Long lines of communication
d. Unable to handle complex questions quickly
e. Tons of paperwork

Line and staff - Advantages
a. Expert advice from staff to line personnel
b. Establishes lines of authority
c. Encourages cooperation and better communication at all levels

Disadvantages
a. Potential overstaffing
b. Potential overanalyzing
c. Lines of communication can get blurred
d. Staff frustrations because of lack of authority

Matrix - Advantages
a. Flexible
b. Encourages cooperation among departments
c. Can produce creative solutions to problems
d. Allows organizations to take on new projects without adding to the organization structure

Disadvantages
a. Costly and complex
b. Can confuse employees
c. Requires good interpersonal skills and cooperative managers and employees
d. Difficult to evaluate employees and to set up reward systems

26. Areas such as safety, quality control, computer technology, human resource management, and investing would be considered staff.

27. Both line, and line and staff structures have a certain amount of inflexibility.

28. Both types of organizations have established lines of authority and communication and both work well in companies with a relatively unchanging environment and slow product development.

29. In a matrix organization, specialists from different parts of the company are brought together to work on specific projects, but remain a part of a line and staff organization.

30. The matrix system works effectively in high-tech firms, and is used in banking, management consulting firms, accounting firms, ad agencies, and school systems.

31. Cross-functional teams are groups of employees from different departments who work together on a semi-permanent basis. Often the teams are empowered to make decisions on their own without seeking approval of management.

32. Cross-functional, self-managed teams - Advantages
    a. Greatly increases interdepartmental coordination and cooperation
    b. Quicker response to customers and market conditions
    c. Increased employee morale and motivation

    Disadvantages
    a. Some confusion over responsibility and authority
    b. Perceived loss of control by management
    c. Difficult to evaluate employees and set up reward systems
    d. Requires self-motivated and highly trained workers

33. Five kinds of teams are:
    a. management teams.
    b. virtual teams.
    c. quality circles.
    d. work teams.
    e. problem-solving teams.

34. An extranet is an extended Internet that connects suppliers, customers, and other organizations via secure Web sites.

35. Intranets are secure communication links within companies that travel over the Internet.

Learning Goal 5 **The Restructuring Process and Total Quality**

36. Continuous improvement means constantly improving the way that the organization does things so that customer needs can be better satisfied. Reengineering is the fundamental rethinking and radical redesign of organizational processes to achieve dramatic improvements in critical measures of performance.

37. When you reengineer a process, jobs evolve from narrow and task-oriented to multidimensional. Employees now make decisions on their own. Managers behave like coaches, and workers focus more on customer needs. Attitudes and values change in response to new incentives.

38.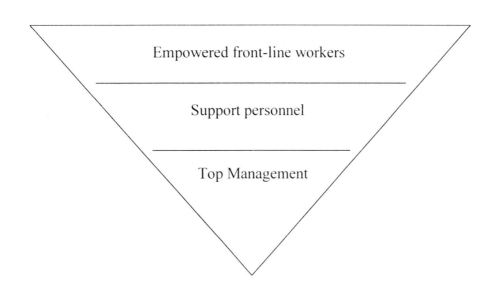

39. Total quality demands that organizations benchmark each function against the best in the world. If an organization can't do as well as the best, the idea is to outsource the function to an organization that is the best. This gives the customer the best the company can offer.

40. Internal customers are created when management sets up buy-sell relationships among teams and business units in the organization.

41. A company will use outsourcing if it can't perform a function as well as the best.

Learning Goal 6 **Establishing a Service Oriented Culture**

42. The best organizations have cultures that emphasize service to others, the atmosphere is one of friendly, concerned, caring people who enjoy working together to provide a good product at a reasonable price. Those companies have less need for close supervision of employees, policy manuals, organization charts and formal rules, procedures and controls.

43. All companies have a(n):

    a. formal organization.   b. informal organization.

44. The formal organization details each person's responsibility, authority and position. The informal organization consists of relationships and lines of authority that develop outside the formal organization.

45. The benefit of a formal organization is that it provides helpful guidelines and lines of authority to follow in routine situations.

46. The drawback of the formal organization is that it is often too slow and bureaucratic to enable an organization to adapt quickly.

47. The informal organization is very effective in generating creative solutions to short-term problems and providing a feeling of camaraderie and teamwork among employees.

48. The drawback of the informal organization is that it is often too unstructured and emotional to allow careful, reasoned decision making on critical matters.

49. The center of the informal organization is the grapevine, the system through which unofficial information flows between employees and managers.

CRITICAL THINKING

Learning Goal 1

1. There will obviously be many different answers to this question. A typical hierarchy in a community college for example may be President, Dean of Instruction, Associate Deans, Department Chairs, and faculty for instruction. For non-instruction areas, there may be Associate Deans, Directors, and non-management positions. There are often many layers of management between the lowest levels and the higher levels, and functional areas are well defined.

Learning Goal 2

2. Colleges may have set up programs for providing high school students with admission and enrollment information, may have developed faculty-student "mentoring" programs, orientation programs, encouraged faculty to be accessible to students, made it easier to apply for financial aid and so forth. Each college will have different programs.

3.
a. Fayol	e. Fayol	i. Weber
b. Fayol	f. Fayol	j. Weber
c. Weber	g. Fayol	k. Weber
d. Weber	h. Weber	l. Fayol

Learning Goal 3

4. A. There could be multiple answers to this question. One suggestion for an organizational chart is:

Lab supervisor
|
10 Researchers

The supervisor's span of control is 10. The reasons for this type of structure are that the researchers probably don't need much supervision, the functions, although complex, are similar in that they are all research related, and all the employees are in the same lab, so are geographically close. Because of the need for coordination of research projects, the supervisor would need to develop an effective communication system.

B. Possible answer

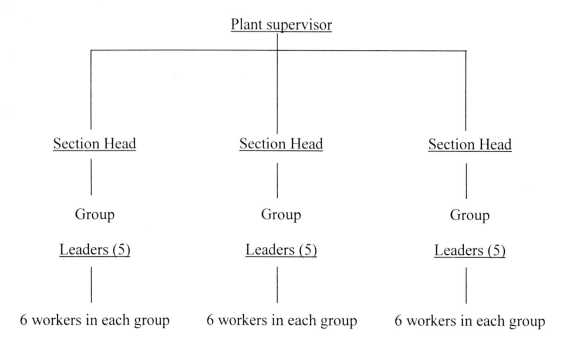

Span of control: Plant supervisor - 3

Section Heads - 5

Group Leaders - 6

Reason: Each group leader can coordinate the work of his group with the other groups in his section, and the section heads can coordinate their sections. The functions in each group are different, so there is a need for a narrower span of control.

NOTE! These are possible answers. Other structures could be utilized, such as self-managed teams.

5. A. Product and function D. Geographic location
   B. Function E. Customer
   C. Process

6. In previous chapters we have learned about the global nature of our economy and of the business sector in particular. We have also read about the focus on productivity, and the search for ways to make firms in the United States more efficient. With globalization comes competition from companies that have been focusing on those productivity issues for quite some time. The disadvantages of the more traditional methods of departmentalization (the functional structure in particular), such as lack of communication, slow response times to external changes and narrowly focused training, can serve to hinder efforts to increase productivity and to better serve an increasingly demanding customer base.

7. Changes in the areas we have been discussing are closely related to the changes we are seeing in the area of decision making. As spans of control widen, and non-traditional ways of grouping workers emerge, decision making is being delegated to lower levels of management, or even to non-management levels. Self-managed teams, which are at the "lowest levels" of the organization, for example, are being given decision-making authority. Today's rapidly changing markets and differences in consumer tastes are favoring a more decentralized structure, with wider spans of control and a team based structure.

8. a. Matrix system cross-functional teams.
   b. Line
   c. Line and staff
   d. Cross-functional

9. Cross-functional teams will have a major impact on organizational designs of the future. Companies will be linked with customers, suppliers, and distributors through these teams, creating an integrated system of firms working together to create products and services designed to exactly meet customers' needs. Firms designed in such a manner will have a real competitive edge over corporations that are more traditional.

10. Managers may resist the move toward teams, and team members themselves may be unsure of what their duties are, how they will be compensated and who is responsible for mistakes. Workers need different skills from working alone, and companies can falter while a change over is in the process. Firms run the risk of overusing teams, which may hinder creativity and problem solving.

Learning Goal 5

11. These organizational changes are all focused on designing the organization with meeting the needs of the customer as the most important objective. Inverted organizations empower front-line workers, who deal directly with customers, and provide them with the information and support needed to satisfy customers. Turning the organization inside out again focuses on customer service because the firm concentrates on its "core competencies," and outsources the functions at which the company is less proficient. The idea of turning the organization inside out is to rate your practices processes and products against the world's best. If you don't measure up, it's important to either outsource the function or reengineer the function.

12. Gallo Winery chooses to stick to what it does best, which is the production and marketing of wine products. Gallo knows its core competencies, and has the most up-to-date information and distribution systems to help them be the best at serving the wine market, without growing grapes.

13. The internal customer "buys" its "product" from another business unit in the organization. If the team (customer) is not happy with products or services provided by the internal unit, the team (customer) can purchase the services from an outside vendor.

Learning Goal 6

14. The best organizations have positive corporate cultures, that emphasize service to customers, have a relaxed atmosphere, and concerned employees who enjoy working together to provide the best product at the best price.

    The text states that companies that have good organizational cultures "have less need for close supervision of employees, policy manuals, organization charts and formal rules, procedures and controls." That would indicate broad spans of control, empowered employees, flatter organizations and a participative leadership style. Employees who need minimal supervision will flourish in self-managed teams, and there is mutual trust between workers and management.

15. The informal organization is the human side of a company that does not show up on the organization chart. It is the system of relationships that develop over time, in a company. At the center of the informal organization is the grapevine, the unofficial flow of information. In a company with a positive culture, the informal organization can help to create a spirit of cooperation between managers and employees. It can strongly reinforce a feeling of teamwork and cooperation and can be an invaluable asset that promotes

harmony among workers. The informal organization can also be disruptive and negative, and powerful in influencing employees to resist management directives.

16. How you would design the organization is up to you. Many of the ideas presented in the chapter could be helpful. This is a small company, so a line organization might be appropriate. We noted earlier that the workers are a "new breed" who don't need a lot of supervision, however, so close monitoring probably could prove to be counter-productive. There doesn't seem to be an immediate need for new product development, so a matrix structure probably wouldn't be necessary. The emphasis on customer service has been apparent throughout the chapter, so however you design the company, the focus should be on whatever design will most effectively help the company to meet customer needs.

PRACTICE TEST

Multiple Choice				True/False			
1.	a	11.	c	1.	T	9.	T
2.	b	12.	a	2.	F	10.	F
3.	c	13.	b	3.	T	11.	T
4.	d	14.	c	4.	F	12.	T
5.	a	15.	d	5.	T	13.	T
6.	d	16.	d	6.	T	14.	F
7.	a	17.	a	7.	F	15.	F
8.	d	18.	d	8.	F		
9.	b	19.	c				
10.	d	20.	b				

CHAPTER 9
USING THE LATEST TECHNOLOGY TO PRODUCE WORLD-CLASS PRODUCTS AND SERVICES

LEARNING GOALS

After you have read and studied this chapter, you should be able to:

1. Describe the production process and explain the importance of productivity.

2. Explain the importance of site selection in keeping down costs and identify the criteria used to evaluate different sites.

3. Classify the various production processes and how materials requirement planning links organizations in performing those processes.

4. Describe manufacturing techniques such as just-in-time inventory control, flexible manufacturing, lean manufacturing, and competing in time.

5. Show how CAD/CAM improves the production process, but can lead to people problems on the plant floor.

6. Illustrate the use of PERT and Gantt charts in production planning.

7. Explain the importance of productivity in all sectors: manufacturing, service and nonprofit.

LEARNING THE LANGUAGE

Listed below are important terms found in the chapter. Choose the correct term for each definition and write it in the space provided.

Analytic system	Mass customization
Assembly process	Enterprise resource planning (ERP)
Computer-aided design (CAD)	Process manufacturing
Computer-aided manufacturing (CAM)	Production
Critical Path	Production and operations management
Flexible manufacturing	Program evaluation and review technique (PERT)
Form utility	Quality control
Gantt chart	Robot
Lean manufacturing	Synthetic system

1. A bar graph that clearly shows what projects are being worked on and how much has been completed on a daily basis is called a _____.

2. The production process known as a(n) _____ either changes raw materials into other products or combines raw materials or parts into a finished product.

3. A computer-based production and operations system called _____ links multiple firms into one integrated production unit.

4. A production process called a(n) _____ puts together components.

5. _____ is the creation of finished goods and services using the factors of production: land, labor, capital, entrepreneurship and information.

6. A computer-controlled machine called a _____ is capable of performing many tasks requiring the use of materials and tools.

7. The use of computers helping in the design of products is called _____.

8. A concept known as _____ means tailoring products to meet the needs of individual customers.

9. _____ is all the activities managers do to create goods and services.

10. The process known as a(n) _____ breaks down raw materials into components to extract other products.

11. A method for analyzing tasks involved in completing a given project known as _____, includes estimating the time needed to complete each task, and identifying the minimum time needed to complete the total project.

9-2

12. Involving computers directly in the production process is called _____.

13. In the process of _____ products and services are measured against set standards.

14. The value added by the creation of finished goods and services using raw materials, components and other inputs is called _____.

15. The production process known as _____ physically or chemically changes materials.

16. Totally automated production centers called _____ can perform a variety of functions to produce different products.

17. _____ is the production of goods using less of everything compared to mass production: half the human effort, half the manufacturing space, half the investment in tools, half the engineering time to develop a new product in half the time.

18. The _____ is the sequence of tasks that takes the longest time to complete.

RETENTION CHECK

Learning Goal 1 **America's Manufacturing Base**

1. What are 7 things U.S. manufacturers have done to regain a competitive lead in the world marketplace?

    a. _____

    b. _____

    c. _____

d. _____

e. _____

f. _____

g. _____

2. What must be done in the future to keep U.S. manufacturers number one?

3. What is the difference between "production" and "productivity?"

Learning Goal 2 **Keeping Costs Low: Site Selection**

4. What are three major reasons why firms shift facilities from one area to another?

    a. _____

    b. _____

    c. _____

5. What are some issues surrounding moving to foreign countries in search of cheap labor?

6. Why would companies choose to remain in areas, such as Chicago, New York or California?

7. What elements are giving firms flexibility in choosing locations, while remaining competitive?

Learning Goal 3 **Production Processes**

8. What are the three basic requirements of production, according to Andrew Grove?

   a. _____

   b. _____

   c. _____

9. What are two types of manufacturing processes?

   a. _____

   b. _____

10. What are two types of synthetic manufacturing systems?

    a. _____   b. _____

11. What is the difference between synthetic systems and analytic systems?

12. What are two types of production processes?

    a. _____   b. _____

13. What is the difference between a continuous production process and an intermittent process?

14. Why do most manufacturers today use intermittent processes?

15. What did MRP do for manufacturers?

Learning Goal 4   **Modern Production Techniques**

16. What will be the benefit of programs such as ERP?

17. What is the main reason why companies must make a wide variety of high quality, custom products at a very low cost?

18. What are 5 major developments which have radically changed the production process in the United States?

   a. _____   d. _____

   b. _____   e. _____

   c. _____

19. How does a JIT program work?

20. What does ERP, in combination with JIT systems, provide?

21. How does a company become "lean?"

22. What is the benefit flexible manufacturing systems provide to manufacturers?

Learning Goal 5   **Computer-Aided Design and Manufacturing**

23. What one development changed production techniques more than any other?

24. What has CAD/CAM made possible?

25. What is CIM?

Learning Goal 6 **Control Procedures: PERT and Gantt charts**

26. List the four steps in designing a PERT chart.

    a. _____

    b. _____

    c. _____

    d. _____

27. How are PERT Charts generally developed?

28. What is the difference between a Gantt Chart and a PERT Chart?

29. What can a manager do with a Gantt Chart?

30. How was quality control handled in the past?

31. How are things different today with regard to quality control?

32. What are three steps involved in the quality control process?

   a. _____

   b. _____

   c. _____

Learning Goal 7   **Measuring Productivity in the Service Sector**

33. Where is the greatest productivity problem in the United States?

34. Why is productivity in the service sector difficult to measure?

35. What are some examples of how technology has begun to improve productivity in the service sector?

36.   How is the Internet changing the service industry?

37.   How do the changes in technology affect workers outside of work?

CRITICAL THINKING EXERCISES

Learning Goal 1

1.   You have been reading throughout the text of the move toward a global marketplace, and the need for U.S. firms to make changes to be competitive. How are production and productivity fundamental to the process?

Learning Goal 2

2.   "One of the major issues of the 1990s has been the shift of manufacturing and service organizations..."

   Businesses may choose to locate close to where the buying power for their product is located, where labor is inexpensive and/or skilled, or where land and resources are inexpensive and readily available.

   Evaluate the area in which you live based on the site-selection criteria listed and discussed in the text. Does your area have an advantage in the variables considered for site selection? If so, which ones? Are you located close to markets? What could you say to convince a producer or service business to locate in your area?

Learning Goal 3

3. In manufacturing there are synthetic systems and analytic systems. Synthetic systems

   a) change materials, which is process manufacturing, or

   b) put together components, which is assembly process.

   Analytic systems break down raw materials into components to extract other products. In addition, production processes are either: continuous or intermittent. Match the correct type of production process to each of the following, according to the description:

   a. In the meat processing industry, a firm produces various cuts of meat, glue from horns and hooves, and leather from hides. _____

   b. the steel industry never shuts down its ovens. _____

   c. In the furniture industry, a store will sell custom designed furniture and pass the order on to the manufacturer, who custom makes each piece.
   _____

   d. The Macintosh computer is assembled piece by piece along an assembly line.
   _____

   e. In the steel industry, ore is melted down, poured into forms, then cooled.
   _____

4. Music-stor is beginning to really gear up for production. It has 2 main product lines: a component part, for built-in tape and CD storage, designed to be installed during the automotive assembly process, and an "after-market" product, to be sold in auto parts stores which can be installed by the consumer. Music-stor buys the raw material from a plastic supplier. They then melt the plastic down and pour it into molds, which are then allowed to cool. During the process, color is added, that's coded to the colors offered by the car company they have contracted with. Later, clips and other parts are added which are needed for installation. The process is similar for both product lines, with some alterations needed for the retail version. What type of production process is Music-stor likely to be using? How can the company ensure their product is available when the assembly plant needs it, and when the retailer wants to sell it?

Learning Goal 4

5. How do Flexible Manufacturing Systems, lean manufacturing and mass customization reflect the customer orientation we have discussed in earlier chapters?

6. Five radically different production techniques have emerged in recent years:

    Just-in-time inventory control   Mass customization   Lean manufacturing

    Flexible manufacturing   Competing in time

    Distinguish the differences between each technique in the following:

    a. The Chrysler plant in Fenton, Missouri receives shipments about every four hours from its seat supplier, (located in a neighboring town), and literally hundreds of other parts continually. There is virtually no storage space in the plant.
    _____

    b. Volvo uses modular construction in their plants, where workers are grouped into autonomous teams working on mobile assembly platforms that carry the cars to the workers. Each worker has been trained to do a whole cluster of tasks. This system enabled Volvo to build quality cars with fewer workers in more space efficient plants, and has reduced the number of hours need to assemble a car.
    _____

    c. Because of increased competition from its Japanese counter parts, Xerox implemented a program designed to cut its new product development time in half.
    _____

    d. Levi's markets a service which enables any customer to order a custom-made pair of jeans from any retailer at any time. The jeans cost $10 more than an "off-the-rack" pair. _____

    e.   At Dynalink Industries, 15 machines are used to make, test and package component parts for stereo and quadraphonic sound systems. The parts are never touched by human hands. _____

Learning Goal 5

7. How does the concept of teams fit into the modular construction process used to make the Saturn, which is described in the text ?

8. How does CAD/CAM relate to mass customization?

9. Help! There are problems on the shop floor! You work for a highly progressive and until now, successful company. Recently, in an effort to further improve their competitive position, the company has installed some high-tech, very sophisticated production technology. The workers that were not laid off received one-half day of training before being put to work on the new machines. Managers, supervisors and workers alike are expressing concern, and customer complaints have begun to trickle in. To make matters worse, even with the new equipment, productivity has begun to slip. Your job is to find out what's wrong and fix it! What's your plan?

Learning Goal 6

10. You have learned in earlier chapters that one advantage small businesses often have over larger, less flexible companies, is the ability to move quickly to serve the needs of their markets and provide more customized service. As increasing numbers of large businesses implement the modern production techniques discussed in this chapter, what potential impact could this have on small businesses?

11. PERT, Critical Path and Gantt charts are control measures used to ensure that products are manufactured and delivered on time.

    Draw a PERT Chart for cooking and serving a breakfast of 3-minute eggs, buttered toast and coffee and identify the critical path.

12. In the past, quality control in U.S. firms was often done at the end of the production line. How does the concept of "total quality" change the old way of thinking about quality?

Learning Goal 7

13. How have changes in service automation affected you? What services do you use which have been changed by implementing new technologies in to the service sector.

PRACTICE TEST

Multiple Choice: Circle the best answer.

1. What statement does not fit in when describing the trend in manufacturing in the United States?

    a. The heart of the free enterprise system has always been manufacturing.
    b. Manufacturing produces less than one-fourth of the U.S. Gross Domestic Product.
    c. Traditional manufacturing leaders have declined through much of the last 2 decades.
    d. Foreign competition has not affected U.S. manufacturers.

2. New production techniques have:

    a. been difficult and costly to implement, and so have been largely ignored.
    b. made it possible to virtually custom-make products for individual industrial buyers.
    c. have been implemented primarily by foreign manufacturers.
    d. have not been shown to be effective in making U.S. manufacturers competitive.

3. Music-Stor is beginning to see some competition for their portable compact disc storage units. In order to remain competitive, Music-Stor must be sure to:

    a. replace all workers with automated equipment.
    b. move all manufacturing to foreign countries.
    c. train all salesmen in aggressive selling techniques.
    d. keep the costs of inputs down.

4. Which of the following is not considered a strong reason for companies to move production facilities from one area to another?

    a. availability of cheap labor
    b. cheaper natural resources
    c. the level of unemployment in a geographic area
    d. reducing the time it takes to deliver products to the market

5. What are the benefits manufacturers see in locating close to larger markets, according to the text?

   a. businesses can lower transportation costs and be more responsive to customers
   b. more availability of skilled labor
   c. guaranteed lower tax rates in the suburban areas
   d. cheaper natural resources

6. Boiling an egg is an example of:

   a. assembly process.
   b. process manufacturing.
   c. analytic system.
   d. continuous process.

7. Music-Stor wants to link its resource planning and manufacturing with its suppliers in order to develop a more integrated system. Music-Stor could use:

   a. enterprise resource planning.
   b. continuous process manufacturing.
   c. PERT charts.
   d. total quality control.

8. Tony Ruggali is in the process of opening a new restaurant. Tony wants to be sure that his new place, The Fresh Place, always has the freshest ingredients, and will always be known for being the "freshest place in town." He also wants to devote most of the space in the restaurant to tables for diners, not for storing produce. Tony could make use of:

   a. analytic production.
   b. Gantt charts.
   c. just in time inventory.
   d. mass production.

9. _____ enable manufacturers to custom-make goods as quickly as mass-produced items once were.

   a. PERT techniques
   b. Flexible manufacturing systems
   c. Lean manufacturing
   d. Computer aided design

10. Quon Ho believes that there must be a way to cut down on the amount of resources his company uses in the production process. Quon feels that the company uses more space, tools and time to make their product than is necessary. Quon should examine the benefits of:

   a. lean manufacturing.
   b. CAD/CAM.
   c. mass customization.
   d. competing in time.

11. A _____ is a bar graph that shows which projects are being worked on and how much has been completed.

   a. PERT chart
   b. flexible manufacturing system
   c. Gantt chart
   d. CAD/CAM system

12. Munchin A. Pickle is a production supervisor at the local cucumber processing plant. Munchin is looking at a chart which illustrates for him the sequence of tasks involved in processing the cukes. He is especially interested in the sequence of tasks that take the longest time to complete. Munchin is interested in the:

   a. Gantt chart.
   b. total quality management process.
   c. critical path.
   d. lean manufacturing process.

13. Which of the following is not a part of the TQM process?

   a. continual employee evaluations
   b. analyzing the consumer to determine quality demands
   c. incorporating quality features into the product design
   d. ensuring quality standards are met during the entire production process

14. What is the difficulty in measuring productivity growth in the service sector?

   a. incorporating automation
   b. unemployment caused by using computers in services
   c. measuring improvements in quality of service provided
   d. finding trained workers

15. The success of service organizations in the future depends upon:

    a. keeping out foreign competition.
    b. automating even more elements of providing the service.
    c. listening to consumers in order to adapt to consumer demands more quickly.
    d. training workers in how to sell services to customers.

TRUE/FALSE

1. ____ It could be said that we are actually in a new era in the industrial revolution.

2. ____ The key to success in the future is for U.S. producers to combine effective marketing with effective production and management.

3. ____ Form utility is the value added by the creation of finished goods and services using raw materials, components and other inputs.

4. ____ Many firms in the U.S. are moving to the Northeast in the search for inexpensive labor.

5. ____ Telecommuting has not had much impact on site selection.

6. ____ Eventually, suppliers will be linked with manufacturers and retailers in a completely integrated system to facilitate the smooth flow of goods to the consumer.

7. ____ Global competition has had little impact on U.S. manufacturers.

8. ____ Flexible manufacturing systems are so flexible that a special order, even a single item can be produced without slowing down the manufacturing process.

9. ____ It is likely that robots will totally replace manufacturing workers in the future.

10. ____ Computer-integrated manufacturing allows computer-aided design machines to "talk" to computer-aided manufacturing machines.

11. ____ A Gantt computer program will allow a manager to trace the production process minute by minute to determine which tasks are on time and which are behind.

12. ____ In manufacturing, it is still the company itself which determines what the standard for quality should be.

13. ____ Productivity in the service sector is going down.

14. ____ The government doesn't yet know how to measure productivity gains in the service sector.

15. ____ One of the results of technology in the workplace will be that people will need more contact with people outside the work environment.

ANSWERS

Learning the Language

1. Gantt chart	7. Computer-aided design (CAD)	13. Quality control
2. Synthetic system	8. Mass customization	14. Form utility
3. Enterprise resource planning (ERP)	9. Production and operations management	15. Process manufacturing
4. Assembly process	10. Analytic system	16. Flexible manufacturing
5. Production	11. PERT	17. Lean manufacturing
6. Robot	12. Computer-aided manufacturing (CAM)	18. Critical path

RETENTION CHECK

Learning Goal 1 **America's Manufacturing Base**

1. Manufacturers today have:
   a. Taken a customer focus
   b. Created cost savings through site selection
   c. Used flexible manufacturing for a faster response to the market
   d. Saved on the plant floor through lean manufacturing
   e. Used computer-aided manufacturing and other modern practices
   f. Implemented total quality management
   g. Imposed better control procedures

2. To keep U.S. manufacturers number one, they must get closer to customers to find out what their product needs are. Effective marketing must be then combined with effective production and management.

3. Production is a broad term that describes the creative process in all industries that produce goods and services. Productivity is the term used to describe output per unit of input.

Learning Goal 2   **Keeping Costs Low: Site Selection**

4. Firms shift facilities from one site to another for these reasons:
   a. cheap labor or the right kind of skilled labor
   b. cheaper natural resources
   c. reducing time-to-market

5. Cheap labor is a key reason why less technologically advanced producers move their plants to foreign locations. This has caused problems for some firms, as they have been charged with using child labor and unsafe labor practices in other countries. It is important for firms to maintain the same quality standards and fair labor practices wherever they produce.

6. Companies would choose to locate or remain in highly populated areas such as Chicago or New York in order to stay close to customers. Much of the buying power of the United States is still centered in the Northeast, Midwest and Far West. By locating close to customers, businesses lower transportation costs and can be more responsive to customer service needs.

7. New developments in information technology, such as computers, modems, e-mail, voice mail and so forth are enabling firms and employees to be more flexible in choosing locations while remaining competitive. These innovations have made telecommuting a major trend in business.

Learning Goal 3   **Production Processes**

8. According to Andrew Grove, the 3 basic requirements of production are:
   a. Build and deliver products in response to demands of a customer at a scheduled delivery time.
   b. Provide an acceptable quality level.
   c. Provide everything at the lowest possible cost.

9. Two types of manufacturing processes are:
   a. Synthetic systems.
   b. Analytic systems.

10. Two types of synthetic manufacturing processes are:
    a. process manufacturing.
    b. assembly process.

11. Synthetic systems either change raw materials into other products or combine raw materials or parts into a finished product. Analytic systems, on the other hand, break down raw materials into components to extract other products.

12. Two types of production processes are:
    a. continuous.
    b. intermittent.

13. A continuous process is one in which long production runs turn out finished goods over time. An intermittent process is an operation where the production run is short and the machines are changed frequently to produce different products.

14. Most new manufacturers use intermittent processes because the use of computers, robots, and flexible manufacturing processes make it possible to make custom-made goods almost as fast as mass-produced goods were once made.

15. MRP allowed manufacturers to make sure that needed parts and materials are available at the right place and the right time.

Learning Goal 4 **Modern Production Techniques**

16. Programs such as ERP will link suppliers, manufacturers and retailers in a completely integrated manufacturing and distribution system that will be constantly monitored for the smooth flow of goods from the time they're ordered to the time they reach the ultimate consumer.

17. Companies must make a wide-variety of high-quality custom-designed products at a very low cost because of global competition.

18. These developments have changed the production process in the U.S.:
    a. just-in-time inventory control.
    b. flexible manufacturing.
    c. lean manufacturing.
    d. mass customization.
    e. competing in time.

19. In a JIT program, a manufacturer sets a production schedule using enterprise resource planning or a similar system, and determines what parts and supplies will be needed. It then informs its suppliers of what will be needed. The supplier delivers the goods just in time to go on the assembly line. The supplier becomes more like another department in the firm because it is linked to the manufacturer by computer.

20. ERP in combination with JIT makes sure the right materials are at the right place at the right time at the cheapest cost to meet customer needs and production needs. This is the first step in modern production innovation.

21. A company becomes lean by continuously increasing the capacity to produce more, higher quality products with fewer resources.

22. Flexible manufacturing systems enable manufacturers to custom-make goods as quickly as mass-produced items were once made. This enables producers to more closely meet the wants and needs of customers.

Learning Goal 5 **Computer-Aided Design and Manufacturing**

23. The one development which has changed production techniques more than any other has been the integration of computers into the design and manufacture of products.

24. CAD/CAM has made it possible to custom-design products to meet the needs of small markets with very little increase in cost. A producer can program the computer to make a simple design change, and that change can be incorporated directly into the production line.

25. Computer integrated manufacturing is software that enables machines involved with computer-aided design to "talk" with machines involved with computer–aided manufacturing.

Learning Goal 6   **Control Procedures: PERT and Gantt charts**

26. Steps involved in developing a PERT chart include:
    a. Analyze and sequence tasks that need to be done.
    b. Estimate the time needed to complete each task.
    c. Draw a PERT network illustrating the 2 previous steps.
    d. Identify the critical path.

27. PERT charts are generally developed by computer.

28. A PERT chart analyzes the tasks involved in completing a given project, estimating the time needed to complete each task, and identifying the minimum time needed to complete the total project. A Gantt chart is more basic, and is used to measure production progress using a bar chart that shows what projects are being worked on and how much has been completed.

29. A manager can trace the production process minute by minute to determine which tasks are on time, and which are behind so that adjustments can be made to stay on schedule.

30. In the past quality control was often done at the end of the production line in the quality control department.

31. Today, quality means satisfying customers by building in and ensuring quality from product planning to production, purchasing, sales, and service.

32. A total quality program involves:
    a. analyzing the consumer to see what quality standards need to be established.
    b. ensuring quality is designed into products.
    c. specifying products must meet the quality standards every step of the way in the production process.

Learning Goal 7   **Measuring Productivity in the Service Sector**

33. The greatest productivity problem in the United States is reported to be in the service economy.

34. The increase in productivity in the service sector has been in quality, not in quantity, and quality increases are hard to measure with traditional productivity measurements.

35. Technology has changed productivity in the service sector in a number of ways. ATMs have made banking easier, and the new system of universal product codes has allowed computerized retail checkout so the process goes much faster. In the airline industry, computers are used to process reservations, secure prepackaged meals on board, and to help with handling luggage, passengers and so on. Tax preparers can use software packages that speed up the completion and filing of returns. Electronic tax return filing is even available, for relatively simple returns. The registration process for this class was made easier by using computers, and you may have paid with money electronically transferred or deposited into your account. The postal service makes use of machines that are able to process upwards of 10,000 pieces of mail an hour. The list is endless!

36. The Internet has changed retailing in particular. A greater variety of books and CDs is available on the Internet than in the retail stores, for example. Jet travel has enabled FedEx to deliver goods overnight. Computer databases enabled AT&T to have individualized customer service.

37. Technology will allow for a greater standard of living and new opportunities. In the future, people will need more contact with people outside of work. There will be new demands for recreation, social clubs, travel and other diversions.

CRITICAL THINKING EXERCISES

Learning Goal 1

1. Production is the creation of finished goods (output) using the factors of production, (inputs) while productivity measures how efficiently the output has been created. To be competitive in world markets, manufacturers must keep the cost of production (inputs) low while output must be relatively high. The fundamental question is: How does a producer keep costs low and still produce more? In other words, how do manufacturers increase productivity?

Learning Goal 2

2. The area in which you live may meet a number of important criteria. Look for a population that may be willing to work hard for less pay, such as new immigrants. What kind of skilled labor is available in your area? Is your state a "right to work" state or a heavily unionized state? That affects labor cost. Are you in a rural, suburban or urban area? That affects the availability and costs of land.

   If you live in a large urban area, such as Chicago, New York, northern New Jersey or much of California, businesses may be attracted because that's where their customers are. However land is more expensive, so a large production facility may not be built there. There may be lots of opportunity for a service-based business to locate in that area. Government support will vary from one area to another, in the form of tax incentives and zoning laws.

Learning Goal 3

3.
   a. analytic
   b. continuous
   c. intermittent assembly process
   d. synthetic - assembly process
   e. synthetic - process manufacturing

4. It sounds like Music-stor uses the synthetic process manufacturing system to create the product. This would most likely be an intermittent process, as the machines or molds may need to be changed when they go from producing the retail version to the built-in version, or when they change colors according to manufacturer.

   Music-stor needs to keep track of its own inventory, as well as that of the auto assembly plants and their retail customers. Enterprise resource planning is a sophisticated computer-based operations system that would link Music-stor with their suppliers, as well as with their customers. With this system, Music-stor could track the availability of the plastic they need from their supplier. They could monitor their own inventory to ensure adequate stock at crucial times, and be sure that their customers have what they need when they need it to keep production flowing smoothly, and sales at the retail level from slacking off.

Learning Goal 4

5. Flexible manufacturing systems, lean manufacturing and mass customization are all ways companies have available to put customer needs first. Manufacturers can custom-make goods at a very low cost very quickly, which is exactly what consumers want!

6. a. Just-in-time inventory control
   b. Lean manufacturing
   c. Competing in time
   d. Mass customization
   e. Flexible-manufacturing system

Learning Goal 5

7. Modular construction means that most parts are preassembled into a few large components called modules. Workers no longer work individually but are grouped at workstations. So, workers are grouped into teams who perform a whole cluster of tasks. These teams have become an integral part of American companies.

8. CAD/CAM is the integration of computers into the design and manufacture of products. This process has enabled manufacturers to tailor products to meet the needs of individual consumers at very little or no extra cost. A simple design change can be incorporated directly into the production line. It is what has enabled the Levi Strauss Company to offer "custom made" jeans at very little additional cost. CAD/CAM systems have revolutionized the production process and have essentially created and allowed for the concept of mass customization.

9. Like many others, managers at your firm may have believed that high tech equipment and processes are the only way to move into the future and remain competitive. Recent studies have indicated, however, that the manufacturing companies that did the best job of improving productivity have been those that have had a strong people orientation combined with the new technology.

    One of the first places to start may be in the area of customer service. Workers need to be made aware of the importance of focusing on the customer, fast response and delivery time of high quality products in an increasingly competitive marketplace.

    Further, these workers need more training time, or perhaps more highly skilled workers need to be hired. The workers need to have training in working in teams and to understand the concepts of total quality and continuous improvement.

    Managers need to be trained to deal with workers who are more highly skilled, and who demand a more participative management style.

    The company may also need to work with its suppliers. If the company has implemented such programs as JIT, or plans to implement a program along the lines of enterprise resource networking, adjustments need to be made, and open communication with suppliers is a must.

Learning Goal 6

10. As bigger businesses increase the use of sophisticated manufacturing technology, they will be able to meet the changing needs of their markets much more quickly. This weakens one advantage small businesses have had, which has been the ability to adapt quickly to changing customer markets. Additionally, big businesses are now able to customize their products, enabling them to meet the needs of smaller target markets, traditionally a stronghold for smaller businesses.

11. To cook a breakfast of 3-minute eggs, buttered toast and coffee, a PERT chart may look like this:

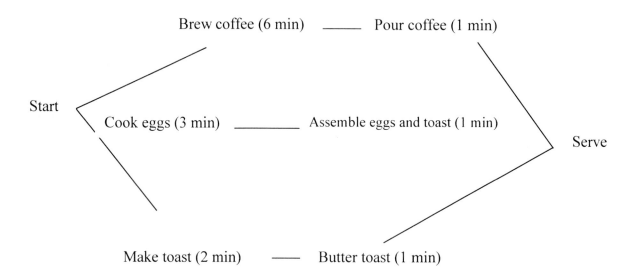

The critical path is the brewing and pouring of the coffee, as it takes the longest time to complete.

12. Total quality means satisfying customers by building in and ensuring quality from product planning to production, purchasing, sales, and service. In essence, the customer is ultimately the one who determines what the standard for quality should be, so emphasis is placed on customer satisfaction, and the fact that quality is everyone's concern. A total quality management program begins by analyzing what the consumer expects in terms of quality, and then continues by designing that level of quality into the products. Every product must meet those standards every step of the way in the production process.

Learning Goal 7

13. Your answers to this question will vary, but think about the kinds of services you make use of every day. At the grocery store, your groceries are probably checked out by using a bar code reader, and you can use your ATM at the grocery store as well as at the gas station.

    Have you ever bought a book or any other item over the Internet? Have you registered for a class electronically, watched the movie *Toy Story*, *Titanic*, or some other movie which used digital imaging? The ways technology has affected each of us are myriad, and will continue to increase!

PRACTICE TEST

Multiple Choice				True/False			
1.	d	9.	b	1.	T	9.	F
2.	b	10.	a	2.	T	10.	T
3.	d	11.	c	3.	T	11.	T
4.	c	12.	c	4.	F	12.	F
5.	a	13.	a	5.	F	13.	F
6.	b	14.	c	6.	T	14.	T
7.	a	15.	c	7.	F	15.	T
8.	c			8.	T		

CHAPTER 10
MOTIVATING EMPLOYEES AND BUILDING SELF-MANAGED TEAMS

LEARNING GOALS

After you have read and studied this chapter, you should be able to:

1. Explain Taylor's scientific management.

2. Describe the Hawthorne studies and relate their significance to human-based management.

3. Identify the levels of Maslow's hierarchy of needs and relate its importance to employee motivation.

4. Differentiate among Theory X, Theory Y and Theory Z.

5. Distinguish between motivators and hygiene factors identified by Herzberg.

6. Explain how job enrichment affects employee motivation and performance.

7. Identify the steps involved in implementing a management by objectives (MBO) program.

8. Explain the key factors involved in expectancy theory.

9. Examine the key principles of equity theory.

LEARNING THE LANGUAGE

Listed below are important terms found in the chapter. Choose the correct term for each definition and write it in the space provided.

Esteem needs	Job simplification
Equity theory	Management by objectives (MBO)
Expectancy theory	Motion economy
Extrinsic reward	Motivators
Goal-setting theory	Physiological needs
Hawthorne effect	Safety needs
Hygiene factors	Scientific management
Intrinsic reward	Self-actualization needs
Job enlargement	Social needs
Job enrichment	Time-motion studies
Job rotation	

1. Elements of a job called _____ cause dissatisfaction if missing, but do not motivate if increased.

2. The process of _____ produces task efficiency by breaking down the job into simple steps and assigning people to each of those steps.

3. The needs for peace and security are called _____.

4. _____ are studies of the tasks performed to complete a job and the time needed to do each task.

5. An _____ is the good feeling you have when you have done a job well.

6. The need for self-confidence and status is called _____.

7. A system of goal setting and implementation known as _____ involves a cycle of discussion, review, and evaluation of objectives among top and middle-level managers, supervisors, and employees.

8. A strategy known as _____ combines a series of tasks into one assignment that is more challenging, interesting and motivating.

9. The needs to feel loved, accepted and part of the group are called _____.

10. An _____ is reinforcement from someone else as recognition for good work, including pay increases, praise and promotions.

11. Efforts to make jobs more interesting, challenging and rewarding are known as _____.

12. Factors known as _____ provide satisfaction and motivate people to work.

13. _____ is the idea that setting specific, attainable goals can motivate workers and improve performance if the goals are accepted, accompanied by feedback and facilitated by organizational conditions.

14. The needs for basic life-giving elements such as food, water and shelter are known as _____.

15. The _____ refers to the tendency for people to behave differently when they know they are being studied.

16. Known as _____, this is a job enrichment strategy involving moving employees from one job to another.

17. _____ are the needs to achieve and be all that you can be.

18. The theory of _____ is that every job can be broken down into a series of elementary motions.

19. Victor Vroom's _____ indicates that the amount of effort employees exert on a specific task depends on their expectations of the outcome.

20. The study of workers to find the most efficient way of doing things and then teaching people those techniques is known as _____.

21. _____ is the theory that employees try to maintain perceived balance between inputs and outputs compared to others in similar positions.

RETENTION CHECK

Learning Goal 1   **The Importance of Motivation**

1. What is the difference between an intrinsic reward and an extrinsic reward?

2. Who is known as the Father of Scientific Management?

3. What three elements were basic to Taylor's Scientific Management?

   a. _____   b. _____   c. _____

4. What did Taylor believe was the key to improving productivity?

5. What is Gantt known for?

6. What contribution to scientific management was made by Frank and Lillian Gillbreth?

7. What view of workers was held by proponents of scientific management?

Learning Goal 2 **The Hawthorne Studies (Mayo)**

8. What did the Hawthorne Experiments set out to test?

9. What was the problem with the initial experiments?

10. Why did the experimenters believe the Hawthorne Experiments were a failure after the second series of experiments?

11. List three conclusions drawn from the Hawthorne Experiments.

   a. _____

   _____

   b. _____

   _____

   c. _____

   _____

12. What is the Hawthorne effect?

13. How did research change after the Hawthorne Experiments?

Learning Goal 3   **Motivation and Maslow's Hierarchy of Needs**

14. What did Maslow believe about motivation?

15. What are the five need levels on Maslow's Hierarchy?

   a. _____ d. _____

   b. _____ e. _____

   c. _____

16. According to Maslow, what kinds of needs are people motivated to satisfy?

17. What must U.S. firms do with regard to motivation, in order to successfully compete?

Learning Goal 4   **McGregor's Theory X and Theory Y**

18. List the assumptions of a Theory X manager.

   a. _____

   b. _____

   c. _____

   d. _____

19. How do the attitudes of a Theory X manager affect his/her behavior?

20. What are the assumptions of a Theory Y manager?

   a. _____

   b. _____

   c. _____

   d. _____

   e. _____

   f. _____

   g. _____

21. How does this manager's attitude affect his/her behavior toward employees?

22. What steps should management follow in order to use "empowerment" as a motivator?

   a. _____

   b. _____

   c. _____

23. What is the management trend in today's companies? Why?

24. List the major elements of Ouchi's Theory Z.

    a. _____

    b. _____

    c. _____

    d. _____

25. How well have Theory Z principles been accepted in the U.S.?

26. Why have U.S. firms had this result with Theory Z?

Learning Goal 5 **Herzberg's Motivating Factors**

27. What did Herzberg's research find were the most important factors that motivate workers?

   a. _____   h. _____

   b. _____   i. _____

   c. _____   j. _____

   d. _____   k. _____

   e. _____   l. _____

   f. _____   m. _____

   g. _____   n. _____

28. Identify Herzberg's motivators.

   a. _____

   b. _____

   c. _____

   d. _____

   e. _____

29. List Herzberg's hygiene factors.

   a. _____

   b. _____

   c. _____

   d. _____

   e. _____

30. What impact do hygiene factors have on workers?

31. What conclusions come from combining Theory Y with Herzberg's motivating factors?

Learning Goal 6   **Job Enrichment**

32. How is job enrichment implemented?

33. List the five characteristics of work important in affecting individual motivation and performance.

   a. _____

   b. _____

   c. _____

   d. _____

   e. _____

34. What is the difference between job enlargement and job rotation?

Learning Goal 7 **Goal Setting Theory and Management By Objectives**

35. What is the basic principle of goal-setting theory?

36. What four things must a manager do in an MBO program?

   a. _____

   b. _____

   c. _____

   d. _____

37. What are the six steps in an MBO program?

   a. _____

   b. _____

   c. _____

   d. _____

   e. _____

   f. _____

38. What is the difference between helping and coaching?

Learning Goal 8   **Meeting Employee Expectations: Expectancy Theory**

39. According to expectancy theory, what are three questions employees ask before exerting maximum effort to a task?

   a. _____

   b. _____

   c. _____

40. What are the steps to improving employee performance, according to expectancy theory?

   a. _____

   b. _____

   c. _____

   d. _____

   e. _____

Learning Goal 9   **Treating Employees Fairly: Equity Theory**

41. What is the basic principle of equity theory?

42. What do people do when they perceive an inequity?

43. What's a key point to remember about equity theory?

44. What are three general ways companies can encourage open communication

    a. _____

    b. _____

    c. _____

45. What are two things companies with highly motivated work forces have done?

46. What is meant by "re-inventing work?"

   a. _____

   b. _____

   c. _____

   d. _____

   e. _____

47. Describe the lessons learned about motivation from the Miller Brewery Company and the Mary Kay examples?

   a. _____

   b. _____

   c. _____

48. Where will motivation come from in the future?

49.   What four attitudes correlate with higher profits?

   a. _____

   b. _____

   c. _____

   d. _____

CRITICAL THINKING EXERCISES

Learning Goal 1

1.   Early management studies were conducted by:

   Frederick Taylor
   Frank and Lillian Gilbreth
   H.L. Gantt
   Elton Mayo Hawthorne studies

   Read the following and indicate which ideas are being described.

   a.   Conducted a series of experiments designed to measure the effect of working conditions on worker productivity. _____

   b.   These studies became the basis for human-based management. _____

   c.   Developed "therbligs". _____

   d.   Created time-motion studies to measure output over time. _____

   e.   Discovered that worker productivity could increase despite adverse conditions. _____

f. Believed the way to improve productivity was to scientifically study the most efficient way to do things, then teach people those methods. _____

g. Developed a chart plotting employees' work a day in advance. _____

h. The principle of motion economy was based on his theory. _____

i. Developed the principle of scientific management. _____

j. Discovered that when workers are involved in planning and decision making, productivity tends to increase. _____

k. Found that workers were motivated in an informal atmosphere where they could interact with supervisors. _____

l. Believed people would be motivated primarily by money. _____

m. Identified the tendency for people to behave differently when they know they are being studied. _____

n. Developed the idea that every job could be broken down into a series of elementary motions which could then be analyzed to make it more efficient. _____

o. His findings led to new assumptions about employees, including the idea that pay is not the only motivator for workers. _____

Learning Goals 1, 2

2. How did Taylor and other proponents of Scientific Management view workers?

   How does that compare to Mayo's Hawthorne Studies?

Learning Goal 3

3. The principle behind Maslow's ideas is that only unmet needs are motivators, and that needs could be arranged in a hierarchy.

   Complete the illustration shown below, and give two examples for each need level.

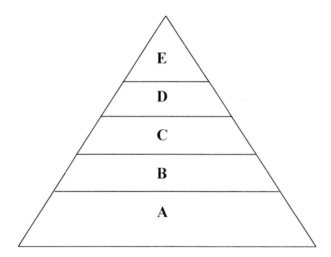

A._____   D._____

    1._____   1._____

10-19

    2. _____   2. _____

B. _____   E. _____

    1. _____   1. _____

    2. _____   2. _____

C. _____

    1. _____

    2. _____

4. Read the following statements, and determine which need on Maslow's Hierarchy is being described.

    a. Ryan Raley gets home from school and immediately raids the refrigerator. _____

    b. Jan Stahl joins as many campus organizations as she can fit into her schedule. _____

    c. Bill Cook wins "Zone Manager of the Month" in his sales office, in recognition of his outstanding performance. _____

    d. Wendy Armstrong, a 33 year old student with severe cerebral palsy, receives her bachelor's degree, a lifelong dream. _____

    e. A union contract negotiator makes sure that layoffs will be made on the basis of seniority. _____

5. In developed countries, people seek to fill social, esteem, and self-actualization needs at work. Give two actions that a company or a manager could take to fill each of these higher-level needs. What would motivate you?

   a. Social _____

   b. Esteem _____

   c. Self-actualization _____

Learning Goal 4

6. McGregor observed that managers had two different attitudes toward workers, which led to different management styles. He called these styles Theory X and Theory Y.

   Which type of manager would make each of the following statements?

   a. "Joe is pretty good at solving these kinds of problems. Let's get his input on this." _____

   b. "Ann, I know you'd like that promotion. Keep up the good work and I think you'll be the next new product manager." _____

   c. "Tell that secretary that if she values her job, she'll keep those coffee breaks down to 15 minutes!" _____

   d. "I think that secretary takes long coffee breaks because she gets her work done so quickly and then doesn't have much to do. She's been asking about working on the new product project. I'll talk to her about it and see what she thinks." _____

   e. "Ann, new product managers have to work a lot of weekends and evenings. If you think you want that job, you'll have to prove to me you're willing to work those extra hours." _____

7. What kind of leadership style would a Theory X manager use most often?

   Theory Y? Why?

8. What is empowerment, and how does it fit into Theory X/Y?

9. There have been questions as to the effectiveness of a Theory Z approach in "typical" U.S. firms. You have been learning about all the changes taking place in "typical" U.S. firms, and of the many changes made necessary by increasing global competition. Compare the philosophy of Theory Z to those changes and to the ideas in this chapter. Do you see any similarities?

Learning Goal 5

10. Workers at Universal Industries are among the best paid in the industry. Their factories are clean and workers seem to get along well with one another. "The bosses are okay," one worker is quoted as saying, "but they sure do hang around us a lot." The union has made sure that everyone has a secure position. Management at Universal is aware that their competitive position is in jeopardy, as several foreign firms have been making inroads into their market. Management is also aware that while there doesn't seem to be any problems with the workers, they don't seem to be motivated. Using Herzberg's theory of motivators and hygiene factors, discuss what the problem may be.

11. Make your own personal ranking of the 14 job-related factors listed in the text. Relate them to a job you have had, or currently have, to explain why you were or were not motivated!

1. _____   8. _____

2. _____   9. _____

3. _____   10. _____

4. _____   11. _____

5. _____   12. _____

6. _____   13. _____

7. _____   14. _____

Learning Goals 4, 5, 6

12. Using the outline below, illustrate the relationship between Maslow, Herzberg and where McGregor's X and Y managers would fall.

MASLOW   HERZBERG   MCGREGOR

13. What kind of leadership (or management) style would these theories indicate is best for motivating employees?

Learning Goal 6

14. Four job-design strategies are:

    job enrichment   job enlargement

    job simplification   job rotation

    Which of the following is being illustrated in each of the following examples?

    a. Employees at Published Image, a financial newsletter, are combined into a team so that one team has the entire responsibility of selling, advertising, writing, proofing, editing and distributing the newsletter to their own group of clients. While each member will specialize in a certain area, each member of the team knows enough about all the jobs to get the product out.

    b. New zone managers at Ford Motor Company move from one job to another during their training program, to familiarize themselves with the operations of the district sales office.

    c. At the Pasta House Company restaurant, you are either an expediter, a host, a busser or a server. The job lines don't cross, and are distinct from one another.

    d. At the Hosin Manufacturing Company, production is such that each worker makes an entire motor, instead of working only on separate parts.

15. Keeping in mind the five characteristics of work important in affecting motivation and performance, design an "enriched" job for publishing campus newsletters or for another area with which you are familiar.

16. How does job enrichment relate to Herzberg and Maslow?

17. Things have really been happening at Music-stor. Lots of changes have been made and it would seem like things ought to be going smoothly. However, there are problems with the workers, and you just can't figure out what's wrong. People don't seem to be motivated, although they are being paid well. You have been in charge, made the decisions you thought were best for the company and the workers, and have even pitched in and shown people how you want things done from time to time. Everybody has their own job, and they know exactly how it's supposed to be done. You have heard some people complain that their job is boring, but you know that the way you have shown them is the best way to get things done. People come in late, and sometimes seem to actually resent your help! You would really like the employees of this company to feel like they are a team. How will you solve this problem?

   Re-read your answer - Are you a Theory X or a Theory Y manager?

Learning Goal 7

18. Review the six steps of implementing an MBO program described in the text. How does an MBO program fit into the ideas of Maslow and Herzberg? Why is the third step a key step in the program? What are some potential problems with MBO?

Learning Goal 8

19. Think about expectancy theory and how it works for you. What is something you really want? How likely is it that you can reach the goal? Will the hard work be worth the effort? For example:

    What kind of job do you want as a career? (or, go back and review the exercise you completed in Chapter 6 on planning, when you were asked to write out some long-range and short-range goals for yourself)

    What do you need to do to get that kind of job? Is it possible to get that job if you exert the effort?

    What intrinsic and extrinsic benefits will you get from this kind of job?

20. Hal Yard is in marketing with a major manufacturer of sailboats. He has been happy with his job since he started there 3 years ago. He has received several raises, and has always gotten very good reviews. He is in line for a good promotion, which he should know about soon. Hal recently went to lunch with a new co-worker, Donna Telli. Donna just got her degree at night school, and this is her first "real" job. During the course of their conversation, Donna mentioned her starting salary is only $50 per month lower than Hal's!

How would you feel if you were Hal? Why? What would you do? What theories of motivation may come into play here?

21. In the end, who is most likely to motivate any individual? Where does a manager fit in?

PRACTICE TEST

Multiple Choice – Circle the best answer

1. Time and motion studies, methods of work and rules of work were all part of the ideas of _____.

    a. Maslow's hierarchy of needs
    b. Herzberg's two factor theory
    c. Taylor's scientific management
    d. the Hawthorne experiments

2. Which of the following was not determined as part of the Hawthorne experiments:

    a. Workers enjoyed the atmosphere of their special room.
    b. The workers thought of themselves as a social group.
    c. The workers were not involved in the planning of the experiment.
    d. Workers felt their ideas were respected.

3. Frederick Taylor believed the best way to improve worker productivity was to:

    a. scientifically determine the most efficient way to do things and then teach people.
    b. design jobs to be interesting and challenging.
    c. determine people's needs at work and find ways to meet those needs.
    d. give people the authority to make decisions.

4. Which of the following is not included as one of Maslow's needs?

    a. self-actualization
    b. social
    c. monetary
    d. esteem

5. Harry Leggins has worked for Shavem Up for a number of years. He has just been passed over for promotion, again, and is considering leaving because it seems that his managers don't appreciate his abilities. The only problem is that he really likes his co-workers, and they have an undefeated softball team. Harry is concerned with filling:

    a. esteem needs
    b. social needs
    c. self-actualization needs
    d. safety needs

6. Douglas McGregor believed that managers with a Theory X attitude believed:

    a. workers prefer to be directed.
    b. people seek responsibility.
    c. people will use imagination in problem solving.
    d. workers like work.

7. At Flo Valley Manufacturing, workers are encouraged to find their own solutions to problems, and to implement their solutions when practical. They work with little supervision because management feels they are committed workers, and that the workers are pretty creative. Flo Valley reflects a _____ attitude about workers.

    a. Theory Z   c. scientific
    b. autocratic   d. Theory Y

8. _____ emphasizes lifetime employment, collective decision making and few levels of management.

    a. Theory Z   c. Theory Y
    b. Theory X   d. Theory M

9. Herzberg motivators include:

    a. job security   c. working conditions
    b. salary   d. recognition

10. According to Herzberg, workers felt that good pay and job security

    a. are the most important motivators for most workers.
    b. were important for participative management.
    c. provided a sense of satisfaction, but did not motivate them.
    d. were the best way to keep jobs interesting and to help them achieve their objectives.

11. Which statement does not fit with the ideas of Herzberg and McGregor regarding the most effective way to motivate workers?

    a. Employees work best when mangers assume employees are self-motivated.
    b. The best way to motivate employees is to make sure they know exactly what to do and how to do it.
    c. Interesting jobs is one of the best ways to motivate workers.
    d. It is important to recognize achievement through advancement and added responsibility.

12. The strategy of making work interesting and motivating employees by moving them from one job to another is called:

    a. job enlargement
    b. job simplification
    c. job rotation
    d. job enrichment

13. The degree to which a job has a substantial impact on the work of others in the company is called:

    a. skill variety
    b. task identity
    c. autonomy
    d. task significance

14. At the NOVA car manufacturing company, workers are grouped into self-managed teams, which are responsible for completing a significant portion of the automobile. Unlike the typical assembly plant, the car stops along the way, and the team completes their portion of the car before the vehicle moves on. The team is given the freedom to decide who does which job, and they receive constant feedback from the company. NOVA is using a job strategy of:

    a. job rotation
    b. job enlargement
    c. job enrichment
    d. job simplification

15. Management by objectives calls for managers to do all of the following except:

    a. set goals for employees
    b. commit employees to goals
    c. monitor results
    d. reward accomplishment

16. Which of the following is not one of the questions employees will ask themselves before committing a maximum effort toward a task?

    a. Can I accomplish this task?
    b. Is the reward worth the effort?
    c. What do I need to do to accomplish this task?
    d. If I do accomplish the task, what is the reward?

17. Expectancy theory indicates that:

    a. people's needs affect their level of motivation.
    b. the amount of effort an employee puts forth depends on their expectations of the outcome.
    c. the perception of fairness will affect an employee's willingness to perform.
    d. employees expect to be involved in setting objectives.

18. According to equity theory, when workers perceive an inequity, they will

    a. try to reestablish an equitable feeling in a number of ways.
    b. always reduce their efforts in the future.
    c. always increase their effort in the future.
    d. generally be mistaken in their perceptions.

19. In most traditional organizations most communication:

    a. flows upward, from employees to management.
    b. flows laterally between departments and peers.
    c. flows downward from mangers to employees.
    d. flows both upward and downward.

20. To create an atmosphere of "us working together" and encourage open communication, managers should do everything but:

    a. provide feedback.
    b. eliminate separate facilities for managers.
    c. develop precise job descriptions so that everyone knows what to do.
    d. reward all upward communication, even if the discussion is negative.

21. According to the text, companies with highly motivated work forces have:

    a. open communication and self managed teams.
    b. autocratic leadership and bureaucratic structures.
    c. upward communication and Theory Z management styles.
    d. centralized decision making and interesting work.

22. The experiences of Mary Kay and Miller Brewing Company tell us:

    a. the future of industry and business depends upon advanced technology.
    b. motivation is best provided by managers.
    c. the first step to a motivation program is open communication.
    d. workers are primarily motivated by money and job security.

TRUE-FALSE

1. ____ The problem with the initial experiments of the Hawthorne study was that the productivity of the experimental group actually decreased when lighting was changed.

2. ____ The satisfaction you feel when you have finished a term paper and done a good job is an example of an extrinsic reward.

3. ____ Frank and Lillian Gilbreth developed the principle of motion economy and therbligs.

4. ____ The Hawthorne experiments led to new assumptions about workers, including that pay was not the only motivator.

5. ____ According to Maslow, people will always try to satisfy higher-level needs before they focus on lower-level needs.

6. ____ In developed countries, basic needs such as those for food and shelter dominate workers' motivation.

7. ____ A Theory X manager believes that employees should be involved in both defining problems and in designing the solutions.

8. ____ Theory Z principles have been widely adopted by American companies.

9. ____ Herzberg's research results showed that the most important factors that motivate workers were a sense of achievement and earned recognition.

10. ____ Goal-setting theory is based on the notion that managers should set specific goals to be reached.

11. ____ The basic principle of expectancy theory is that workers try to maintain equity when they compare what they expect to gain to people in similar situations.

12. ____ The concept of re-inventing work involves respecting workers, rewarding good work, developing worker skills and decentralizing authority.

ANSWERS

LEARNING THE LANGUAGE

1. Hygiene factors	8. Job enlargement	15. Hawthorne effect
2. Job simplification	9. Social needs	16. Job rotation
3. Safety needs	10. Extrinsic reward	17. Self-actualization needs
4. Time-motion studies	11. Job enrichment	18. Motion economy
5. Intrinsic reward	12. Motivators	19. Expectancy Theory
6. Esteem need	13. Goal-setting theory	20. Scientific management
7. Management by objectives	14. Physiological needs	21. Equity theory

RETENTION CHECK

Learning Goal 1 **The Importance of Motivation**

1. An intrinsic reward is a good feeling after having done a job well. It comes from within. An extrinsic reward is something given to you by someone else as recognition for good work

2. Frederick Taylor is known as the Father of Scientific Management.

3. The three basic elements of scientific management are:

   a. time   b. methods   c. rules of work

4. The way to improve productivity according to Taylor was to scientifically study the most efficient way to do things and then teach people those methods.

5. Gantt is known for charts which managers use to plot the work of employees a day in advance down to the smallest detail.

6. Frank and Lillian Gilbreth used Taylor's ideas to develop the principle of motion economy, which showed that every job could be broken down into a series of elementary motions called therbligs.

7. Scientific management viewed people largely as machines that needed to be programmed. There was little concern for psychological or human aspects of work.

Learning Goal 2   **The Hawthorne Studies (Mayo)**

8. Elton Mayo and his colleagues wanted to test the degree of lighting associated with optimum productivity.

9. The problem with the initial experiments was that productivity of the experimental group compared to other workers doing the same job went up regardless of whether the lighting was bright or dim.

10. The second series of experiments added a number of other environmental factors to the experiment, such as temperature and humidity. Productivity went up with each experiment. No matter what the experimenters did, productivity went up thus proving the initial ideas were invalid.

11. a. People in work groups think of themselves as a social group.
    b. Involving employees in decision making motivates them.
    c. Job satisfaction increases with a friendly atmosphere and additional compensation.

12. The Hawthorne Effect refers to the tendency for people to behave differently when they know they're being studied.

13. After the Hawthorne Experiments, the emphasis of research shifted away from Taylor's scientific management to a new human-based management.

Learning Goal 3   **Motivation and Maslow's Hierarchy of Needs**

14. Maslow believed that motivation arises from need.

15. The need levels of Maslow's Hierarchy are:

   a. Physiological
   b. Safety
   c. Social
   d. Self-esteem
   e. Self-actualization

16. Maslow believed that people are motivated to satisfy unmet needs. Needs that have been satisfied do not provide motivation.

17. To compete successfully, U.S. firms must create a work environment that motivates the best and brightest workers. This means establishing a work environment that includes goals such as social contribution, honesty, reliability, service, quality, dependability, and unity.

Learning Goal 4 **McGregor's Theory X and Theory Y**

18. A Theory X manager assumes:

   a. The average person dislikes work and will avoid it if possible.
   b. The average person must be forced, controlled, directed or threatened with punishment to make him/her work.
   c. The average worker prefers to be directed, wants to avoid responsibility, has little ambition and wants security.
   d. Primary motivators are money and fear.

19. A Theory X manager will hang over people, telling them what to do and how to do it. Motivation will take the form of punishment for bad work, rather than reward for good work. Workers are given little responsibility, authority, or flexibility.

20. A Theory Y manager assumes:

   a. The average person likes work, and feels it is as natural as play or rest.
   b. The average person naturally works toward goals to which they are committed.
   c. How committed a person is to goals depends on the rewards for achieving them.
   d. Under certain conditions, the average person accepts and seeks responsibility.
   e. People are capable of creativity, cleverness, and imagination.
   f. The average person's intellectual potential is only partially used in industry.
   g. People are motivated by a variety of rewards, unique to each worker.

21. A Theory Y manager will emphasize a more relaxed atmosphere, in which workers are free to set objectives, be creative, be flexible, and go beyond the goals set by management. A key factor in this environment is empowerment, which gives employees the ability to make decisions and the tools to implement the decisions they make.

22. In order to use empowerment as a motivator, a manager must:

    a. Find out what people think the problems in the organization are.
    b. Let them design the solutions.
    c. Get out of the way and let them put the solutions into action.

23. The trend today is toward a Theory Y management style. There are two basic reasons for this: Many service industries are finding Theory Y is more conducive to dealing with on-the-spot customer problems, and a more flexible management style may help U.S. firms meet and beat foreign competition.

24. The major elements of Ouchi's Theory Z are:

    a. virtually life-time employment
    b. emphasis on collective decision making
    c. slow evaluation and promotion
    d. few levels of management

25. Theory Z principles have never been widely accepted in the United States.

26. Theory Z principles go against some common cultural elements fundamental to the United States. We are more used to having the opportunity to move up quickly through the ranks. There are fewer management positions under a Theory Z style, and the chance to move up is what often motivates U.S. workers.

27. According to Herzberg's research, factors that motivate workers are:

   a. sense of achievement
   b. earned recognition
   c. interest in the work
   d. opportunity for growth
   e. opportunity for advancement
   f. importance of responsibility
   g. peer and group relationships
   h. pay
   i. supervisor's fairness
   j. company policies and rules
   k. status
   l. job security
   m. supervisor's friendliness
   n. working conditions

28. Herberg's motivators are:

   a. The work itself
   b. Achievement
   c. Recognition
   d. Responsibility
   e. Growth and advancement

29. Herberg's hygiene factors are:

   a. Company policy and administration
   b. Supervision
   c. Working conditions
   d. Interpersonal relations
   e. Salary

30. Workers felt that the absence of good pay, job security, friendly supervisors, and the like could cause dissatisfaction, but the presence of those factors did not motivate them; they just provided satisfaction and contentment in the work situation.

31. Employees work best when management assumes that employees are competent and self motivated. Theory Y calls for a participative style of management. The best way to motivate employees is to make the job interesting, help them to achieve their objectives, and recognize that achievement through advancement and added responsibility.

Learning Goal 6   **Job Enrichment**

32. In a program of job enrichment, work is assigned to individuals so that they have the opportunity to complete an identifiable task from beginning to end. They are held responsible for successful completion of the task.

33. Characteristics of work that affect motivation and performance are:

   a. Skill variety
   b. Task identity
   c. Task significance
   d. Autonomy
   e. Feedback

34. Job enlargement combines a series of tasks into one assignment that is more challenging, interesting, and motivating. Job rotation also makes work more interesting, but does so by moving employees from one job to another.

Learning Goal 7   **Setting Theory and Management by Objectives**

35. Goal-setting theory is based on the notion that setting specific but attainable goals will lead to high levels of motivation and performance if goals are accepted, accompanied by feedback and facilitated by organizational conditions.

36. Management by objectives calls on managers to:

   a. formulate goals in cooperation with everyone in the organization
   b. commit employees to those goals
   c. monitor results
   d. reward accomplishment

37. Steps in an MBO program are:

   a. Managers set goals in cooperation with subordinates and provide the means to meet them.
   b. Objectives are set for each department, including deadlines.
   c. Managers sit down with workers to discuss objectives which the workers commit to in writing.
   d. Constant two-way communication and review to show employees how they are doing.
   e. Objectives are matched with results, and corrections are made if necessary.
   f. Reward employees for achieving the goals.

38. Helping means working with the subordinates and doing part of the work if necessary. Coaching means acting as a resource, teaching, guiding and recommending, but not participating or actively doing the task.

Learning Goal 8   **Meeting Employee Expectations: Expectancy Theory**

39. Before exerting maximum effort employees will ask:

    a. Can I accomplish the task?
    b. If I do accomplish it, what's my reward?
    c. Is the reward worth the effort?

40. To improve employee performance according to expectancy theory, managers should:

    a. determine what rewards are valued by employees.
    b. determine the employee's desired performance standard.
    c. ensure performance standards are attainable.
    d. guarantee rewards are tied to performance.
    e. be certain rewards are considered adequate.

Learning Goal 9   **Treating Employees Fairly: Equity Theory**

41. The basic principle of equity theory is that workers try to maintain equity between inputs and outputs compared to people in similar positions.

42. When workers perceive an inequity, they will try to make the situation more equitable. They may change their behavior or rationalize the situation in some way.

43. A key element to equity theory is that equity, or inequity, is based upon perception of reality. Workers often overestimate their own contributions, and so they are often going to feel that there is a lot of inequity.

44. Open communication can be encouraged by:

    a. Creating an organizational culture that rewards listening by being listeners themselves, and by facilitating discussion.
    b. Training supervisors and managers in listening.
    c. Getting rid of barriers to open communication, such as separate offices, parking spaces, bathrooms, and other facilities for various levels of management and workers.

45. Companies with highly motivated work forces have established open communication and implemented self-managed teams.

46. Re-inventing work means:

   a. respecting workers.
   b. providing interesting work.
   c. rewarding good work.
   d. developing workers' skills.
   e. allowing autonomy.
   f. decentralizing authority.

47. The lessons learned from Miller Brewing and Mary Kay are:

   a. The future growth of industry and business in general depends on a motivated productive work force.
   b. Motivation is largely internal, generated by the workers themselves.
   c. The first step in any motivation program is to establish open communication among workers and managers, so that the feeling is one of cooperation and teamwork.

48. Motivation in the future will come from the job itself rather than from external punishments or rewards.

49. The four attitudes that correspond with high profits are:

   a. workers feel they are given the opportunity to do what they do best every day.
   b. they believe their opinions count.
   c. they sense that their fellow workers are committed to quality.
   d. the workers have made a connection between their work and the company's mission.

CRITICAL THINKING EXERCISES

Learning Goal 1

1.
   a. Mayo
   b. Hawthorne studies
   c. Gilbreths
   d. Taylor
   e. Mayo/Hawthorne studies
   f. Taylor
   g. Gantt
   h. Taylor
   i. Taylor
   j. Mayo/Hawthorne studies
   k. Mayo/Hawthorne studies
   l. Taylor
   m. Mayo/Hawthorne studies
   n. Gilbreths
   o. Mayo

Learning Goals 1, 2

2. Taylor and the other proponents of scientific management viewed people largely as machines which, properly programmed, could perform at a high level of effectiveness. Time and motion specialists studied every move a worker made, and standardized every motion. The most important tools were a stopwatch and observation. Taylor believed that workers would perform effectively with a high enough pay level because money would allow them to meet their basic needs.

   Although the Hawthorne studies grew out of Taylor's research, they came to a very different conclusion. Mayo began by studying environmental effects on worker productivity, with the idea of determining the degree of lighting associated with optimum productivity. When productivity increased regardless of the amount of illumination, a second series of experiments was conducted. When those, too, failed, Mayo guessed that some human or psychological factor was involved. When workers were interviewed about their feelings Mayo recognized that people were motivated at work by a relaxed atmosphere, being involved in decision making, and by being in a social group <u>as well as</u> by additional compensation.

   The Hawthorne Studies, then, recognized the human and psychological factors that impact worker productivity. This was different from scientific management, which ignored the human aspect of work.

Learning Goal 3

3. A. Physiological
      1. Food
      2. Rest
    B. Safety
      1. Locks on your doors
      2. Job security
    C. Social
      1. Belonging to a club
      2. Family life
    D. Esteem
      1. Winning an award
      2. Getting a desired promotion
    E. Self-actualization
      1. Accomplishing a goal
      2. Getting an "A" in a difficult class

4. a. Physiological
    b. Social
    c. Esteem
    d. Self-actualization
    e. Safety

5. a. To fill social needs companies could sponsor baseball teams, hold picnics, implement self-managed work teams, etc.
b. Esteem needs can be met by recognition programs, recognizing an employee's achievement in a company newsletter, allowing employees to participate in decision making.
c. To help fill self-actualization needs, companies could offer tuition assistance programs, provide job training, allow people to set their own goals, implement self-managed work teams, provide appropriate rewards for accomplishing objectives.

Learning Goal 4

6. a. Y   e. Y
   b. Y   f. X
   c. X

7. A Theory X manager would most likely use an autocratic style of leadership. When a manager believes that workers prefer to be told what to do, and do not want to assume responsibility, they are not likely to involve workers in decision making. A Theory X manager will make decisions, then announce the decision to his/her workers.

   A Theory Y manager is more likely to use a more democratic or participative leadership style. Employee input will be important to a Y manger, who believes that people are creative and seek responsibility. A Theory Y manager may also lean toward a laissez-faire leadership style.

8. Empowerment means giving employees the right to make decisions and the tools to implement those decisions. Theory Y emphasizes a "freer" managerial style where workers are free to set goals and reach them. In essence Theory Y empowers employees to reach their potential.

9. The changes we have learned about in this and previous chapters would appear to be fundamentally similar to the philosophy found in a Theory Z type corporation. We are seeing more worker participation in decision making, for example, which could be similar to collective decision making. As companies downsize and re-organize, they are reducing layers of management, and attempting to create a "team" atmosphere. With programs such as job enrichment and self-managed work teams, managers have had to place more trust and responsibility in workers. The figure comparing Theories X, Y and Z will show that many of the characteristics of Theory Z are found in the "new" management philosophies we have been learning about.

Learning Goal 5

10. From Herzberg's perspective, it looks like management and the union both have been concentrating on hygiene factors, while ignoring those factors which would motivate workers to greater productivity. The workers are apparently satisfied, as there are no problems, according to management. This means that the workers are content with pay, supervision, working conditions and interpersonal relations, as is indicated throughout the story. If management wants motivated workers, they should continue what they are doing now, but also find ways to give workers a sense of achievement, make the work more interesting, give workers more responsibility, a chance for growth and advancement. According to Herzberg, these are factors which will motivate workers.

11. The way you have ranked the 14 job-related factors Herzberg researched will be unique to you. Look, however, to see which type of things you ranked near the top, and near the bottom. Are motivators more important to you? Or did you focus on those factors Herzberg listed as hygiene factors? If the motivators ranked highest, you may want to look at firms that are using the "new" approach to management. If hygiene factors ranked highest, you may be happier in a more traditional organizational setting.

Learning Goals 4, 5, 6

12. Comparing Maslow, Herzberg and McGregor

MASLOW	HERZBERG	MCGREGOR
	Motivators	
self-actualization	challenge	Theory Y
	work itself	
self-esteem	achievement	participative management
	recognition	style
	responsibility	
	growth	
	Hygiene	
social	interpersonal relations	
safety	company policy	Theory X
	supervision	Autocratic management
	working conditions	style
physiological	salary	

13. Generally, these theories indicate that a participative or democratic management style is most effective in motivating most employees. Employees work best when management assumes that employees are competent and self motivated.

14. a. job enrichment c. job simplification
    b. job rotation d. job enlargement

15. An "enriched" job would include skill variety, task identity, task significance, autonomy and feedback. For publishing a newsletter, you could create self-managed teams, with each team member trained to do all the jobs necessary to get the newsletter out on deadline: editing, proofing, research, layout, selling, advertising, fielding questions. The team members will be responsible for deciding which member will do what job, what the deadline needs to be, how to coordinate with the other teams, and evaluation of their own performance. This meets all the criteria identified.

16. With job enrichment, work is assigned to individuals or groups so that they have the opportunity to complete an identifiable task from beginning to end. They are held responsible for successful completion of the task. The motivation comes from the opportunities for personal achievement, challenge and recognition, which are Herzberg's motivators, and which meet the higher-level needs on Maslow's hierarchy.

17. How you would solve these problems is a matter of personal style. However, there are some suggestions. You may want to sit down with these people and find out exactly what they think the problem is, or even if they recognize that there is a problem. It will help to listen to them, ask for their suggestions about how to solve the problems and implement those suggestions.

    It sounds like you have been making most of the decisions yourself, and not generally trusting these workers to be responsible. In other words, sounds like you have used a Theory X approach focusing on Herzberg's hygiene factors as a way to increase productivity. This may be appropriate in some instances, but you recall from previous chapters that these are the "new breed" of workers, who may prefer less direction and "bossing" and more "coaching." You can act as a resource, teaching, guiding and recommending, but not actively participating in doing work. Allow them to decide the most appropriate way of designing their jobs. Programs such as job enlargement may be appropriate, or job rotation. You may also consider self-managed teams. Many of the programs and theories described in this chapter may provide the solution to your problems.

Learning Goal 7

18. MBO programs fill upper-level needs on Maslow's hierarchy and serve as motivators in Herzberg's terms, by giving workers responsibility, a chance for growth and helping them to meet their own personal goals. The third step is a key one because it focuses on the participative management aspects of MBO, which is the type of leadership or management style these theories support.

    The key to effective goal-setting theory is involving everyone in setting the goals. This motivates them by making them feel part of the team.

Learning Goal 8

19. The answer to this question will depend on what your goals are, and how hard you are willing to work to reach them. The level of motivation you feel will be determined, according to expectancy theory, by how strongly you value what you say your goals are, and whether or not you feel like you can "make the grade," or get the kind of job you want. And lastly, in the end, your motivation will be determined by whether or not you feel that the effort would actually be worth it.

20. If you were Hal, you may feel like there is an inequity in your level of compensation compared to Donna's. This is equity theory at work! After all, she is new, and you have been a good employee for three years. What you would do will depend upon your own view of how big the inequity is. You may choose to talk to your boss, work harder to get promoted and recognized, work a little less for a while, rationalize the inequity in some way, or take the afternoon off!

21. In the end, it is really the individual that motivates him or herself. The manager's job is to understand that all workers are different and respond to different motivational styles. Managers will have to get to know each worker as an individual and fit the "reward" to each individual. Rewards will come from the job itself, rather that from external rewards. Managers need to give workers what they need to do a good job: the right tools, the right information and the right amount of cooperation.

PRACTICE TEST

Multiple Choice				True/False			
1.	c	12.	c	1.	F	12.	T
2.	c	13.	d	2.	F		
3.	a	14.	c	3.	T		
4.	c	15.	a	4.	T		
5.	a	16.	c	5.	F		
6.	a	17.	b	6.	F		
7.	d	18.	a	7.	F		
8.	a	19.	c	8.	F		
9.	d	20.	c	9.	T		
10.	c	21.	a	10.	F		
11.	b	22.	c	11.	F		

CHAPTER 11
HUMAN RESOURCE MANAGEMENT

LEARNING GOALS

After you have read and studied this chapter, you should be able to:

1. Explain the importance of human resource management and describe current issues in managing human resources.

2. Summarize the six steps in planning human resources.

3. Describe methods companies use to recruit new employees and explain some of the problems that make recruitment challenging.

4. Outline the six steps in selecting employees.

5. Illustrate the use of various types of employee training and development methods.

6. Trace the six steps in appraising employee performance.

7. Summarize the objectives of employee compensation programs and describe various pay systems and fringe benefits.

8. Explain scheduling plans managers use to adjust to workers' needs.

9. Describe the ways employees can move through a company: promotion, reassignment, termination, and retirement.

10. Illustrate the effects of legislation on human resource management.

LEARNING THE LANGUAGE

Listed below are important terms found in the chapter. Choose the correct term for the definition and write it in the space provided.

Affirmative action	Job analysis	On-the-job training
Apprenticeship	Job description	Performance appraisal
Cafeteria-style fringe benefits	Job sharing	Recruitment
Compressed workweek	Job simulation	Reverse discrimination
Core time	Job specifications	Selection
Employee orientation	Management development	Training and development
Flextime plan	Mentor	Vestibule training

| Fringe benefits | Networking | |
| Human resource | Off-the-job training | |

1. The set of activities called _____ are used to obtain a sufficient number of the right people at the right time to select those who best meet the needs of the organization.

2. The written summary of the qualifications required of a worker to do a particular job is called the _____.

3. A work schedule known as _____ gives employees some freedom to adjust when they work, as long as they work the required number of hours.

4. Employment activities designed to increase opportunities for minorities and women are known as _____.

5. A program known as a(n) _____ involves training a new worker alongside a master technician to learn the skills and procedures of a job.

6. The process of _____ is the training and educating of employees to become good managers and then developing managerial skills over time.

7. Known as _____, these include sick-leave pay, vacation pay, pension plans, and health plans that provide additional compensation to employees.

8. The feeling of unfairness that unprotected groups may have when protected groups are given preference in hiring and promoting is called _____.

9. An experienced employee known as a(n) _____ is one who supervises, coaches and guides selected lower-level employees by introducing them to the right people and groups and generally becomes their organizational sponsor.

10. The process of evaluating human resource needs is called _____, which involves finding people to fill those needs, and getting the best work from each employee by providing the right incentives and job environment, all with the goal of meeting organizational objectives.

11. A(n) _____ is a work schedule that involves the same number of hours per week in fewer days.

12. A(n) _____ is a study of what is done by employees who fill various job titles.

13. The process of _____ involves establishing and maintaining contacts with key managers in one's own organization and in other organizations and using those contacts to weave strong relationships that serve as informal development systems.

14. The process of gathering information to decide who should be hired, under legal guidelines, for the best interests of the individual and the organization is known as _____.

15. A program known as _____ consists of internal and external programs to develop a variety of skills and to foster personal development away from the workplace.

16. A(n) _____ is a summary of the objectives of a job, the type of work to be done, the responsibilities of the job, the necessary skills, the working conditions and the relationship of the job to other functions.

17. The _____ refers to the period when all employees are present in a flextime system.

18. An arrangement known as _____ is one whereby two part-time employees share one full-time job.

19. The program known as _____ is one where the employee immediately begins his or her tasks and learns by doing, or watches others for a while and then imitates them, right at the workplace.

20. _____ includes all attempts to improve employee performance by increasing an employee's ability to perform through learning.

21. The activity known as _____ initiates new employees to the organization, to fellow employees, to their immediate supervisors, and to the policies, practices and objectives of the firm.

22. A(n) _____ is an evaluation of the performance level of employees against established standards to make decisions about promotions, compensation, and additional training.

23. A type of training known as _____ is done in schools where employees are given instructions on equipment similar to that used on the job.

24. A program called _____ is a fringe benefits plan which allows employees to choose the benefits they want up to a certain dollar amount.

25. A training method that uses equipment that duplicates job conditions and tasks so that trainees can learn skills before attempting them on the job is _____.

RETENTION CHECK

Learning Goal 1   **Working With People is Just the Beginning**

1.   Identify the six functions of human resource management.

   a. _____   d. _____

   b. _____   e. _____

   c. _____   f. _____

2.   How has the role of human resource management changed in recent years?

3.   What are the challenges facing human resources management?

   a. _____

   b. _____

   c. _____

   d. _____

   e. _____

   f. _____

   g. _____

   h. _____

i. _____

j. _____

k. _____

4. Why has human resource management received increased attention in recent years?

Learning Goal 2 **Determining Your Human Resources Needs**

5. List the steps in human resource planning.

a. _____ d. _____

b. _____ e. _____

c. _____ f. _____

6. What information is included in a human resources inventory?

7. What's the difference between a job description and job specifications?

8. What affects future demand for employees?

9. What is likely to happen regarding supply of future employees?

Learning Goal 3   **Recruiting Employees From a Diverse Population**

10. What are some reasons recruiting has become more difficult?

    a. _____

    b. _____

    c. _____

11. What are three activities used in recruiting?

    a. _____

    b. _____

    c. _____

12. What are two general sources for recruiting?

   a. _____

   b. _____

13. What are some internal methods of recruiting?

   a. _____

   b. _____

   c. _____

14. What are some external sources of recruiting?

   a. _____

   b. _____

   c. _____

   d. _____

   e. _____

   f. _____

   g. _____

15. What are some of the newest tools used to recruit employees?

Learning Goal 4   **Selecting Employees Who Will Be Productive**

16. List the six steps in selecting employees.

    a. _____

    b. _____

    c. _____

    d. _____

    e. _____

    f. _____

17. Why is the selection process such an important element in the human resources program?

18. How do legal issues make the steps in the selection process more challenging?

19. What is the important element of employment tests?

20. What is the benefit of a trial period?

21. What are "contingent workers"?

22. What are the reasons firms hire contingent workers?

   a. _____

   b. _____

   c. _____

   d. _____

   e. _____

   f. _____

   g. _____

23. What are the ups and downs of being a contingent worker?

Learning Goal 5 **Training and Developing Employees for Optimum Performance**

24. What are three steps in the process of creating training and development programs?

    a. _____

    b. _____

    c. _____

25. What is the difference between training and development?

26. Identify seven types of training programs.

    a. _____

    b. _____

    c. _____

    d. _____

e. _____

f. _____

g. _____

27. In what type of situation is on-the- job training effective?

28. What types of jobs would you train for in an apprenticeship?

29. When is vestibule training used?

30. What kinds of jobs use job simulation type training?

31. What are the two basic elements of management development?

   a. _____

   b. _____

32. List four types of training included in management training programs.

   a. _____

   b. _____

   c. _____

   d. _____

33. What are three reasons for companies to develop mentoring and networking programs for women and minorities in the workplace?

   a. _____

   b. _____

   c. _____

Learning Goal 6 **Appraising Employee Performance**

34. What are the steps followed in a performance appraisal?

   a. _____

   b. _____

   c. _____

   d. _____

   e. _____

   f. _____

35. What three characteristics must performance standards have?

   a. _____ b. _____ c. _____

36. What decisions are based upon a performance appraisal?

37. What is the latest form of performance appraisal?

Learning Goal 7   **Compensating Employees**

38. Why have compensation and benefit packages become a major challenge in the 1990s?

39. List several objectives that can be accomplished by a well-managed compensation and benefit program.

   a. _____

   b. _____

   c. _____

   d. _____

   e. _____

   f. _____

40. Identify the various types of pay systems.

   a. _____

   b. _____

   c. _____

d. _____

e. _____

f. _____

41. What types of jobs are compensated on a commission basis?

42. Who gets bonuses?

43. What are two types of bonuses?

44. What is the Hay system of compensation?

45. What is the problem with paying members of a team based upon individual performance?

46. What are two types of pay systems based on team performance?

    a. _____

    b. _____

47. Describe a skill-based pay system for teams.

48. What are two problems with skill-based pay systems?

    a. _____

    b. _____

49. Describe a profit-sharing, or gain sharing, system of compensation for teams.

50. Where does individual compensation fit into these team-based plans?

51. What are some of the things included in a fringe benefits package?

52. Why have companies implemented cafeteria-style benefits packages?

Learning Goal 8 **Scheduling Employees**

53. What are 4 alternatives for job scheduling?

    a. _____

    b. _____

    c. _____

    d. _____

54. What are some benefits to flextime?

55. What are the disadvantages of flextime?

56. What is a disadvantage of a compressed work week?

57. What are the benefits to working at home?

   a. _____

   b. _____

   c. _____

   d. _____

   e. _____

58. What are four benefits to job sharing?

   a. _____

   b. _____

   c. _____

   d. _____

59. What are some disadvantages to job sharing for employers?

Learning Goal 9 **Moving Employees Up, Over, and Out**

60. What are four ways of moving employees through the organization?

   a. _____   c. _____

   b. _____   d. _____

61. What events have created a need for managers to manage layoffs and firings?

62. Why are companies hesitant to re-hire permanent employees?

63. What is the doctrine of "employment at will"?

64. How has the "employment at will" doctrine changed?

65. What are two tools used to downsize companies?

66. What are two advantages of early retirement programs?

Learning Goal 10 **Laws Affecting Human Resource Management**

67. What are six laws enacted to prevent discrimination in the workplace?

    a. _____

    b. _____

    c. _____

d. _____

e. _____

f. _____

68. What is the EEOC?

69. What powers does the EEOC have?

a. _____

b. _____

c. _____

70. What was the purpose of affirmative action programs?

71. What does Title VII of the Civil Rights Act of 1964 do?

72. What did the Civil Rights Act of 1991 do?

73. Who does the Vocational and Rehabilitation Act of 1973 protect?

74. What does the ADA require?

75. What difficulties are companies having in conforming to the ADA?

76. What did the Age Discrimination in Employment Act do?

77. Identify four important aspects of the impact of legislation on human resource management.

   a. _____

   b. _____

   c. _____

   d. _____

CRITICAL THINKING EXERCISES

Learning Goal 1

1. Six functions of human resource management are:

Human resource planning	Training and development
Recruitment	Evaluation
Selection	Compensation

   You have read in previous chapters of the changing structure of American business and about population trends occurring in the United States. In this chapter, we read about the challenges in human resource management. For each of the following, identify at least one area of human resource management that could be affected and how companies could respond to the change.

	AREA AFFECTED	COMPANY RESPONSE
a. Shortages of trained workers	_____	_____

b. An aging workforce   _____   _____
                                                     _____
                                                     _____

c. Increases in single parent
and two-income families   _____   _____
                                                     _____
                                                     _____

d. Changing attitude toward
work   _____   _____
                                                     _____
                                                     _____

e. Complex laws   _____   _____
                                                     _____
                                                     _____

f. Concern over work
environment and equality   _____   _____
                                                     _____
                                                     _____

Learning Goal 2

2.   Six steps in human resource planning are:

     Forecasting human resource needs.   Assessing future demand.

     Current human resource inventory.   Assessing future supply.

     Job analysis, description, specification.   Establishing a strategic plan.

Match the correct step to each of the following:

a. A large West Coast two-year college recently required its clerical staff to identify all the tasks involved in their jobs and to show how each job related to the other areas of their department. _____

b. Ford periodically requests employees to update information in their personnel file, for such things as recent courses taken, recent training programs and other employee information. _____

c. Chrysler anticipates that its plant managers will need to develop updated skills in new management techniques as technology changes. _____

d. Chrysler makes arrangements with a local college for on-site training for its plant managers, and arranges to retrain workers at state-sponsored retraining programs. _____

e. The human resources manager of a large East Coast firm gets statistics on the educational background of the graduating MBA classes of several East Coast colleges, including two schools with a large minority enrollment and two high-tech schools. _____

f. Based on a five-year strategic plan, a small business owner determines that he will need at least three additional sales people within the next two years, and one more office person with a computer background. _____

Learning Goal 3

3. Prepare a resume! Think about the kind of information you need to include on a resume that would make you "look" better than other people applying for the same job. Who do you think you should send this resume to? Talk to someone you know who is in charge of hiring. Ask them about the recruitment process, the selection process, and how new employees are trained at their company. What kind of fringe benefits does this company offer? What do they look for in new employees? What kind of questions does an interviewer ask a prospective employee?

4. Be observant! Look around you and observe how many ways you can notice that firms are using to recruit employees. Newspapers, radio, signs in windows, college placement office? What ways would you use to look for a job?

Learning Goal 4

5. A typical selection process may involve six steps:

   Complete an application.　　　　　　Background investigations.

   Initial and follow-up interviews.　　　Physical exams.

   Employment tests.　　　　　　　　　Trial periods.

   Match each of the following to the correct step in the selection process:

   a. Contributes to the high cost of turnover, but enables a firm to fire incompetent employees after a certain period of time. _____

   b. Helps a firm to determine the information about an employee that is pertinent to the requirements of the job. Legal guidelines limit what companies can ask. _____

   c. An investigation of previous work records and school records, and follow-up on recommendations. _____

   d. These have been criticized because of charges of cultural discrimination. They are most often used to measure specific job skills. _____

   e. Used to screen applicants after the application form has been reviewed. Gives the company an opportunity to assess communication skills. _____

   f. A major controversy in this step is preemployment drug testing to detect drug or alcohol abuse, and AIDS screening. _____

Learning Goals 1, 2, 3, 4

6. Music-stor needs the human resources manager to begin developing some job descriptions, identify the various skills needed to perform the different jobs in the company and to start to develop a recruitment and selection process. Select at least one job that will be a part of Music-stor's organization, write a job description, job specifications, and develop a plan for recruiting and selecting job candidates.

Learning Goal 5

7. Firms have several types of training programs available:

   Employee orientation.   Vestibule training.

   On-the-job training.   Job simulation.

   Apprentice programs.   Management development.

   Off-the-job training.

   Match the correct type of training program to each situation described:

   a. Before Tom Hershberger went to work for a construction firm, he had a lot of training on how to use the heavy equipment he was assigned to operate. _____.

   b. Bill Martin is a plumber. Before he became a journeyman, he had to work for several years alongside another plumber to learn the skills and procedures for the job. _____

   c. Maria Alvarez went on a sales call her second day on the job. She basically "learned by doing." _____

   d. Scott Toblin is learning to fly the newest, and largest, commercial aircraft, a 797. Before he takes it up in the air, he will work the control panel, and "land" on the runways of virtually every airport in the United States, all while staying right on the ground. _____

e. Bernie Breen spent three weeks at a seminar learning effective communications and human relations skills for his job as a middle manager in a major corporation.
   _____

f. In his first day on the job, Hong Nyu was introduced to several department managers, studied a corporate brochure describing all the company's products and saw a video of the history of his company. He was even assigned a mentor.
   _____

8. The text discusses networking, and its importance in business. How could networking become even more important in the future, and how can you start now to develop a "network?"

Learning Goal 6

9. You are the newly appointed sales manager for Music-stor, and your job is to develop a new appraisal system that is effective and objective. This is the first real test of your skills as a manager. What, specifically, do you think you should do? In other words, what kinds of things will you include on an appraisal form, and then what will you do after that's completed?

10. Right now at Music-stor, you have a salesperson who doesn't seem to be performing the way she should. You know something must be done. This is a real test of your management skills. What will you do?

Learning Goal 7

11. In the competitive environment of the 1990s, compensation and fringe benefit packages are being given special attention. A good program can accomplish several benefits for an organization.

    Basic pay systems include:

Salary systems.	Commission plans.
Hourly wage.	Bonus plans.
Piecework.	Profit-sharing.

    Give a suggested pay system for each situation described below. Your suggestion can be a combination of systems:

    a. A sales job that includes a variety of nonselling functions such as advising, keeping records and setting up displays. _____

    b. An assembly-line operation in which each worker completes several tasks before the product moves to the next station. _____

    c. An office manager just starting out with new office equipment designed to increase productivity. _____

    d. The president of a small firm that makes computer chips. _____

    e. A worker in a garment factory, making shirts. _____

12. How can a company ensure its benefits programs meet the needs of a changing workforce? Why is that important?

Learning Goal 8

13. Changing workforces mean changing schedules for many companies and their employees. Some alternative work schedules are:

    Job sharing.   Compressed work weeks.

    Flextime plans.   In-home work.

    What kind of program is being described:

    a. This type of program can give an employee a break, and lets them sleep in once in a while! _____

    b. At Readers Guide, employees work 35 hours in 4 days for each week in May, giving everyone a three day weekend. _____

    c. At St. Lukes Hospital, Julie Andersen works as an accountant every morning, and Mary Krull takes over each afternoon. _____

    d. Felicia Hill has a fax, modem, and a computer that she carries with her wherever she goes, but she doesn't have an office. _____

    e. Some of the benefits of this schedule include a reduction in absenteeism and tardiness, because people can handle their other duties in off hours. _____

    f. With this program, John and Elena Morina can schedule their days so that one of them is home to see their children off in the morning, and the other is home when the children come home from school. _____

g. One of the disadvantages of this program is the need to hire, train and supervise twice as many people. _____

h. Gil Pfaff likes this schedule, because it allows him to avoid the heavy morning traffic during his commute to work. _____

i. Manager David Whitsell likes this program because he has found workers who take advantage of it are often more productive and it's easier for him to schedule people into peak demand periods for his department. _____

j. Debbie Rhodes schedules doctor's appointments on days when she comes in early and leaves early. _____

14. How have the changes in the workforce and in the workplace, discussed in this and other chapters, affected the ways companies move employees around?

15. How have changes in the "make-up" of the workforce - more immigrants, more minorities, more women, and so on, affected corporations from a legal perspective?

PRACTICE TEST

Multiple Choice: Circle the best answer.

1. Human resources management does not include:

    a. leading
    b. evaluation
    c. recruitment
    d. selection

2. Which of the following would not be included in a discussion of the challenges faced by human resource managers?

    a. Shortages of people trained to work in growth areas
    b. A growing population of workers who need retraining
    c. Challenges from an overseas labor pool available for lower wages
    d. Fewer older workers, and too many of them that want to retire, making it difficult to fill their jobs

3. A human resource inventory will provide information about:

    a. what is done by various employees who fill different job titles.
    b. whether or not the labor force is paid adequately.
    c. the strategic plan for recruiting, selecting, training and development.
    d. education, capabilities, training and specialized skills to determine if the company' labor force is technically up-to-date.

4. "Clerical worker, with responsibilities of answering phones, greeting clients, and filing for human resources department. Some weekends required." This is an example of a:

    a. job analysis.
    b. job specification.
    c. job description.
    d. job evaluation.

11-33

5. According to the text, the greatest advantage of hiring from within is:

   a. it is quick.
   b. it requires less training.
   c. it helps maintain employee morale.
   d. it keeps the firm from having an oversupply of workers trained in certain areas.

6. Which of the following is not included in a list of reasons why recruiting has become difficult?

   a. Sometimes people with necessary skills aren't available.
   b. The number of available recruiting tools has begun to shrink.
   c. The emphasis on participative management makes it important to hire people who fit in with the corporate culture.
   d. Some companies have unattractive work places and policies which make it difficult to recruit.

7. What is the first step in the selection process?

   a. completing an application form
   b. contacting an employment agency
   c. background investigation
   d. interviews

8. Background investigations:

   a. are no longer legal.
   b. help weed out candidates that are not likely to succeed.
   c. include an investigation of skills
   d. are not good predictors of who will be successful.

9. The use of contingent workers

   a. is more expensive than hiring full time workers.
   b. is appropriate when jobs require minimum training.
   c. is declining.
   d. is not a good way to find good employees.

10. Internal and external programs to develop a variety of skills and to foster personal development away from the job is called:

    a. off-the-job training.
    b. vestibule training.
    c. an apprentice program.
    d. employee orientation.

11. _____ is a type of training that exposes managers to different functions of the organization by giving them assignments in a variety of departments.

    a. Understudy positions
    b. On-the-job coaching
    c. Job enlargement
    d. Job rotation

12. In developing a performance appraisal, standards should have all of the following characteristics except:

    a. They should be specific.
    b. They should be subject to measurement.
    c. They should be easily attainable.
    d. They should be reasonable.

13. The latest form of performance appraisal requires feedback from up, down and around the employee and is called a:

    a. 360 degree review.
    b. turnaround review.
    c. complete feedback review.
    d. total review.

14. Ima Gogetter is interested in making a lot of money! He is a very good salesperson. People tell him he could sell ice to an Eskimo! He is a very hard worker, and is willing to work a lot of hours to make the kind of money he wants. Ima should look for the kind of job that is paid:

    a. on salary with overtime.
    b. hourly.
    c. with profit sharing.
    d. on commission.

15. Studies of compensation for teams have shown that:

    a. it is recommended that pay should be based on team performance.
    b. team-based pay programs are pretty well developed and need not be changed.
    c. team members should be compensated as individuals.
    d. skill-based pay programs are relatively easy to apply.

16. A program that gives employees freedom to adjust when they work, as long as they work the required number of hours is called:

    a. job sharing.
    b. flextime.
    c. a compressed workweek.
    d. home based work.

17. Which of the following is not a benefit of job sharing?

    a. reduced absenteeism
    b. ability to schedule people into peak demand periods
    c. a high level of enthusiasm and productivity
    d. less supervision

18. The effect of downsizing on human resources management has been that:

    a. fewer layers of management make it more difficult for employees to be promoted to higher levels of management.
    b. companies are now scrambling to re-hire those workers who were laid off.
    c. a decrease in the level of complexity of managing human resources.
    d. less need to adhere to employment law.

19. Affirmative action programs:

    a. are no longer legal and have had to be thrown out.
    b. were designed to "right past wrongs" endured by females and minorities.
    c. came into being as a result of the ADA.
    d. refer to problems experienced with reverse discrimination.

20. Title VII of the Civil Rights Act:

    a. requires that disabled applicants be given the same consideration for employment as people without disabilities.
    b. prevents businesses from discrimination against people with disabilities on the basis their physical or mental handicap.
    c. prohibits discrimination in hiring, firing, and other areas on the basis of race, religion, creed, sex or national origin.
    d. gives the victims of discrimination the right to a jury trail and punitive damages.

TRUE-FALSE

1. ____ Qualified labor is more scarce today, which makes recruiting and selecting more difficult.

2. ____ Job descriptions are statements about the person who does the job.

3. ____ The newest tools used to recruit employees are Internet online services.

4. ____ The application form and the initial interview are good ways for a company to find out about an applicant's family and religious backgrounds.

5. ____ It can be more cost effective for a company to hire contingent workers rather than hire permanent employees when more workers are needed.

6. ____ In an apprentice program, a worker immediately begins his or her tasks and learns by doing.

7. ____ In a mentoring program, an older, more experienced worker will coach and guide a selected lower-level manager by introducing him or her to the right people and groups.

8. ____ Decisions about promotions, compensation, additional training and firing are all based upon performance evaluations.

9. ____ While compensation and benefits packages are important to keep employees, these programs play little role in attracting qualified employees.

10. ____ Most companies have found that compensating teams is a relatively straightforward issue.

11. ____ Some companies have found that telecommuting has helped the company to save money.

12. ____ Legislation to prevent employer abuse in firing workers has restricted management's ability to terminate workers as it increased workers' rights to their jobs.

13. ____ While early retirement programs are a more expensive strategy of downsizing than laying off employees, it can increase the morale of remaining employees.

14. ____ Legislation and legal decisions have had little effect on human resource management.

15. ____ The EEOC is charged with enforcing affirmative action programs.

ANSWERS

KEY TERMS AND DEFINITIONS

1. Recruitment	14. Selection
2. Job specifications	15. Off-the-job training
3. Flextime plan	16. Job description
4. Affirmative action	17. Core time
5. Apprenticeship	18. Job sharing
6. Management development	19. On-the-job training
7. Fringe benefits	20. Training and development
8. Reverse discrimination	21. Employee orientation
9. Mentor	22. Performance appraisal
10. Human resource management	23. Vestibule training
11. Compressed work week	24. Cafeteria-style benefits
12. Job analysis	25. Job simulation
13. Networking	

RETENTION CHECK

Learning Goal 1   **Working With People Is Just the Beginning**

1.
   a. Human resource planning
   b. Recruitment
   c. Selection
   d. Training and development
   e. Evaluation
   f. Compensation

2. Historically firms assigned the functions of human resources management, such as recruiting, selecting, training and so on, to various functional departments. "Personnel" was viewed mostly as a clerical function responsible for screening applications, keeping records, processing payroll and finding people when necessary. Today the job of human resource management has taken on a new role in the firm. It has become so important that it is a function of all managers.

3. Challenges of human resource management include:
   a. Shortages of people trained to work in growth areas.
   b. Large numbers of workers from declining industries who need retraining.
   c. A growing population of new workers who are poor and undereducated.
   d. A shift in the age composition of the work force, including older workers and baby boomers.
   e. Complex laws in human resource management.
   f. Increasing numbers of single parent and two-income families who need programs like day care, job sharing and family leave.
   g. Changing employee attitudes toward work with leisure having a greater priority.
   h. Downsizing and its effect on morale and need for contingency workers.
   i. Challenges from an overseas labor pool.
   j. Increased demand for benefits tailored to the individual.
   k. Growing concern for issues such as health care, elder care and employment for people with disabilities.

4. Human resources management has received greater attention recently because in the past, labor, or "human resources" was plentiful, and there was little need to nurture and develop the labor force. If you needed qualified people, all you had to do was hire them. If they didn't work out, you could simply hire others. Qualified labor is scarcer today, and that makes the whole area of human resources management more challenging.

Learning Goal 2   **Determining Your Human Resources Needs**

5. The steps in human resource planning are:
   a. Forecast human resource needs.
   b. Prepare an inventory of current human resource information.
   c. Prepare job analyses, job descriptions, and job specifications.
   d. Determine future demand, including what training programs may be needed.
   e. Determine the future supply of human resources with needed skills.
   f. Establish a strategic plan for recruiting, selecting, training, evaluating and scheduling.

6. A human resources inventory includes ages, names, education, capabilities, training, specialized skills and other information pertinent to the organization, such as languages spoken. This information reveals whether or not the labor force is technically up-to-date and thoroughly trained.

7. A job description specifies the objectives of the job, the types of work to be done, responsibilities and duties, working conditions and the relationship of the job to other functions. Job specifications specify the qualifications of the individual, need to fill the job. In other words, the job description is about the job, and job specifications are about the person who does the job.

8. The demand for employees will be affected by changing technology. Often training programs must be started long before the need is apparent.

9. There are likely to be increased shortages of some skills in the future, and an oversupply of other types of skills.

Learning Goal 3 **Recruiting Employees From a Diverse Population**

10. Recruiting has become difficult because:
    a. Sometimes people with the right skills are not available, and must be hired and trained internally.
    b. The emphasis on culture, teamwork, and particitipative management makes it important to hire the right kind of people.
    c. Some organizations have unattractive workplaces, policies that demand promotion from within or other situations that make recruiting and keeping employees difficult.

11. Activities used in recruiting are:
    a. Finding.　　　　　b. Hiring.　　　　　c. Training.

12. Sources for recruiting are:
    a. Internal sources.　　　　　b. External sources.

13. Internal methods of recruiting are:
    a. Transfers.　　　　　b. Promotions.　　　　　c. Employee recommendations.

14. External sources of recruiting are:
    a. Advertisements.
    b. Public and private employment agencies.
    c. College placement bureaus.
    d. Management consultants.
    e. Professional organizations.
    f. Referrals.
    g. Applicants who appear at the workplace.

15. Some of the newest tools used to recruit employees are Internet online services.

Learning Goal 4   **Selecting Employees Who Will Be Productive**

16. Steps in selecting employees are:

    a. Completion of an application form.   d. Background investigations.

    b. Initial and follow-up interviews.   e. Physical exams.

    c. Employment tests.   f. Trial periods.

17. The selection process is so important because the cost of selecting and training employees has become so high.

18. Legal issues affect the selection process in a number of ways. Today, legal guidelines limit the kinds of questions one can ask on an application or in an interview. Employment tests have been challenged because of discrimination, so tests must be directly related to the job. Some states will only allow physical examinations after an offer of employment has been accepted, and such tests must be given to everyone applying for the same position. Conditional employment, where a company gives an employee a trial period, have made it easier to fire inefficient or problem employees.

19. As noted above, employment tests must be directly related to the job.

20. During a trial period, a person can prove his or her worth to the firm. After the trial period, a firm has the right to discharge an employee based upon performance evaluations, so it is easier to fire inefficient employees.

21. Contingent workers are workers who do not have the expectation of regular, full-time employment. These workers include part-time workers, seasonal workers, temporary workers, independent contractors, interns and co-op students.

22. Firms have contingent workers because:
    a. There is a varying need for employees.
    b. Full-time employees experience downtimes.
    c. There is a peak demand for labor.
    d. Qualified contingent workers are available.
    e. Jobs require minimum training.
    f. Quick service to customers is a priority.

23. Contingent workers are often offered full-time positions, but as contingent workers they receive few health, vacation and pension benefits. They also earn less than permanent workers.

Learning Goal 5   **Training and Developing Employees for Optimum Performance**

24. Steps in creating training and development programs are:
    a. Assessing the needs of the organization and the skills of the employees to determine training needs.
    b. Designing the training activities to meet the needs.
    c. Evaluating the effectiveness of the training.

25. Training is short-term skills oriented, while development is long-term career oriented.

26. The types of training programs are:
    a. Employee orientation
    b. On-the-job training
    c. Apprenticeship
    d. Off-the-job training
    e. Vestibule training
    f. Job simulation
    g. management training

27. On the job training is the most fundamental type of training. It is the easiest kind of training to implement, and can be effective where the job is easily learned, such as clerking in a store, or performing repetitive physical tasks.

28. As an apprentice, you would train for a craft, such as a bricklaying or plumbing.

29. Vestibule training is used when proper methods and safety procedures must be learned before using equipment on the job.

30. Job simulation is the use of equipment that duplicates job conditions and tasks so trainees can learn skills before attempting them on the job. It differs from vestibule training in that simulation attempts to duplicate the exact conditions that occur on the job.

31. Basic elements of management development are:
    a. Training and educating employees to become good managers.
    b. Developing managerial skills over time.

32. Types of training used in management training programs are:
    a. On-the-job coaching.
    b. Understudy positions.
    c. Job rotation.
    d. Off-the-job courses and training.

33. Companies taking the initiative to develop female and minority mangers understand that:
    a. Grooming women and minorities for management positions is a key to long-term profitability.
    b. The best women and minorities will become harder to attract and retain in the future.
    c. More women and minorities at all levels means that businesses can serve female and minority customers better.

Learning Goal 6 **Appraising Employee Performance**

34. The steps of performance appraisal are:
    a. Establish performance standards.
    b. Communicate the standards.
    c. Evaluate performance.
    d. Discuss results with employees.
    e. Take corrective action.
    f. Use the results to make decisions.

35. Performance standards must be:

    a. understandable   b. subject to measurement   c. reasonable

36. Decisions about promotions, compensation, additional training or firing are all based on performance evaluations.

37. The latest form of performance appraisal is called the 360-degree review, because it calls for feedback from superiors, subordinates and peers.

Learning Goal 7   **Compensating Employees**

38. Compensation and benefits packages have become a main marketing tool used to attract qualified employees. At the same time, employee compensation is one of the largest operating costs for many organizations, and the firm's long-term survival may depend on how well it can control employee costs, while still attracting and keeping qualified personnel.

39. Objectives accomplished by a well-managed compensation and benefits program include:
    a. Attracting the kind of people the organization needs.
    b. Providing employees with incentives.
    c. Keeping valued employees from leaving.
    d. Maintaining a competitive position in the marketplace.
    e. Protecting employees from unexpected problems.
    f. Assuring employees a sense of financial security through insurance and retirement benefits.

40. Types of pay systems include:

    a. Salary systems.   d. Commission plans.
    b. Hourly wage or daywork.   e. Bonus plans.
    c. Piecework.   f. Profit-sharing plans.

41. Commission plans are often used to compensate sales people.

42. Bonus plans are for executives, sales people and other employees who earn bonuses for accomplishing or surpassing certain objectives.

43. Two types of bonuses are monetary and cashless. Cashless rewards include written thank-you notes, sending appreciation notes to an employee's family, movie tickets, flowers, time off, gift certificates, shopping sprees awards and other types of recognition.

44. The Hay system is a compensation system that is based on job tiers, each of which has a strict pay range.

45. The problem with paying members of a team based on individual performance is that it erodes team cohesiveness and makes it less likely that the team will meet its goals as a collaborative effort.

46. Two types of pay systems for teams are:
    a. skills-based pay   b. profit sharing

47. Skill-based pay is related to the growth of the individual and of the team. Base pay is raised when team members learn and apply new skills.

48. The drawbacks of the skill-based pay system are:
    a. Its complexity.
    b. Difficulty of correlating skill acquisition to bottom-line gains.

49. In a profit-sharing, or gain-sharing system, bonuses are based on improvements over a previous performance baseline.

50. Outstanding team players that go beyond what is required and make an outstanding individual contribution to the firm should be separately recognized for their additional contribution. A good way to avoid alienating recipients who feel team participation was uneven is to let the team decide which members get what type of individual award.

51. Fringe benefits include sick-leave pay, vacation pay, pension plans, and health plans. They can also include everything from paid vacations to health-care programs, recreation facilities, company cars, country club memberships, day care services and executive dining rooms, dental care, eye care, elder care, legal counseling, mental health care and shorter workweeks.

52. Firms have begun to offer cafeteria-style benefits to counter the growing demand for different kinds of benefits. Today employees are more varied and need different kinds of benefits. The key to cafeteria style benefits is flexibility, where individual needs can be met.

Learning Goal 8 **Scheduling Employees**

53. a. Flextime c. Home-based scheduling
    b. Compressed work week d. Job sharing

54. Flextime plans are designed to allow employees to adjust to demands on their time, and have freedom to adjust when they work, as long as they work the required number of hours.

55. One disadvantage of flextime is that it doesn't work in assembly-line processes where everyone must work at the same time. In addition, managers often have to work longer days to be able to assist and supervise employees. Flextime can make communication more difficult, as certain employees may not be at work when you need to talk to them. Further, some employees could abuse the system, and that could cause resentment.

56. A disadvantage to a compressed work week is that some employees get tired working such long hours, and productivity could decline.

57. Benefits to working at home include:
    a. Workers can choose their own hours.
    b. Work can be interrupted for child care and other tasks.
    c. Workers can take time out for personal reasons.
    d. It can be good for your career.
    e. Telecommuting can be a cost saver for employers.

58. Benefits to job sharing can be:
    a. employment opportunities to those who cannot or prefer not to work full-time.
    b. a high level of enthusiasm and productivity.
    c. reduced absenteeism and tardiness.
    d. ability to schedule people into peak demand periods.

59. The disadvantages to job sharing include having to hire, train, motivate and supervise twice as many people and to prorate some fringe benefits.

Learning Goal 9   **Moving Employees Up, Over and Out**

60. a. Promotions   c. Reassignment
    b. Terminations   d. Retirement

61. Downsizing and restructuring, increasing customer demands for value, the pressure of global competition and shifts in technology have made human resource managers struggle.

62. Companies are hesitant to rehire permanent employees because the cost of terminating employees is so high that managers choose to avoid the cost of firing by not hiring in the first place. Instead, companies are using temporary employees or outsourcing.

63. "Employment at will" is an old doctrine that meant that managers had as much freedom to fire workers as workers had to leave voluntarily.

64. Most states now have written employment laws that limit the "at will" doctrine to protect employees form wrongful firing.

65. Two tools used to downsize are to offer early retirement benefits and to lay off employees.

66. Two advantages of early retirement programs are the increased morale of surviving employees and greater promotion opportunities for younger employees.

Learning Goal 10   **Laws Affecting Human Resource Management**

67. Laws that prevent discrimination in the workplace are:
    a. Civil Rights Act of 1964.
    b. Equal Employment Opportunity Act.
    c. Vocational Rehabilitation Act.
    d. Age Discrimination Act.
    e. Americans with Disabilities Act.
    f. Civil Rights Act of 1991.

68. The EEOC, the Equal Employment Opportunity Commission, is a regulatory agency created by the Civil Rights Act in 1964. The job of the EEOC is to enforce programs put forth by various legislation.

69. The EEOC has the power to:
    a. issue guidelines for acceptable employer conduct in administering equal employment opportunity.
    b. enforce mandatory record-keeping procedures.
    c. ensure that mandates are carried out.

70. The purpose of affirmative action was to "right past wrongs" endured by females and minorities in the administration of human resources management.

71. Title VII of the Civil Rights Act of 1964 prohibits discrimination based on race, religion, creed, sex, national origin or age in all areas of human resource management. The Equal Employment Opportunity Commission was established with this act.

72. The Civil Rights Act of 1991 expanded the remedies available to victims of discrimination. Now victims have the right to a jury trial and punitive damages.

73. The Vocational Rehabilitation Act of 1973 extended protection from discrimination, in all areas of human resource management, to people with disabilities.

74. The Americans with Disabilities Act of 1990 requires that disabled applicants be given the same consideration for employment as people without disabilities. Companies must make "reasonable accommodations" to people with disabilities including modifying equipment or making structural changes.

75. Most companies are not having trouble making structural changes to be accommodating. What companies are finding difficult are the cultural changes.

76. The Age Discrimination in Employment Act outlawed mandatory retirement in most organizations before the age of 70.

77. Impact of legislation on human resource management include:
    a. Employers must be sensitive to the legal rights of all groups in the workplace.
    b. Legislation affects all areas of human resource management.
    c. It is clear that it is sometimes legal to go beyond providing equal rights for minorities and women to provide special employment and training to correct past discrimination.
    d. New court cases and legislation change human resource management almost daily.

CRITICAL THINKING EXERCISES

Learning Goal 1.

1.

	AREA	COMPANY RESPONSE
a. Shortages of trained workers	Training, Recruitment	Training programs, aggressive recruiting programs
b. Aging work force	Compensation, Planning	Demand for good retirement programs will change benefits packages. Companies will also need to plan for replacement of workers in the future. Also family leave programs needed for workers to care for older parents.
c. Increases in single-parent and two-income families	Compensation, Planning	Companies will need to look at offering day care, continuing to offer cafeteria style benefits will be especially important as companies experience shortages of trained workers.

d. Changing attitudes about work	Planning	Need to look at flextime, and compressed work weeks to meet needs of future workers.
e. Complex laws	Selection, Recruitment, Compensation	These laws will require companies to look at their policies regarding hiring, promotion and termination.
f. Concern over work environment and equality	Planning, Compensation	Companies will begin to offer programs to help employees deal with issues regarding eldercare. Accommodate the work place as to accessibility for disabled workers.

Learning Goal 2

2. Steps in human resource planning are:
   a. Job analysis.
   b. Human resource inventory.
   c. Assessing future demand.
   d. Establishing a plan.
   e. Assessing future supply.
   f. Forecasting future human resource needs.

Learning Goal 3

3. What your resume will include is obviously going to be unique to your own experiences and qualifications. A good place to look for information on creating a good resume is your college placement office. However, a good resume is only the first step in "getting recruited." Additional factors include creating your own network, becoming involved in extra-curricular activities, maintaining a good grade-point average and developing good interviewing skills. A good way to find out what employers are looking for is to talk to people who do the hiring for the companies they work for, and practice interviewing.

4. You will probably notice a number of ways that companies are trying to recruit new employees. One good reason to develop a "network" is that employers often use current employees to find new hires. The newspaper, especially on Sundays, may have several pages of employment opportunities. On your college campus, there may be signs in windows, ads in the college newspaper, ads on electronic bulletin boards among a myriad of other ways that companies are using to look for qualified employees.

Learning Goal 5

5. a. Trial periods
    b. Complete an application
    c. Background investigations
    d. Employment tests
    e. Initial and follow-up interviews
    f. Physical exams

Learning Goal 6

6. Your answer will depend upon what kind of job you have chosen. There are many different jobs which will be a part of Music-stor : Sales, production, marketing, accounting, and clerical, to name a few. For a sales job, a job description may be: Sales for a small manufacturing company, calling on automotive manufacturers and/or automotive after market dealers. Sales territory will be primarily based on geographic location. Duties will include sales calls, follow-up reports, working directly with production manager, direct input into marketing program development. Compensation will be salary plus commission.

   Skills required include familiarity with electronic communication equipment, teamwork skills, good oral and written communications skills, presentation skills, and a bachelor's degree, preferably in marketing or a related area.

   You may make use of any of the recruiting tools listed in the text. Good sources may include current employees, local colleges, a local professional marketing organization, or simply advertising. The selection process should include several interviews, in particular with the people with whom the salesperson will work, production manager, other marketing people, other members of the team he/she will work with.

7. a. Vestibule training
    b. Apprenticeship
    c. On-the-job training
    d. Job simulation
    e. Management development
    f. Employee orientation

8. As corporations downsize and layers of management "thin out," your network of co-workers, friends and professional associations could become especially important. To get the kind of job that meets your needs, you may have to do a lot of searching; to "move up the ladder" in the face of declining numbers of management positions, you may have to find the right mentor.

   In college, you can begin to develop a network in a number of ways. If there are student chapters of professional business organizations, such as The American Marketing Association or The American Management Association, for example, you could take advantage of student membership rates and attend monthly meetings and meet people already working in the field. Your professors may have contacts in the area you are interested in, also. Further, you could begin a series of "informational interviews". Make appointments with managers in corporations you may have an interest in working for in the future, and find out exactly what kind of skills they are looking for, what kinds of jobs they think will be available in the future and a little bit about the company. Lastly, network with your fellow students. You never know who may be the future CEO of the company you're dying to work for!

9. The first thing you need to do in developing this appraisal system is decide exactly what elements of the salespeople's' jobs will be included in the system. For example, you will probably include: sales volume, number of sales calls, number of sales compared to number of sales calls (called the closing ratio), dollar amount per sale, number of units per sale, sales expenses, average dollar volume per customer, and so on, as well as what time frame will be used for evaluations, six months or a year, for example. After that, you will want to decide what is an acceptable and reasonable standard for each of those areas - i.e. how many sales calls per month is enough? What's an acceptable dollar amount per sale? What is an acceptable sales volume in the given period?

Lastly, these standards must be communicated to each salesperson, explained clearly and precisely. Each individual must know exactly what is expected of them.

10. How you would deal with an employee who is not performing well is a matter of individual style. However there are a number of suggestions to make the process more effective. The most important thing to do first is to discuss the problem with the employee and determine what is causing the problem. There may be a problem in her territory, family problems that took her away from work or inadequate support from the company. Figure 11-4 gives you some specific suggestions about conducting an effective appraisal. It will be important to get agreement from the employee that there is a problem, and suggestions from her about how to take corrective action. It may be a good idea to give her a period of time to improve, and then re-evaluate.

Learning Goal 7

11. These are some suggested answers:
    a. Salary or salary plus commission.
    b. Hourly wages plus profit sharing.
    c. Salary plus bonus for meeting objective.
    d. Salary plus profit sharing, or bonus for meeting profit objective.
    e. Piecework, plus profit sharing.

12. To counter growing demands for more individualized benefits, companies have begun to offer cafeteria-style benefits. The key to this type of program is providing enough choices so that employees can meet their varied needs, while still maintaining cost effectiveness. These types of programs are particularly important in light of the predicted difficulty in finding skilled employees.

Learning Goal 8

13.
    a. Flextime
    b. Compressed work week
    c. Job sharing
    d. In-home work
    e. Job sharing
    f. Flextime
    g. Job sharing
    h. Flextime
    i. Job sharing
    j. Flextime

14. As downsizing has created flatter organizational structures, there are fewer opportunities for employees to be promoted. To keep morale from sagging, and to keep employees productive, it is common today for companies to reassign workers rather than move them up. This kind of transfer allows employees to develop and display new skills. Downsizing has also forced companies to struggle with layoffs and terminations. Many companies are reluctant to rehire permanent workers because of the high cost involved. Legislation has also made firing more difficult, in light of wrongful discharge lawsuits, and some companies find it more cost effective to use part-time workers to replace permanent workers when the need arises.

    As an alternative to layoffs, companies have offered early retirement to entice older employees to resign, and allow younger workers to move up. As the workforce gets older, these programs will enable companies to reduce the number of older, more expensive workers. However, if skilled workers are in short supply, companies may need experienced workers, and could reconsider offering early retirement plans.

15. As the workforce becomes more culturally diverse, laws protecting minorities from discrimination will be carefully monitored. These areas have become very complex, and a diverse workforce makes enforcement even more complex. However, as more women and minorities with the necessary skills enter the workforce, compliance with these laws may actually become less an issue than in the past.

A major issue for the 1990s has been providing equal opportunity for people with disabilities. Companies are finding that making structural accommodations is less difficult than understanding the difference between the need to be accommodating and the need to be fair to all employees. As the workforce ages, age discrimination may become an issue.

PRACTICE TEST

Multiple Choice				True/False			
1.	a	11.	d	1.	T	11.	T
2.	d	12.	c	2.	F	12.	T
3.	d	13.	a	3.	T	13.	T
4.	c	14.	d	4.	F	14.	F
5.	c	15.	a	5.	T	15.	T
6.	b	16.	b	6.	F		
7.	a	17.	d	7.	T		
8.	b	18.	a	8.	T		
9.	b	19.	b	9.	F		
10.	a	20.	c	10.	F		

CHAPTER 12
EMPLOYEE-MANAGEMENT ISSUES: UNIONS, EXECUTIVE COMPENSATION, AND OTHER ISSUES

LEARNING GOALS

After you have read and studied this chapter, you should be able to:

1. Trace the history of organized labor in the United States and discuss the major legislation affecting labor unions.

2. Outline the objectives of labor unions.

3. Describe the tactics used by labor and management during conflicts and discuss the role of unions in the future.

4. Explain some of the controversial employee-management issues such as executive compensation, comparable worth, child care and elder care, AIDS, drug testing, violence in the workplace, and employee stock ownership plans. (ESOPs).

LEARNING THE LANGUAGE

Listed below are important terms found in the chapter. Choose the correct term for the definition and write it in the space provided.

Agency shop agreement	Injunction
American Federation of Labor (AFL)	Knights of Labor
Arbitration	Lockouts
Bargaining zone	Mediation
Certification	Negotiated labor-management agreement
Closed-shop agreement	Open shop agreement
Collective bargaining	Primary boycott
Congress of Industrial Organizations (CIO)	Right-to-work laws
Comparable worth	Secondary boycott
Cooling-off period	Sexual harassment
Craft union	Shop steward
Decertification	Strike
Employee stock ownership plans (ESOP)	Strikebreakers

Givebacks	Unions
Golden parachute	Union security clause
Grievance	Union shop agreement
Industrial unions	Yellow-dog contract

1. The _____ is the range of options between the initial and final offer that each party will consider before a union will strike or before management will close a plant.

2. The time known as a _____ is a period when workers return to their jobs while the union and management continue negotiations.

3. The process known as _____ is one in which workers take away a union's right to represent them.

4. A charge by employees that management is not abiding by the terms of the negotiated labor agreement is called a(n) _____.

5. This tactic known as a(n) _____ puts pressure on unions by closing the business.

6. A tactic called a(n) _____ occurs when the union encourages its members not to buy the products of a firm involved in a labor dispute.

7. Employee organizations known as _____ have the main goal of representing members in employee-management bargaining about job-related issues.

8. A clause in a labor-management agreement whereby employers may hire nonunion workers who are not required to join the union but must pay a union fee is called an _____.

9. The issue of _____ is the demand for equal pay for jobs requiring similar levels of education, training and skills.

10. The use of a third party to encourage both sides of a contract dispute to continue negotiating is called _____.

11. Known as _____ this is unwelcome sexual advances, requests for sexual favors, and other conduct of a sexual nature.

12. A(n) _____ was an agreement in which employees had to agree not to join a union as a condition of employment.

13. A(n) _____ is a labor official who works permanently in an organization and represents employee interests on a daily basis.

14. A provision in a negotiated labor-management agreement known as a(n) _____ stipulates that employees who reap benefits from a union must either join or pay dues to the union.

15. An organization known as the _____ consisted of craft unions that championed basic labor issues, and was formed in 1886.

16. Concessions made by unions to help employers remain competitive and save jobs are called _____.

17. Under this type of agreement, known as a(n) _____ workers in right-to-work states have the option to join or not join the union, if one exists in their workplace.

18. Workers who are hired to do the jobs of striking employees until the labor dispute is resolved are called _____.

19. The process of union's becoming recognized by the NLRB as the authorized bargaining agent for a group of employees is called _____.

20. A sizable severance package known as a(n) _____ is for corporate managers whose jobs may be threatened by a takeover by another firm.

21. Labor organizations called _____ consist of unskilled workers in mass production related industries such as automobiles and mining.

22. This clause in a labor-management agreement called a(n) _____, indicates that workers do not have to be members of a union to be hired, but must agree to join the union within a prescribed period.

23. The process known as _____ is where union representatives reach a negotiated labor-management agreement.

24. The first national labor union was the _____.

25. A(n) _____ is an attempt by labor to convince others to stop doing business with a firm that is the subject of a primary boycott.

26. The agreement to bring in an impartial third party to render a binding decision in a labor dispute is called _____.

27. The clause in a labor-management agreement known as a(n) _____ specified that workers had to be members of a union before being hired.

28. A program called a(n) _____ is a plan whereby employees can buy part or total ownership of the firm where they work.

29. A(n) _____ is a settlement which sets the tone and clarifies the terms under which management and labor agree to function over a period of time.

30. Legislation which gives workers the right, under an open shop agreement to join or not join a union if it is present are called _____.

31. A union strategy known as a(n) _____ means that workers refuse to go to work to further their objectives after an impasse in collective bargaining.

32. The _____ is the union organization of unskilled workers which broke away from the AFL in 1935 and rejoined it in 1955.

33. A labor organization of skilled specialists ina particular craft or trade is a(n) _____.

34. An _____ is a court order directing someone to do something or to refrain from doing something.

RETENTION CHECK

Learning Goal 1 **Employee Management Issues**

1. What triggered the union movement of today?

2. How long have labor unions existed in the United States?

3. What impact did the Industrial Revolution have on the economic structure of the U.S.?

4. What were working conditions like during the Industrial Revolution?

5. What was the first national labor organization?

6. What was the intention of this labor union?

7. What is the AFL?

8. Why did the AFL limit membership?

9. What is the CIO? Why was it formed?

10. How did the AFL-CIO form?

11. Name five major pieces of labor-management legislation.

   a. _____

   b. _____

   c. _____

   d. _____

   e. _____

12. What did the Wagner Act provide for organized labor?

13. Why did Samuel Gompers of the AFL support collective bargaining?

14. What does the NLRB do?

15. What are the major elements of the Norris-LaGuardia Act?

16. What is the Fair Labor Standards Act?

17. What did the Taft-Hartley Act provide for?

18. What is the Landrum-Griffin Act?

Learning Goal 2 **Objectives of Organized Labor**

19. What were the primary objectives of labor unions in the 1970s?

    a. _____

    b. _____

20. What was the focus of unions in the 1990s?

   a. _____

   b. _____

21. List the general topics covered in labor-management agreements.

   a. _____ g. _____

   b. _____ h. _____

   c. _____ i. _____

   d. _____ j. _____

   e. _____ k. _____

   f. _____

22. Identify four different forms of union contracts.

   a. _____ c. _____

   b. _____ d. _____

23. What is a "right-to-work" state?

24. What will be the focus of union negotiations in the future?

   a. _____

   b. _____

   c. _____

   d. _____

   e. _____

25. What are three methods used to resolve labor-management disputes?

   a. _____

   b. _____

   c. _____

26. What are generally the sources of grievances?

   a. _____

   b. _____

   c. _____

   d. _____

   e. _____

27. When does mediation become necessary?

28. What does a mediator do?

29. How does arbitration differ from mediation?

Learning Goal 3   **Tactics Used in Labor Management Conflicts**

30. What are the tactics used by labor in labor-management disputes?

   a. _____   c. _____

   b. _____   d. _____

31. What does a strike provide?

32. What is the difference between a primary boycott and a secondary boycott?

33. What are the tactics available to management in these disputes?

   a. _____   c. _____

   b. _____

34. What will unions have to do in order to grow in the future?

Learning Goal 4 **Controversial Employee Management Issues**

35. Identify several controversial non-union employee-management issues.

   a. _____

   b. _____

   c. _____

   d. _____

   e. _____

   f. _____

g. _____

h. _____

36. What does management consultant Peter Drucker say regarding the level of executive compensation?

37. How does the pay of U.S. executives compare to executive pay in other countries?

38. How does comparable worth differ from "equal pay for equal work"?

39. What explains the disparity between women's pay and men's pay?

40. What is the idea of "pay equity"?

41. A person's conduct on the job could be considered sexually harassing if:

   a. _____

   b. _____

   c. _____

42. What is the concept of a "hostile workplace?"

43. What is a problem companies have with sexual harassment policies?

44. What does the Family and Medical Leave Act permit?

45. Identify two questions surrounding the child care debate.

   a. _____

   b. _____

46. List five kinds of programs companies are providing to help with the child care problem.

   a. _____

   b. _____

   c. _____

   d. _____

   e. _____

47. Why has the issue of elder care become important in today's workplace?

48. Why is HIV and AIDS a concern to employers?

49. What is a controversial employee-management policy regarding HIV/AIDS?

50. Identify the kinds of costs which could be incurred by an employer of an AIDS-afflicted employee.

    a. _____   c. _____

    b. _____   d. _____

51. What is the estimated the loss to business due to substance abuse?

52. Why don't many companies provide formal training for dealing with violence in the workplace?

53. What is the theory behind employee stock ownership programs?

54. What benefits have companies experienced from ESOPs?

55. What have been some problems with ESOPs?

CRITICAL THINKING EXERCISES

Learning Goal 1

1. What were the issues which concerned the early crafts unions, before and during the Industrial Revolution?

2. How do those issues compare with modern day work issues?

3. Five major pieces of legislation which have had an impact on the development of labor unions are the:

    Norris-LaGuardia Act 1932.
    National Labor Relations Act (Wagner Act) 1935.
    Fair Labor Standards Act 1938.
    Labor-Management Relations Act (Taft-Hartley Act) 1947.
    Labor-Management Reporting and Disclosure Act (Landrum-Griffin Act) 1959.

    Identify which act is being discussed in each of the following:

    a. Texas, Florida, Georgia, Iowa, Kansas and 16 other states have passed right-to-work laws. _____

b. The AFL-CIO and Teamsters file financial reports every year with the U.S. Department of Labor. _____

c. Union members picketed the Price Chopper grocery stores to protest the stores' use of non-union labor. _____

d. A retail store in Michigan is prevented from getting an injunction against a worker who is trying to organize a union. _____

e. In 1997, workers at a General Motors plant in Ohio went on strike, forcing closings at another plant which needed parts supplied by the striking plant. _____

f. A grocery store in Illinois carries products produced by a company the AFL-CIO is striking. Under this law, the AFL-CIO cannot call for a boycott of the grocery store. _____

g. Voter fraud was alleged in the election of a Teamster union official, and is being investigated. _____

h. In an attempt to avoid a strike, union and management officials in the automotive industry begin negotiating a year in advance of the end of the current contract. _____

i. In the mid-1990s Congress raised the minimum wage to $5.15 per hour. _____

4. There are four types of labor agreements:

a. closed shop agreemen.t   c. union shop agreement.
b. agency shop agreement.   d. open shop agreement.

Identify each of the following:

a. When Tom Oswalt worked in an automotive factory for the summer in Michigan, he chose not to join the local union. However, he was still required to pay a fee to the union under a union-security clause. _____

b. After the Wagner Act was passed, unions sought security with this type of agreement. With passage of the Taft-Hartley Act in 1947, however, these types of agreements were made illegal. _____

c. When Peter Tobler went to work at Tyson Foods in Springdale, Arkansas, he was not required to join the union, and did not have to pay any fees to the union. _____

d. Gary Reese took a job with the Saint Louis plant of Anheuser-Busch in August. He had until October to join the union. _____

Learning Goals 2, 3

5. In the mid 1990s, the National and American League baseball players went on strike, and ended the baseball season for the year. While player representatives continued to negotiate with team owners (sporadically), the strike was still not resolved by the opening of the season in the spring of the following year. Even President Bill Clinton could not convince the owners and players to come to the bargaining table and talk to one another. What options are available to labor and management for resolving agreements, which could have been used before the players went on strike, or while they were on strike?

6. When the collective bargaining process breaks down, both management and labor have specific tactics available to them to reach their objectives.

Management	**Labor**
Injunction	Strike
Lockout	Picketing
Strikebreakers	Primary boycotts
	Secondary boycotts

Match the tactic being used in each of the following descriptions:

a. In the past, members of various unions have mounted campaigns to persuade consumers not to buy Coors Beer, because Coors does not use union labor. _____

b. When contract negotiations broke down, the owners of the National Hockey clubs refused to allow players to play, and delayed the start of the 94-95 season by several weeks. _____

12-19

c. While the hockey players were being prevented from working, the baseball players were refusing to work. _____

d. In order to start a season anyway, the baseball club owners hired replacement players, bringing many up from the minor leagues. _____

e. During a strike against AT&T, union members attempted to raise public awareness and sympathy for their cause by gathering outside their places of employment carrying signs outlining their grievances. _____

f. To prevent a sympathy strike by its machinists, TWA obtained a court order making it illegal for the machinists to strike during a strike by the flight attendants. _____

g. Although they are illegal, the employee of an airline threatened this action against the railways. _____

7. How do unions fit into the concepts we have discussed in previous chapters, such as self-managed teams, continuous improvement, and so on?

Learning Goal 4

8. What justifications can be given for the high level of executive pay in the United States?

9. What are the negative aspects of the high level of executive pay in the United States?

10. The issue of comparable worth centers on comparing the value of jobs traditionally held by women with the value of jobs traditionally held by men. What do comparisons of "men's jobs" with "women's jobs" show? How are things changing?

11. As more women have entered the workforce, the issue of sexual harassment has become increasingly visible. What are the problems surrounding this issue, and what are companies doing about it?

12. In some countries the federal government has stepped in to provide help for workers who need day care. In the United States, the federal child-care assistance has risen significantly. Why has this issue of day care become so important in today's workplace?

13. What are the issues surrounding?

    a. Elder care

    b. AIDS

    c. Drug testing

    d. Violence in the workplace

14. What are the goals of ESOPs and why have some problems developed with the ESOP programs?

PRACTICE TEST

Multiple Choice: Circle the best answer.

1. Most historians agree that today's union movement is an outgrowth of:

    a. the Great Depression.
    b. the Civil War.
    c. the Industrial Revolution.
    d. the Revolutionary War.

2. The first national labor organization was the:

    a. Knights of Labor.
    b. American Federation of Labor.
    c. Congress of Industrial Organizations.
    d. United Mine Workers.

3. The minimum wage and maximum hours for workers requirements were established by the:

    a. Norris-LaGuardia Act.
    b. Taft-Hartley Act.
    c. Landrum-Griffin Act.
    d. Fair Labor Standards Act.

4. When Joe Kerr began working at his local bakery, he felt there was a need for the workers to sit down with management and talk about some of the problems facing the workers at their job. Joe found out there was a union for the bakery workers, but that management didn't take them seriously, and refused to sit down with the union and negotiate. After some research Joe found out that under the _____, workers had the right to expect management to negotiate with them.

    a. Norris-LaGuardia Act
    b. Wagner Act
    c. Fair Labor Standards Act
    d. Taft-Hartley Act

5. When Dave Sutton went to work for a printing shop, he thought he was going to have to join the union representing the shop. However on his first day of work he was told that while there was a union representing the workers, he was not required to join, and he didn't have to pay any dues to the union if he chose not to join. Dave works in a _____ shop.

   a. union
   b. agency
   c. closed
   d. open

6. When baseball players went on strike, an individual was brought in to help resolve the dispute between management and players. This third party was involved to make suggestions, but he did not make any decisions about how the players dispute should besettled. This is an example of:

   a. arbitration.
   b. grievance.
   c. mediation.
   d. a bargaining zone.

7. When organized labor encourages its members not to buy products made by a firm in a labor dispute, it is encouraging a(n):

   a. strike.
   b. primary boycott.
   c. secondary boycott.
   d. injunction.

8. Which of the following is not a tactic used by management in a labor dispute?

   a. lockout
   b. injunction
   c. use of strikebreakers
   d. secondary boycott

9. For unions to grow in the future, they will have to:

   a. continue to grant givebacks to management.
   b. begin to organize foreign workers.
   c. adapt to a more culturally diverse, white collar workforce.
   d. take up the fight against continuous improvement and employee involvement.

10. When compared to their European and Japanese counterparts, U.S. corporate executives:

   a. are making considerably more than executives in other countries.
   b. are being paid much less than their counterparts, considering how much more they work.
   c. are compensated better when times are good, but worse when the company isn't doing as well.
   d. are at about the same level in terms of compensation.

11. The issue of comparable worth deals with:

   a. paying equal wages to men and women who do the same job.
   b. equal pay for different jobs that require similar levels of training and education or skills.
   c. assuring that men and women have equal opportunity in the job market.
   d. ensuring that executive pay is not more than 20 times the pay of the lowest paid worker.

12. Which of the following is not a type of sexual behavior which would be considered sexually harassing?

   a. An employee must submit to behavior as a condition of employment.
   b. Submission or rejection of behavior is used as a basis for employment decisions.
   c. Behavior interferes with job performance or creates a hostile working environment.
   d. Reporting of behavior results in job dismissal.

13. Which of the following is not true regarding the issue of childcare for workers?

   a. Federal child-care assistance has declined significantly and is expected to continue to do so.
   b. Workplace changes have taken place with the Family and Medical Leave Act.
   c. The number of companies providing some kind of childcare services is growing.
   d. Parents have made it clear they will not compromise on the issue of childcare.

14. Companies have responded to requests for assistance in child-care with all of the following except:

    a. discount arrangements with national child care chains.
    b. vouchers that offer payment toward the kind of child-care the employee prefers.
    c. on-site child-care centers.
    d. increases in the number of allowable sick leave days for employees to use when a child is ill.

15. One of the more controversial employee-management policies concerns:

    a. sexual harassment policies.
    b. policies against violence in the workplace.
    c. mandatory testing for the AIDS antibody.
    d. offering ESOPs to all employees.

16. Employee stock ownership programs allow employees to:

    a. gain a voice in running the company thorough voting.
    b. buy ownership in the company.
    c. gain more job security.
    d. have a secure path to file grievances.

TRUE/FALSE

1. _____ During the Industrial Revolution, issues such as low wages and the use of child labor made the workplace ripe for the emergence of national labor unions.

2. _____ The CIO, Congress of Industrial Organizations, grew out of the Knights of Labor.

3. _____ Yellow dog contracts, preventing workers from joining a union as a condition of employment, were outlawed by the Fair Labor Standards Act.

4. _____ In arbitration, an impartial third party will make a binding decision in a labor dispute.

5. _____ Strikebreakers are often used to replace strikers during a prolonged strike until the dispute is resolved.

6. _____ Unions have begun to take a leadership role in encouraging cooperation of employees in employee involvement programs.

7. _____ In the past, the primary explanation for the disparity between men and women's pay has been that women often aren't as educated as men.

8. _____ Women file the majority of sexual harassment cases.

9. _____ The issue of elder care is expected to decline in importance in coming years.

10. _____ Many companies and executives don't take workplace violence seriously.

ANSWERS

LEARNING THE LANGUAGE

1. Bargaining zone	18. Strikebreakers
2. Cooling-off period	19. Certification
3. Decertification	20. Golden parachute
4. Grievance	21. Industrial unions
5. Lockout	22. Union shop agreement
6. Primary boycott	23. Collective bargaining
7. Unions	24. Knights of Labor
8. Agency shop agreement	25. Secondary boycott
9. Comparable worth	26. Arbitration
10. Mediation	27. Closed shop agreement
11. Sexual harassment	28. Employee stock ownership program (ESOP)
12. Yellow dog contract	29. Negotiated labor agreement
13. Shop steward	30. Right-to-work laws
14. Union security clause	31. Strike
15. American Federation of Labor (AFL)	32. Congress of Industrial Organizations (CIO)
16. Givebacks	33. Craft union
17. Open shop agreement	34. Injunction

RETENTION CHECK

Learning Goal 1 **Employee-Management Issues**

1. Most historians agree that the union movement of today is an outgrowth of the economic transition caused by the Industrial Revolution. The workers who worked in the fields suddenly became dependent upon factories for their living.

2. Labor unions have existed in the United States as early as 1792, when shoemakers met to discuss the work issues of pay, hours, conditions and job security.

3. The Industrial Revolution changed the economic structure of the United States.

4. Workers were faced with the reality that if you failed to produce you lost your job. Often workers went to work when they were ill or had family problems. The average workweek expanded to 60 or as many as 90 hours per week. Wages were low and the use of child labor was common.

5. The first national labor union was the Knights of Labor

6. The intention of the Knights of Labor was to gain significant political power and eventually restructure the entire U.S. economy.

7. The American Federation of Labor, AFL, is an organization of craft unions that champions fundamental labor issues.

8. The AFL limited membership to skilled workers, assuming they would have better bargaining power in getting concessions from employers.

9. The Congress of Industrial Organizations, CIO was formed to organize both craftspeople and unskilled workers.

10. The AFL and the CIO merged in 1955 after each organization struggled for leadership for several years.

11.   a. Norris-LaGuardia Act 1932
    b. National Labor Relations Act (Wagner Act) 1935
    c. Fair Labor Standards Act 1938
    d. Labor Management Relations Act (Taft-Hartley Act) 1947
    e. Labor Management Reporting and Disclosure Act (Landrum-Griffin Act) 1959

12. The Wagner Act gave employees the right to form or join labor organizations, and the right to collectively bargain with employers. It also gave workers the right to engage in strikes, picketing, and boycotts. It also prohibited certain unfair labor practices by management, and established the National Labor Relations Board.

13. Gompers believed that collective bargaining was the key to attaining a fairer share of the economic pie for workers. He further believed that collective bargaining would enhance the well being of workers by improving working conditions on the job.

14. The NLRB provides guidelines and offers legal protection to workers that seek to vote on organizing a union to represent them in the workplace.

15. The major elements of the Norris-LaGuardia Act are that it prohibited courts from issuing injunctions against nonviolent union activities and it outlawed yellow dog contracts.

16. The Fair Labor Standards Act set a minimum wage and maximum basic hours for workers.

17. The Taft-Hartley Act amended the Wagner Act. It permitted states to pass right to work laws, and set up methods to deal with strikes affecting national health and security. The act also prohibits secondary boycotts, closed- shop agreements, and featherbedding.

18. The Landrum-Griffin Act amended the Taft-Hartley Act and the Wagner Act. It guaranteed individual rights of union members in dealing with their union, and required annual financial reports to be filed with the U.S. Department of Labor.

Learning Goal 2 **Objectives of Organized Labor**

19. The primary objectives of labor unions in the 1970s were:
    a. additional pay.
    b. additional benefits.

20. The focus of unions in the 1990s was on:
    a. job security.
    b. global competition and its effects.

21. The general topics covered in labor-management agreements are:
    a. Management rights.
    b. Union recognition.
    c. Union security clause.
    d. Strikes and lockouts.
    e. Union activities and responsibilities.
    f. Wages.
    g. Hours of work and time-off policies.
    h. Job rights and seniority principles.
    i. Discharge and discipline.
    j. Grievance procedures.
    k. Employee benefits, health and welfare.

22. Forms of union contracts include:
    a. Union shop.
    b. Agency shop.
    c. Closed shop.
    d. Open shop.

23. In a right-to-work state workers are required to work under the open shop agreement that gives them the option to join or not join a union if one is present.

24. In the future unions will focus on:
    a. child and elder care.
    b. worker retraining.
    c. two-tiered wage plans.
    d. employee empowerment.
    e. integrity and honesty testing.

25. Methods used to resolve labor-management disputes include:
    a. Grievances.
    b. Mediation.
    c. Arbitration.

26. Sources of grievances are:
    a. overtime rules.
    b. promotions.
    c. layoffs.
    d. transfers.
    e. job assignments.

27. Mediation becomes necessary if labor-management negotiators aren't able to agree on alternatives within the bargaining zone.

28. A mediator will encourage both sides to continue negotiating and makes suggestions for resolving a work dispute. Mediators make suggestions not decisions about how a dispute should be settled.

29. In arbitration, an impartial third party will render a binding decision in the labor dispute. A mediator can only make suggestions.

Learning Goal 3   **Tactics Used in Labor-Management Conflicts**

30. Tactics used by labor in labor-management disputes include:
    a. Strikes.
    b. Pickets.
    c. Primary boycotts.
    d. Secondary boycotts.

31. A strike provides public focus on a labor dispute and at times causes operations in a company to slow down or totally shut down.

32. A primary boycott is when labor encourages its membership not to buy the product of a firm involved in a labor dispute. A secondary boycott is an attempt to convince others to stop doing business with a firm that is the subject of a primary boycott.

33. Tactics used by management in labor-management disputes include:
    a. Lockouts.
    b. Injunctions.
    c. Strikebreakers.

34. For unions to grow, they will have to adapt to a work force that is increasingly culturally diverse, white collar, female, foreign born and professional. Increased global competition, advanced technology, and the changing nature of work have changed and threatened the jobs of many workers.

Learning Goal 4   **Controversial Employee-Management Issues**

35. Controversial non-union employee-management issues include:
    a. Executive compensation.
    b. Golden parachutes.
    c. Pay equity.
    d. Sexual harassment.
    e. Child care.
    f. Elder care.
    g. AIDS, drug testing and violence.
    h. Employee stock ownership plans.

36. Management consultant Peter Drucker suggests that CEOs should not earn much more than 20 times as much as the company's lowest-paid employee.

37. American CEOs typically earn two to three times as much as executives in Europe and Canada. In Japan, the CEO of a large corporation makes about 40 times what the average factory worker makes, compared to 209 times for the American CEO.

38. Equal pay for equal work requires that men and women doing the same job should be paid the same. Comparable worth centers on comparing the value of jobs traditionally held by women with jobs traditionally held by men. The idea is equal pay for different jobs that require similar levels of education, training, or skills.

39. In the past the primary explanation for the pay disparity between men and women was that women only worked a portion of their available years once they left school, whereas men worked all of those years. This has changed, and now the explanation is that many women try to work as well as have families, and so fall off the career track. Other women opt for lower paying jobs. Still others say that the labor market still has some degree of gender bias.

40. The idea of pay equity is to correct past discrimination by raising the pay in so-called "women's" jobs.

41. Conduct can be considered sexually harassing if:
    a. an employee's submission to such conduct is made either explicitly or implicitly a term of employment.
    b. an employee's submission to or rejection of such conduct is used as the basis of employment decisions affecting the worker's status.
    c. the conduct interferes with a worker's job performance or creates an unhealthy atmosphere.

42. A hostile workplace implies a work atmosphere or behavior that would offend a reasonable male or female.

43. A major problem companies have had with sexual harassment policies is that workers and managers often know a policy exists but have no idea what it says.

44. The Family and Medical Leave Act permits up to 12 weeks of unpaid leave per year to qualified workers upon the birth of a child.

45. Two questions surrounding child care are:
    a. who should provide child-care services.
    b. who should pay for them.

46. Companies have responded to the need for safe, affordable day care by providing:
    a. Discount arrangements with national child-care chains.
    b. Vouchers that offer payments toward whatever child care the employee chooses.
    c. Referral services that help identify quality child-care facilities.
    d. On-site child-care centers.
    e. Sick-child care.

47. The issue has become important because the number of households with at least one adult providing elder care has tripled in the past ten years. It is expected that over the next five years, 18 percent of the U.S. workforce will be involved in the task of caring for an aging relative.

48. These illnesses are a concern for employers because HIV and AIDS are a leading cause of death for Americans between the ages of 25-44, a group which represents almost half of the nation's workforce.

49. One of the more controversial employee-management policies concerns the mandatory testing for the AIDS antibody.

50. Costs incurred by an employer of an AIDS-afflicted employee:

    a. insurance.   c. increased absenteeism.

    b. losses in productivity.   d. employee turnover.

51. The U.S. Department of Health and Human Services estimates that businesses lose up to $312 billion a year due to substance abuse in the workplace.

52. Many executives and managers don't take workplace violence seriously and believe it is media hype. This is why many companies don't provide formal training for dealing with violence in the workplace.

53. The theory behind the ESOPs programs is that no matter how hard workers fight for better pay, they will never become as wealthy as people who actually own the company.

54. Giving employees a share in the profits of the firm motivates them to enhance their involvement and increases morale. It can also encourage workers to increase productivity.

55. Some problems are that ESOPs have been used to refinance a firm with employee money without giving employees added participation or more job security. Employees generally have no representation on the company's board and no voting rights.

CRITICAL THINKING EXERCISES

Learning Goal 1

1. The development of crafts unions, beginning in 1792 came about to discuss work issues such as pay, hours, work conditions and job security. The Industrial Revolution led to changes and problems for workers in terms of productivity, hours of work, wages and unemployment. If you failed to produce, you lost your job. Hours worked increased to as many as 80 hours per week.

2. The issues unions face today are similar to those that concerned the early labor unions. However, union negotiators today also address such issues as drug testing, benefits such as day care and elder care, violence in the workplace and employee stock ownership programs.

3. Legislation regarding labor unions include:
   a. Taft Hartley Act.
   b. Landrum-Griffin Act.
   c. Wagner Act.
   d. Norris-LaGuardia Act.
   e. Wagner Act.
   f. Taft Hartley Act.
   g. Landrum-Griffin Act.
   h. Wagner-Act.
   i. Fair Labor Standards Act.

4. a. Agency shop agreement
   b. Closed shop agreement
   c. Open shop agreement
   d. Union shop agreement

Learning Goals 2, 3

5. There are three options available for resolving labor disputes. The players union could have filed grievances against the owners before going on strike, in an attempt to resolve their differences without putting an end to the season. Either side could have brought in a mediator, before or during the strike. The mediator's job is to make suggestions for resolving the dispute. Lastly, arbitration could have been used. In arbitration, the parties agree to bring in a third party to make a binding decision, a decision that both parties must adhere to. The arbitrator must be acceptable to both parties. In fact, an arbitrator was discussed between the players and the owners, but neither side could agree on the choice of an arbitrator.

6.   a. Primary boycott   e. Picketing
       b. Lockout   f. Injunction
       c. Strike   g. Secondary boycott
       d. Strikebreakers

7. The role of unions is likely to be much different from that of the past. Union leadership is aware of the need to be competitive with foreign firms. Unions have taken a leadership role in introducing such concepts as continuous improvement, constant innovation and employee involvement programs. In the future, unions will help management in training, work design and in recruiting and training foreign workers, unskilled workers and others.

Learning Goal 4

8. U.S. executives are responsible for billion dollar corporations. They often work 70 or more hours per week. Many can show stockholders that they have turned potential problems into profitable success. Further, many top performers in sports, movies and entertainment are paid large sums, so is it therefore out of line that CEOs of major corporations should be compensated in the same way? The high level of executive pay creates incentives for lower level managers to work hard to get those jobs.

9. The drawbacks of the high level of pay are most noticeable when an executive makes staggering sums, while the financial performance of the company may be lagging. Lavish compensation for executives who are ordering cutbacks, layoffs and corporate austerity for everyone else makes other stakeholders, employees, small investors and unions angry. In comparison to our global competitors, U.S. executives earn substantially more than their counterparts. In the U.S. the average CEO earns 209 times what the average factory worker earns, while in Japan the CEO of a large corporation makes about 40 times the average factory worker. American CEOs typically earn two to three times as much as executives in Europe and Canada.

10. A comparison of jobs traditionally held by men with jobs traditionally held by women show that women earn about 71 percent of what men earn. In the past, this disparity could be explained by the fact that women only worked 50 to 60 percent of their available years after they left school, whereas men worked all of those years. As fewer women left the work force for an extended period, this changed. Another explanation for the disparity may be that many women try to work as well as care for families, and thus do not move ahead in their careers as quickly as men. Others opt for lower paying jobs that are less demanding.

11. The major question surrounding the issue of sexual harassment is the fact that while managers and workers may know that their company has a sexual harassment policy, they don't know what it says. The definition of sexual harassment is unwelcome sexual advances, requests for sexual favors, and other conduct of a sexual nature. The conduct becomes illegal when: 1) an employee's submission to such conduct is made either explicitly or implicitly a term of employment, 2) an employee's submission to or rejection of such conduct is used as the basis of employment decisions affecting the worker's status or 3) the conduct interferes with a worker's job performance or creates an unhealthy atmosphere. Companies are becoming more sensitive to comments and behavior of a sexual nature. Suggestions are more management training, mandatory sexual harassment workshops for all employees and a revamping of the human resource department if necessary to ensure compliance.

12. The need for day care in today's workplace has risen considerably with the continuing increase in the number of working women. According to statistics, a large percentage of women in the labor force will have children during their working years. The major questions are, "Who should provide day care and who should pay for it?" Working parents have made it clear that safe, affordable child-care is an issue on which they will not compromise. Companies have responded by providing a variety of arrangements designed to meet the needs of these valued workers.

13. a. The elder care issue has arisen because the workforce of the U.S. is aging. Older workers are more likely to be concerned with finding care for elderly parents than with finding day care for children. Some predict that elder care will have a greater impact on the workplace than child-care. Businesses do not seem to be responding to the need for elder care as quickly as they could, even though it is estimated that elder-care givers cost employers billions of dollars in lost output and replacement costs.
b. Because of the spread of AIDS, businesses are directing their attention to this serious problem. The most controversial employee-management policy concerns the mandatory testing for the AIDS antibody, as more firms are insisting upon that testing. A major reason for the testing is the cost to an employer that an AIDS afflicted employee can incur in terms of insurance, losses in productivity, increased absenteeism and employee turnover. Many firms have gone beyond pre-employment testing and suggested that all employees should be tested for the antibody.

c. Some companies feel that alcohol and drug abuse is an even more serious problem than AIDS, because so many more workers are involved. Drug testing is growing at a rapid pace.

d. Violence in the workplace is a growing trend. Still, many companies don't offer formal training for dealing with prevention of violence in the workplace, because managers are not taking the issue seriously.

14. The goals of ESOPs are employee ownership, employee pride, and better customer relations. However, while the goals of ESOPs are positive, the major problem stems from implementation of the program. In most ESOPs employees do not have voting rights. They do not have a strong voice on the company's board of directors and are helpless when it comes to major decision making.

PRACTICE TEST

Multiple Choice

1.	c	9.	c
2.	a	10.	a
3.	d	11.	b
4.	b	12.	d
5.	d	13.	a
6.	c	14.	d
7.	b	15.	c
8.	d	16.	b

True/False

1.	T	6.	T
2.	F	7.	F
3.	F	8.	T
4.	T	9.	F
5.	T	10.	T

CHAPTER 13
MARKETING: BUILDING CUSTOMER AND STAKEHOLDER RELATIONSHIPS

LEARNING GOALS

After you have read and studied this chapter, you should be able to:

1. Define marketing and summarize the steps involved in the marketing process.

2. Describe marketing's changing role in society and the merging of the marketing concept with total quality management.

3. Describe how relationship marketing differs from traditional marketing.

4. List the four Ps of marketing.

5. Apply the four parts of the marketing research process to a business problem.

6. Differentiate between consumer and industrial markets and compare the various forms of market segmentation.

LEARNING THE LANGUAGE

Listed below are important terms found in the chapter. Choose the correct term for the definition and write it in the space provided.

Brand name	Marketing mix
Business to business marketing	Marketing research
Cognitive dissonance	Mass marketing
Consumer market	Niche marketing
Focus group	Primary data
Green product	Product
Market	Promotion
Market segmentation	Relationship marketing
Marketing	Secondary data
Marketing concept	Target marketing
Marketing management	Test marketing

13-1

1. A word, letter or group of words or letters is a _____ that differentiates the goods and services of a seller from those of a competitor.

2. All the techniques sellers use to motivate people to buy products or services is called _____.

3. Already-published research reports called _____ come from journals, trade associations, the government, information services, libraries, and so forth.

4. All individuals and organizations that want goods and services to produce other goods and services or to sell, rent or supply goods to others is known as the _____.

5. The process known as _____ is when an organization tests products among potential users.

6. The process called _____ calls for planning and executing the conception, pricing, promotion, and distribution of ideas, goods and services to create mutually beneficial exchanges.

7. A _____ is any physical good, service or idea that satisfies a want or need.

8. Facts and figures known as _____ are not previously published and you gather them on your own.

9. A three-part business philosophy called the _____ involves (1) a customer orientation, (2) service orientation, and (3) a profit orientation.

10. A _____ is a small group of people who meet under the direction of a discussion leader to communicate their opinions about an organization, its products, or other important issues.

11. The process known as _____ calls for finding very small, but profitable market segments and designing custom-made products for those groups.

12. Consumer doubts after a purchase about whether or not the purchase was the best product at the best price is called _____.

13. The ingredients that go into a marketing program are the _____ that include product, price, place, and promotion.

14. A product is called a _____ when the production, use, and disposal don't damage the environment.

15. The process known as _____ is how an organization decides which market segments it can profitably serve.

16. The process called _____ is used to determine what consumer and industrial clients want and need to select the most effective way to satisfy those wants and needs.

17. Establishing and maintaining mutually beneficial exchange relationships with internal and external customers and all the other stakeholders of the company is called _____.

18. The _____ consists of all the individuals or households who want goods and services for personal consumption or use.

19. The process of _____ is determining customer wants and needs and then providing customers with goods and services that meet or exceed their expectations.

20. A _____ consists of people with unsatisfied wants and needs who have both the resources and the willingness to buy.

21. The process of dividing the total market into several groups that have similar characteristics is called _____.

22. Developing products and promotions that are designed to please large groups of people is known as _____.

RETENTION CHECK

Learning Goal 1   **What is Marketing?**

1. How does a database help in the marketing of products?

2. List the eight steps in the marketing process.

   a. _____

   b. _____

   c. _____

   d. _____

   e. _____

   f. _____

   g. _____

   h. _____

3. What is meant by "concept testing"?

4. What are prototypes?

5. What are marketing middlemen?

6. What are four promotion techniques?

   a. _____

   b. _____

   c. _____

   d. _____

Learning Goal 2 **Total Quality and the Marketing Concept**

7. What are the three basic elements of the marketing concept?

   a. _____

   b. _____

   c. _____

8. What is a customer orientation?

9. What is a service orientation?

10. What is a profit orientation?

11. What is meant by "delighting customers"?

12. How does marketing relate to cross functional teams?

13. What does a company do with its profits?

Learning Goal 3 **Relationship Marketing**

14. How does a mass marketer "operate?"

15. What is the goal of relationship marketing?

16. How is a "community of customers" established?

Learning Goal 4 **Marketing Management and the Marketing Mix**

17. What is a mutually beneficial exchange?

18. List the four Ps of the marketing mix.

   a. _____

   b. _____

   c. _____

   d. _____

19. What does a marketing manager do? What is marketing management?

20. What three elements are necessary for a market?

    a. _____

    b. _____

    c. _____

Learning Goal 5   **Determining What Customers Want**

21. What are three things which marketing research helps to determine?

    a. _____

    b. _____

    c. _____

22. What are the four steps of the marketing research process?

    a. _____

    b. _____

    c. _____

    d. _____

23. What is the difference between primary and secondary data?

24. What is the observation method of collecting data?

25. What are six general sources of secondary data?

   a. _____   d. _____

   b. _____   e. _____

   c. _____   f. _____

26. What are five sources of primary data?

   a. _____   d. _____

   b. _____   e. _____

   c. _____   f. _____

27. What do marketers need to do in order to do effective marketing research?

28. Why is the need for research even greater for international markets?

29. What are the steps in the consumer decision-making process?

   a. _____

   b. _____

   c. _____

   d. _____

   e. _____

30. List the four types of influences on the consumer decision making process.

   a. _____

   b. _____

   c. _____

   d. _____

31. What is "culture"?

32. What impact does learning have on our buying behavior?

33. What is a "reference group"?

Learning Goal 6   **Recognizing Different Markets: Consumer and Business-to-Business**

34. What are two major markets in marketing?

35. What determines if a product is a business-to-business product or a consumer product?

36. How does a company segment the consumer market?

37. What has made "niche marketing" possible?

38. What is one-to-one marketing?

39. How does business-to-business marketing differ from consumer marketing?

40. What are five factors that differentiate business-to-business marketing from consumer marketing?

   a. _____

   b. _____

   c. _____

   d. _____

   e. _____

CRITICAL THINKING EXERCISES

Learning Goal 1

1. Todd Whitman was a full-time student at a community college in the St. Louis area. In addition to going to school, Todd also worked for a company out of Idaho (Todd's home state) that made ice cream. As Todd tells it: "Alan Reed owns a potato farm in Idaho. He was looking for another market for his potatoes when he realized that the chemical makeup of the potato was such that it could be used in making a tasty ice cream without using any sugar - i.e. a sugar free ice cream. He figured there had to be a market for that kind of product, one made without any artificial products to sweeten, so he made a few batches and tried it on his friends, without telling them it was made from potatoes." He called the ice cream Al and Reed's. This is where Todd came in. While in St. Louis, Todd's job was to attempt to get the product sold to St. Louisans. His employer shipped him a few gallons (as much as he could hold in his home freezer). Todd started trying to sell Al and Reed's to local grocery store chains, and ultimately got one of them to carry the ice cream in a couple of stores on a trial basis. He also brought some samples into his Introduction to Business class, after persuading his teacher to allow a taste test. The product went over well, until the students found out it was made from potatoes.

Todd continued his promotional efforts with grocery stores, calling on them whenever he could. He left promotional pamphlets that explained the concept and production of ice cream made from potatoes, and offered the stores discounts for buying in volume.

a. What steps in the marketing process did Todd and Alan Reed take?

b. Did Alan "find a need and fill it"?

c. What potential problem might they encounter with this product? How could Todd and Alan use the last step of the marketing process to overcome the problem?

Learning Goal 2

2. The goal of the marketing concept in the past was to provide customer satisfaction. How have firms gone beyond that goal with TQM?

3. We read in earlier chapters about the latest concepts of organizational design such as cross-functional, self managed teams, and continuous improvement. What does all that have to do with marketing?

Learning Goal 3

4. How has technology enabled companies to go from mass marketing to more customized marketing?

Learning Goals 1, 2, 3, 4

5. We have been "creating" a company, and its product, Music-stor throughout several chapters. Now is the time to begin developing a marketing plan for our product. We will become more specific in the following chapters. Generally,

    a. What need did Eric see when he came up with the idea of Music-stor?

    b. Who/what do you think should be Music-stor's customers?

    c. How could concept testing have helped Eric?

    d. How do the various elements of the marketing environment affect Music-stor?

e. Could Music-stor make use of "customized marketing?"

6. Marketing research is conducted to determine the needs of the market and the best ways to fill those needs. Using the four steps outlined in your book, suggest a market research project that might be of use to Music-stor:

a.

b.

c.

d.

Learning Goal 5

7. Harry Allen turned on his stereo to listen to music while he was studying, and all he heard was a loud buzzing coming from his speakers. "Oh no! Now what?" thought Harry. Well, Harry found the problem, and realized that the system was shot. "Well, we've got to have tunes for the party coming up in two weeks, so I'm going to have to get a new player" Harry said to his roommate on the way to class. Harry looked through the ads in the Sunday paper, and saw several sales at a couple of different stores. He spent part of the weekend, and part of a few days the following week looking at different component pieces, comparing each for price and sound quality and talking to sales people about which system was the best value. A couple of friends gave Harry their opinions of the brands, based on their experience with the specific brand Harry was looking at. Harry knew this brand was a good one, because his sister had purchased it last year. He bought the new stereo system the following weekend, before the sale went off. He felt somewhat uneasy at how much he had spent, but when he saw an ad for that same system in an upscale magazine for $100 more, he felt better.

    Identify the steps in the decision making process that Harry took, and what factors influenced his decision, using Figure 13-6 in your text.

8. The buyer's reason for buying and the end use of the product are what determine whether a product is considered a consumer product or an industrial product. Determine whether the following describes a consumer or an industrial product.

    1. Monsanto buys apples to sell in its company cafeteria. _____

    2. Jeff Walter buys a lawn mower for his lawn mowing business. _____

    3. Darlene Knott buys a lawn mower to mow her lawn. _____

    4. Marti Galganski buys apples for her daughter's lunch. _____

9. How would you classify Music-Stor's product? What characteristics of the business-to-business market will affect Music-stor's marketing efforts, and why?

10. Let's continue helping Music-stor develop a marketing plan:

   a. Who would you choose as Music-stor's target market?

   b. If you choose to target the consumer market, what are some variables that you would want to consider?

   c. How would marketing your product to an industrial market differ from marketing the product to the consumer market?

PRACTICE TEST

Multiple Choice: Circle the best answer.

1. If a "customer is king", then _____ must come first in business activities.

    a. production
    b. distribution
    c. marketing
    d. planning

2. The basis of marketing is to:

    a. find a need and fill it.
    b. produce as many products as possible.
    c. look for a market, then make a product.
    d. find a good product and make it available at a reasonable price.

3. When McDonald's considered adding pizza to their menu, the company made pizza available in some of their markets, to determine customer reactions. That process is called:

    a. promotion.
    b. test marketing.
    c. outsourcing.
    d. concept testing.

4. Which of the following would not be included in a discussion of the marketing concept?

    a. A customer orientation
    b. Training employees in customer service
    c. Profit orientation
    d. Establish a market

5. When a firm is in the business of "delighting" the customer, what are they doing?

    a. Charging the lowest possible price
    b. Using advertising that is attractive and humorous
    c. Providing products that exceed the customer expectations
    d. Making products available in unexpected places

6. Businesses have learned that employees won't provide first class goods and services to customers unless they:

   a. receive first class treatment themselves.
   b. are paid wages considerably above average.
   c. are members of cross functional, self-managed teams.
   d. are given regular promotions.

7. Balancing the wants and needs of all a firm's stakeholders, such as employees, suppliers, dealers and the community is known as:

   a. a consumer orientation.
   b. relationship marketing.
   c. mass marketing.
   d. forming a community of buyers.

8. At one time, companies developed products and promotions to please large groups of people, and tried to sell as many products to as many people as possible. This is known as:

   a. relationship marketing.
   b. a consumer orientation.
   c. forming a community of buyers.
   d. mass marketing.

9. A mutually beneficial exchange occurs when:

   a. the company gets the price it wants.
   b. the marketing mix has been satisfied.
   c. both the company and its stakeholders believe they have received good value for their efforts.
   d. a marketing manager has designed a marketing program that effectively combines the marketing mix variables.

10. Which of the following is not considered one of the marketing mix variables?

    a. Producing a want satisfying product
    b. Promoting the product
    c. Simplifying the production process
    d. Setting a price for the product

11. Alonzo Wilder has just been hired as the marketing manager for the L. Ingalls farming co-op. In his job as marketing manager, Alonzo's primary responsibility will be to:

    a. make sure the product is priced reasonably.
    b. manage the primary sales force.
    c. monitor production and make sure the product is in the right place at the right time.
    d. manage the marketing mix variables to ensure an effective marketing program.

12. Which of the following is not a requirement for a "market"?

    a. People with unsatisfied wants and needs
    b. People who have the authority to buy
    c. People who have the resources to buy
    d. People who have the willingness to buy

13. Marketing research helps determine all of the following except:

    a. how customer needs will change.
    b what customers have purchased in the past.
    c. what changes have occurred to change what customers want.
    d. what customers are likely to want in the future.

14. What is the first step in the marketing research process?

    a. Analyze data   c. Define the problem
    b. Collect data   d. Develop potential solutions

15. Curious George went to the library to look up government statistics on the amount of bananas imported into the U.S. during the previous year. Curious was making use of:

    a. primary data.
    b. secondary data.
    c. the observation method.
    d. focused research.

16. What must be done in order to do effective marketing research?

    a. Develop a good understanding of the mass market.
    b. Make sure that all research is up-to-date.
    c. Use as many secondary sources as possible to keep costs down.
    d. Get out of the office and close to customers to determine their needs.

17. Kelly Butler is out looking for a new car. Kelly is an aspiring lawyer, and she is looking for a car that will help her to project that "lawyer " image. Kelly is influenced by:

    a. a cultural influence.
    b. a reference group.
    c. cognitive dissonance.
    d. the consumer market.

18. After Kelly bought her car, she realized just how much money she had spent! She spent some time wondering if she had made the right decision. Kelly seems to be suffering from:

    a. cognitive dissonance.
    b. consumer behavior.
    c. self-doubt.
    d. psychological influences.

19. The company that makes the Nautica brand licensed with the Stride-Rite company to make an athletic shoe to compete with Nike. The company wants the shoe to be used for athletics, not worn just for style. Nautica is making use of:

    a. market analysis.
    b. market segmentation.
    c. niche marketing.
    d. one-to-one marketing.

20. Which of the following is NOT descriptive of the business-to-business market?

    a. There are relatively few customers in the industrial market.
    b. Industrial customers are relatively large.
    c. Industrial buyers are generally more rational than consumer buyers.
    d. Industrial markets tend to be geographically scattered.

TRUE/FALSE

1. _____ The role of marketing is to make a good or service, and then make sure people want to buy it.

2. _____ Marketing middlemen are organizations that traditionally are in the middle of a series of organizations that distribute goods from producers to consumers.

3. _____ According to the text, most organizations have reached the goal of delighting customers.

4. _____ Competitive benchmarking means that companies will only concentrate on those activities which they do best, and they will outsource those functions at which they do not excel.

5. _____ Relationship marketing leads away from mass production toward more custom-made goods and services.

6. _____ The four marketing mix variables are product, price, packaging and promotion.

7. _____ One goal of marketing research is to determine exactly what consumers want and need.

8. _____ To minimize costs, it is best to use secondary data first, when possible.

9. _____ In determining the best solution in the marketing research process, companies should consider what's the right thing to do as well as the profitable thing to do.

10. _____ The process of dividing the total market into several groups is called target marketing.

11. _____ The reason for distinguishing between consumer markets and the business to business market is because the strategies for reaching the market are different, because the buyers are different.

12. _____ Industrial sales tend to be less direct than consumer sales, because industrial buyers use more middlemen.

ANSWERS

KEY TERMS AND DEFINITIONS

1. Brand name	8. Primary data	15. Target marketing
2. Promotion	9. Marketing concept	16. Marketing research
3. Secondary data	10. Focus group	17. Relationship marketing
4. Business to business market	11. Niche marketing	18. Consumer market
5. Test marketing	12. Cognitive dissonance	19. Marketing
6. Marketing management	13. Marketing mix	20. Market
7. Product	14. Green product	21. Market segmentation
		22. Mass marketing

RETENTION CHECK

Learning Goal 1 **What Is Marketing?**

1. The role of marketing is to determine exactly what customers want and then to provide products that fill those needs. Because purchases are recorded in a database, knowing what customers want is much easier. Using the information in the database, stores can send out coupons and advertisements specifically designed to appeal to certain groups.

2. The steps in the marketing process are:
   a. Find a need.
   b. Conduct research.
   c. Design a product to meet the need, based upon research results.
   d. Test the product.
   e. Determine brand name, design packaging and set a price.
   f. Select a distribution system.
   g. Design a promotional program.
   h. Build a relationship with your customers.

3. In concept testing, an accurate description of a product is developed, and then people are asked whether the concept appeals to them.

4. Prototypes are samples of the product that you take to consumers to test their reactions.

5. Marketing middlemen are organizations that specialize in distributing products. They are called middlemen because they're in the middle of a series of organizations that distribute goods from producers to consumers.

6. Promotion techniques include:
   a. advertising.
   b. personal selling.
   c. publicity.
   d. sales promotion.

Learning Goal 2 **Total Quality and the Marketing Concepts**

7. The elements of the marketing concept are:
   a. A service orientation.
   b. A service orientation.
   c. A profit orientation.

8. A customer orientation is to find out what customers want and provide it for them.

9. A service orientation involves training employees from all areas in customer service to ensure customer satisfaction.

10. In pursuing a profit orientation a firm will market those goods and services that will earn the firm a profit and enable it to survive and expand to serve more customers.

11. The goal of some total quality firms is to delight customers by providing goods and services that exactly meet their requirements or exceed their expectations. The objective then is to make sure that the response to customer wants and needs is so fast and courteous that customers are truly surprised and pleased by the experience.

12. Businesses have learned that employees won't provide first class goods and services to customers unless they receive first-class treatment themselves. Marketers therefore must learn to work with others in the firm to help make sure that employees are pleased. Barriers between departments must fall, and then marketers need to form cross-functional teams with designers, engineers, production personnel and others in the firm to develop quality products.

13. When a firm makes a profit, it can use that profit to satisfy other stakeholders of the firm such as stockholders, environmentalists, and the local community.

Learning Goal 3   **Relationship Marketing**

14. A mass marketer tries to sell products to as many people as possible, using mass media such as TV, radio and newspapers. Many marketing managers will get so caught up with their products and competition that they become less responsive to the market.

15. Relationship marketing leads away from mass production toward more custom-made goods and services. The goal is to keep individual customers over time by offering them more products that exactly meet their requirements. It is more concerned with retaining old customers than creating new ones. This is done with special deals, fantastic service, loyalty programs and maintaining databases that enable companies to custom-make products for customers.

16. A community of customers is established by creating a database so that every contact with customers results in more information about them. Over time, the seller knows more and more about consumers. Companies establish web sites where customers can provide their input and talk to other customers. Some companies will have events where the manufacturer sends merchandise, staff, information, and give-away items. Community bonding leads to a strong commitment to the company and its products.

Learning Goal 4   **Marketing Management and the Marketing Mix**

17. A mutually beneficial exchange means that both parties to the exchange believe they have received good value for their efforts.

18. The four Ps of the marketing mix are:
    a. Product.
    b. Price.
    c. Promotion.
    d. Place.

19. A marketing manager designs a marketing program that effectively combines the ingredients of the marketing mix in order to please customers. Marketing management is the process of planning and executing the conception, pricing, promotion, and distribution of goods and services to create mutually beneficial exchanges.

20. A market must have:
   a. people with unsatisfied wants and needs.
   b. people who have the resources to buy.
   c. people who have the willingness to buy.

Learning Goal 5   **Determining What Customers Want**

21. Marketing research helps to determine:
   a. what customers have purchased in the past.
   b. what situational changes have occurred to change what customers want.
   c. what they're likely to want in the future.

22. The steps of the marketing research process are:
   a. Define the problem and determine the present situation.
   b. Collect data.
   c. Analyze the research data.
   d. Choose the best solutions.

23. Primary data are statistics and information not previously published that you gather on your own through observation, surveys, and personal interviews or focus groups. Secondary data are published reports and research from journals, trade associations, the government, information services and others. Secondary data would be used before primary whenever possible.

24. In the observation method, data are collected by observing the actions of potential buyers.

25. Sources of secondary data include:
   a. Government publications.
   b. Commercial publications.
   c. Magazines.
   d. Newspapers.
   e. Internal company sources.
   f. Internet searches.

26. Sources of primary data include:
   a. Observation.
   b. Surveys.
   c. Experiments.
   d. Focus groups.
   e. Questionnaires.

27. Effective marketing research calls for getting out of the office and getting close to customers to find out what they want and need. Laboratory research and consumer panels can never replace going into people's homes, watching them use products, and asking them what improvements they would like.

28. In international markets, one must learn the culture of the people and talk with them directly. To find a need and fill it in the international market, marketers must adapt to all the customs and beliefs of the people with whom they are dealing

29. The steps in the consumer decision-making process are:
    a. Problem recognition.
    b. Information search.
    c. Alternative evaluation.
    d. Purchase decision.
    e. Postpurchase decision (cognitive dissonance).

30. Types of influence on consumer decision-making include:
    a. Marketing mix influences—product, price, promotion, place.
    b. Sociocultural influences—Reference groups, family, social class, culture, subculture.
    c. Situational influences—Type of purchase, social surroundings, physical surroundings, previous experience.
    d. Psychological influences—Perception, attitudes, learning, motivation.

31. Culture is the set of values, attitudes and ways of doing things transmitted from one generation to another.

32. Learning involves a change in a person's behavior that results from previous experiences and information.

33. A reference group is the group that an individual uses as a reference point in the formation of their beliefs, attitudes, values, or behavior.

Learning Goal 6   **Recognizing Different Markets: Consumer and Business-to-Business**

34. The two major markets in marketing are the consumer market and the business to business market.

35. The buyer's reason for buying and the end use of the product determine whether a product is considered a consumer product or an industrial product.

36. The consumer market can be segmented by demographic variables such as sex, and age, by geographics and by different wants and needs of consumers.

37. New manufacturing techniques make it possible to develop specialized products for small market groups. This is called niche marketing.

38. One-to-one marketing means developing a unique mix of goods and services for each individual customer. Travel agencies often develop such packages. This is easier to do in industrial markets where customers buy in large volume.

39. The strategies differ between consumer marketing and business to business marketing.

40. Factors that differentiate business-to-business marketing from consumer marketing include:
    a. The number of customers in the industrial market is relatively few.
    b. The size of industrial customers is relatively large.
    c. Industrial markets tend to be geographically concentrated.
    d. Industrial buyers generally are more rational than individual consumers are.
    e. Industrial sales tend to be direct.

CRITICAL THINKING EXERCISES

Learning Goal 1

1. a. Alan recognized the need for a sugar free ice cream. (Step 1). At least he thought he did. We don't know how much research he did on the actual demand for a sugar free ice cream. (2)He did test the concept by making small batches and testing it with his friends. (3)He made the product in small batches at first. (4)Todd did some research in his business class. You could say the concept testing was combined with the test marketing stage, or that St. Louis served as a test market. (5)The brand name stemmed from the originator's name, Alan Reed (Al and Reed's). (6)The marketing middlemen are Todd, and then the grocery stores which finally agreed to sell the product through Todd's efforts. (7)Promotion was done primarily through pamphlets and personal selling by Todd. There is no mention made of any effort to build a relationship with the customer.

b. From the story, it doesn't sound as if Al found a need for a sugar free ice cream and then found a way to develop it. It sounds more like he had extra potatoes and needed to find a novel way to sell them! It would appear that Alan Reed took a "production orientation."

c. Probably the biggest potential problem is the negative reaction to the product. It could be that consumers will not be attracted to ice cream made from potatoes, and would wonder about the taste. The students actually liked the taste of the ice cream until they found out it was made from potatoes. By talking with consumers, grocery store managers (who are consumers too, and must be convinced), Todd and Alan may have found ways to overcome the perception that ice cream made from potatoes must taste terrible.

Learning Goal 2

2. The marketing concept includes finding out what customers want and then providing them with a product that satisfies their needs, training all employees in customer satisfaction and maintaining a profit orientation by selling goods and services which will earn a profit. TQM has taken those concepts further by making the goal not just one of providing customer satisfaction, but of pleasing, dazzling and delighting customers by exactly meeting their needs.

3. It has become clear that everyone in a firm has to work together to please, delight and dazzle customers. Companies have begun to see that employees will not provide first-class goods and services to customers unless they receive first-class treatment from their employer. Therefore, we have seen changes in organizational design, and a focus on the "internal" customer. Cross functional teams, discussed in previous chapters, are practicing continuous improvement, and uniting employees in a joint effort to produce goods and services which will both please customers and assure a profit for the firm.

Learning Goal 3

4. With sophisticated information technology, marketers are able to find out what customers are buying, and what they will want to buy in the future. With such programs as CAD/CAM, flexible manufacturing, and mass customization, companies can more readily meet smaller, more individualized markets. With new production and information technology, companies will be able to both establish and maintain long-term relationships with customers.

Learning Goals 1, 2, 3, 4

5.   a. Eric may have seen that more people are listening to tapes and compact discs in their cars. Compact discs especially are growing in popularity. When people want to listen to their own music in the car, a convenient place to store several tapes or CDs would be a real benefit.
b. We have discussed two types of customers, the automotive manufacturers, for installation as an option in new cars, and the after-market dealers, like auto supply stores, for people who want to install their own.
c. Asking people if they need a product such as this would have given Eric a feel for what demand might have been. He would have to be sure to ask the right questions of the right people to get an accurate idea. He could have given prototypes to friends, or potential customers, for use, to "field test" or test market the product.
d. The <u>social</u> environment consists of trends and population shifts, for example. The trend toward installing compact disc players in autos, for example, contributes to a positive outlook for Music-stor's product. As the population ages, more people may prefer to listen to music they bring along, rather than the radio. Since that type of equipment comes only in certain kinds of cars, <u>economic</u> factors such as disposable income, and unemployment would affect demand for the cars, and thus for Music-stor's product. With a rapidly expanding <u>global</u> market, there may be possibilities outside the United States, as well as potential competition. <u>Technology</u> has affected Music-stor simply by virtue of the fact that CD players are a fact of life in cars today. Further, new high-tech production techniques will help Music-stor to produce more products with fewer people at a lower cost.
e. Can Music-stor adopt customized marketing? Basically, the product must be made to suit many different models of car, with different interior shapes, different interior colors. The product is "custom made" for "customized marketing."

6.   a. Music-stor may want to determine what kind of demand there will be for their product in the next five years. They may want to find out if their primary market should be younger or older drivers, and relate that to the type of car being driven. They may also want to determine if there are other markets they could enter. For example, over-the-road truckers could make use of this product, but it may have to be of a different size and shape to fit into the cab of a semi.
b. Collecting secondary data for the automotive market may be easily done to determine potential demand for autos and related products in the automotive market. Trade journals and government publications would provide sales forecasts for the type of cars Music-stor is targeting. The truck market may require some primary research, such as focus groups or some kind of survey, possible distributed through the mail or directly to truckers in some way.
c. Analysis of the data may indicate there is a bigger market for the product for truckers than for the automotive market. Alternatively, it may indicate that sales are predicted to go flat for the kinds of cars Music-stor has targeted, indicating that the company may want to target a different car segment, or another market altogether.
d. Choosing the best solution would entail choosing the market that will be the most profitable for Music-stor and still meet the needs of their stakeholders.

Learning Goal 5

7. Problem recognition came when Harry realized his system couldn't be fixed! Harry searched for information through the newspaper ads, and also by going to the stores and talking to salespeople. He was evaluating the alternatives by comparing each component piece for value and sound. When he finally made his purchase, he felt "cognitive dissonance," until he saw an ad for the same brand at a more expensive price.

   Along the way, several factors influenced Harry's decision. He spoke to friends, which could be considered a reference group. Family may have been an influence, as Harry's sister has the same brand. There was a cultural influence as well, by the fact that Harry felt it necessary to have a new stereo system for his party, rather that use a less expensive tape player or some other alternative. The price variable of the marketing mix was an influence, as the system was on sale. You could also consider the psychological influence of learning, as Harry's friends had learned, that this was a good brand through experience, and passed that information along. You may have thought of other influences as well.

8.
   a. Industrial
   b. Industrial
   c. Consumer
   d. Consumer

9. Music-stor's product could be classified as both a consumer product and a product for the business-to-business market. If Eric sells the storage case through after market auto equipment retailers, the product would be considered a consumer good. In attempting to reach automobile manufacturers, Eric is developing a business-to-business marketing relationship. The characteristics of the business-to-business market listed in your book will affect Music-stor in a number of ways. First, the primary market is the automotive industry, which has relatively few customers compared to the consumer market. The few car manufacturers are very large corporations, among the largest in the world, each with significant buying power. The domestic car market, at least, is concentrated in one geographic area. If Eric were to try to appeal to buyers for foreign manufacturers, he would have to do some more travelling. These buyers will consider Eric's product based on the "total product offer," including how much more marketable Music-stor will make their product, in addition to factors such as quality and price. If the customer is the auto industry, Eric won't need to use wholesalers or retailers, but will instead sell directly to the car companies. For the consumer market, he will have to use at least a retail distribution center.

10. Keep in mind these are suggested answers, and you may come up with a totally different plan.

a. We have often mentioned two target markets for Music-stor: the automotive equipment market, to be installed as cars are assembled; and a consumer market, through auto parts stores for people who want to install the product later. You may have decided on another way to approach the market.

b. If you chose the consumer market, many variables need to be considered. Demographic and geographic factors must be considered as well as other related variables. This is where research can really come in handy.

c. To market to the industrial market, Music-stor must focus on personal selling, in a very concentrated market. The automobile industry has few domestic producers, some foreign manufacturers with production facilities here in the United States. You would have to focus on quality, be able to meet the volume required to sell to the industrial market, and meet delivery requirements that may include dealing with a just-in-time inventory control system. This would require a sophisticated production and delivery system on the part of Music-stor.

PRACTICE TEST

Multiple Choice				True/False			
1.	c	11.	d	1.	F	7.	T
2.	a	12.	b	2.	T	8.	T
3.	b	13.	a	3.	F	9.	T
4.	d	14.	c	4.	F	10.	F
5.	c	15.	b	5.	T	11.	T
6.	a	16.	d	6.	F	12.	F
7.	b	17.	b				
8.	d	18.	a				
9.	c	19.	b				
10.	c	20.	d				

CHAPTER 14
DEVELOPING AND PRICING QUALITY PRODUCTS AND SERVICES

LEARNING GOALS

After you have read and studied this chapter, you should be able to:

1. Explain the difference between a product and a value package.

2. Describe how businesses create product differentiation for their goods and services in both the consumer and industrial markets.

3. List and describe the six functions of packaging.

4. Give examples of a brand, a brand name, and a trademark, and explain how to prevent a brand name from becoming generic.

5. Explain the role of product managers and the five steps of the new-product development process.

6. Identify and describe the stages of the product life cycle and describe marketing strategies at each stage.

7. Give examples of various pricing objectives and show how break-even analysis helps in pricing decisions.

LEARNING THE LANGUAGE

Listed below are important terms found in the chapter. Choose the correct term for the definition and write it in the space provided.

Brand	Product life cycle
Brand associations	Product line
Brand awareness	Product manager
Brand equity	Product mix
Brand loyalty	Shopping goods and services
Break-even analysis	Skimming pricing strategy
Convenience goods and services	Specialty goods and services
Dealer brands (private brands)	Total fixed costs
Generic goods	Trademark
Generic name	Unsought goods and services
Industrial goods	Value package

Manufacturer's brand	Value pricing
Penetration strategy	Variable costs
Product differentiation	

1. The process used to determine profitability at various levels of sales is called _____.

2. The method of pricing known as a(n) _____ is when a product is priced low to attract more customers and discourage competitors.

3. The term _____ is used to describe the combination of product lines offered by a manufacturer.

4. A(n) _____ consists of everything that consumers evaluate when deciding whether or not to buy something.

5. The degree to which customers are satisfied, like the brand, and are committed to further purchases is called _____.

6. The four-stage theoretical model called the _____ is depiction of the process from birth to death of a product class: introduction, growth, maturity, and decline.

7. A strategy known as a(n) _____ is a method of pricing the product high to make optimum profit while there is little competition.

8. A brand that has been given exclusive legal protection for both the brand name and the pictorial design is called a(n) _____.

9. The linking of a brand to other favorable images is called _____.

10. Products called _____ are used in the production of other products.

11. Known as _____, these are all the costs that remain the same no matter how many products are sold.

12. A strategy known as _____ means offering consumers brand name goods and services at fair prices.

13. A(n) _____ is a name, symbol, or design that identifies the goods or services of one seller or group of sellers and distinguishes them from those of competitors.

14. A(n) _____ coordinates all the marketing efforts for a particular product or brand.

15. Products called _____ are products that consumers want to purchase frequently with a minimum of effort.

16. The name for a product category is a(n) _____.

17. Products called _____ do not carry the manufacturer's name, but carry the name of a distributor or retailer instead.

18. Products that have a special attraction to consumers who are willing to go out of their way to obtain them are called _____.

19. When your product is the first recalled when a product category is mentioned your product has _____.

20. A group of products known as the _____ are physically similar or are intended for a similar market.

21. Nonbranded products called _____ usually sell at a sizable discount from national or private brands, have very basic packaging, and are backed with little or no advertising.

22. The creation of real product differences or perceptions that make one product seem superior to others is called _____.

23. Products known as _____ are products that consumers are unaware of, haven't necessarily thought of buying, or find that they need to solve an unexpected problem.

24. Consumers buy _____ only after comparing value, quality, and price from a variety of sellers.

25. A combination of factors called _____ includes awareness, loyalty, perceived quality, the feeling and images and any other emotion people associate with a brand name.

26. The brand names of manufacturers that distribute a product nationally are called _____.

27. Costs known as _____ change according to the level of production.

RETENTION CHECK

Learning Goal 1 **Product Development and the Value Package**

1. What must marketers do today to satisfy customer?

2. What are the factors that make up the "value package" of a product?

   a. _____   g. _____

   b. _____   h. _____

   c. _____   i. _____

   d. _____   j. _____

   e. _____   k. _____

   f. _____

3. How can businesses keep customers?

4. What is the difference between a product line and a product mix?

Learning Goal 2 **Product Differentiation**

5. How does a marketer create product differentiation?

6. What are questions to ask when determining how to improve a customer's experience with your product?

   a. _____

   b. _____

   c. _____

   d. _____

7. List the four different classes of consumer goods and services. Give an example of each kind.

   a. _____

   b. _____

   c. _____

   d. _____

8. What are three variables important to marketers of convenience goods?

   a. _____ b. _____ c. _____

9. What can marketers of shopping goods emphasize?

10. How are specialty goods marketed?

11. Where are unsought goods often displayed?

12. What's the best way to market convenience goods?

   a. _____

   b. _____

13. What are the best appeals for promoting shopping goods?

   a. _____

   b. _____

   c. _____

14. What do makers of specialty goods rely on to appeal to their markets?

    a. _____

    b. _____

    c. _____

15. What determines how a good is classified?

16. What distinguishes a consumer good from an industrial good?

17. Can a good be classified as both? How?

18. What are two general categories of industrial goods?

    a. _____

    b. _____

19. What are categories of production goods?

   a. _____

   b. _____

   c. _____

20. What are categories of support goods?

   a. _____   c. _____

   b. _____   d. _____

Learning Goal 3   **Packaging Changes the Product**

21. How can packaging change a product?

22. Identify the functions of packaging.

   a. _____

   b. _____

   c. _____

   d. _____

   e. _____

   f. _____

Learning Goal 4 **Building Brand Equity**

23. What are four categories of brands?

    a. _____   c. _____

    b. _____   d. _____

24. How can a brand name become a generic brand?

25. List the important elements of brand equity.

    a. _____

    b. _____

    c. _____

    d. _____

    e. _____

26. What's the difference between brand awareness and brand preference?

27. Why is perceived quality an important part of brand equity?

Learning Goal 5 **Product Management**

28. What are four reasons for product failure?

   a. _____   c. _____

   b. _____   d. _____

29. Identify the steps in the new product development process.

   a. _____   d. _____

   b. _____   e. _____

   c. _____

30. What are four sources of new product ideas for consumer products?

   a. _____   c. _____

   b. _____   d. _____

31. What are four sources of new product ideas for industrial goods?

   a. _____   c. _____

   b. _____   d. _____

32. What is product screening?

33. What is concept testing?

34. What are two important elements for commercialization?

   a. _____

   b. _____

35. What must U.S. firms do with the new product development process to compete internationally?

Learning Goal 6 **The Product Life Cycle**

36. What are the four stages of the product life cycle?

    a. _____

    b. _____

    c. _____

    d. _____

37. What's important about the product life cycle?

38. Complete the following chart.

	Product	Price	Promotion	Place
Introduction				
Growth				
Maturity				
Decline				

Learning Goal 7 **Competitive Pricing**

39. What are six pricing objectives?

   a. _____   d. _____

   b. _____   e. _____

   c. _____   f. _____

40. Name two ways used to set prices.

   a. _____   b. _____

41. In the long run, who or what determines price?

42. What is the difference between cost-based pricing, price led pricing, and value pricing?

43. How do service industries use the same pricing tactics as goods-producing firms?

44. What is a break-even point?

45. What is the formula for determining a break-even point?

46. Describe five pricing strategies for new products.

   a. _____   d. _____

   b. _____   e. _____

   c. _____

47. At what level is price set in a skimming strategy? Why?

48. At what level are prices set in a penetration strategy? Why?

49. What is demand oriented pricing?

50. What is competition oriented pricing?

51. What will determine the price level when using competition oriented pricing?

52. What is likely to spur on non-price competition?

53. How do firms compete using something other than price?

54. What are three strategies for avoiding price wars?

   a. _____

   b. _____

   c. _____

CRITICAL THINKING EXERCISES

Learning Goal 1

1. In Chapter 13 you read about the importance of the marketing process. Explain the relationship of the marketing concept to the importance of developing new products, as it is described in the text.

2. When people buy a product, they evaluate and compare the product on several dimensions:

For each product below, identify some of the dimensions that may influence the buyer.

a. Bicycle - _____
_____

b. Toothpaste - _____
_____

c. A new suit - _____
_____

3. What is the relationship between the "value" package of the product and the other marketing mix variables?

4. Identify 3 product lines that General Motors sells, and a specific item in each line. What other products may make up their product mix?

   Product line _____   Item _____

   Product line _____   Item _____

   Product line _____   Item _____

Learning Goal 2

5. The two major product classifications are consumer goods and services and industrial goods and services.

   A. Classify the following products according to the most common use:

   1. Milk _____

   2. Steel _____

   3. Tickets to the Olympics _____

   4. Dry cleaners _____

   5. Diesel engines _____

   6. Flashlight batteries _____

   7. Auto repair _____

   8. Heart surgeon _____

   9. Management consultant _____

   10. Winter coat _____

B. Consumer goods and services are further classified as either: convenience, shopping, specialty or unsought. Indicate the correct class for each of the **consumer** items you identified above.

1. _____   5. _____

2. _____   6. _____

3. _____   7. _____

4. _____

Learning Goal 3

6. Packaging is carrying the promotional burden for products more than ever, and performs a number of functions: attract attention, describe contents, explain benefits, provide information, indicate price, value, and uses, and protect goods. Evaluate the importance of packaging, and which function(s) are the most important for the following:

   a. Lunch meat (like bologna) _____

   _____

   _____

   _____

   b. Children's cereal (like Fruit Loops) _____

   _____

   _____

   _____

c. Potato chips (like Ripples) _____

_____

_____

_____

Learning Goals 1, 2, 3

7. You are in conference with the marketing manager of Music-stor, and are still in the process of developing a marketing plan. In evaluating the disc and tape storage product produced by Music-stor, you want to know

   a. What dimensions customers might consider in purchasing Music-stor from a retailer?

   b. What is the total product offer?

   c. How can we differentiate the product?

   d. How would Music-stor be classified?

   e. Will packaging be an important consideration for Music-stor?

Learning Goal 4

8. Brand categories include manufacturer's brands and dealer (private) brands. Some brand names have become generic, and have come to describe an entire product category.

a. Identify a manufactuere brand and a dealer brand for each of the following:

		MANUFACTURER'S BRAND	DEALER BRAND
1.	Orange juice		
2.	Soft drinks		
3.	Small tools		
4.	Peanut butter		
5.	Blue jeans		
6.	Pain reliever		

b. How do you think customer perception of these products differs by the brand name? Why is this important?

c. What is the problem with a brand name becoming a generic name?

d. What are the important elements of brand equity, and how can brand equity be built?

Learning Goal 6

9. The product life cycle is a model of what happens to classes of products over time. It consists of four stages. Label the following illustration.

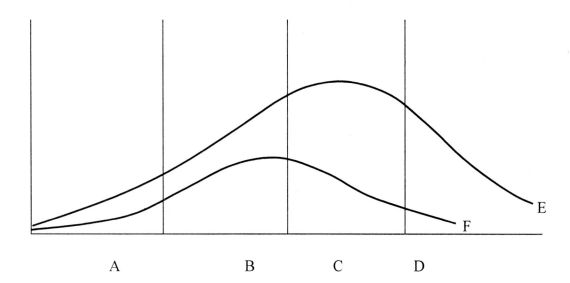

A. _____ D. _____

B. _____ E. _____

C. _____ F. _____

10. There are different marketing strategies used in each stage of the product life cycle. Using your text, give a specific example of a marketing strategy from one of the four Ps which could be used for the following products.

14-22

MARKETING STRATEGY

	Stage	Product	Marketing Strategy
a.	Introduction	Electric cars	_____
b.	Growth	Cellular phones	_____
c.	Maturity	Fast food	_____
d.	Decline	Black and white T.V.	_____

Learning Goal 7

11. Among the objectives that firms use in setting prices are:

    Achieve a target profit   Increase sales

    Build traffic   Create an image

    Achieve greater market share   Social objectives

Match the correct pricing objective to each of the following statements.

a. Kroger's advertises eggs at 10 cents a dozen. _____

b. Ralston Purina changes a price that gives them a 25% profit on dog food, higher than they need. Consumers are willing to pay the high price for this particular dog food. _____

c. Farmers in Arkansas receive subsidies on their grain products, so they can keep their prices artificially low. This keeps prices on derivative products low enough for a larger market to purchase. _____

d. Retailers, facing several dismal Christmas seasons in a row, slashed prices on a wide variety of merchandise for a number of years. _____

e. "Polo Crest", a cologne for men by Ralph Lauren, costs $45 for a small bottle in most upscale retail stores. _____

f. If you go to Midas Muffler with a bid from a competitor, Midas will meet that price in order to keep your business. _____

12. Using the concept of break-even analysis:

a. How many units will Music-stor have to sell to break even if their costs are $800,000 and the revenue from each unit is $25? _____

b. How much profit will Music-Stor make if they sell 45,000 units?
_____

c. What would the break even point (the number of units which need to be sold in order to break even) be if Music-stor raised their price to $40?
_____

d. The marketing department has said that at a price of $40, Music-stor would be able to sell about 19,000 units. Should they raise their price? Why or why not?

13. After determining which pricing objectives fit with the firm's objectives, a business can use any of several different strategies.

    Skimming   Price leadership

    Penetration   Competition oriented

    Demand oriented

    Match the correct pricing strategy to each of the following:

    a. Home-automation systems run as high as $15,000, and there are only a few companies offering the systems. _____

    b. Hotel and motel prices at Disney World are lower from September to Thanksgiving, from January to March, and from April to June, times which Disney defines as their "off" seasons. _____

    c. The sticker price of similarly equipped Lexus, Infiniti and Accura automobiles is just about the same. _____

    d. Carl Godwin is just starting out in the home remodeling and construction business. When he makes a bid, it is often significantly lower than the bids of any of his competition, as Carl wants the business. _____

    e. During the summer months, and at other peak times, the price of gasoline at most retail stations goes up, and virtually all stations charge the same price for a gallon of gas. _____

14. Many companies will try to sell their products by promoting something other than price. Identify three types of products in the marketplace that are promoted using nonprice competition. What are the companies using to promote their products?

    a.

    b.

    c.

PRACTICE TEST

Multiple Choice: Circle the best answer.

1. Which of the following would not be included in the overall value package of benefits consumers consider when they purchase a product?

    a. Price
    b. Image created by advertising
    c. Brand name
    d. Buyer's income

2. Ford Motor Company produces cars, and trucks, provides financing and has interest in a major bank. These products are part of Ford's:

    a. product mix.
    b. product depth.
    c. product width.
    d. product line.

3. Which of the following is not included in a list of questions to ask when determining how a consumer's experience with a company can be improved?

    a. How do consumers become aware of a need?
    b. How do consumers find your product?
    c. How do consumers order your product?
    d. How do consumers feel about the economy?

4. Small businesses often have an advantage in product differentiation because:

    a. they have fewer products, so they can spend more time working on them.
    b. they are more flexible in adapting customer wants and needs.
    c. larger businesses aren't as interested in getting close to the customer.
    d. larger businesses don't have to differentiate their products.

5. Which of the following is not one of the classifications of consumer products?

    a. Convenience goods and services
    b. Unsought goods and services
    c. Shopping goods and services
    d. Desired goods and services

6. Which of the following would be considered a shopping good?

   a. Toothpaste.
   b. Funeral services.
   c. Washing machine.
   d. Bank.

7. When a manufacturer buys a personal computer for use at work, the computer would be considered a(n):

   a. industrial good.
   b. specialty good.
   c. consumer good.
   d. shopping good.

8. The Jolly Green Giant would be an example of a:

   a. brand name.
   b. generic name.
   c. trademark.
   d. knockoff brand.

9. Xerox is working to make sure that when people refer to photocopying, they don't use the name Xerox to refer to the process. Xerox is afraid that their brand name will become a:

   a. generic name.
   b. knockoff brand.
   c. private brand.
   d. trademark.

10. Because products are often being sold in self-service outlets, rather than by salespersons:

    a. brand names have become less important.
    b. packaging has become more important, as a way to promote the product.
    c. the popularity of generic products has declined.
    d. packaging has become less important, because consumers want to see what they are buying.

11. The first step in the product development process is:

    a. development.
    b. product screening.
    c. commercialization.
    d. idea generation.

12. Which of the following is not an important criterion for screening products?

    a. How the product fits with current products
    b. Profit potential
    c. Personnel requirements
    d. Ease of production

13. The process of taking a product idea to consumers to test their reactions is known as:

    a. test marketing.
    b. concept testing.
    c. product screening.
    d. business analysis.

14. In order for the U.S. to remain competitive in the new product development proces:

    a. managers must continually develop new ideas to test.
    b. companies must look at what foreign competitors are offering.
    c. managers must go out into the market and interact with dealers and customers.
    d. the new product development process must be shortened.

15. Which of the following is not one of the stages of the product life cycle?

    a. Introduction
    b. Growth
    c. Maturity
    d. Saturation

16. The importance of the product life cycle is that:

    a. different stages in the product life cycle call for different marketing strategies.
    b. most brands follow the same pattern in the product life cycle.
    c. all products go through the product life cycle in the same length of time.
    d. in the growth stage, marketers will differentiate their product from competitors.

17. During the _____ stage of the product life cycle, marketers will keep the product mix limited, adjust the price to meet competition, increase distribution, and do significant competitive advertising.

    a. introduction
    b. growth
    c. maturity
    d. decline

18. Which of the following is not included in a list of pricing objectives?

    a. Iincreasing sales
    b. Increasing market share
    c. Create an image
    d. Beat the competition

19. The pricing strategy of determining what the market will pay, and then designing a product to fit the price is known as:

    a. demand-oriented pricing.
    b. cost-based pricing.
    c. price-led pricing.
    d. value pricing.

20. If fixed costs are $100,000, variable cost per unit is $40 and the selling price is $60, how many units must be sold for the firm to break even?

    a. 10,000
    b. 1,000
    c. 2500
    d. 5000

21. When the Japanese entered the videotape recorder market, they priced the product lower than the U.S. makers in order to capture a large share of the market quickly. This strategy is called a:

   a. skimming strategy.
   b. demand-oriented strategy.
   c. price leadership.
   d. penetration strategy.

TRUE/FALSE

1. _____ In today's market, marketers must learn to listen to consumers and adapt to a constantly changing market.

2. _____ An organization can use low price to create an attractive value package.

3. _____ It is often easier for larger companies to establish a close relationship with customers because they have representatives in most parts of the country.

4. _____ An example of a convenience good would be a candy bar.

5. _____ The importance of packaging is declining in relation to the marketing mix variables.

6. _____ Brand loyalty means that your product comes to mind when a product category is mentioned.

7. _____ The Internet has become an important variable in the commercialization step of the new product development process.

8. _____ Global marketers today are using cross-functional teams to develop new products.

9. _____ A firm may have several pricing strategies all at once.

10. _____ Pricing objectives generally will have no effect on the other marketing mix variables.

11. _____ The break-even point is the point where sales revenue is equal to profits.

12. _____ When movie theaters charge lower rates for children, and companies give discounts to senior citizens, they are using demand-oriented pricing.

13. _____ Most pricing depends upon what the competition is charging.

14. _____ Marketers will often compete on product attributes other than price.

ANSWERS

LEARNING THE LANGUAGE

1. Breakeven analysis	15. Convenience goods and services
2. Penetration strategy	16. Generic name
3. Product mix	17. Dealer brands (private brands)
4. Value package	18. Specialty goods and services
5. Brand loyalty	19. Brand awareness
6. Product life cycle	20. Product line
7. Skimming pricing strategy	21. Generic goods
8. Trademark	22. Product differentiation
9. Brand association	23. Unsought goods and services
10. Industrial goods	24. Shopping goods
11. Total fixed costs	25. Brand equity
12. Value pricing	26. Manufacturer's brand
13. Brand	27. Variable costs
14. Product manager	

RETENTION CHECK

Learning Goal 1 **Product Development and the Value Package**

1. To satisfy consumers, marketers must learn to listen and to adapt constantly to changing market demands, and to price challenges from competitors. Products must be perceived to have the best value – high quality at a fair price.

2.
   a. Price
   b. Package
   c. Store surroundings
   d. Image created by advertising
   e. Guarantee
   f. Reputation of the producer
   g. Brand name
   h. Service
   i. Buyers' past experience
   j. Speed of delivery
   k. Accessibility of marketer (e.g. on the "net")

3. One way to keep customers is to establish a dialogue with them and keep the information they provide in a database. One of the easiest ways to do this is to establish a Web site where a consumers can ask questions, get information and chat with others.

4. A product mix is the combination of products that a company has available for sale. The product mix consists of a company's product lines. Product lines are groups of products that are similar or are intended for a similar market.

Learning Goal 2 **Product Differentiation**

5. Marketers use a mix of pricing, advertising and packaging to create a unique attractive image to differentiate their products.

6. a. How do customers become aware of a need for your product?
   b. How do customers find your product?
   c. How do customers order your product?
   d. How quickly do you deliver your product?

7. Classes of consumer goods and services are:
   a. Convenience – bread.
   b. Shopping – furniture.
   c. Specialty - Rolex watch.
   d. Unsought – emergency car towing.

8. Variables important to marketers of convenience goods are:
   a. location.
   b. brand awareness.
   c. image.

9. Marketers of shopping goods can emphasize price differences, quality differences or a combination of the two.

10. Specialty goods are often marketed through specialty magazines and through interactive Web sites.

11. Unsought goods are often displayed at the checkout counter in a store.

12. The best way to market convenience goods is:
    a. make them readily available.
    b. create the proper image.

13. The best appeal for promoting shopping goods is:
    a. price.
    b. quality.
    c. service.

14. Makers of specialty goods rely on:
    a. advertising.
    b. the Internet.
    c. creative and highly visible displays.

15. Whether a good or service falls into a particular class depends on the individual customer. For example, what is a shopping good for one customer could be a specialty good for another.

16. Consumer goods are purchased for personal consumption, while industrial goods are products used in the production of other products.

17. A product can be classified as both a consumer good or an industrial good depending upon the end use of the product.

18. Two general categories of industrial goods are: a. production goods b. support goods.

19. Three categories of production goods are:
    a. raw materials.
    b. component parts.
    c. production materials.

20. Support goods are classified as:
    a. installations.
    b. accessory equipment.
    c. supplies.
    d. service.

Learning Goal 3   **Packaging Changes the Product**

21. Packaging changes the product by changing its visibility, usefulness, or attractiveness.

22. The functions of packaging are:
    a. Attract the buyer's attention.
    b. Describe the contents of the product.
    c. Explain the benefits of the product.
    d. Provide information on warranties or warnings.
    e. Give an indication of price, value, and uses.
    f. Protect the product from damage, be tamperproof and easy to open and use.

Learning Goal 4   **Building Brand Equity**

23. a. Manufacturers' brands
     b. Private brands
     c. Knockoff brands
     d. Generic "brands"

24. A brand name can become generic when a name becomes so popular, so identified with the product that it loses its brand status and becomes the name of the product category. Examples include aspirin, nylon, escalator, and zipper.

25. The elements of brand equity are:
    a. Brand loyalty.   d. Feelings and images.
    b. Perceived quality.   e. Emotions people associate with a brand name.
    c. Brand awareness.

26. Brand awareness means that your product comes to mind when a product category is mentioned. Brand preference means that consumers prefer one brand to another because of perceptions determined by a price, appearance, and reputation.

27. Perceived quality is an important part of brand equity because a product that is perceived as better quality than its competitors can be priced higher and thus improve profits.

Learning Goal 5 **Product Management**

28. Reasons for product failure include:
    a. Products don't deliver what they promise.
    b. Poor positioning.
    c. Not enough differences from competitors.
    d. Poor packaging.

29. The steps in new product development are:
    a. Idea generation.
    b. Screening and analysis.
    c. Development.
    d. Testing.
    e. Commercialization.

30. Sources of new product ideas for consumer products include:
    a. Analysis of the competition.
    b. Company sources other than research and development.
    c. Consumer research.
    d. Research and development.

31. Sources of new product ideas for industrial products include:
    a. Company sources other than research and development.
    b. Analysis of the competition.
    c. Research and development.
    d. Product users.

32. Product screening is designed to reduce the number of ideas being worked on at any one time. Criteria needed for screening include whether the product fits in well with present products, profit potential, marketability and personnel requirements.

33. Concept testing involves taking a product idea to consumers to test their reactions.

34. Two important elements for commercialization are:
    a. Promoting the product to distributors and retailers to get wide distribution.
    b. Developing strong advertising and sales campaigns to generate and maintain interest.

35. To stay competitive in world markets, U.S. businesses must develop an entirely new product development process. Keeping products competitive requires continuous, incremental improvements in function, cost, and quality. Attention must be given to developing products in cooperation with their user. Managers must go out into the market and interact closely with their dealers and their ultimate customers. Changes are made over time to make sure that the total product offer exactly meets customers needs.

Learning Goal 6   **The Product Life Cycle**

36. The stages of the product life cycle are:
    a. Introduction.
    b. Growth.
    c. Maturity.
    d. Decline.

37. The product life cycle is important because different stages in the product life cycle call for different strategies. It can provide some basis for anticipating future market developments and for planning marketing strategies.

38.

	Product	Price	Promotion	Place
Introduction	Offer market-tested product	High price	Selective distribution	Primary advertising sales promotion
Growth	Improve product	Adjust to meet competition	Increase distribution	Competitive advertising
Maturity	Differentiate to satisfy different segments	Reduce price further	Intensify distribution	Emphasize brand name and product benefits and differences
Decline	Cut product mix, develop new products	Consider increase	Drop some outlets	Reduce advertising

Learning Goal 7   **Competitive Pricing**

39. Pricing objectives include:
    a. Achieve a target profit.
    b. Build traffic.
    c. Achieve a greater market share.
    d. Increase sales.
    e. Create an image.
    f. Social objectives.

40. Ways to set prices include:
    a. Cost-based pricing.
    b. Value pricing.

41. In the end, the market determines what the price of a product will be.

42. Cost-based pricing bases the end-selling price upon the cost of manufacturing the product plus some margin of profit. It does not take into consideration what the consumer believes is a fair price. Price led costing, used by the Japanese, determines what the market is willing to pay for a product, and then designs a product which can be sold for that price. Value pricing means providing quality, name brand goods at "value" prices.

43. Service industries can use the same pricing tactics as goods-producing firms by cutting costs as much as possible. Then they determine what services are most important to customers. Those services that aren't important are cut. An example is cutting meal service on airlines. The idea is to give the consumer value.

44. The break-even point is the point where revenues from sales equal all costs.

45. Break even point = $\dfrac{\text{Fixed costs}}{\text{(Price per unit) minus (variable cost per unit)}}$

46. Pricing strategies for new products include:
    a. Skimming pricing, setting a high initial price.
    b. Penetration pricing, setting a low initial price.
    c. Demand-oriented pricing, reflecting consumer demand rather than cost or some other calculation.
    d. Price leadership, where all competitors follow similar pricing practices, usually those of a dominant firm in the industry.
    e. Competition-oriented pricing based upon all competitors.

47. A skimming price strategy sets initial prices high to make optimum profit while there is little competition.

48. A penetration strategy sets prices low, which attracts more buyers and discourages other companies. This enables the firm to penetrate or capture a large share of the market quickly.

49. Demand-oriented pricing is used when price is set on the basis of consumer demand rather than cost or some other calculation. An example is movie theaters with low rates for children or during certain times of the day.

50. Competition-oriented pricing is a strategy based on what all the other competitors are doing.

51. In competition pricing, the price will depend on customer loyalty, perceived differences and the competitive climate.

52. Non-price competition will rise as the level of price competition is affected by the availability of products on the Internet.

53. Firms using nonprice competition will stress product images and consumer benefits such as comfort, style, convenience, and durability.

54. Strategies for avoiding price wars include:
    a. Add value.
    b. Educate consumers.
    c. Establish relationships.

CRITICAL THINKING EXERCISES

Learning Goal 1

1. The initial stages of the marketing process include finding a need, conducting research and designing a product to meet the need. Knowing consumer preferences is crucial to the new product development process. Companies must constantly monitor the marketplace to determine customer preferences and how they are changing. To continually satisfy customers, marketers must adapt their products to meet the needs they identify in the marketplace. The marketing process and new product development process it would seem, go hand in hand, and are on going functions of marketing.

2. a. In the purchase of a bicycle, a consumer may evaluate the product in terms of price, guarantee, reputation of the producer, brand name, past experience, and the service the retailer may provide.
b. In buying toothpaste, a purchaser may look at price, package, image created by advertising, brand name and the buyer's past experience.
c. For a new suit, the dimensions may be price, store surroundings, image of the store, brand name, guarantee, and past experience.

3. With a "value package" concept, all of the marketing mix variables take on equally important dimensions. A high price may indicate a high quality product. Store surroundings, the place variable, are important to contribute to the image of the product. Guarantees of satisfaction can increase the product's value in the mind of the consumer, as can a well known brand name. Advertising, a part of the promotion variable, creates an attractive image. Word of mouth will affect the product's reputation.

4. Possible answers:
Product line – Chevrolet.   Item – Corvette.
Product line – Pontiac.   Item - Grand Am.
Product line – Cadillac.   Item – Seville.

Learning Goal 2

5. A. 1. Consumer   6. Consumer
       2. Industrial   7. Consumer
       3. Consumer   8. Consumer
       4. Consumer   9. Industrial
       5. Industrial   10. Consumer

   B   1. Milk- Convenience
       2. Tickets to the Olympics - Specialty
       3. Dry cleaners - Probably convenience service but could be shopping service
       4. Flashlight batteries- Convenience
       5. Auto repair - Unsought
       6. Heart surgeon - Unsought
       7. Winter coat - Shopping

Learning Goal 3

6.   a. For lunch meat like bologna, the primary consideration would be protecting the product from spoiling, and enabling the buyer to see what they are getting. The price or uses won't be listed on the package, but the package may need to attract the buyer's attention, as it is a crowded market. The main problem with the package is that once it is opened, most lunchmeat packages don't easily close, and so the product becomes stale more quickly.
b. For a children's cereal, the most important variable would be attracting the children's attention! For the parent, nutrition information would be important to include on the package. Further, keeping the product fresh would be important. For the most part, most kids' cereals do a great job of attracting children's attention, and by law must provide nutrition information on each box. As with lunchmeat, the problem with most of these packages is that once they are opened, they are difficult to re-close, and the cereal may turn stale quickly.
c. One of the considerations for potato chips is protection from damage, as chips break easily. (That consideration was one of the factors Procter & Gamble looked at when they introduced Pringles.) The package needs to attract attention, as it is a crowded market. Most companies have not found a good way of keeping chips from breaking, and the same old problem arises: once they are opened, the package doesn't close very well, and the product can get stale quickly.

Learning Goal 1, 2, 3

7.   a. Customers may look at price, image, guarantee, and service. The retailer will be an important variable in this combination. Will the retailer install the case? Will the store take it back if it breaks?
b. Total product offer is convenience, image, and the kind of store in which the product is sold, in addition to such product considerations as the size, color, and fit of Music-stor.
c. Music-stor could differentiate the product by giving it an image of not only convenience, but of the "ultimate," kind of auto accessory that everyone needs to have in today's cluttered world. You could create the perception that this product isn't merely a luxury, but a <u>necessity</u>. Advertising could be aimed at the end consumer, with the idea of people asking for the product when they go to the dealership to buy the car.
The main consideration for an auto manufacturer will be price, how much it will add to the sticker price of the car, guarantee, and speed of delivery and reputation of Music-stor. The ease of installation at the factory will also be a factor - where does it fit into the car? Color will also be a consideration.
d. Music-stor would be classified as a consumer good, and could be marketed as either a shopping good or a specialty good. It is also an industrial good, when it is marketed to manufacturers for direct installation on the assembly line.

e. Packaging could be an important variable for Music-stor for the consumer portion of the market. We may want to attract attention to our product on the shelf, give consumers an idea of what it is, and protect it from being scratched or broken. These decisions depend upon our perception of the product as a shopping good or as a specialty good. The package will be less important for the industrial market, the focus being primarily on protection during shipping and handling.

Learning Goal 4

8. a. Sample answers - The private brand name will vary by city, area, or region. These examples come from the Saint Louis area.

		Manufacturer's Brand	**Dealer Brand**
1.	Orange juice	Tree Sweet	President's Choice
2.	Soft Drinks	Coca-cola	Super S
3.	Small tools	Black & Decker	Craftsman
4.	Peanut butter	Jif	Schnuck's brand (Grocery brand)
5.	Blue jeans	Levi's	Arizona
6.	Pain reliever	Tylenol	Good Sense

b. Customer perception of brand names often affects their purchase decision. People are often impressed by certain brand names, although they may realize that there may be little or no difference between brands. This makes it important for a producer to create brand recognition, and develop positive associations with their brand.

c. The problem with a brand name becoming generic is that the producer must then come up with a new brand name, and begin the process of developing brand awareness and brand loyalty all over again.

d. The important elements of brand equity are brand loyalty, brand awareness, perceived quality image and brand association. For a start, Brand equity can be built by creating a good relationship with your customers, and encouraging brand loyalty. Further, advertising can be used to build strong brand awareness, as well as other kinds of sales promotion designed to keep your name in front of the public. Creating a quality product, and communicating the message of quality to your consumers is also important. Further associating your product with other favorable images reinforces the image of your product in the consumer's mind.

Learning Goal 6

9.   a. Introduction   d. Decline
     b. Growth   e. Industry product sales
     c. Maturity   f. Industry profits

10. Possible strategies:
    a. High price.
    Promote as a necessity for driving safety in upscale publications.
    b. Change advertising to change product image.
    Add distribution outlets.
    Decrease price, or give price "deals".
    c. Add new menu items, such as healthier versions of standard items.
    Look for new target markets.
    d. Reduce advertising.
    Limit the product variations.
    Reduce the number and kind of distribution outlets.

Learning Goal 7

11.   a. Build traffic   d. Increase sales
      b. Achieve a target profit   e. Create an image
      c. Social objectives   f. Achieve a greater market share

12.   a. The number of units Music-stor would have to sell to break even is 32,000.
      b. If they sold 45,000 units, profit would be $325,000.
      c. If Music-stor raised their price to $40, the break-even point would be 20,000 units.
      d. No, they should not raise their price to $40. If they will break even at 20,000 units, but can only sell 19,000 units at that price, they will be losing money. They should, then, price below $40, at some point where they can sell enough units to make a profit.

13.   a. Skimming pricing
      b. Demand pricing
      c. Price leadership
      d. Penetration pricing
      e. Competition pricing

14. There are multiple answers. Some examples of companies trying to sell their products by promoting something other than price include:
    a. Cosmetics - Promoted by showing how the product enhances looks.
    b. Food items - Promoted by emphasizing flavor, freshness, convenience.
    c. Gasoline - Promoted by emphasizing quality or service.

PRACTICE TEST

Multiple Choice				**True/False**			
1.	d	12.	d	1.	T	8.	T
2.	a	13.	b	2.	T	9.	T
3.	d	14.	c	3.	F	10.	F
4.	b	15.	d	4.	T	11.	F
5.	d	16.	a	5.	F	12.	T
6.	c	17.	b	6.	F	13.	F
7.	a	18.	d	7.	T	14.	T
8.	c	19.	c				
9.	a	20.	d				
10.	b	21.	d				
11.	d						

CHAPTER 15
DISTRIBUTION, WHOLESALING, AND RETAILING

LEARNING GOALS

After you have read and studied this chapter, you should be able to:

1. Explain the value of marketing intermediaries.

2. Give examples of how middlemen perform the five utilities.

3. Discuss how a manufacturer can get wholesalers and retailers in a channel system to cooperate by the formation of systems.

4. Describe in some detail what is involved in physical distribution management.

5. Describe the various wholesale organizations that assist in the distribution system.

6. List and explain the ways that retailers compete.

7. Explain the various kinds of non-store retailing.

LEARNING THE LANGUAGE

Listed below are important terms found in the chapter. Choose the correct term for the definition and write it in the space provided.

Administered distribution system	Intensive distribution
Cash and carry wholesaler	Limited-function wholesaler
Channel captain	Marketing middlemen
Channel of distribution	Materials handling
Contractual distribution system	Physical distribution
Corporate distribution system	Rack jobber
Drop shipper	Retailer
Efficient consumer response	Selective distribution
Electronic data interchange (EDI)	Supply chain management
Exclusive distribution	Telemarketing
Freight forwarder	Wholesaler
Full service wholesaler	

1. In a(n) _____ members are bound to cooperate through contractual agreements.

2. A(n) _____ is a merchant wholesaler that performs only selected distribution functions.

3. A marketing middleman known as a _____ sells to organizations and individuals, but not to final consumers.

4. A(n) _____ is a distribution system in which all the marketing functions at the retail level are managed by producers.

5. The movement of goods within a warehouse factory or store is _____.

6. Software called _____ enables the computers of producers, wholesalers and retailers to "talk" with each other.

7. The distribution strategy known as _____ puts products into as many retail outlets as possible, including vending machines.

8. The sale of goods and services by telephone is called _____.

9. A(n) _____ is the organization in the channel of distribution that gets all the channel members to work together in a cooperative effort.

10. A merchant wholesaler called a(n) _____ performs all distribution functions.

11. The overall process of minimizing inventory and moving goods through the channel faster by using computers to improve communication among the channel members is called _____.

12. The distribution strategy known as _____ uses only one retail outlet in a given geographic area.

13. The system known as _____ is the movement of goods from producers to industrial and consumer users.

14. Marketing middlemen in the _____ are wholesalers and retailers who join together to transport and store goods in their path from producers to consumers.

15. A(n) _____ is a marketing middleman that sells to ultimate consumers.

16. A distribution system called a(n) _____ is one in which all the organizations in the channel are owned by one firm.

17. A distribution strategy that uses only a preferred group of the available retailers in an area is called _____.

18. A system known as _____ is the linking of firms to provide more efficient response to consumer needs.

19. Organizations called _____ assist in the movement of goods and services from producer to industrial and consumer users.

20. A full-service wholesaler known as a(n) _____ furnishes racks or shelves full of merchandise to retailers, displays products, and sells on consignment.

21. A(n) _____ is a marketing intermediary that puts many small shipments together to create a single, large shipment that can be transported more cost-efficiently to the final destination.

22. A limited-function wholesaler called a(n) _____ solicits orders from retailers and other wholesalers and has the merchandise shipped directly from a producer to a buyer.

23. A limited-function wholesaler that serves mostly smaller retailers with a limited assortment of products is a(n) _____ wholesaler.

RETENTION CHECK

Learning Goal 1   **The Role of Distribution in Business**

1. What are the functions and activities that are included in physical distribution?

   a. _____   d. _____

   b. _____   e. _____

   c. _____   f. _____

2. What are two types of marketing intermediaries?

   a. _____

   b. _____

3. What is the value chain, and why is it important?

4. What is meant by the term "quick response"?

5. How is response time minimized?

6. How have companies such as Procter & Gamble, Xerox and Nabisco cut inventory and improved service?

7. What is ECR?

8. Why do we have marketing intermediaries?

9. How do marketing intermediaries add efficiency to the distribution system?

10. How does the Internet affect distribution?

11. What are three important points to remember about middlemen?

   a. _____

   b. _____

   c. _____

Learning Goal 2 **How Intermediaries Add Utility To Goods**

12. List five utilities created by intermediaries.

   a. _____   d. _____

   b. _____   e. _____

   c. _____

13. How does an intermediary add time utility?

14. How do intermediaries add place utility?

15. What is possession utility?

16. How do intermediaries add information utility?

17. How is service utility provided?

18. Which of these is becoming the most important utility for retailers? Why?

Learning Goal 3 **Building Cooperation in Channel Systems**

19. Identify four types of distribution systems.

   a. _____

   b. _____

   c. _____

   d. _____

20. What are three types of contractual distribution systems?

   a. _____

   b. _____

   c. _____

21. Distinguish between the three types of systems.

22. Why do retailers cooperate with producers in an administered distribution system?

23. What makes a value chain efficient?

Learning Goal 4 **Physical Distribution (Logistics) Management**

24. What is a "mode" in the language of distribution?

25. What does a logistics system involve?

26. What is JIT? What are two things it means for manufacturers?

   a. _____

   b. _____

27. What are some problems associated with JIT?

28. What is the primary concern for distribution managers regarding selecting a mode of transportation?

   a. _____

   b. _____

29. List five transportation modes used in physical distribution.

   a. _____   d. _____

   b. _____   e. _____

   c. _____

30. What is meant by a "piggyback" system?

31. Name six criteria used to evaluate transportation modes.

   a. _____   d. _____

   b. _____   e. _____

   c. _____   f. _____

32. What is intermodal shipping?

33. What are two kinds of warehouses?

   a. _____

   b. _____

34. What is the difference between the two kinds of warehouses?

Learning Goal 5   **Wholesale Intermediaries**

35. What is the difference between a "retail sale" and a "wholesale sale?"

36. Identify two types of merchant wholesalers.

    a. _____

    b. _____

37. What is the difference between the types of merchant wholesalers?

38. List three types of limited-function wholesalers.

    a. _____

    b. _____

    c. _____

39. What does a rack jobber do?

40. How does a cash and carry wholesaler function?

41. What does a drop shipper do?

Learning Goal 6   **Retail Intermediaries**

42. What are five ways retailers compete?

   a. _____   d. _____

   b. _____   e. _____

   c. _____

43. How can smaller, independent retailers compete with discount stores and warehouse stores?

44. What is involved in service competition?

45. What is a category killer store?

46. How do smaller retailers compete with category killers?

47. What is a total quality retailer?

48. Name three retail distribution strategies.

   a. _____

   b. _____

   c. _____

49. What is the difference between each of these distribution strategies?

Learning Goal 7 **Nonstore Retailing**

50. What are five types of non-store retailing?

   a. _____   d. _____

   b. _____   e. _____

   c. _____

51. What are the benefits of kiosks and carts?

52. What are an "upliner" and a "downliner" in multilevel marketing?

53. What are 2 attractions of multilevel marketing?

    a. _____

    b. _____

54. What are some of the activities included in direct retail marketing?

    a. _____

    b. _____

    c. _____

    d. _____

CRITICAL THINKING EXERCISES

Learning Goal 1

1. What is the relationship between the first two "Ps" in the marketing mix, product and price, and the third "P", place, or distribution?

2. What do you think is the channel of distribution for:

a. cars   _____

                                                         _____

                                                         _____

b. soft drinks   _____

                                                         _____

                                                         _____

c. business forms (like blank invoices)   _____

                                                         _____

3. Joe Dell and his friend Woody were complaining as they were shopping for suits about how expensive they seemed to be. "Man" said Joe, "If we just had one of those outlet malls where we could avoid the middleman, we'd be better off. That outlet store down at the Lake of the Ozarks is always advertising about how much lower their prices are because they get shipments direct from the manufacturer. Wouldn't it be a better deal if we just didn't have to deal with these expensive stores!" Woody replied "Well Joe, I understand what you mean, but in my business class we've talked about marketing intermediaries, or middlemen, and they're not as bad as you think! Besides, if you go to an outlet store, you're still using a middleman!" What did Woody mean?

Learning Goal 2

4. Marketing intermediaries add value to products by creating five utilities:

   Time.   Possession.   Service.

   Place.   Information.

   Match the correct response to each example:

   a. St. Lukes's Hospital sponsors a "pediatric party" every Saturday for its young patients to show what will happen while they are in the hospital for surgery. _____.

   b. Two years after being spun-off by a division of the May Company, Venture Stores began offering their own credit card. _____.

   c. Many colleges are offering classes at off-campus locations, in late afternoon and on Saturdays and Sundays to meet the needs of a diverse student body. _____.

   d. McDonald's restaurants can be found in some Wal-Mart superstores, where you can order your meal from the Wal-Mart check-out counter. _____.

Learning Goals 1, 2, 3

5. Music-stor is looking at the distribution function. You and the marketing manager must make a proposal soon. In general, what kind of marketing intermediaries should we consider? How does the classification of Music-stor as either a convenience good, shopping good or a specialty good affect the answer to this question? What would the channel of distribution look like? Is there a need for a marketing intermediary if we target primarily the automotive manufacturers? What kind of utilities will our customers find most important?

Learning Goal 3

6. A further look at Music-stor's distribution shows the need to consider the kind of cooperation necessary for us to create an efficient system.

    In what kind of distribution system (corporate, contractual or administered) will Music-stor take part? Who will most likely be the channel captain, at least initially?

7. How does supply chain management relate to what we have learned earlier about technology and customer service?

Learning Goal 4

8. Five basic modes of transportation are:

    Railroad.   Ship (water).

    Truck.   Airplane.

    Pipeline.

    A. Using the figure in your text, determine which mode of transportation would likely be used in the following situations when:

        1. Speed of delivery is the most important criterion, and cost is not a essential element. _____

        2. There is a need to serve multiple locations fairly quickly.
           _____

3. Products are bulky, cost is a major consideration and speed of delivery is not an essential element. _____

4. There is a need for constant or steady delivery to a minimal number of locations; speed of delivery is not important. _____

5. There are multiple locations, bulky products, and cost and speed of delivery are of equal but moderate importance. _____

B. Which do you think would be the best choice of transportation mode for Musicstor? Why?

Learning Goal 5

9. There are several types of merchant wholesalers:

   Rack jobbers.   Drop shippers.

   Cash and carry wholesalers.   Truck jobbers.

Identify the correct type of wholesaler with the following:

a. These wholesalers have begun selling to the public in warehouse clubs, like "Sam's". _____

b. L'Eggs are displayed in the store on a rack. When the product is sold, the company shares the profit with the retailer. _____

c. This type of wholesaler will deliver milk and yogurt to your local supermarket. _____

d. Peabody Coal will sell their product to this wholesaler, who will then make arrangements for the coal to be shipped from the mine to a Union Electric facility in southern Missouri. _____

Learning Goal 6

10. Fast Eddy's is a retailer going downhill fast! Eddy has turned to you to help him turn the store around and make it profitable again. Fast Eddy's has been selling general merchandise for years, with the gimmick of using sales associates on roller skates, to provide "fast service." The store looks a little run down, and Eddy knows he has to do something about that, but he just can't seem to figure out what to do to compete "with the big guys." How can you advise him?

11. The three types of retail distribution strategies are intensive, selective and exclusive. Which strategy would likely be used for:

a. Chewing gum _____.   d. Tickets to the Olympics _____.

b. Athletic shoes _____.   e. Ski chalets _____.

c. Potato chips _____.   f. Winter coats _____.

12. There are several types of nonstore retailing:

   Telemarketing. Multilevel marketing.

   Vending machines, kiosks and carts. Direct marketing.

   Direct selling.

   Determine which is being described in each of the following:

   a. Catalogs, telemarketing, and on-line shopping all help to make this form of retailing very convenient for consumers. _____

   b. In Japan, everything from bandages and face cloths to salads and seafood are retailed this way. _____

   c. Lingerie, artwork, baskets, jewelry and plastic bowls are sold at "parties" held at a customer's home or work place. _____

   d. Companies "reach out and touch someone" using this form of marketing, to supplement or replace in-store selling. _____

   e. Retailers like this form, as it lends an outdoor marketplace atmosphere to the mall in which they are located. _____

   f. Using this form of retailing, a new salesperson's job is to sell the products provided by the company and to recruit several people who will use the product and recruit others to sell and use the product. _____

PRACTICE TEST

Multiple Choice: Circle the best answer.

1. Which of the following is an activity that would not be considered a physical distribution function?

    a. Storage
    b. Transportation
    c. Inventory
    d. Production

2. Minimizing inventory and moving goods more quickly, using computers and other technology is called:

    a. supply chain management.
    b. channels of distribution.
    c. electronic data interchange.
    d. quick response.

3. Which of the following statements is accurate regarding marketing intermediaries?

    a. Intermediaries add cost to products, but not value:
    b. Intermediaries must adopt the latest technology to maintain their competitive position.
    c. The functions performed by marketing intermediaries are easily eliminated.
    d. Intermediaries have never performed their job efficiently, that's why they are being eliminated.

4. In some areas of the country, Wal-Mart stays open 24 hours a day, most days of the year. This is an example of:

    a. service utility.
    b. place utility.
    c. time utility.
    d. possession utility.

5. McDonald's, Baskin-Robbins, and other franchisors are examples of a(n):

    a. corporate distribution system.
    b. contractual distribution system.
    c. retail cooperative.
    d. administered distribution system.

6. A value chain is efficient because:

   a. organizations within the chain are electronically linked so information flow is smooth.
   b. one organization is performing most of the activities, so things happen faster.
   c. the activities begin only after the products are made and shipped to the wholesaler.
   d. each organization signs a written contract, and has agreements with a union.

7. Because of improved, more customer-oriented logistics systems:

   a. wholesalers have become obsolete.
   b. businesses carry less inventory, and costs have decreased significantly.
   c. certain transportation modes have been eliminated.
   d. final customers are now able to go direct to the manufacturer, or to the wholesaler.

8. The largest percentage of goods are shipped by:

   a. air.
   b. ship.
   c. truck.
   d. rail.

9. When Hans Kaupfmann bought his car while on a trip to Germany, he wasn't sure how it would be shipped. The dealer assured him that many people buy cars and have them shipped, and it's a smooth transition from land to sea and back to land, by trucking the car to the port, loading the entire truck trailer on to the ship, then trucking again to the destination. This process is known as:

   a. piggyback.
   b. fishyback.
   c. bi-modal transportation.
   d. transatlantic transportation.

10. A _____ gathers, then redistributes products.

    a. distribution warehouse
    b. storage warehouse
    c. full-service wholesaler
    d. drop shipper wholesaler

11. The major difference between wholesalers and retailers is that:

    a. retailers sell only in certain parts of the country, while wholesalers are nationwide.
    b. wholesale organizations are generally more profitable than retail organizations.
    c. retailers sell only consumer goods, and wholesalers sell business to business goods.
    d. retailers sell to final consumers, while wholesalers sell to another member of the channel of distribution, not final consumers.

12. A(n) _____ is an independently-owned wholesaler, that takes title to the goods they handle.

    a. broker   c. merchant wholesaler
    b. agent   d. manufacturer's agent

13. Sam's Club sells to retailers, but doesn't offer credit or transportation. Sam's will also allow a final consumer to shop, but charges an annual fee, does not allow customers to use credit, and the store will not deliver. Sam's is an example of a:

    a. rack jobber.   c. drop shipper.
    b. truck wholesaler.   d. cash and carry wholesaler.

14. Discount stores such as Wal-Mart, K-Mart and Target are hard to compete against, because these stores are the best at:

    a. selection competition.   c. location competition.
    b. price competition.   d. total quality competition.

15. A _____ offers a very wide selection of a specific product category at prices that smaller retailer can't match.

    a. category killer   c. discount store
    b. department store   d. franchised store

16. Which of the following is not true regarding retailing over the Internet and the use of computers in general?

    a. Most small retailers can get away without using computers.
    b. The Internet has helped to boost sales for many small retailers.
    c. Computers will allow smaller retailers to restock quickly.
    d. Computers can allow retailers to carry less inventory.

17. After a few years of relying on the Internet to market their product, management at The Flying Noodle, a pasta company, has decided that it is time to get their product into the supermarket. This kind of basic pasta product will do best with:

    a. selective distribution.
    b. intensive distribution.
    c. exclusive distribution.
    d. nonstore retailing distribution.

18. Nonstore retailing, or, out of store shopping is:

    a. declining as the Internet takes over.
    b. growing as the types of nonstore retailing grow.
    c. not a profitable method of retailing for most companies.
    d. consists primarily of vending machines and telemarketing.

19. Which of the following would not be an example of direct marketing?

    a. Ordering a book from Amazon.com online.
    b. Buying Avon from your neighborhood Avon representative.
    c. Sending in an order form from an advertising supplement in the newspaper.
    d. Buying a soda from the vending machine at school.

TRUE/FALSE

1. ____ A channel of distribution consists of marketing intermediaries who join together to store and transport goods in their path from producer to consumer.

2. ____ Companies are now able to carry lower levels of inventory because of supply-chain management.

3. ____ Generally, it is much less expensive and much faster when we can avoid the use of a marketing intermediary and go straight to the producer.

4. ____ Providing service utility is becoming the most important utility for retailers, because without personal service they could lose business to other forms of retailing.

5. ____ In a corporate distribution system, a retailer signs a contract to cooperate with a manufacturer.

6. ____ Just-in-time inventory means that manufacturers can cut back substantially on the inventory in their warehouses.

7. ____ The primary concern of physical distribution managers is keeping costs down, regardless of anything else.

8. ____ Railroads could experience an increase in use if energy prices go up.

9. ____ Merchant wholesalers do not buy what they sell, they primarily match buyers with sellers.

10. ____ The Internet has made wholesalers obsolete.

11. ____ Consumers will often pay a bit more for goods and services if a retailer will offer outstanding service.

12. ____ Smaller retailers can compete with category killer stores by offering lower prices and better store hours.

13. ____ Telemarketing is expected to be one of the fastest growing areas in marketing.

14. ____ Multilevel marketing is not a good way to make money, because it costs to much to get into.

ANSWERS

LEARNING THE LANGUAGE.

1. Contractual distribution system	13. Physical distribution
2. Limited function wholesaler	14. Channel of distribution
3. Wholesaler	15. Retailer
4. Administered distribution system	16. Corporate distribution system
5. Materials handling	17. Selective distribution
6. Electronic data interchange (EDI)	18. Efficient consumer response
7. Intensive distribution	19. Marketing middlemen
8. Telemarketing	20. Rack jobber
9. Channel captain	21. Freight forwarder
10. Full service wholesaler	22. Drop shipper
11. Supply chain management	23. Cash & carry
12. Exclusive distribution	

RETENTION CHECK

Learning Goal 1   **The Role of Distribution in Business**

1.
   a. Transportation
   b. Storage
   c. Purchasing goods
   d. Receiving goods
   e. Moving goods through the plant
   f. Inventorying goods

2. The types of marketing intermediaries are:
   a. Wholesalers.
   b. Retailers.

3. The value chain comes from the supply chain management process, which is the process of minimizing inventory and moving goods throughout the channel faster by using computers and other technology to improve the flow of goods and information among the channel members. The improvement has been so dramatic that the system is called the value chain, because the value created by such an efficient system is so great. This enables producers to get products to customers faster, and more economically than in the past.

4. Quick response is the term used to describe the efforts by producers and suppliers to send goods to retailers and to each other as quickly as possible.

5. Response time can be minimized by linking retailers with suppliers and producers by computer, so that suppliers and producers can send replacement stock quickly when something is needed. Computerized checkout machines read the bar codes on goods that are sold and send that information to suppliers instantly so that a replacement good can be on the way immediately.

6. Companies such as Procter & Gamble, Xerox and Nabisco have cut inventory and improved service by using supply system management. They implement the system by working together on a variety of functions. Data are shared among firms so the whole system can operate as a unit, and so globally competitive products can be sent through the system in the fastest time.

7. Efficient consumer response is the term used in the grocery industry to describe linking firms to provide more efficient response to consumer needs.

8. We have marketing intermediaries because it is usually faster and cheaper to use intermediaries to perform certain marketing functions, such as transportation, storage, selling, and advertising. The intermediaries can perform these functions more effectively and efficiently than manufacturers could.

9. Marketing intermediaries add efficiency to the distribution system by reducing the number of transactions necessary to get products from the producer to the consumer.

10. Technology has made it possible for manufacturers to reach consumers more efficiently. Some manufacturers, such as Dell Computer reach consumers directly on the Internet. Retailers, too, are so closely linked to manufacturers that they can get delivery as often as once or twice a day. All this means that there is often no need for a wholesaler to perform functions such as storage and delivery. Wholesalers are not yet obsolete, but they need to change their functions to remain viable in today's rapidly changing distribution systems.

11. Important points to remember about middlemen include:
    a. Marketing middlemen can be eliminated, but their activities cannot.
    b. Middlemen survive because they perform marketing functions more efficiently than others can perform them.
    c. Middlemen add costs, but the costs are offset by the value they create.

Learning Goal 2   **How Intermediaries Add Utility to Goods**

12. The utilities created by intermediaries are:
    a. Time.
    b. Place.
    c. Possession.
    d. Information.
    e. Service.

13. Intermediaries add time utility to products by making them available when they're needed.

14. Place utility is added to products by having them where people want them.

15. Possession utility is added by doing whatever is necessary to transfer ownership from one party to another, including providing credit. Activities include delivery, installation, guarantees, and follow-up service.

16. Intermediaries add information utility by opening two-way flows of information between marketing participants.

17. Service utility is added by providing fast, friendly service during and after the sale and teaching customers how to best use products over time.

18. Service utility is becoming the more important utility because without personal service they could lose business to electronic marketing or direct marketing. Personalized service is what distinguishes retailers from other types of nonstore marketing.

Learning Goal 3   **Building Cooperation in Channel Systems**

19. The four types of distribution systems are:
    a. Corporate system.
    b. Contractual systems.
    c. Administered systems.
    d. Value chains.

20. The three types of contractual distribution systems are:
    a. Franchise systems.
    b. Wholesaler-sponsored chains.
    c. Retail cooperatives.

21. In a franchise system, the franchisee agrees to all of the rules, regulations, and procedures established by the franchisor. In wholesaler-sponsored chains, each store signs an agreement to use the same name, participate in chain promotions and cooperate as a unified system of stores, even though each store is independently owned and managed. In retail cooperatives, the arrangement is much like a wholesaler-sponsored chain except it's initiated by the retailers.

22. Retailers cooperate with producers in an administered distribution system because they get so much help for free.

23. A value chain is efficient because the various organizations are linked electronically so that information flows among firms are as smooth as information flows were within a single firm.

Learning Goal 4   **Physical Distribution (Logistics) Management**

24. A mode refers to the various means used to transport goods, such as trucks, trains, planes, ships, and airplanes.

25. A logistics system involves activities such as processing orders and inventorying products, as well as transporting products. It is whatever it takes to see that the right products are sent to the right place quickly and efficiently.

26. JIT stands for just in time inventory control. It means that manufacturers can cut back substantially on their inventory in warehouses and count on suppliers to deliver needed parts and materials just in time to go onto production lines.

27. Some problems with JIT concern heavy traffic flows, and problems with weather and other circumstances that hinder the smooth flow of goods.

28. The primary concern for distribution managers is selecting a transportation mode that will:
    a. minimize costs.
    b. ensure a certain level of service.

29. The five transportation modes are:
    a. Railroad.
    b. Trucks.
    c. Pipeline.
    d. Ships (water).
    e. Airplane.

30. A piggyback system means that a truck trailer is detached from the cab, loaded onto a railroad flatcar and taken to a destination where is will be offloaded, attached to a truck and driven to customers' plants.

31. Criteria used to evaluate transportation modes include:
    a. Cost.
    b. Speed.
    c. On-time dependability.
    d. Flexibility in handling products.
    e. Frequency of shipments.
    f. Reach.

32. Intermodal shipping uses multiple modes of transportation, including highway, air, water and rail to complete a single long-distance movement of freight.

33. The two kinds of warehouses are:
    a. storage warehouses.
    b. distribution warehouses.

34. A storage warehouse stores products for a relatively long time, such as what is needed for seasonal goods. Distribution warehouses are facilities used to gather and redistribute products.

Learning Goal 5 **Wholesale Intermediaries**

35. A retail sale is a sale of goods and services to <u>consumers</u> for their own use. A wholesale sale is the sale of goods and services to <u>businesses and institutions</u> for use in the business or for resale.

36. Two types of merchant wholesalers are:
    a. Full-service.
    b. Limited-function.

37. Full-service wholesalers perform all distribution functions, such as transportation, storage, risk bearing, credit, market information, grading, buying, and selling. Limited function wholesalers perform only selected functions.

38. Three types of limited-function wholesalers are:
    a. Cash and carry.
    b. Drop shippers.
    c. Truck jobbers.

39. Rack jobbers furnish racks or shelves full of merchandise, display products, and sell on consignment to retailers.

40. A cash-and-carry wholesaler serves mostly smaller retailers with a limited assortment of products. Retailers go to them, pay cash, and carry the goods home.

41. A drop shipper solicits orders from retailers and other wholesalers and has the merchandise shipped directly from a producer to a buyer. They own the merchandise but don't handle, stock or deliver it.

Learning Goal 6 **Retail Intermediaries**

42. Retailers compete by:
    a. Price.
    b. Service.
    c. Location.
    d. Selection.
    e. Total quality.

43. Smaller independent retailers have to offer truly outstanding service and selection to compete with giant retailers such as Office Depot.

44. Retail service involves putting the customer first. This requires that all front-line people be courteous and accommodating to customers. It also means follow-up service such as on-time delivery, guarantees, and fast installation. Customers are frequently willing to pay a little more for goods and services if the retailers offer outstanding service.

45. Category killer stores offer a wide selection of a certain category of products at competitive prices. Examples are Toys R Us and Borders Books.

46. Smaller retailers compete with category killers by offering more selection within a smaller category of items. You may have successful smaller stores selling nothing but coffee or party products. Smaller retailers also compete with more personalized service.

47. A total quality retailer offers low price, good service, wide selection and total quality management.

48. Retail distribution strategies include:
    a. Intensive distribution.
    b. Selective distribution.
    c. Exclusive distribution.

49. Intensive distribution puts products into as many retail outlets as possible. Selective distribution is the use of only a preferred group of the available retailers in an area. Exclusive distribution is the use of only one retail outlet in a given geographic area.

Learning Goal 7   **Nonstore Retailing**

50. Types of nonstore retailing includes:
    a. Telemarketing.
    b. Vending machines, kiosks and carts.
    c. Direct selling.
    d. Network marketing.
    e. Direct marketing.

51. Kiosks and carts have lower costs than stores. Therefore they can offer lower prices on items such as T-shirts and umbrellas. Mall owners often like them because they are colorful and create a marketplace atmosphere. Customers enjoy interactive kiosks because they dispense coupons and provide information when buying products.

52. In multilevel marketing, an "upliner" is an individual who has recruited others to sell for them. The "downliners" are the people who have been recruited to sell.

53. The main attractions of multilevel marketing are:
    a. great potential for making money.
    b. low cost of entry.

54. Direct retail marketing includes:
    a. direct mail.
    b. catalog sales.
    c. telemarketing.
    d. on-line shopping.

CRITICAL THINKING EXERCISES

Learning Goal 1

1. The type of product will determine what kind of transportation and storage will be called for, and what kinds of stores (retailers) will carry the product. The type of transportation mode and the kind of storage will be a part of the final price of the product, as well as the kind of store - i.e. the image of the store and its pricing policies.

2. The channel of distribution for:

    a. <u>cars</u>.
       manufacturer.
       retailer.
       consumer.

    b. <u>soft drinks</u>.
       manufacturer.
       bottler.
       retailer.

    c. <u>business forms</u>.
       manufacturer.
       business user.
       consumer.

3. What Woody was trying to tell Joe is that, first, the outlet store is a type of middleman, called a retailer. Further, retailers and the other type of middlemen, wholesalers, add many things to a product that would be difficult to replace. In the first place, Joe would have to drive to wherever the suit he chose was manufactured, if he were to really avoid a middleman. That could be as far away as Asia! The retailer is much closer. Secondly, if he decided to have the manufacturer ship the suit to him, he would have to pay for shipping the suit to his home, which could be expensive. He would have to contact the manufacturer during working hours, which for a manufacturer would probably be Monday - Friday, between 8a.m. and 5 p.m. Then he would have to try it on, and figure out any alterations, perhaps ship the suit back to be altered, or find someone to alter it for him. Further, Joe would not be able to see the suit before it was sent, or would have to spend hours looking through the manufacturer's warehouse looking through hundreds of suits. In short, middlemen provide value through adding convenience such as transportation and storage, and enable us to shop for and find exactly what we want, at times convenient for us with far less effort.

    Therefore, while middleman organizations can be eliminated, their functions cannot.

Learning Goal 2

4.   a. Information
       b. Possession
       c. Time and place
       d. Place and possession

Learning Goal 1, 2, 3

5. Initially we may use some kind of wholesaler, who will then sell to a retailer. If we primarily target the auto industry, we will not necessarily need a wholesale middleman, unless we use a broker in lieu of employing our own sales force. The channel of distribution will look like this:

Music-stor.	Music-stor.
wholesaler.	auto manufacturers.
retailer.	
consumer.	

   The most important utility for the end consumer may be information utility, as the consumer may need to know more about the product. Place utility is important, but is affected by our classification of Music-stor as either a shopping good or specialty good. This affects the kind of store we will choose, as shopping goods may be found in several kinds of stores and specialty goods will be found in fewer, different kinds of stores.

   For the auto manufacturers, time and place utility will be important, as they will need the product delivered when they need it, where they need it.

Learning Goal 3

6. Music-stor will most likely be a part of an administered distribution system when we are using retailers. As a new company, we can't afford to own our own retail stores right away, which cuts out a corporate distribution system. Moreover, for this type of product, a corporate distribution system would not be practical. The same is true of a contractual distribution system. A franchise system is not appropriate without many more product lines. Wholesaler-sponsored chains and retail cooperatives don't fit either.

   As a new company, however, we will want to provide our retailers with as much service as we can until we become better known. In this case, the retailers would be the channel captains.

   In the case of the auto manufacturers, <u>they</u> will be the channel captains.

7. Supply chain management is the process of minimizing inventory and moving goods through the channel faster by using computers. This allows members of the channel to save money and serve customers much faster. A way to minimize inventory, for example, is just-in-time inventory control. Inventory control is also the point of electronic data interchange, which makes it possible for retailers to be directly linked to their supplier. Faster service at less cost allows firms to better serve customers, which has been the focus of the changes we are observing in today's corporations.

8. A.
   1. Air
   2. Truck
   3. Water
   4. Pipeline
   5. Railroad

   B. The best transportation mode for Music-stor would probably be by truck to both the auto manufacturers and the retailers. For auto manufacturers which are located a considerable distance from Music-stor, a combination of rail and truck could be used for flexibility, number of deliveries and speed. The major problem with trucks is the cost, but it serves the other needs best.

Learning Goal 5

9. a. Cash and carry wholesaler:
   b. Rack jobber.
   c. Truck jobber.
   d. Drop shipper.

Learning Goal 6

10. Possible answer:

    Eddy's gimmick of using sales associates on roller skates may actually be the key he is looking for. He apparently already knows that service is important to his customers, he may just need another way of approaching the idea! Retailers compete based on price, service, selection, location, or total quality. Eddy needs to decide what is most important to his customers, what may draw new customers in, and what his strengths and weaknesses are. As a small retailer, he may be better able to specialize in a market, and compete with larger retailers by offering more selection within a smaller category of items. It is difficult for smaller retailers to compete with "category killers" based on price, but outstanding service may allow Eddy to charge a price that will help him stay in business and make a profit.

11. a. Intensive
    b. Selective
    c. Intensive
    d. Exclusive
    e. Exclusive
    f. Selective

12. a. Direct marketing
     b. Vending machines
     c. Direct selling
     d. Telemarketing
     e. Kiosks, carts
     f. Multilevel marketing

PRACTICE TEST

	Multiple Choice				**True/False**		
1.	d	11.	d	1.	T	8.	T
2.	a	12.	c	2.	T	9.	F
3.	b	13.	d	3.	F	10.	F
4.	c	14.	b	4.	T	11.	T
5.	b	15.	a	5.	F	12.	F
6.	a	16.	a	6.	T	13.	T
7.	b	17.	b	7.	F	14.	F
8.	d	18.	b				
9.	b	19.	d				
10.	a						

CHAPTER 16
PROMOTING PRODUCTS USING INTEGRATED AND INTERACTIVE MARKETING COMMUNICATION

LEARNING GOALS

After you have read and studied this chapter, you should be able to:

1. List and describe the various elements of the promotion mix.
2. Illustrate the seven steps of the selling process.
3. Describe the functions of the public relations department and the role of publicity.
4. Explain the importance of word of mouth and sales promotion as promotional tools.
5. Describe the advantages and disadvantages of various types of advertising and explain the latest advertising techniques.
6. Compare and contrast push and pull strategies.
7. Describe integrated marketing communication and the role of interactive communications within it.

LEARNING THE LANGUAGE

Listed below are important terms found in the chapter. Choose the correct term for each definition and write it in the space provided.

Advertising	Prospecting
Direct marketing	Public relations
Infomercials	Publicity
Integrated marketing	Pull strategy
Integrated marketing communication system	Push strategy
Mass customization	Sales promotion
Personal selling	Trade shows
Promotion	Word-of-mouth promotion
Promotion mix	

1. The design of custom-made product and promotions is called _____ and includes advertising.

2. The promotional tool known as _____ stimulates consumer purchasing and dealer interest by means of short-term activities.

3. Paid, nonpersonal communication, or _____, goes through various media by organizations and individuals who are in some way identified in the promotional message.

4. The management function of _____ evaluates public attitudes, develops policies and procedures consistent with the public interest, and takes steps to earn public understanding and acceptance.

5. A(n) _____ uses promotional tools to motivate consumers to request products from stores.

6. Events called _____ are where many marketers set up displays and potential customers come to see the latest in goods and services.

7. The _____ is the combination of promotion tools that an organization uses.

8. Consumers talking about products they like or dislike is called _____.

9. The process of _____ is the merging of all organizational efforts to please customers, employees, and other stakeholders.

10. Researching potential buyers and choosing those most likely to buy is called _____.

11. The technique of _____ allows customers to buy products by interacting with various advertising media without meeting a salesperson face-to-face.

12. The form of promotion known as _____ is any information about an individual, a product, or an organization that is distributed to the public through the media and that is not paid for, or controlled by, the sponsor.

13. A(n) _____ is the use of promotional tools to convince wholesalers and retailers to stock and sell merchandise.

14. TV programs that are devoted exclusively to promoting goods and services are known as _____.

15. _____ is the face-to-face presentation and promotion of products and services plus searching out prospects and providing follow-up service.

16. The process of _____ is an attempt by marketers to inform people about products and to persuade them to participate in an exchange.

17. A formal mechanism known as a(n) _____ is a method for uniting all the promotional efforts in an organization to make it more responsive to its customers and other stakeholders.

RETENTION CHECK

Learning Goal 1 **The Importance of Marketing Communication and Promotion**

1. What are the elements of the promotion mix?

   a. _____   d. _____

   b. _____   e. _____

   c. _____   f. _____

Learning Goal 2   **Personal Selling**

2. How do we define "effective selling"?

3. What are the seven steps in the personal selling process?

   a. _____   e. _____

   b. _____   f. _____

   c. _____   g. _____

   d. _____

4. In personal selling, what does it meant to qualify a customer?

5. What activities take place in the preapproach?

6. What is the objective of an initial sales call during the approach stage?

7. What does the salesperson do during the presentation?

8. What activities are involved in closing a sale?

9. Identify the activities involved in the follow up.

10. How has technology aided the salesperson today?

11. How does a salesperson selling to commercial accounts find customers?

12. How does technology help business to business salespeople?

Learning Goal 3   Public Relations and Publicity

13. Identify the three steps in creating a good public relations campaign.

    a. _____

    b. _____

    c. _____

14. What is the responsibility of a public relations department? Why?

15. What are three benefits that publicity has over other promotion mix variables?

    a. _____

    b. _____

    c. _____

16. What are three drawbacks of publicity?

    a. _____

    b. _____

    c. _____

Learning Goal 4 **Sales Promotion and Word of Mouth**

17. List 10 types of sales promotions.

   a. _____   f. _____

   b. _____   g. _____

   c. _____   h. _____

   d. _____   i. _____

   e. _____   j. _____

18. What are sales promotion programs designed to do?

19. Identify two targets of sales promotion.

20. What is internal sales promotion designed to do?

21. What comes after internal sales promotion?

22. What is the benefit of sampling as a sales promotion tool?

23. What is the best way to generate good word of mouth?

   a. _____

   b. _____

   c. _____

24. List three elements of effective word-of-mouth promotion.

   a. _____

   b. _____

   c. _____

Learning Goal 5 **Advertising**

25. How is advertising different from the other elements of the promotion mix?

26. How does the public benefit from advertising?

27. List eight advertising media.

   a. _____   e. _____

   b. _____   f. _____

   c. _____   g. _____

   d. _____   h. _____

28. List some of the advantages and disadvantages of each form of advertising media.

		Advantages	Disadvantages
a.	Newspapers	_____	_____
		_____	_____
		_____	_____
		_____	_____
b.	Television	_____	_____
		_____	_____
		_____	_____
		_____	_____
c.	Radio	_____	_____
		_____	_____
		_____	_____
		_____	_____
d.	Magazines	_____	_____
		_____	_____
		_____	_____
		_____	_____

e. Outdoor _____ _____

_____ _____

_____ _____

_____ _____

f. Direct mail _____ _____

_____ _____

_____ _____

_____ _____

g. Yellow pages _____ _____

_____ _____

_____ _____

_____ _____

h. Internet _____ _____

_____ _____

_____ _____

_____ _____

29. What are the benefits of infomercials?

30. How has technology changed advertising?

31. What are the challenges of advertising products in foreign markets?

32. What is the trend in advertising today regarding advertising to different groups?

Learning Goal 6 **Preparing the Promotion Mix**

33. What is the best way to reach:

   a. large homogenous groups?

   b. large organizations?

34. What is the idea of a push strategy?

35. What is the idea of a pull strategy?

36. What is a total systems approach to marketing?

37. What is interactive marketing?

Learning Goal 7 **Integrated Marketing Communication (IMC)**

38. What is an interactive marketing communication system?

39. What are the steps necessary to develop an interactive marketing communications system?

   a. _____

   b. _____

   c. _____

40. Why are smaller firms capturing markets from large firms?

41. What are the advantages of interactive marketing on the Internet?

   a. _____

   b. _____

   c. _____

   d. _____

42. Why is marketing services more difficult on the Internet?

43. What is fax on demand?

44. What elements are blended in integrated marketing communications?

45. What is disk-based advertising?

46. What impact could new technologies have on TV and mass advertising?

47. What impact will the Internet have on traditional mall retailing?

CRITICAL THINKING EXERCISES

Learning Goal 2

1. While we haven't yet decided on a promotion mix for Music-stor, (that will come shortly) it will most likely include some form of personal selling. Using the seven steps in your text, prepare an outline for a sales presentation to your automotive manufacturing customers.

2. How will the presentation differ for selling Music-stor to a retailer?

Learning Goal 3

3. The Fox affiliate in large Midwestern city added a news broadcast to its lineup. In order to compete with the larger affiliates, the Fox affiliate (Channel 30) decided to air their program at 9:00 p.m. Before the news broadcast went on the air, the station surveyed viewers regarding their likes and dislikes about the current local news broadcasts. Shortly before the new show was to premiere, the station began promoting the show, the news anchors, and how this show was going to be different from current shows.

   One of the changes the new show made was to avoid, as much as possible, the real "bad news" stories as leads to the broadcast, leaving them until later in the show. They have made a point of finding "good news" stories about the city and the inhabitants. During the broadcast, just before a commercial break, a screen will show with the exact show times of each of the upcoming stories, in response to customer complaints that other stations will use upcoming stories as "hooks" but actually not air the story until much later in the broadcast. In promoting the show, and during the news broadcast, mention is made of the way the station is responding to viewer requests. Further, during the broadcast, the station's telephone number is flashed, and viewers are encouraged to call with complaints, requests, or suggestions.

   How do these actions by the television station demonstrate a "good" public relations program?

Learning Goal 4

4. How do the other elements of the promotion mix affect word of mouth promotion?

   a. Product _____

   b. Sales promotion _____

   c. Advertising _____

   d. Publicity _____

   e. Personal selling _____

5. Identify three main groups that are the focus of sales promotion efforts, and a technique used to reach each group.

                Group   Technique

    a. _____ _____

    b. _____ _____

    c. _____ _____

6. Consumers are frequently the targets of sales promotion techniques. What kinds of sales promotion have you been involved in recently?

Learning Goal 5

7. There is a variety of media available to use for advertising. Using the chart in your text, determine what might be the most appropriate form of advertising media for: (there may be more than one answer for each).

    a. A rock concert at an outdoor theater _____

    b. Sales at the local mall _____

    c. Products aimed specifically at women _____

    d. A local news show _____

    e. Long distance telephone service _____

    f. Credit cards _____

    g. Computer software _____

h. A storage case for CDs and tapes for the car _____

8. In today's marketplace, there are many alternatives to advertising in the traditional media such as print, television, and radio. Compare the benefits of advertising using infomercials, the Internet, and other forms of technology.

Learning Goals 1-6

9. Now that we have covered the promotion mix variables, you are an expert in designing an effective promotion campaign. What do you think would be the most effective promotion mix for Music-stor to use? Will it be more important to use a push or a pull strategy, a combination, or a "total systems" approach?

10. The Barucci family has run Barruci's Restaurant for 17 years. Most of the time it has only been marginally profitable, although the whole family worked diligently. After Papa Barucci died, the restaurant stared to falter. No one seemed to be in charge, no one knew the suppliers, the inventory system or much about managing the restaurant, as Papa had taken care of all that. Maria Barucci knew she had to do something fast. She began by finding out as much about the business as she could. She talked to the employees, looked at company records and other internal files. She asked the employees for their insights and recommendations. They gave her information about how the business was run, and many ideas for improvements. Maria kept all her information on her home computer and implemented the improvements her employees suggested.

Maria also talked to her competitors, other restaurant owners as well as suppliers and salespeople from several computer firms. From them, she learned the newest restaurant management techniques and technology. Maria and her employees learned how to implement many additional changes from some of the salespeople, which helped to make their job helping her, easier.

Maria spent a lot of time talking to customers, asking questions and seeking suggestions. She implemented many of those suggestions, too. Finally, Maria, along with her employees and others, began an advertising campaign, with the theme "You asked for it! You got it!" with advertisements in local newspapers and on the radio. She also included coupons with a bulk mailing company.

Lastly, Maria found a new company, just getting started, which agreed to develop a simple Internet-based advertisement for the restaurant, showing menus, specials, hours of operation and so forth. She contacted several web servers and began negotiations for advertising on the Web, on her city's Web page and other appropriate formats. Maria also bought a fax machine, and started accepting take-out orders.

The atmosphere at the restaurant became open, friendly, and helpful. A positive relationship between Maria, her employees, and her suppliers developed. The positive atmosphere carried over to the customers, who felt that the Barucci employees were among the most helpful and friendliest of any local restaurant. Barucci's became a bigger success than it had in the past.

A. How did Maria Barucci implement an integrated marketing communication system?

B. What advantages does a small business like Barucci's have in developing an integrated marketing communication system?

PRACTICE TEST

Multiple Choice: Circle the best answer.

1. _____ allows customers to buy products by interacting with various advertising media without meeting a sales person face-to-face.

    a. Target marketing   c. Direct marketing
    b. Market segmentation   d. Promotion

2. Promotion is an attempt by marketers to:

    a. help retailers sell products.
    b. inform and persuade people to buy.
    c. segment markets to reach them more effectively.
    d. search for new prospects.

3. In personal selling, the relationship must continue for a long time, as the salesperson responds to new requests for information from current customers. This is an important part of the _____ step in personal selling.

    a. prospecting   c. follow up
    b. closing   d. presentation

4. Which of the following is true regarding personal selling today?

    a. Technology has had a big impact on personal selling with the use of high-tech hardware and software.
    b. The objective of an initial sales call is to make a sale immediately.
    c. Big customers should always be treated with more care than small ones.
    d. It is more difficult to find customers in the business-to-business market than in the consumer market.

5. Which of the following is not a part of developing a good public relations program?

    a. Listen to the public.
    b. Inform people of the fact you're being responsive.
    c. Develop policies and procedures in the public interest.
    d. Advertise in a way that promotes positive word-of-mouth.

6. Which of the following is not considered a benefit of publicity?

    a. Publicity may reach people who wouldn't read an advertisement.
    b. Publicity may be placed on the front page of a newspaper.
    c. You can control when the publicity release will be used.
    d. Publicity is more believable than other forms of promotion.

7. When Mary Lynn went to the grocery store last week, she took with her several coupons she had received in the mail that week. While at the store, Mary Lynn was offered samples of several food items and actually bought a few, using the in-store coupons. She also bought a particular brand of toothpaste, because the tube came with a free toothbrush. Mary Lynn is taking advantage of:

    a. word of mouth.
    b. sales promotion.
    c. advertising.
    d. publicity.

8. Which of the following is not true regarding sales promotion efforts?

    a. Sales promotion efforts are aimed first at salespersons, then at the end consumer.
    b. Sales promotion can be done both internally and externally.
    c. Sales promotion programs are designed to supplement other promotion efforts.
    d. Sales promotion efforts are designed to create long-term relationships.

9. Mama Barucci's Restaurant has had a big increase in business since Mama implemented an integrated marketing communications system. Mama has learned that much of the new business is coming from customers who have recommended the restaurant to their friends and associates. People seem to be hearing about Mama Barucci's and want to try if for themselves. Mama's is benefiting from:

    a. publicity.
    b. advertising.
    c. word of mouth.
    d. sales promotion.

10. Which of the following is an advantage of Internet advertising over other media?

    a. Targets a specific audience
    b. Local market focus
    c. No competition from other material
    d. Inexpensive global coverage

11. Which of the following would not be included in a discussion of the benefits of advertising using infomercials?

    a. They can show the product in great detail.
    b. Infomercials are low in cost.
    c. It is the equivalent of sending your best salesperson into the home.
    d. Infomercials provide the opportunity to show the public how a product works.

12. Technology has:

    a. had little impact on the area of advertising.
    b. affected other areas of business more than advertising.
    c. had a tremendous impact on advertising.
    d. decreased the need for personal selling.

13. The city of San Antonio has made an effort to develop promotional materials for travel agents and bus tour companies that are within a 300-mile radius of the city. City officials are hopeful that these efforts will encourage tourism in the area when agents suggest the city to their clients. San Antonio is making use of a:

    a. push strategy.   c. segmentation strategy.
    b. pull strategy.   d. targeting strategy.

14. Microsystems advertises in several software publications, as well as the Internet. Their sales people call on computer stores, and often leave brochures and other materials describing their products and customer service programs. The company has a Web site where the customers can purchase products on-line. These efforts are part of the company's:

    a. marketing mix.   c. push strategy.
    b. promotion mix.   d. corporate platform.

15. Which of the following is not one of the basic steps of developing an interactive marketing communication system?

    a. Make it possible for customers to access information they need to make a purchase.
    b. Respond quickly to customer information by designing wanted products.
    c. Gather data about the groups affected by the organization.
    d. Develop a promotion mix to satisfy the needs of interactive customers.

16. Which statement would not be included in a discussion of the advantages of interactive marketing on the Internet?

   a. Customers can access information any time they want.
   b. Large companies can reach the markets more effectively than smaller companies.
   c. Buyers and sellers can engage in a dialog.
   d. Electronic ads and catalogs do not have to be printed, stored or shipped.

17. What is likely to be the impact of technology on television and other forms of mass advertising?

   a. The Internet has probably peaked as a form of advertising, and will not have a further impact on any other forms of advertising.
   b. There will be a big drop off in TV and other mass advertising.
   c. Technology will be a complementary effort, but will not increase in use as a tool for advertising.
   d. Infomercials will probably replace the Internet as the primary form of promotion.

TRUE/FALSE

1. _____ Most data indicate that personal selling is not a major force in our economy.

2. _____ It is said that 50 percent of a sale's negotiation's outcome is determined before you meet a customer face to face.

3. _____ The idea of public relations is to establish a dialogue with stakeholders.

4. _____ One of the problems with publicity is that it is not believable.

5. _____ Sales promotion can be used as an attempt to keep salespeople enthusiastic about the company.

6. _____ The best way to generate positive word of mouth is to have a good product and provide good service.

7. _____ Word-of-mouth is really another form of advertising.

8. _____ Evidence supports the theory that promotional efforts specifically designed for individual countries are not any more successful than more general advertising.

9. _____ When using a pull strategy, advertising and sales promotion efforts are directed at consumers.

10. _____ Small firms are capturing markets from large firms because small firms tend to be better listeners and more responsive to changes in the market.

11. _____ The promotion of services is often harder than for goods because the product is intangible.

12. _____ Disk-based advertising may take the place of infomercials in the future.

ANSWERS

LEARNING THE LANGUAGE

1. Mass customization	10. Prospecting
2. Sales promotion	11. Direct marketing
3. Advertising	12. Publicity
4. Public relations	13. Push strategy
5. Pull strategy	14. Infomercials
6. Trade shows	15. Personal selling
7. Promotion mix	16. Promotion
8. Word-of-mouth promotion	17. Integrated marketing communication system
9. Integrated marketing	

RETENTION CHECK

Learning Goal 1 **The Importance of Marketing Communication and Promotion**

1. The elements of the promotion mix are:
   a. Personal selling.
   b. Word-of-mouth.
   c. Sales promotion.
   d. Public relations.
   e. Publicity.
   f. Advertising.

Learning Goal 2 **Personal Selling**

2. Effective selling is a matter of persuading others to buy and helping others to satisfy their wants and needs.

3. The steps of the personal selling process are:
   a. Prospect and qualify.
   b. Preapproach.
   c. Approach.
   d. Make presentation.
   e. Answer objections.
   f. Close sale.
   g. Follow-up.

4. To qualify customers means to make sure that they have a need for the product, the authority to buy, and the willingness to listen to a sales message. People who meet these criteria are called prospects.

5. Before making a sales call, the sales representative must do further research, which is done during the preapproach. As much as possible should be learned about customer's wants and needs.

6. The objective of an initial sales call is to give an impression of professionalism, create rapport and to build credibility.

7. During the sales presentation, the sale representative matches the benefits of his or her value package to the client's needs. The presentation will be tailored to the customer's needs, and will be relatively easy to present because the sales representative has done the homework of getting to know the customer.

8. Closing techniques include getting a series of small commitments and then asking for the order and showing the client where to sign.

9. The follow-up includes handling customer complaints, making sure that the customer's questions are answered, and supplying what the customer wants.

10. Companies are providing many high-tech aids to help salespeople in their job. Salespeople often have laptop computers that connect to databases. Using the computers, sales people can track orders, get product information and search for other information. Sales force automation includes over 400 software programs that help salespeople design products, close deals, tap into company intranets and more. Some salespeople can even conduct virtual reality tours of the manufacturing plant for the customer.

11. Business to business sales people can find customers more easily because the government classifies business customers using the Standard Industrial Classification codes. Books with such codes are available at most libraries. Once a salesperson has found one customer industry, he or she can easily find other customers with the same SIC code.

12. Sales force automation helps business-to-business salespeople by providing laptop computers, modems, e-mail, fax software, and scanners. Salespeople can get specifications by e-mail, get product announcements from the company and then e-mail them to customers, scan documents and fax them to customers, find information in databases and use that data in sales presentations.

Learning Goal 3 **Public Relations and Publicity**

13. Steps in creating a public relations campaign are:
    a. Focus on customer satisfaction and quality.
    b. Deliver on promises.
    c. Target opinion leaders.

14. It is the responsibility of the public relations department to maintain close relationships with the media, community leaders, government officials, and other corporate stakeholders. The idea is to establish and maintain a dialogue with those stakeholders so that the company can respond to questions, complaints, and suggestions quickly.

15. The benefits of publicity are:
    a. It's free, if the material is interesting or newsworthy.
    b. It may reach people who would not read an advertisement.
    c. It's believable.

16. The drawbacks of publicity are:
    a. No control over how or when the media will use the story.
    b. The story may be altered, and could end up not as positive as the original.
    c. Once a story has run, it won't be repeated.

Learning Goal 4 **Sales Promotion and Word of Mouth**

17. Types of sales promotion are:
    a. Displays.
    b. Contests.
    c. Samples.
    d. Trade shows.
    e. Incentives.
    f. Lotteries.

      g. Catalogs.
      h. Special events.
      i. Exhibits.
      j. Sweepstakes.

18. Sales promotion programs are designed to supplement the other promotion mix variables by creating enthusiasm for the overall promotional program.

19. Sales promotion targets can be both internal, within the company, and external, outside the company.

20. Internal sales promotion efforts are directed at salespeople and other customer contact people. It is an attempt to keep salespeople enthusiastic about the company through sales training and the development of sales aids, and participation in trade shows where salespeople can get leads.

21. After the company's employees have been motivated, the next step is to promote to final consumers using samples, coupons, cents-off deals, displays, store demonstrations, premiums, and other incentives like contests, trading stamps and rebates.

22. Sampling is a quick effective way of demonstrating a product's superiority at the time when consumers are making a purchase decision.

23. The best way to generate word of mouth is to:
    a. Have a good product.
    b. Provide good services.
    c. Keep customers happy.

24. The elements of an effective word-of-mouth promotion are:
    a. Focusing on customer satisfaction and quality
    b. Delivering on promises
    c. Targeting opinion leaders

Learning Goal 5 **Advertising**

25. Advertising is paid, nonpersonal communication through various media. Word-of-mouth is not a form of advertising because it doesn't go through media, is not paid for, and is personal. Publicity isn't advertising because the media space isn't paid for. Personal selling is face-to-face communication and doesn't go through media.

26. The public benefits from advertising because ads are informative. It provides us with free TV and radio because advertisers pay for the production costs. Advertising also covers the major costs of producing newspapers and magazines.

27. Advertising media include:
    a. Newspapers.
    b. Television.
    c. Radio.
    d. Magazines.
    e. Outdoor.
    f. Direct mail.
    g. Yellow pages.
    h. Internet.

28.

a.	Newspapers	Good local coverage; ads placed quickly; high acceptance; ad can be clipped and saved	Ads compete with other features; poor color; ads get thrown away
b.	Television	Sight, sound, motion reaches all audiences; high attention with no competition	High cost; short exposure time; takes time to prepare ads.
c.	Radio	Low cost; can target specific audiences; flexible; good for local marketing	People may not listen; short exposure time; audience can't keep ad.
d.	Magazines	Target specific audiences; good use of color; long life ad can be clipped and saved	Inflexible; ads must be placed weeks before publication; cost is relatively high
e.	Outdoor	High visibility and repeat exposures; low cost; local market focus	Limited message, low selectivity of audience

f. Direct mail	Best for targeting specific markets; very flexible; ad can be saved	High cost; consumer rejection as junk mail; must conform to postal regulations
g. Yellow pages	Great coverage of local markets; widely used by consumers; available at point of purchase	Competition with others; cost may be too high for very small businesses
h. Internet	Inexpensive global coverage; available at any time; interactive	Relatively low readership

29. Infomercials allow the seller to show the product in detail, which helps the product to sell itself. They allow for testimonials and for showing the customer how the product actually works, and allow for the use of drama, demonstration, graphics, and other advertising tools.

30. Technology is having a major impact on advertising. Promoters are using interactive TV to carry on a dialogue with customers, and using CD-ROM technology to provide more information. Salespeople are using hand-held computers to place orders and to help consumers design custom-made products. Customers can request information via e-mail or fax and can reach service people from almost any location.

31. Evidence supports the theory that promotional efforts specifically designed for individual countries often work best. The challenge is to conduct the research needed to determine the wants, needs and culture of each specific country and then designing appropriate ads and testing them.

32. Much advertising today is moving from the trend toward globalism, or one ad for everyone in the world, to regionalism, which calls for specific ads for each country and for specific groups within a country. In the future, marketers will prepare more custom-designed promotions to reach smaller audiences.

Learning Goal 6 **Preparing the Promotion Mix**

33. a. Large homogeneous groups of consumers are usually most efficiently reached through advertising.
    b. Large organizations are best reached through personal selling.

34. In a push strategy, the producer uses promotion tools to convince wholesalers and retailers to stock and sell merchandise. If it works, consumers will walk into the store, and see the product and buy it. The idea is to push the product through the distribution system to the stores.

35. In a pull strategy, heavy advertising and sales promotion efforts are directed toward consumers so they'll request the products from retailers. If it works, consumers will go to the store and order the products. Seeing demand, the storeowner will then order them from the wholesaler. The wholesaler in turn will order from the producer. The idea is to pull products down through the distribution system.

36. A total systems approach to marketing is when promotion is a part of supply-chain management. In such cases retailers would work with producers and distributors to make the supply chain as efficient as possible. Then a promotional plan would be developed for the whole system. The idea would be to develop a value package that would appeal to everyone.

37. Interactive marketing is the use of new information technologies such as fax on demand, 900 telephone service, the Internet, databases, e-mail, and CD-ROMs. Marketers are now able to establish and maintain a dialogue with customers over time. Control over promotional messages is being shifted from the seller to the buyer.

Learning Goal 7   **Integrated Marketing Communication (IMC)**

38. An interactive marketing communication system is one where consumers can access company information on their own and supply information about themselves in an on-going dialogue.

39. Steps to develop an interactive marketing communications systems are:
    a. Gather data constantly about the groups affected by the organization and keep the information in a database. Make it available to everyone.
    b. Respond quickly to information by adjusting company policies and practices and by designing wanted products and services for target markets.
    c. Make it possible for customers and potential customers to access information that they may need to make a purchase.

40. Small firms are capturing markets from large firms because small firms tend to be better listeners, have fewer layers of management in which information gets lost, and are more responsive to changes in the market.

41. Advantages of interactive marketing on the Internet are:
    a. Customers can access information 24 hours a day. A company can reach markets anywhere in the world.
    b. Electronic ads and catalogs don't have to be printed, stored or shipped, and can be easily updated, continuously.
    c. Small companies have an equal or better chance to reach consumers as larger firms.
    d. Buyers and sellers can engage in a dialogue over time, so both feel they are getting the best deal.

42. Marketing services on the Internet is more difficult than marketing goods because the product is intangible and customers can't visualize all the benefits they may receive.

43. Fax on demand means that a company gives a customer a telephone number to call. When consumers call, they are given a series of numbers to dial in to receive whatever information they desire. That information is then faxed to them immediately.

44. Integrated marketing communication blends with interactive communications when phones, faxes, e-mail, television and radio are all combined in one promotion.

45. Disk-based advertising is information provided on a CD-ROM or computer disk. That information can be in graphic form and accompanied by sound. Consumers can search the disks for whatever information they want. They can contact the company by phone, fax, e-mail or letter to order the product they want.

46. The net result of the new technology is that companies will have to totally rethink how marketing and promotion will be done in the future. There is likely to be a big drop off in TV and other mass advertising. There will be a huge increase in the use of the Internet as a promotional and marketing tool. The same is true of e-mail, fax, and other communication tools.

47. Soon there may be as many Internet malls as there are regional malls. Shoppers will be able to request information from multiple firms, compare prices and make purchases from their homes.

CRITICAL THINKING EXERCISES

Learning Goal 2

1. A sales presentation for Music-stor will have to begin with prospecting. Which carmakers are you going to target? Are you going to go after just one carmaker, or several? Initially, you will probably be wise to begin with just one. The question then becomes which maker to go after. After research, you may be able to make that decision more easily. Then, the preapproach will call for learning as much as possible about the products your customer sells. Which models will be the best suited for Music-stor? Which of the models could be most easily adapted? What's the production volume on those models? What's the competition doing? How could Music-stor benefit your customer? Making the approach will involve making an appointment with the right person, the decision-maker. You will need to look professional, have a prototype of the product with you. Come prepared with questions geared to help you find out what they may be looking for. During the presentation, you will have to show the car maker how Music-stor will make their cars better than the competition. You could discuss the benefits of convenience, luxury, and have something the competition doesn't have. You could come prepared with visuals demonstrating how easily Music-stor would fit into the interior of the car (with the magic of computer graphics). You will also want to know something about who your customer's customers are, in order to be able to demonstrate how Music-stor will appeal to them. Objections will have to be overcome by showing how easily Music-stor will fit into existing models, perhaps by driving a car (one of their models of course) with Music-stor installed, and taking the customer for a ride to show them Music-stor convenience. You could show them how easily the interior could be adapted for Music-stor by using your computer graphics presentation. Eventually you will have to close the sale, perhaps by asking to make Music-stor an available option, or asking your customer to put Music-stor in some of their cars. Finally, always be available for questions, "hand-holding," and problems that may arise. Keep in mind that this process will take a lot of time, and won't be accomplished in one sales call.

2. In order to convince retailers to sell the product, you will need to convince them that the shelf-space you are asking for will pay off. You will still need to determine which type of retailer will be most appropriate (prospecting and qualifying), and research retailers in terms of who their customers are, the needs of the retailer, and exactly what they want from the products they carry. During the presentation, you will need to convince the retailer that this is a product consumers will want, why they will want it (convenience and the ability to store more tapes and CDs) and how carrying the product will benefit the retailer. You will need to have a sample of Music-stor with you and show the retailer how it works easily with most interiors and how easily it can be detached to take out of the car if needed.

Learning Goal 3

3. It sounds like the station really wanted to know what people thought of their programming, and what people wanted in a news program. The first step of a good public relations program is to do research to evaluate public attitudes, which is exactly what the station did, by researching the market before the premier, and by publishing the station's phone numbers and encouraging viewers to call. The station also seems to have responded by avoiding, as much as possible, the "bad news" stories as lead ins, which is in the public interest, especially as the broadcast is at 9:00 p.m. when it is possible that children could be watching. They also seem to have avoided the scandalous stories upon which many TV news programs seem to thrive. This is also illustrated by the fact that they tell the viewers exactly when a news story will air, allowing viewers to change the channel if children are likely to be watching a story that parents don't want them to see. Lastly, during the broadcast and in their advertising they are mentioning the specific ways in which they have responded to viewer requests, which is the third step in a good public relations program.

4. a. Product—A good product will generate positive word of mouth because customers will be happy with the product and pass the word along.
b. Sales promotion—Techniques such as special events and contests often create positive word of mouth promotion
c. Advertising—When an advertisement is easily remembered or funny it will often create positive word of mouth. A good technique is to advertise to people who already use your product.
d. Publicity—A news story can create word of mouth by stimulating the public's interest in the product.
e. Personal selling—A good sales person can help the customer to develop a positive image of the product, thus creating positive word of mouth.

5. Suggested answers:

	Group.	Technique.
a.	Salespeople.	Sales training, conventions, trade shows.
b.	Dealers.	Catalogues, special events, "deals".
c.	Customers.	Coupons, sweepstakes, displays, samples.

6. You may have received free samples at the store or coupons in the mail, entered a contest, bought a glass at a fast food restaurant, sent in a rebate to a manufacturer, gone to a trade show or even received a free pen with a company name on it.

Learning Goal 5

7.
   a. Radio, newspaper
   b. Newspaper, radio
   c. Magazines, direct mail
   d. Outdoor, local TV, radio
   e. TV, direct mail
   f. Direct mail
   g. Magazines, direct mail
   h. Newspaper, TV, direct mail

8. Technology has changed advertising in terms of the way the message can be delivered to the customer. Interactive TV allows promoters to carry on a dialogue with customers. CD-ROM allows promoters to follow up with even more information using the latest in multimedia. Hand-held computers can be used to place orders, and to help customers design custom-made products. Information can be received over E-mail, and can reach service people using cellular telephones and pagers.

Further, companies are making use of such on-line services as Prodigy, America Online and CompuServe to provide information. Potential customers can go online with sellers and get information immediately.

Infomercials allow producers to provide more in-depth information about their products and offer testimonials, demonstrations and more.

Learning Goal 1-6

9. Your response to this question will really depend upon whom you have selected as your primary target market. If you have decided to go after the automotive manufacturers as your primary market, then most likely your promotion mix will include lots of personal selling, some advertising in the form of brochures, aimed at the car dealerships who will be selling the cars with your product installed. If your research has been done, and a need for this kind of product has been established, you could design a public relations campaign for the auto manufacturer, indicating that the company listened to your need for a product like Music-stor, then made the product in response.

    If your primary market is the retail market, then you must design a campaign aimed at encouraging the retailers to carry the product. Some kind of sales promotion will be appropriate such as price deals, incentives for the retailers selling the most product, and so on. You could participate in trade shows, featuring the latest car models, which are held all over the United States and are attended by thousands of consumers. You could use some advertising, after the retailers have been convinced to carry Music-stor. Any form of publicity could be useful, as will the word of mouth generated by satisfied customers.

    You may have your own web site, with attractive graphics, interactive sales techniques. You may be able to advertise on-line, on Web sites that appeal to a younger market, for example, which may be more likely to purchase your product for their car. You may also consider direct marketing, such as order forms in music magazines.

    Most likely you will use a combination of a push and pull strategy for the product. You will be using primarily a push strategy if you are aiming at the automotive manufacturers. A combination will be most effective if you are aiming at the consumer market. Probably the best approach, once you are an established company, will be to work with your customers, retailers and develop a value package that will appeal to everyone, the manufacturers, retailers and consumers.

10. A. Maria Barucci implemented an integrated marketing communication system first by developing a list of all her "stakeholders," all those groups affected by her company. She started the process by talking with and listening to her employees, and responded by implementing their suggestions. This committed the employees to the rest of the changes she wanted to make. Maria communicated with customers and other stakeholders, and implemented the changes they suggested. She kept a database of this information, so that the information could be continually updated. Further, she let her customers know she was responding by developing an ad campaign with the theme "You asked for it! You got it!" which tells customers that Maria has responded to their suggestions. She is using new technology to make it easy for customers to know what changes they have made, what is on the menu and so forth.

The new, more relaxed atmosphere created by these changes carried over to the customers in the restaurant. Although there is no mention made, it is probable that the open, helpful atmosphere created positive word of mouth, and customers responded by patronizing the restaurant and by telling others.

B. As discussed earlier, small businesses have the advantage of being closer to the customer, and of being able to respond more quickly to suggested changes. Small businesses may also find it easier to develop relationships that are more personal with their suppliers and other stakeholders. Small businesses are more flexible than big businesses and the decision making process takes less time. Small firms tend to be better listeners and have fewer layers of management, which enables them to be more responsive to market changes.

PRACTICE TEST

Multiple Choice				True/False			
1.	c	10.	d	1.	F	7.	F
2.	b	11.	b	2.	T	8.	F
3.	c	12.	c	3.	T	9.	T
4.	a	13.	a	4.	F	10.	T
5.	d	14.	b	5.	T	11.	T
6.	c	15.	d	6.	T	12.	T
7.	b	16.	b				
8.	d	17.	b				
9.	c						

CHAPTER 17
USING TECHNOLOGY TO MANAGE INFORMATION

LEARNING GOALS

After you have read and studied this chapter, you should be able to:

1. Outline the changing role of business technology.

2. Compare the scope of the Internet, intranets, and extranets as tools in managing information.

3. List the steps in managing information and identify the characteristics of useful information

4. Review the hardware most frequently used in business and outline the benefits of the move toward computer networks.

5. Classify the computer software most frequently used in business.

6. Evaluate the human resource, security, and privacy issues in management that are affected by information technology.

7. Identify the careers that are gaining or losing workers due to the growth of information technology.

LEARNING THE LANGUAGE

Listed below are important terms found in the chapter. Choose the correct term for the definition and write it in the space provided.

Communication software	Internet 2
Cookies	Intranet
Data processing (DP)	Knowledge technology (KT)
Database programs	Message center software
Extranet	Network computing system (client/server computing)
Firewall	Public domain software
Groupware	Push technology
Information systems (IS)	Shareware
Information technology (IT)	Spreadsheet program
Integrated software (suites)	Virtualization
Internet	Virus

1. Technology called _____ supports existing business, used primarily to improve the flow of financial information.

2. A type of software known as a _____ creates a table made up of rows and columns, which enable a manager to organize information.

3. Computer software called _____ allows people to work collaboratively and share ideas.

4. This type of technology known as _____ adds a layer of intelligence to filter appropriate information and deliver it when it is needed.

5. The type of software called _____ makes it possible for different brands of computers to transfer data to each other.

6. Accessibility through technology, or _____, allows business to be conducted independent of location.

7. A semiprivate network known as a(n) _____ uses Internet technology and allows more than one company to access the same information or allows people on different servers to collaborate.

8. Computer software that is copyrighted but distributed to potential customers free of charge is called _____.

9. A piece of programming code known as a _____ is inserted into other programming to cause some unexpected and, for the victim, usually undesirable event.

10. Technology called _____ helps companies to do business.

11. A computer software package called _____ offers two or more applications in one package.

12. Computer software called _____ allows users to store and manipulate information that is normally keep in lists such as names and addresses, schedules, and inventories.

13. Computer systems that allow personal computers to obtain needed information from huge databases in a central computer are called a(n)_____.

14. Technology called _____ helps companies to change business by its applications to new methods of doing business.

15. A connection of tens of thousands of interconnected computer networks called the _____ includes 1.7-million host computers.

16. Web software called _____ delivers information tailored to a previously defined user profile; thus, it appears that the information is "pushed "by the Web rather than "pulled "by the user.

17. The new Internet system known as the _____ links government supercomputer centers and a select group of universities; it runs many times faster than today's public infrastructure and supports heavy-duty applications.

18. A new generation of programs called _____ uses fax/voice modems to receive, sort, and deliver phone calls, e-mail, and faxes.

19. Computer hardware and/or software that prevent unauthorized users from accessing an intranet is called a(n) _____.

20. A companywide network called an _____ is closed to public access, and uses Internet-type technology.

21. A piece of information such as registration information or user preferences, known as _____ is sent by a web server over the Internet to a web browser that the browser software is expected to save and send back to the server whenever the user returns to that web site.

22. Software that is free for the taking is _____.

RETENTION CHECK

Learning Goal 1   **The Role of Information Technology**

1. What is the difference between data and information?

2. What was the primary role and use of data processing?

3. How did Information Systems differ from data processing?

4. What does Information Technology allow businesses to do?

5. What two barriers to doing business are being broken by Information technology?

6. How does breaking these barriers change the way business is done?

7. What is a virtual office?

8. What is the difference between information technology and knowledge technology?

9. How does knowledge technology change the flow of information?

Learning Goal 2 **Road to Knowledge: The Internet, Intranets and Extranets**

10. What is a key issue for business today regarding information?

11. What are some applications of an intranet?

12. How have companies solved the problem of competitors getting into their intranets?

13. How is an intranet different from an extranet?

14. How does the Internet change the way we do business?

15. What is a problem being encountered with using the Internet?

16. What is the Internet 2 to be used for?

Learning Goal 3 **Managing Information**

17. What is "infoglut"?

18. List four qualities of useful information.

   a. _____   c. _____

   b. _____   d. _____

19. What does push technology do?

20. What is important to remember about information overload?

Learning Goal 4   **The Enabling Technology: Hardware**

21. What are some hardware components?

22. How is a network computing system different from mainframe computing?

23. Identify the major benefits of computer network systems.

   a. _____

   b. _____

   c. _____

Learning Goal 5 **Software**

24. What are six major business uses of software?

   a. _____

   b. _____

   c. _____

   d. _____

   e. _____

   f. _____

25. What is word processing used for?

26. What is desktop publishing?

27. Name three of the most popular word processing programs.

   a. _____

   b. _____

   c. _____

28. What is a spreadsheet?

29. What are three of the most popular spreadsheet programs?

   a. _____

   b. _____

   c. _____

30. What does a database program allow you to do?

31. What are the leading database programs?

   a. _____   e. _____

   b. _____   f. _____

   c. _____   g. _____

   d. _____

32. What is a personal information manager (PIM)?

33. What can a graphics program add to a presentation?

34. What are the most popular graphics programs?

   a. _____   d. _____

   b. _____   e. _____

   c. _____   f. _____

35. What does communications software enable a computer to do?

36. What are some popular communications software programs?

   a. _____   c. _____

   b. _____   d. _____

37. What is the next generation of communications software?

38. What are three message center software programs?

   a. _____   c. _____

   b. _____

39. What is accounting software used for?

40. Name three accounting/finance software programs.

    a. _____

    b. _____

    c. _____

41. What can you do with integrated software packages?

42. Name three integrated software packages.

    a. _____

    b. _____

    c. _____

43. What does groupware make possible?

44. Name four groupware programs.

    a. _____   c. _____

    b. _____   d. _____

Learning Goal 6   Effects of Information Technology on Management

45. What are three areas that are being affected by the growing reliance on information technology?

   a. _____

   b. _____

   c. _____

46. Name two ways that computers will change the structure of organizations and jobs.

   a. _____

   b. _____

47. What are some benefits of telecommuting?

48. What are some drawbacks telecommuting?

49. How are companies attempting to alleviate the problems of telecommuting?

50. What is a hacker?

51. How are computer viruses spread?

52. Why are antivirus programs not always effective? How do you avoid the problem?

53. What kind of personal information can be obtained from certain Web sites?

54. What is a key issue being debated over Internet privacy?

55. What does a cookie do?

Learning Goal 7   **Technology and You**

56. What are some of the reasons being computer illiterate could be "occupational suicide?"

57. What will be the consequences of a shortage of information technology workers?

CRITICAL THINKING EXERCISES

Learning Goal 1

1. Describe how business technology changed from the 1970's to the 1980's to the present.

2. We have read in several previous chapters of the need to meet increasing global competition, and the movement toward customized products and marketing. How does information technology change business to make those jobs possible?

Learning Goal 2

3. Compare the Internet, intranets and extranets. Do you know a company that has an intranet? How is it used? What are the applications in this company?

4. What is one of the biggest problems with the age of information technology in terms of managing the information?

Learning Goal 3

5. Help! You are swamped by the data, reports, facts, figures, and tons of paper and e-mail being sent to you! It's your job as a low level sales employee to manage the dissemination of all this "stuff" and make sure it makes sense to everyone who gets it. In other words, your job is to manage all that information! What can you do to make this information useful? How does push technology help to solve information overload?

Learning Goal 4

6. How could a network computing system help with information overload?

Learning Goal 5

7. Major uses for software include:

    Writing (word processing).   Integrated software groupware.

    Manipulating numbers (spreadsheets).   Presenting information visually (graphics).

    Filing and retrieving data (databases).   Communicating.

Match the application being used to the following examples:

a. Richard Bolt uses this software to record his students' grades, average the grades and total the grades at the end of the semester. It's easy to change scores if an error is made, because the computer will automatically recalculate averages and totals when the new score is recorded. _____

b. Ray Smith uses Microsoft Mail to send and retrieve messages from work. _____

c. Randy Langston is a marketing manager who uses this type of software to keep track of all his sales people. He has all the information regarding territories, sales quotas, expenses, sales calls and more right at his fingertips. _____

d. Ryan Charles used this software to create a more interesting report for his science project. After he had finished writing the report, he created a pie chart and a bar chart to illustrate the findings of his research. _____

e. Lin Stallings works in a law office. Whenever there is a need for a certain kind of document for a specific case, all Lin has to do is pull the document up on her screen and insert the relevant information. _____

f. Julie Andersen uses this to complete her accounting worksheet, design a chart that graphically represents her information, and write a report summarizing all the information, all with one software package. _____

g. The Ford Mustang re-design team used this type of software to work together on their project all at the same time. Every time someone had a good idea, they put it into memory for retrieval by anyone on the team at any time.

Learning Goal 6

8. What has happened to organizational structures as a result of the increased use of technology?

9. What are some of the security and privacy issues that are important to recognize with the increasing use of information technology?

10. What careers will be shrinking in the next 10 years? Why will they be shrinking?

    What careers will be growing? How can computers be used for such jobs as a physical therapist or a special education teacher?

PRACTICE TEST

Multiple Choice: Circle the best answer.

1. In the 1980's, business technology changed from supporting business, to doing business by using _____.

    a. data processing   c. information systems
    b. information technology   d. knowledge technology

2. Using _____ a new employee can sit at a workstation and let the system take over doing everything from laying out a checklist of each thing required on a shift to answering questions and offering insights that once would have taken up a supervisor's time.

    a. data processing   c. knowledge technology
    b. information technology   d. virtualization

3. At MEMC Electronics, employees can update their addresses, submit requisitions, timesheets and payroll forms online. The company's system is closed to public access, but all employees have access. MEMC is using an _____.

    a. intranet   c. internet
    b. extranet   d. electronic data interchange system

4. A problem managers have with the rapid advance of information technology has been

    a. the skyrocketing cost of information.
    b. the hardware and software products available can't keep up with the expansion.
    c. the increased layers of management.
    d. information overload, with the deluge of information available.

5. Which of the following is not included in a list of characteristics of useful information?

    a. Timeliness   c. Completeness
    b. Quality   d. Accessibility

6. When facing information overload a manger should

   a. set goals and do the best he or she can.
   b. hire an intern to take care of information which is not needed.
   c. look for a system which will handle the information more readily.
   d. make use of a file management system.

7. _____ includes pagers, cellular phones, printers and scanners and personal digital assistants.

   a. Software   c. Extranets
   b. Multimedia   d. Hardware

8. In recent years, businesses have moved from:

   a. network computing systems to mainframe systems.
   b. client/server computing to network computing systems.
   c. database systems to information processing.
   d. mainframe systems to network computing systems.

9. Which of the following is not a benefit of networks?

   a. More information is available
   b. Saving time and money
   c. Networks provide easy links across boundaries
   d. Companies can see their products more clearly

10. Which of the following projects would be best suited to a spreadsheet program?

    a. Personalizing a standardized letter to clients
    b. Recording the sales figures from several different stores, and calculating profits
    c. Updating lists and schedules, keeping track of inventory
    d. Making a presentation more appealing with sound clips, video clips, and clip art

11. A major difference between groupware and other types of software is that groupware

    a. is less expensive than other forms of software because it is distributed free.
    b. can replace more management functions than others.
    c. allows computers to talk to one another.
    d. runs on a network and allows several users to work on the same project at the same time.

12. Perhaps the most revolutionary effect of computers and increased use of the Internet is

    a. the amount of information which has been made available to managers.
    b. the ability to allow employees to work from home.
    c. the spread of viruses.
    d. the amount of personal information available and people who can access it.

13. Which of the following is not considered a benefit of telecommuting?

    a. Saves money by retaining valuable employees during long leaves
    b. It involves less travel time and cost
    c. Can increase productivity
    d. Avoids isolation of workers

14. In the movie Sneakers, two young guys broke into a government computer and accessed some sensitive government documents. The term to describe these young guys would be:

    a. hackers.   c. cookies.
    b. viruses.   d. computer illiterates.

15. One of the problems with today's direct, real-time communication is

    a. existing laws do not address the legal issues.
    b. public information is more difficult to obtain.
    c. communication is not face to face.
    d. having to be careful to constantly update antivirus programs.

16. What is expected to happen to the demand for information technology workers?

    a. Thousands of technology jobs will go unfilled in the next few years.
    b. Demand is expected to level off within the next 10 years.
    c. Supply of workers will probably meet demand for workers.
    d. There will be more workers than jobs by the year 2005.

17. Which of the following job categories will shrink by the next century?

    a. Systems analysts
    b. Special education teachers
    c. Physical therapists
    d. Computer operators

TRUE/FALSE

1. _____ A virtual office would include cellular phones, pagers, laptop computers and personal digital assistants.

2. _____ Information technology creates organizations and services that are independent of location.

3. _____ An extranet is a companywide network which is closed to everyone outside the specific company using the intranet.

4. _____ Only the largest companies can use the Internet to do business.

5. _____ The Internet 2 will support heavy-duty applications, such as videoconferencing, research, distance education and other sophisticated applications.

6. _____ With the increased use of the Internet, information has become easier to manage.

7. _____ Push technology will allow for customized news delivery to your computer after sorting through thousands of new sources.

8. _____ Companies are moving toward mainframe computer systems for the next century.

9. _____ A computer network will help a company file, store and access data more easily.

10. _____ Desktop publishing combines word processing with graphics capabilities.

11. _____ Personal information mangers are actually word processing programs.

12. _____ Message center software teams up with modems to provide a way of making certain that phone calls, e-mail and faxes are received, sorted and delivered on time.

13. _____ Computers have created more middle management layers.

14. _____ Antivirus programs need to be updated on a regular basis.

15. _____ In the future, being computer illiterate will be "occupational suicide."

ANSWERS

LEARNING THE LANGUAGE

1. Data processing (DP)	12. Database programs
2. Spreadsheet	13. Network computing system
3. Groupware	14. Information technology
4. Knowledge technology	15. Internet
5. Communications software	16. Push technology
6. Virtualization	17. Internet 2
7. Extranet	18. Message software center
8. Shareware	19. Firewall
9. Virus	20. Intranet
10. Information systems	21. Cookies
11. Integrated software (suites)	22. Public domain software

RETENTION CHECK

Learning Goal 1   **The Role of Information Technology**

1. Data are raw, unanalyzed, and unsummarized facts and figures. Information is the processed and summarized data that can be used for managerial decision making.

2. The primary role of data processing was to support existing business by improving the flow of financial information.

3. Information Systems went from supporting business to actually doing business, through such means as ATMs and voice mail.

4. Information technology allows businesses to deliver products and services where and when it is convenient for the customer.

5. Information technology breaks time and location barriers.

6. Breaking these barriers creates organizations and services that are independent of location. Being independent of location brings work to people instead of people to work. With Information technology, businesses can conduct work around the world continuously.

7. A virtual office includes cellular phones, pagers, laptop computers, and personal digital assistants. This technology allows you to access people and information as if you were in an actual office.

8. Knowledge technology is information charged with enough intelligence to make it relevant and useful. It adds a layer of intelligence to filter appropriate information and deliver it when it is needed. Information technology makes information available, as long as you know how to use it and where to find it. Knowledge technology brings the information to the individual. It will "think" about individual needs and reduce the amount of time finding and getting information.

9. Knowledge technology changes the traditional flow of information from an individual going to the database to the data coming to the individual. Using KT business training software a company can put a new employee at a workstation and then let the system take over.

Learning Goal 2 **Road to Knowledge: The Internet, Intranets and Extranets**

10. The key issue for business today is how to get the right information to the right people at the right time. Knowledge is now the key to successful competition.

11. Intranet applications can include allowing employees to update their addresses or submit company forms such as requisitions, timesheets, or payroll forms online.

12. To solve the problem of other companies getting into an intranet, companies can construct a "firewall" between themselves and the outside world to protect corporate information from unauthorized users. A firewall can be hardware, software, or both.

13. An intranet is only within the company. An extranet is a semiprivate network that uses Internet technology so that more than one company can access the same information or so that people on different servers can collaborate.

14. Almost all companies can use the Internet to share and process data such as orders, specifications, invoices, and payments. The Internet creates a critical mass of people who can exchange data over the network. The Internet also makes it easier for small businesses to sell their goods and services globally.

15. The capacity of the Internet is finite, and the more people who use Internet technology, the slower it becomes. So, there are traffic jams on the information highway. Remote and mobile workers trying to connect to the corporate networks are also adding to the congestion. Traffic on the Internet has become so intense that many have found they are unable to access, transmit, and manipulate data the way they would like.

16. The Internet 2 will support heavy-duty applications, such as videoconferencing, collaborative research, distance education, digital libraries, and full-body simulation environments known as tele-immersion.

Learning Goal 3 **Managing Information**

17. Infoglut refers to information overload resulting from a deluge of information from a variety of sources.

18. a. Quality
    b. Completeness
    c. Timeliness
    d. Relevance

19. Push technology consists of software and services that filter information so that users can get the customized information they need. Push technology pushes the information to you so you don't have to pull it out. These services deliver customized news to your computer after sorting through thousands of news sources to find information that suits your identified needs.

20. The important thing to remember when facing information overload is to relax. Set goals for yourself and do the best you can.

Learning Goal 4   **The Enabling Technology: Hardware**

21. Hardware components include computers, pagers, cellular phones, printers, scanners, fax machines, and personal digital assistants.

22. In a mainframe system, the central computer performed all the tasks and sent the results to a terminal that could not perform the task itself. In the network computing system, the tasks, such as searching sales records, are handled by personal computers. The information needed to complete the tasks is stored in huge databases controlled by the server. Networks connect people to people and people to data.

23. Computer network systems:
    a. Save time and money
    b. Provide easy links to other areas of the company
    c. Permit companies to see their products more clearly

Learning Goal 5   **Software**

24. a. Writing by using word processing
    b. Manipulating numbers using spreadsheets
    c. Filing and retrieving data using databases
    d. Presenting information visually using graphics
    e. Communicating
    f. Accounting and financial information

25. Businesses use word processors to increase office productivity. Standardized letters can be personalized, documents can be updated by changing only the outdated text and leaving the rest intact, and contract forms can be revised to meet the stipulations of specific customers.

26. Desktop publishing software combines word processing with graphics capabilities.

27. a. Corel WordPerfect
    b. Microsoft Word
    c. WordPro

28. A spreadsheet is a table made up of rows and columns that enable a manager to organize information. Using the computer's speedy calculations, managers have their questions answered almost as fast as they can ask them.

29. a. Lotus 1-2-3
    b. Quattro Pro
    c. Excel

30. Database programs allow you to work with information you normally keep in lists: names and addresses, schedules, and inventories for example. Simple commands allow you to add new information, change incorrect information, and delete out-of-date or unnecessary information. Using database programs you can create reports with exactly the information you want and the way you want the information to appear.

31. a. Q & A Access
    b. Approach
    c. Paradox
    d. PFS: Professional File
    e. PC-File
    f. R base
    g. HyperCard

32. Personal information managers, or contact managers, are specialized database programs that allow users to track communication with their business contacts. These programs keep track of people, phone calls, e-mail messages and appointments.

33. Graphics can add sound clips, video clips, clip art, and animations.

34. a. MacDraw
    b. PowerPoint
    c. Harvard Graphics
    d. Lotus Freelance Graphics
    e. Active Presenter
    f. Corel Draw

35. Communications software makes it possible for different brands of computers to transfer data to each other.

36. a. Microsoft Outlook
    b. ProComm Plus
    c. Eudora
    d. Telik

37. Message center software is more powerful than traditional communications packages. This generation of programs has teamed up with fax/voice modems to provide an efficient way of making certain that phone calls, e-mail and faxes are received, sorted, and delivered on time, no matter where you are.

38. Such programs include Communicate, Message Center and WinFax Pro.

39. Accounting software helps users record financial transactions and generate financial reports. Some programs include online banking features that allow users to pay bills through the computer.

40. a. Peach Tree Complete Accounting
    b. Simply Accounting
    c. QuickBooks Pro

41. Integrated software packages offer two or more applications in one package. With these programs, you can share information across applications easily. Most such packages include word processing, database management, spreadsheet, graphics and communications.

42. a. Microsoft Office
    b. Lotus SmartSuite
    c. Corel WordPerfect Suite

43. Groupware runs on a network and allows people to work on the same project at the same time. Groupware also makes it possible for work teams to communicate together over time. Team members can swap leads, share client information, monitor news events, and make suggestions to one another. The computer becomes a kind of team memory.

44.   a. Lotus Notes
        b. Frontier's Intranet Genie
        c. Metainfo Sendmail
        d. Radnet Web Share

Learning Goal 6   **Effects of Information Technology on Management**

45.   a. human resource changes
        b. security threats
        c. privacy concerns

46.   a. Computers will decrease the number of management layers, eliminating middle management functions, and flattening organizational structures.
        b. Computers will allow employees to work at home (telecommuting).

47.   Companies can retain valuable employees while they are on leave and take advantage of the experience offered by retired employees. Workers with disabilities can be gainfully employed, men and women with small children can stay home, and employees can work extra hours at home rather than at work. This may help to improve morale and reduce stress.

48.   Some telecommuters report that a consistent diet of long-distance work gives them a dislocated feeling of being left out of the office loop. Some feel a loss of the increased energy people can get through social interaction. In addition to isolation, the intrusion that work makes into personal lives is an issue. Often people who work from home don't know when to turn off the work.

49.   Companies are using telecommuting as a part-time alternative to alleviate some of the problems and complaints of this kind of work schedule.

50.   A hacker is a person who breaks into computer systems for illegal purposes.

51.   Computer viruses are spread by downloading infected programming over the Internet or by sharing an infected disk.

52. New viruses are being developed constantly, and the antivirus programs may have difficulty detecting them. It is important to keep your antivirus protection program up-to-date and not download files from an unknown source.

53. The Internet allows Web surfers to access all sorts of personal information. For example, Web sites allow a person to search for vehicle ownership from a license number, find real estate property records on individuals, or find the vehicles owned by a person.

54. One of the key issues in the debate over protecting our privacy is: Isn't this personal information already public anyway? The difference is that the Net makes getting public information too easy.

55. A cookie contains your name and password that the Web site recognizes the next time you visit the site so that you don't have to re-enter the same information every time you visit. Other cookies track your movements around the Web and then blend that information with their databases and tailor the ads you receive accordingly.

Learning Goal 7   **Technology and You**

56. Being computer illiterate could be occupational suicide because workers in every industry are exposed somewhat to computers. Nearly 80% of the respondents to a 1997 survey said that they believe it is impossible to succeed in the job market without a working knowledge of technology.

57. A shortage of information technology workers could have severe consequences for American competitiveness, economic growth and job creation.

CRITICAL THINKING EXERCISES

Learning Goal 1

1. In the 1970's, business technology was known as data processing. It was used primarily to support the existing business, to improve the flow of financial information. In the 1980's, the name changed to information systems, and the role changed from supporting business to doing business. Customers interacted with the technology in a variety of ways. In the 1990's, businesses have shifted to using new technology on new methods of doing business, and the role of information technology has become to change business.

2. "In the old days" customers had to go to a business during business hours to meet their needs for consumer products, and employees had to "go to the office" to work. We went to the bank for a loan. Businesses decided when and where we did business with them. Information technology has changed all that. Information technology allows businesses to deliver products and services whenever and wherever it is convenient for the customer. Even further, it has enabled businesses to become better and faster at serving customer needs by reducing product development times, getting customer feedback quickly, allowing companies to make changes in products easily and quickly, allowing companies to solve customer problems instantly by using databases, reducing defects, and cutting expensive product waste. This has allowed businesses to become more customer oriented and thus more competitive.

Learning Goal 2

3. The Internet is a network of computer networks, available to anyone with the right equipment and software. An intranet is a companywide network closed to public access, which uses internet-type technology. An extranet is a semiprivate network that uses Internet technology so more than one company can access the same information, or so people on different servers can collaborate. One of the most common uses of extranets is to extend an intranet to outside customers.

4. One of the biggest problems of information technology and the information highway is the overwhelming amount of information available. Today business people are deluged with information from voice mail, the Internet, fax machines, and e-mail. Businesspeople refer to this information overload as "infoglut."

5. The first thing you need to do is to improve the quality of the information by combining the facts and figures and so on into something that is meaningful. Put sales reports together and summarize weekly or monthly figures. Note any trends in sales over a given period, and double check for accuracy in all the information you use. (Quality)

   Second, you need to make sure that you are using the latest sales reports, and double-check your figures. Since you will be sending this information to various sales managers, check to be sure that you have included all the data needed to give the managers an accurate picture of how sales are going and why. You don't need to include anything that may not be relevant, such as reports from committees or other areas that don't pertain to sales. (Completeness)

   In addition, you need to work fast! If a sales person is not meeting quotas, a few weeks is too long to wait to find out why. With E-mail, your reports can be sent out almost as soon as they're finished. (Timeliness)

   Lastly, be sure that the sales reports you are sending are appropriate to the management level at which they'll be received. Lower level managers will need inventory information perhaps, but not industry trends. Middle level managers may want your sales forecasts based upon past trends, but not vacation schedules for various salespeople. (Relevance)

Learning Goal 4

6. The network would allow you to communicate quickly with other areas of the company through E-mail, which we already mentioned. You may more easily find someone in the company who could either answer questions you may have, or could tell you exactly what kind of information they need, and in what format. Using a network means that you could put all the information you have into a database and anyone who needs it could access it. The network could, in fact, eliminate the need for your job altogether!

7.
   a. Spread sheet—to store and manipulate numbers
   b. Communications—to send and retrieve messages
   c. Database—to store and organize information
   d. Graphics—to make a pictorial presentation
   e. Word processing for writing
   f. Integrated software—to use more than one type of software at one time
   g. Groupware—to allow a team to work on a project simultaneously

Learning Goal 6

8. Computers have often enabled businesses to eliminate middle management functions, and thus flatten organization structures. Perhaps the most revolutionary effect of computers and the increased use of the Internet and intranets may be the ability to allow employees to stay home and do their work from there, or telecommute. Using computers linked to the company's network, workers can transmit their work to the office and back easily.

9. One problem today is hackers, who break into computer systems for illegal purposes. Today, computers not only make all areas of the company accessible, but also other companies with which the firm does business. Another security issue involves the spread of computer viruses over the Internet. Viruses are spread by downloading infected programming over the Internet or by sharing an infected disk. A major concern is a problem with privacy as more and more personal information is stored in computers and people are able to access all sorts of information about you. One of the key issues in the privacy debate is: Isn't this personal information already public anyway?

10. Some careers that will be shrinking are computer operators, billing, posting and calculating machine operators, telephone operators, typists and word processors and bank tellers. The number of jobs in those areas will be shrinking because computers will either take over the job entirely, or will be able to help the companies in those industries do more with fewer workers.

    Careers that will be growing include computer engineers and scientists, systems analysts, physical therapists, special education teachers and operations research analysts.

    Physical therapists will use computer software to help with planning a program of therapy for people with specific injuries, thus "customizing" a therapy program. In the future, computers will also help with a diagnosis as well as with a plan of therapy. Special education teachers will use computers for multimedia presentations in their classrooms, as well as for student use in the classroom, with educational games.

PRACTICE TEST

Multiple Choice				True/False			
1.	c	10.	b	1.	T	10.	T
2.	c	11.	d	2.	T	11.	F
3.	a	12.	b	3.	F	12.	T
4.	d	13.	d	4.	F	13.	F
5.	d	14.	a	5.	T	14.	T
6.	a	15.	a	6.	F	15.	T
7.	d	16.	a	7.	T		
8.	d	17.	d	8.	F		
9.	a			9.	T		

CHAPTER 18
UNDERSTANDING FINANCIAL INFORMATION AND ACCOUNTING

LEARNING GOALS

After you have read and studied this chapter, you should be able to:

1. Understand the importance of financial information and accounting.

2. Define and explain the different areas of the accounting profession.

3. Distinguish between accounting and bookkeeping and list the steps in the accounting cycle.

4. Explain the difference between the major financial statements.

5. Describe the role of depreciation, and LIFO and FIFO in reporting financial information.

6. Explain the importance of ratio analysis and the budgeting process in reporting financial information.

7. Describe how computers are used to record and apply accounting information in business.

LEARNING THE LANGUAGE

Listed below are important terms found in the chapter. Choose the correct term for the definition and write it in the space provided.

Accounting	Fundamental accounting equation
Accounting cycle	Gross margin
Annual report	Income statement
Assets	Independent audit
Auditing	Intangible assets
Balance sheet	Journals
Bookkeeping	Ledger
Budget	Liabilities
Cash flow	LIFO
Certified Internal Auditor	Liquidity
Certified Management Accountant (CMA)	Managerial accounting
Certified Public Accountant (CPA)	Net income

Cost of goods sold	Owner's equity
Current assets	Private accountants
Depreciation	Public accountants
Double-entry bookkeeping	Retained earnings
Expenses	Revenue
FIFO	Statement of cash flows
Financial accounting	Tax accountants
Financial statements	Trial balance
Fixed assets	

1. A yearly statement called the _____ covers the financial condition and progress of an organization covering a one year period.

2. A company's _____ is the difference between cash coming in and cash going out of a business.

3. Resources known as _____ include cash or noncash items that can be converted to cash within one year.

4. A _____ is a financial plan that sets forth management's expectations for revenues and that allocates the use of resources based on those expectations.

5. Resources of a permanent nature, or _____, include items such as land, buildings, furniture and fixtures.

6. A _____ is the book where accounting data are first entered.

7. An accounting method called _____, used for calculating the cost of inventory that assumes that the last goods to come in are the first to go out.

8. Assets minus liabilities is the formula for _____.

9. Creating a _____ involves totaling all the data in the account ledgers to see the figures are correct and balanced.

10. An accountant known as a _____ is trained in tax law and is responsible for preparing tax returns and developing tax strategies.

11. The speed with which an asset can be converted into cash is its _____.

12. An _____ is an evaluation and unbiased opinion about the accuracy of company financial statements.

13. Providing accounting information and analyses to managers within the organization to aid in decision making is called _____.

14. A concept called _____ is a system of writing every transaction in two places.

15. An accountant called a _____ passes a series of examinations established by the American Institute of Certified Public Accountants.

16. The economic resources owned by the firm are called _____.

17. The accounting technique called _____ is a method for calculating the cost of inventory which assumes the first goods to come in are the first to go out.

18. A firm's _____ is how much the firm earned by buying and selling or making and selling merchandise.

19. Preparing financial statements for people outside the firm is _____.

20. Revenue minus expenses is called _____.

21. A financial statement called a _____ reports the financial position of a firm at a specific time.

22. Accountants who work for a single firm, government agency or nonprofit organization are called _____.

23. The recording, classifying, summarizing and interpreting of financial events and transactions, or _____ provides management and other interested parties the information they need to make better decisions.

24. A company's _____ is the value of what is received from goods sold or services rendered.

25. Reviewing and evaluating the records used to prepare the company's financial statements is called _____.

26. A _____ is the summary of all transactions that have occurred over a particular period.

27. The six-step procedure called the _____ results in the preparation and analysis of two major financial statements: balance sheets and income statements.

28. A type of expense called the _____ measures the cost of merchandise sold or cost of raw materials and supplies used for producing items for resale.

29. A _____ is one who provides accounting services to individuals or businesses on a fee basis.

30. Accounts known as _____ measure what the business owes to others.

31. A specialized accounting book known as a _____ is one in which information from accounting journals is accumulated into specific categories and posted so managers can find all the information about one account in the same place.

32. A _____ is a professional accountant who has met certain educational and experience requirements and been certified by the Institute of Certified Management Accountants.

33. The recording of business transactions is called _____.

34. The _____ reports a firm's profit after costs, expenses and taxes; it summarizes all of the resources that have left the firm, and the resulting net income or loss.

35. The systematic write-off of the value of a tangible asset over its estimated useful life is called _____.

36. Items known as _____ include items of value such as patents, and copyrights that have no real physical form.

37. Earnings called _____ are kept in the business and not paid out in dividends.

38. The financial statement called a _____ reports cash receipts and disbursement related to a firm's major activities.

39. A _____ is an accountant who has a bachelor's degree, 2 years of internal auditing experience, and has successfully passed an exam administered by the Institute of Internal Auditors.

40. Assets equal liabilities plus owner's equity is the _____ and is the basis for the balance sheet.

41. Costs such as rent, utilities, and salaries are _____.

RETENTION CHECK

Learning Goal 1   **The Importance of Financial Information**

1. What are the three parts of the accounting system?

   a. _____

   b. _____

   c. _____

2. What are two purposes of accounting?

   a. _____

   b. _____

Learning Goal 2   **Areas of Accounting**

3. List the four key working areas of accounting.

   a. _____   c. _____

   b. _____   d. _____

4. Identify the areas with which managerial accounting is concerned.

5. Who receives financial accounting information?

6. Where can you find the information derived from financial accounting?

7. What are some of the things a public accountant might do?

8. What does it mean when financial reports are prepared in accordance with GAAP?

9. Why are internal audits performed?

Learning Goal 3   **Accounting versus Bookkeeping**

10. What do accountants do with data provided by bookkeepers?

11. What information is recorded in a journal?

12. What is the difference between a journal and a ledger?

13. What are the six steps in the accounting cycle?

   a. _____

   b. _____

   c. _____

   d. _____

   e. _____

   f. _____

Learning Goal 4 **Understanding Key Financial Statements**

14. Identify two key financial statements.

   a. _____

   b. _____

15. List the three major accounts on a balance sheet.

   a. _____

   b. _____

   c. _____

16. What kinds of things are considered assets?

17. List the three categories of assets on a balance sheet.

   a. _____

   b. _____

   c. _____

18. What is the difference between current liabilities and long term liabilities?

19. What are:

   a. accounts payable?

   b. notes payable?

   c. bonds payable?

20. What is "equity"? Shareholder's equity?

21. What is the formula for owner's equity?

22. What is the fundamental accounting equation, or the formula for a balance sheet?

23. What is the formula for developing an income statement?

    a. _____

    b. _____

    c. _____

24. How does one arrange an income statement according to accepted accounting principles?

25.   What is the difference between revenue and sales?

26.   What is the difference in gross margin between a service firm and a manufacturing firm?

27.   What are some kinds of operating expenses?

28.   What is the "bottom line"?

29.   How can cash flow become a problem?

30. List the three major activities for which cash receipts and disbursements are reported on a statement of cash flows.

    a. _____

    b. _____

    c. _____

Learning Goal 5 **Applying Accounting Knowledge**

31. How can depreciation affect a firm's net income?

32. What are two methods of inventory valuation for cost of goods sold?

    a. _____   b. _____

33. What impact do LIFO and FIFO have on net income?

Learning Goal 6 **Using Financial Ratios**

34. What are the four financial issues dealt with using ratio analysis?

35. What are the two primary indicators of a company's liquidity?

   a. _____

   b. _____

36. What do liquidity ratios measure?

37. What is the formula for the current ratio?

38. To what is the current ratio compared?

39. Identify the formula for the acid test ratio.

40. What is a leverage ratio?

41. What is the formula for the debt to equity ratio?

42. What does it mean if a firm has a ratio above "1"?

43. What are profitability ratios?

44. What are three profitability ratios?

   a. _____

   b. _____

   c. _____

45. What is the formula for determining Basic Earnings Per Share?

46. What is the difference between Basic EPS and diluted EPS?

47. What is the formula for return on sales?

48. What is the formula for return on equity?

49. What do activity ratios measure?

50. What is the formula for inventory turnover?

51. What is meant by inventory turnover ratios which are lower than or higher than average?

52. What financial statements form the basis for the budgeting process? Why?

Learning Goal 7 **The Impact of Computer Technology in Accounting**

53. What can computers do for accounting in a business?

CRITICAL THINKING EXERCISES

Learning Goals 1, 2

1. Match the following terms with the definitions listed below.

    Auditing   Managerial accounting

    Certified management accountant (CMA)   Private accountant

    Certified public accountant (CPA)   Public accountant

    Financial accounting   Tax accountant

    Independent audit

    a. The preparation and analysis of financial information for people and organizations outside the firm. _____

    b. They provide business assistance by designing an accounting system for a firm, selecting the correct software and analyzing the financial strength of a firm as well as conduct independent audits. _____

    c. These people work within a firm, as accountants with management responsibilities. _____

d. As the burden of taxes grows, these accountants will become increasingly important to companies. _____

e. This accountant works for a single firm on a full time basis to help the company keep accurate financial information. _____

f. This happens internally, and often continually to ensure that proper accounting procedures and financial reporting are being carried on within the company.
_____

g. These accountants have passed a series of examinations and meet the state's requirement for education and experience. _____

h. This is concerned with measuring and reporting costs of production, marketing and other functions, preparing budgets, checking to see that units are staying within budgets and designing strategies to minimize taxes.
_____

i. This is conducted by a public accountant to determine if a firm has prepared its financial statements according to accepted accounting principles.
_____

Learning Goal 3

2. Music-stor is doing very well! They need a bookkeeper to help them with their paperwork, and an accountant. You have been given the task of writing a brief job description for each job. How would you write the job description for each?

Bookkeeper –

Accountant –

Learning Goal 4

3. A. Two key financial statements are the balance sheet and the income statement.

Indicate whether each of the following accounts would be found on a balance sheet or an income statement.

1. _____ Cash

2. _____ Retained earnings

3. _____ Accounts payable

4. _____ Interest

5. _____ Rent

6. _____ Property

7. _____ Commission revenue

8. _____ Gross sales

9. _____ Common stock

10. _____ Supplies expense

11. _____ Notes payable

12. _____ Accounts receivable

13. _____ Equipment

14. _____ Advertising

15. _____ Wages

16. _____ Land

17. _____ Utilities

18. _____ Cost of goods sold

19. _____ Inventories

20. _____ Gross Margin

    B.   List the liquid assets in order of liquidity.

        1. _____   3. _____

        2. _____

4. The balance sheet reports the financial condition of a firm at a specific time. The basic formula for a balance sheet is:

Assets = Liabilities + Owner's Equity

Total assets consist of current, fixed and intangible assets.

Total liabilities consist of current and long term liabilities.

Owner's equity consists of various types of stock and Retained earnings

Using the following list of accounts, construct an accurate balance sheet for Music-stor, Inc. BE CAREFUL! Not all of the accounts listed will be used for the balance sheet.

MUSIC-STOR, INC.

List of accounts

Accounts payable	$25,000
Net sales	$600,000
Accounts receivable	$110,000
Depreciation expense	$4,000
Inventories	$62,000
Advertising	$28,000
Wages and salaries	$125,000
Notes payable (current)	$15,000
Rental revenue	$3,000
Cost of goods sold	$313,000
Property, plant, equipment	$204,000
Cash	$18,000
Retained earnings	$165,000
Accrued taxes	$40,000
Long-term debt	$60,000
Common stock	$130,000
Utilities	$12,000
Supplies	$3,700
Investments	$45,000
Rent	$35,000

5. The income statement reports all the revenues and expenses of a firm for a specific period of time. The basic formula for an income statement is:

Revenue - Cost of goods sold = Gross profit (gross margin)

Gross profit - operating expenses = Net income (loss) before taxes

Net income before taxes - taxes = Net income (loss)

Using the previous list of accounts construct an accurate income statement for Music-stor. Again, look at each account carefully! For purposes of illustration, assume a 28% tax rate on income.

6. Cash flow problems arise when a firm has debt obligations that must be met before cash from sales is received.

   Prepare a personal cash flow statement for two weeks. Include all projected income and all projected cash disbursements (payments) Do you have a cash flow problem?

Cash flow forecast	**Week one**	**Week two**
Projected income	_____	_____
Projected "outgo"	_____	_____
Surplus (Deficit)	_____	_____

Learning Goal 5

7. Two methods of determining the value of inventory, and therefore the cost of goods sold, are:

   LIFO, last-in, first-out.

   FIFO, first-in, first out.

   The method chosen will directly affect the "bottom line," or profits.

   The basic formula for cost of goods sold is: (See Figure 18.6)

   Beginning inventory + purchases = Cost of goods available

   Cost of goods available - ending inventory = Cost of goods sold

A. Determine the cost of goods sold, using FIFO and LIFO with the following information:

FIFO
Beginning inventory	20,000 units @ $10	$200,000
+ Purchases	7,000 units @ $12	84,000
= Cost of goods available	27,000 units	$284,000
- Ending inventory	5,000 units	_____

LIFO
Beginning inventory	20,000 units @ $10	$200,000
+ Purchases	7,000 units @ $12	84,000
=Cost of goods available	27,000 units	$284,000
- Ending inventory	5,000 units	_____

Cost of goods sold   FIFO _____   LIFO _____

B. What is gross margin on revenues of $450,000 using FIFO? LIFO?

FIFO   LIFO

Learning Goal 6

8. Liquidity ratios measure a firm's ability to pay short-term debt. Using the balance sheet and income statement you calculated earlier:

a. Calculate the current ratio for Music-stor.

b. Calculate the acid-test ratio for Music-stor.

c. What shape does Music-stor appear to be in?

9. Leverage ratios refer to the degree to which a firm relies on borrowed money for its operations.

   a. Calculate the debt to owner's equity ratio for Music-stor.

   b. If the industry average is .75, how does Music-stor compare?

10. Profitability ratios measure how effectively the firm is using its resources.

    a. If Music-stor has approximately 30,000 shares of common stock outstanding, what is their basic earnings per share?

    b. Calculate their return on sales.

    c. What is return on equity?

11. Activity ratios measure the effectiveness of the firm in using the available assets.

    a. If the average inventory for Music-stor is 70,000, what is the inventory turnover rate?

b. If the industry average is 3.5, what does that indicate for Music-stor?

12. What value do computers have in the accounting process? How should software be chosen?

PRACTICE TEST

Multiple Choice: Circle the best answer.

1. The purpose of accounting is to:

    a. allow for government tracking of business activities.
    b. make sure a business is paying its taxes.
    c. help managers evaluate the financial condition of the firm.
    d. provide a method of spending money wisely.

2. Which of the following is not one of the activities associated with accounting?

    a. recording
    b. summarizing
    c. classifying
    d. promoting

3. The type of accounting that is concerned with providing information and analyses to managers within the organization is called:

    a. financial accounting.
    b. managerial accounting.
    c. auditing.
    d. tax accounting.

4. Jim Hopson is an accountant who works for a number of businesses as a "consultant." He has helped to design an accounting system, provides accounting services, and has analyzed the financial strength of many of his clients. Jim is working as a:

    a. private accountant.
    b. certified management accountant.
    c. certified internal auditor.
    d. public accountant.

5. If you were a bookkeeper, the first thing you would do is:

   a. record transactions into a ledger.
   b. develop a trial balance sheet.
   c. prepare an income statement.
   d. divide transactions into meaningful categories.

6. A specialized accounting book in which information is accumulated into specific categories and posted so managers can find all information about one account in the same place is a:

   a. ledger.
   b. journal.
   c. trial balance sheet.
   d. double entry book.

7. The _____ reports the firm's financial condition on a specific day.

   a. income statement
   b. cash flow statement
   c. statement of stockholder's equity
   d. balance sheet

8. Which of the following would be considered a current asset?

   a. accounts payable
   b. accounts receivable
   c. copyrights
   d. buildings

Use the information below to answer questions 9 and 10:

Net sales	30,000
Total Assets	16,000
Taxes	2,300
Cost of goods sold	12,500
Total Liabilities	8,000
Operating expenses	3,200

9. Net income is:

   a. 14,000
   b. 17,500
   c. 14,300
   d. 12,000

10. Stockholder's equity is:

    a. 16,000.
    b. 24,000.
    c. 8,000.
    d. can't determine from information given.

11. Which of the following would not be shown on a statement of cash flows?

    a. cash from operations
    b. cash paid for long term debt obligations
    c. cash raised from new debt or equity
    d. cash paid in donations

12. With regard to depreciation, companies are allowed to:

    a. Choose one method of depreciation, but must stay with that method.
    b. Write off only a certain percentage of depreciation as an expense.
    c. Use one of several techniques, resulting in different net incomes.
    d. Change techniques, as long as net income is not affected.

13. The LIFO method of inventory valuation is a method that:

    a. assumes the newest merchandise is used first.
    b. can make the cost of goods sold appear lower than in other forms of inventory valuation.
    c. assumes the oldest merchandise is used first.
    d. has the lease effect on cost of goods sold.

14. Financial ratios:

    a. are used to calculate profits from one year to the next.
    b. are a poor indicator of a company's financial condition.
    c. are only used by independent auditors.
    d. are helpful to use in analyzing the actual performance of a company.

15. Which kind of ratio is used to determine the ability of a firm to pay its short-term debts?

    a. activity ratios   c. debt
    b. profitability   d. liquidity

16. A debt to equity ratio of over 1 would mean:

    a. the company has more debt than equity.
    b. the company has more equity than debt.
    c. by comparison with other firms, the company is probably in good shape.
    d. the company is in too much debt, and should restructure.

17. Earnings per share, return on sales and return on equity are all:

    a. activity ratios.   c. liquidity ratios.
    b. profitability ratios.   d. debt ratios.

18. Which of the following is not considered a part of the basis for the budgeting process?

    a. ratio analysis statements   c. balance sheets
    b. income statements   d. statement of cash flows

19. Which of the following is not true of the use of computers in accounting?

    a. Most big and small companies use computers to simplify the task of accounting.
    b. Computers can provide continuous financial information for the business.
    c. Computers can make accounting work less monotonous.
    d. Computers have been programmed to make financial decisions on their own.

20. One of the benefits of continuous auditing is:

    a. it allows firms to hire fewer accountants.
    b. it can help prevent financial difficulties by spotting trouble earlier.
    c. it makes financial errors much harder to detect.
    d. it reduces the need for small businesses to hire or consult with accountants.

TRUE/FALSE

1. ____ You must know something about accounting if you want to understand business.

2. ____ A major purpose of accounting is to report financial information to people outside the firm.

3. ____ Financial accounting is used to provide information and analyses to managers within the firm to assist in decision making.

4. ____ A private accountant is an individual who works for a private firm that provides accounting services to individuals or businesses on a fee basis.

5. ____ Trial balances are derived from information contained in ledgers.

6. ____ The fundamental accounting equation is assets = liabilities + owner's equity.

7. ____ The "bottom line" is shown in the balance sheet.

8. ____ Cash flow is generally not a problem for companies that are growing quickly.

9. ____ Depreciation will most often not have any effect on net income.

10. ____ The four types of financial ratios include liquidity, debt, profitability and activity ratios.

11. ____ The higher the risk involved in an industry, the lower the return investors expect on their investment.

12. ____ Often, the accounting needs of a small business are significantly different from the needs of larger companies.

ANSWERS

LEARNING THE LANGUAGE

1. Annual report	22. Private accountants
2. Cash flow	23. Accounting
3. Current assets	24. Revenue
4. Budget	25. Auditing
5. Fixed assets	26. Financial statement
6. Journal	27. Accounting cycle
7. LIFO	28. Cost of goods sold(manufactured)
8. Owner's equity	29. Public accountant
9. Trial balance	30. Liabilities
10. Tax accountant	31. Ledger
11. Liquidity	32. Certified Management Accountant
12. Independent audit	33. Bookkeeping
13. Managerial accounting	34. Income statement
14. Double entry bookkeeping	35. Depreciation
15. Certified Public Accountant (CPA)	36. Intangible assets
16. Assets	37. Retained earnings
17. FIFO	38. Statement of cash flows
18. Gross margin	39. Certified Internal Auditor
19. Financial accounting	40. Fundamental accounting equation
20. Net income	41. Expenses
21. Balance sheet	

RETENTION CHECK

Learning Goal 1 **The Importance of Financial Information**

1. a. Inputs—accounting documents such as sales documents, purchasing documents, payroll records and others
   b. Processing—recording, classifying and summarizing
   c. Outputs—financial statements such as balance sheets and income statements

2.   a. To help managers evaluate the financial condition and the operating performance of the firm so they make better decisions.
    b. To report financial information to people outside the firm such as owners, creditors, suppliers employees and the government.

Learning Goal 2   **Areas of Accounting**

3.
   a. Managerial accounting
   b. Financial accounting
   c. Auditing
   d. Tax accounting

4. Managerial accounting is concerned with measuring and reporting costs of production, marketing, and other functions, preparing budgets, checking whether or not units are staying within their budgets and designing strategies to minimize taxes.

5. Financial accounting differs from managerial accounting because the information and analyses are for people outside the organization. This information goes to owners and prospective owners, creditors, and lenders, employee unions, customers, suppliers, governmental units, and the general public. These external users are interested in the organization's profit, its ability to pay its bills, and other financial information.

6. Much of the information derived from financial accounting is contained in the company's annual report.

7. A public accountant can assist a business by designing an accounting system for a firm, helping select the correct computer and software to run the system and analyzing the financial strength of an organization.

8. The independent Financial Accounting Standards Board defines what are generally accepted accounting principles that accountants must follow. If financial reports are prepared "in accordance with GAAP," users know the information is reported according to standards agreed on by accounting professionals.

9. Internal audits are performed to ensure that proper accounting procedures and financial reporting are being carried on within the company. Public accountants will also conduct independent audits of accounting records. Financial auditors today examine the financial health of an organization and additionally look into operational efficiencies and effectiveness.

Learning Goal 3   **Accounting versus Bookkeeping**

10. Accountants classify and summarize the data provided by bookkeepers. They interpret the data and report them to management.

11. The bookkeeper records the data from the original transaction documents into record books called journals. These are the books where accounting data are first entered.

12. A ledger is a specialized accounting book in which information from accounting journals is accumulated into specific categories and posted so managers can find all the information about one account in the same place.

13.
    a. Analyzing and categorizing documents
    b. Posting into journals.
    c. Posting into ledgers.
    d. Prepare a trial balance.
    e. Prepare an income statement and balance sheet.
    f. Analyze financial statements.

Learning Goal 4   **Understanding Key Financial Statements**

14.
    a. Balance sheets
    b. Income statements

15.
    a. Assets
    b. Liabilities
    c. Owner's equity

16. Assets include productive, tangible items such as equipment, building, land, furniture, fixtures, and motor vehicles that help generate income, as well as intangibles of value such as patents or copyrights.

17. a. Current assets
    b. Fixed assets
    c. Intangible assets

18. Liabilities are what the business owes to others. Current liabilities are payments due in one year or less; long-term liabilities are payments not due for one year or longer.

19. a. Accounts payable is money owed to others for merchandise and/or services purchased on credit but yet not paid. If you have a bill you haven't paid, you have an account payable.
    b. Notes payable is short-term or long-term loans that have a promise for future payment
    c. Bonds payable is money loaned to the firm that it must pay back.

20. The value of things you own, assets, minus the amount of money you owe others, liabilities, is called equity. The value of what stockholders own in a firm minus liabilities is called stockholders' equity.

21. Owner's equity is assets minus liabilities.

22. Assets = Liabilities + Owner's equity

23. a. Revenue - Cost of goods sold = Gross profit
    b. Gross profit - Expenses = Net income (loss) before taxes
    c. Net income before taxes - taxes = Net income (loss)

24. Revenue
    − Cost of Goods Sold
       Gross Margin
    − Operating Expenses
       Net Income before Taxes
    −   Taxes
       Net income (or loss)

25. Revenue is the value of what is received for goods sold, services rendered, and other financial sources. Most revenue comes from sales, but there could be other sources of revenue such as rents received, money paid to the firm for use of its patents, interest earned, and so forth.

26. It's possible in a service firm that there may be no cost of goods sold; therefore, net revenue could equal gross margin. In a manufacturing firm, it is necessary to estimate the cost of goods manufactured.

27. Obvious expenses include rent, salaries, supplies, utilities, insurance, even depreciation of equipment.

28. The "bottom line" is the net income or net loss the firm incurred from operations.

29. In order to meet the demands of customers, more and more goods are bought on credit. Similarly, more and more goods are sold on credit. This can go on until the firm uses up all the credit it has with banks that lend it money. When the firm requests money from the bank to pay a crucial bill, the bank refuses the loan because the credit limit has been reached. All other credit sources may refuse a loan as well. The company needs to pay its bills or else its creditors could force it into bankruptcy.

30. a. Operations
    b. Investments
    c. Financing

Learning Goal 5 **Applying Accounting Knowledge**

31. A firm may use one of several different methods to calculate depreciation. Each method will result in a different depreciation amount, and thus a different expense to be taken from gross profit. This will then result in a different bottom line.

32. a. LIFO, last-in, first-out
    b. FIFO, first-in, first-out

33. If the accountant uses FIFO, the cost of goods sold will be different, usually lower, than if the accountant uses LIFO. In FIFO, older perhaps less expensive merchandise is used to value the cost of goods sold. That means the net income will be higher. In LIFO, newer goods are assumed to be used, so the bottom line will be lower, because costs are higher.

Learning Goal 6 **Using Financial Ratios**

34. Ratio analysis provide insights in important financial issues such as liquidity, debt, profitability and activity.

35. a. Current ratio
    b. Acid-test ratio

36. Liquidity ratios measure the company's ability to pay its short-term debts. The short term debts are expected to be repaid within one year and are of importance to the firm's creditors who expect to be paid on time.

37. $$\frac{\text{Current assets}}{\text{Current liabilities}} = \text{Current ratio}$$

38. The current ratio is compared to competing firms within the industry to measure how the company sizes up to its main competitors. It is also important that the firm evaluate its ratio from the previous year to note any significant changes.

39. $$\frac{\text{Cash + marketable securities + receivables}}{\text{Current liailities}} = \text{Acid test ratio}$$

40. Leverage ratios refer to the degree to which a firm relies on borrowed funds in its operations.

41. $$\frac{\text{Total liabilities}}{\text{Owner's equity}} = \text{Debt to equity ratio}$$

42. A debt to equity ratio above 1 shows that a firm actually has more debt than equity. It's a good bet this firm could be quite risky to both lenders and investors. It's always important to compare ratios to other firms in the same industry because debt financing is more acceptable in some industries.

43. Profitability ratios measure how effectively the firm is using its various resources to achieve profits.

44. a. Earnings per share
    b. Return on sales
    c. Return on equity

45. $$\frac{\text{Net Income}}{\text{Number of Common shares outstanding}} = \text{Basic earnings per share}$$

46. Diluted earnings per share measures the amount of profit earned by a company for each share of outstanding common stock, as does basic EPS. However, diluted EPS takes into consideration stock options, warrants, preferred stock and convertible debt securities which can be converted into common stock.

47. $$\frac{\text{Net income}}{\text{Net sales}} = \text{Return on sales}$$

48. $$\frac{\text{Net Income}}{\text{Total owner's equity}} = \text{Return on equity}$$

49. Activity ratios measure the effectiveness of the firm's management in using assets that are available.

50. $$\frac{\text{Cost of goods sold}}{\text{Average Inventory}} = \text{Inventory turnover}$$

51. A lower than average inventory turnover ratio often indicates obsolete merchandise on hand or poor buying practices. A higher than average ratio may signal lost sales because of inadequate stock. An acceptable turnover ratio is generally determined on an industry-by-industry basis.

52. Financial statements including the balance sheet, income statement, and statement of cash flows form the basis for the budgeting process because financial information from the past is what's used to project future financial needs and expenditures.

Learning Goal 7 **The Impact of Computer Technology in Accounting**

53. Computers can record and analyze data and print out financial reports that can provide continuous financial information for the business. It is possible to have continuous auditing because of computers. Continuous auditing helps prevent cash flow problems and other financial difficulties by spotting trouble earlier.

CRITICAL THINKING EXERCISES

Learning Goals 1, 2

1.
   a. Financial accounting
   b. Public accountant
   c. Certified management accountant (CMA)
   d. Tax accountant
   e. Private accountant
   f. Auditing
   g. Certified public accountant (CPA)
   h. Managerial accounting
   i. Independent audit

Learning Goal 3

2. BOOKKEEPING JOB DESCRIPTION - The bookkeeper for Music-stor will be responsible for collecting all original transaction documents, and dividing them into meaningful categories (sales, purchasing, shipping, and so on). The information will be recorded into journals on a daily basis, using the double-entry method. The bookkeeper will also be responsible for recording the information from the journals into ledgers. Must be familiar with computer accounting applications.

   ACCOUNTANT JOB DESCRIPTION - The accountant for Music-stor will be responsible for classifying and summarizing the data provided by the bookkeeper. He/she will interpret the data, report to management, and suggest strategies for improving the financial condition and progress of the firm. Must be able to suggest tax strategies and be skilled in financial analysis.

Learning Goal 4

3.   A   1. Balance sheet   11. Balance sheet
               2. Balance sheet   12. Balance sheet
               3. Balance sheet   13. Balance sheet
               4. Income statement   14. Income statement
               5. Income statement   15. Income statement
               6. Balance sheet   16. Balance sheet
               7. Income statement   17. Income statement
               8. Income statement   18. Income statement
               9. Balance sheet   19. Balance sheet
               10. Income statement   20. Income statement

B   1. Cash
        2. Accounts receivable
        3. Inventories

4.
MUSIC STOR, INC
BALANCE SHEET
Year ending December 31, 199_

Assets

Current assets

Cash	$18,000	
Investments	45,000	
Accounts receivable	110,000	
Inventory	62,000	
Total current assets		**$235,000**
Property, plant and equipment		
Less: accumulated depreciation		200,000
Total Assets		**$435,000**

Liabilities and stockholders' equity

Liabilities

Current liabilities		
Accounts payable	$25,000	
Notes payable (current)	15,000	
Accrued taxes	40,000	
Total current liabilities		**$ 80,000**
Long-term debt		60,000
Total liabilities		**$140,000**
Stockholders' equity		
Common stock	$130,000	
Retained earnings	165,000	
Total stockholders' equity		**$295,000**
Total liabilities and stockholders' equity		**$435,000**

5.
MUSIC-STOR, INC.
INCOME STATEMENT
Year ending December 31, 199_

Revenues		
Net sales	$600,000	
Rental revenue	3,000	
Total revenues		$603,000
Cost of goods sold		313,000
Gross profit		$290,000
Operating expenses		
Wages and salaries	$125,000	
Rent	35,000	
Advertising	28,000	
Depreciation	4,000	
Utilities	12,000	
Supplies	3,700	
Total operating expenses		$207,700
Net income before taxes		$ 82,300
Less income taxes		23,044
Net income after taxes		$ 59,256

6. Everyone's answer will vary, obviously. The things to look at include your wages for the next two weeks, and any other income you will be receiving within the next two weeks (not including that $10 your friend owes you unless you <u>know</u> they're going to pay you!), and any expenses that will be due within the next two weeks, such as car payments, insurance, rent, groceries, utility bills, tuition, books, and so on.

Learning Goal 5

7. A. **FIFO**

A. Beginning inventory	20,000 @ $10	$200,000
+ Purchases	7,000 @ $12	84,000
=Cost of goods available	27,000 units	$284,000
- Ending inventory	5,000 @ $12	60,000
Cost of goods sold		$224,000

LIFO

Beginning inventory	20,000 @ $10	$200,000
+ Purchases	7,000 @ $12	84,000
Cost of goods available	27,000 units	$284,000
- Ending inventory	5,000 @ $10	50,000
Cost of goods sold		$234,000

B. Gross margin for:

	FIFO	LIFO
Revenues	$450,000	$450,000
COGS	224,000	234,000
Gross margin	$226,000	$216,000

In going from FIFO to LIFO the effect is to reduce gross profit. This will have the effect of reducing operating income, and tax liabilities.

Learning Goal 6

8. a. Current ratio: $\frac{\$235,000}{\$80,000} = 2.9$

   b. Acid-test ratio: $\frac{\$173,000}{\$80,000} = 2.16$

   c. It seems that Music-stor is financially sound from the liquidity perspective, as their ratios are above the benchmark of the 2:1 ratio.

9. a. Debt/Owner's equity ratio: $\frac{\$140,000}{\$295,000} = .47$

   b. Music-stor seems to be in very good shape, and could actually afford to take on slightly more debt, according to the industry average.

10. a. Earnings per share: $\dfrac{\$59{,}256}{30{,}000} = \$1.98$ share

    b. Return on sales: $\dfrac{\$59{,}256}{\$600{,}000} = 10\%$ approximately

    c. Return on equity: $\dfrac{\$59{,}256}{\$295{,}000} = 20.1\%$

11. a. Inventory turnover: $\dfrac{313{,}000}{70{,}000} = 4.47$ times

    b. Music-stor's turnover is high, compared to the industry average. This could indicate that they are running the risk of lost sales from inadequate stock.

12. Computers can record and analyze data and print out financial reports that can provide continuous financial information for a business. It is even possible to have continuous auditing. Software must be chosen which is best suited for a particular company's needs.

PRACTICE TEST

Multiple Choice				True/False			
1.	c	11.	d	1.	T	11.	F
2.	d	12.	c	2.	T	12.	T
3.	b	13.	a	3.	F		
4.	d	14.	d	4.	F		
5.	d	15.	d	5.	T		
6.	a	16.	a	6.	T		
7.	d	17.	b	7.	F		
8.	b	18.	a	8.	F		
9.	d	19.	d	9.	F		
10.	c			10.	T		

CHAPTER 19
FINANCIAL MANAGEMENT

LEARNING GOALS

After you have read and studied this chapter, you should be able to:

1. Explain the role and importance of finance.

2. Describe the responsibilities of financial managers.

3. Outline the steps in financial planning by explaining the process of forecasting financial needs, developing budgets, and establishing financial controls.

4. Recognize the financial needs that must be met with available funds.

5. Distinguish between short-term and long-term financing and between debt capital and equity capital.

6. Identify and describe several sources of short-term financing.

7. Identify and describe several sources of long-term financing.

LEARNING THE LANGUAGE

Listed below are important terms found in the chapter. Choose the correct term for the definition and write it in the space provided.

Budget	Long-term financing
Capital budget	Long-term forecast
Capital expenditures	Master budget
Cash budget	Operating budget
Cash flow forecast	Pledging
Commercial finance companies	Promissory note
Commercial paper	Revolving credit agreement
Debt capital	Risk/return trade-off
Equity capital	Secured bond
Factoring	Secured loan
Finance	Short-term financing
Financial control	Short-term forecast

Financial management	Term-loan agreement
Indenture terms	Trade credit
Inventory financing	Unsecured bond
Leverage	Unsecured loan
Line of credit	Venture capital

1. Organizations called _____ make short-term loans to borrowers who offer tangible assets as collateral.

2. In a process known as _____ actual revenues, costs and expenses are periodically reviewed and compared with projections.

3. Borrowed capital that will be repaid over a specific time period longer than one year is called _____.

4. A line of credit called a _____ is guaranteed by the bank.

5. A _____ is a promissory note that requires the borrower to repay the loan in specified installments.

6. A(n) _____ is a loan that is not backed by any specific assets.

7. A financial plan or a _____ allocates resources based on projected revenues.

8. Funds known as _____ are raised from within the firm or through the sale of ownership in the firm.

9. The process of using inventory as collateral for a loan is _____.

10. A written contract, or _____, is a promise to pay.

11. A _____ is a prediction of revenues, costs, and expenses for a period of one year or less.

12. Funds raised through various forms of borrowing that must be repaid is called _____.

13. An _____ is the projection of dollar allocations to various costs and expenses needed to run or operate the business given projected revenue.

14. A(n) _____ is a loan backed by something valuable, such as property.

15. A prediction of cash inflows and expenses in future periods is a _____.

16. A given amount of unsecured short-term funds or a _____ is what the bank lends to a business provided funds are readily available.

17. A bond backed only by the reputation of the issuer is a(n) _____.

18. Raising needed funds through borrowing is called _____.

19. The process of _____ is selling accounts receivable for cash.

20. A _____ highlights the firm's spending plans for major asset purchases that often require large sums of money.

21. The process of _____ is using accounts receivable or other assets as collateral for a loan.

22. A _____ is a prediction of revenues, costs and expenses for a period longer than one year, sometimes extending 5 or 10 years into the future.

23. An unsecured promissory note of $25,000 and up is known as _____ that matures in 270 days or less.

24. The practice of _____ is buying goods today and paying for them later.

25. The type of financing known as _____ refers to borrowed capital that will be repaid within one year.

26. The _____ is the budget that ties together all the firm's other budgets and summarizes the firm's proposed financial activities.

27. The function in a business called _____ is responsible for acquiring funds for the firm and managing funds within the firm.

28. The _____ means the greater risk a lender takes in making a loan, the higher the interest rate required.

29. A bond issued with some form of collateral is a(n) _____.

30. The terms of the agreement in a bond issue are known as the _____.

31. The _____ estimates a firm's projected cash balance at the end of a given period.

32. The job of managing the firm's resources so it can meet its goals and objectives is called _____.

33. Major investments, or _____, focus on long-term assets such as land, buildings, equipment, or research and development.

34. Money that is invested in new companies that have great profit potential is known as _____.

RETENTION CHECK

Learning Goal 1   **The Role of Finance**

1. What is the difference between an accountant and a financial manager?

2. What are three of the most common ways for any firm to fail financially?

   a. _____

   b. _____

   c. _____

3. To whom is an understanding of finance important?

Learning Goal 2   **What is Finance?**

4. What is financial management?

5. Who is in charge of financial management in a firm?

6. List eight functions of a financial manager.

   a. _____   e. _____

   b. _____   f. _____

   c. _____   g. _____

   d. _____   h. _____

7. Why is the collection of payments and overdue accounts particularly critical to small businesses?

8. Why does tax management fall under the area of finance?

9. What is the role of the internal auditor?

Learning Goal 3   **Financial Planning**

10. What is financial planning? What is the objective of financial planning?

11. What are the three steps involved in financial planning?

   a. _____

   b. _____

   c. _____

12. What is the difference between a short-term forecast and a long-term forecast?

13. What is a cash flow forecast based upon?

14. Identify four types of budgets.

   a. _____   c. _____

   b. _____   d. _____

15. What is determined in an operating budget?

16. What is the primary concern in a capital budget?

17. What information does a cash budget provide?

18. When is a cash budget prepared?

Learning Goal 4   **The Need for Operating Funds**

19. What are four basic financial needs affecting both small and large businesses?

   a. _____

   b. _____

   c. _____

   d. _____

20. What is the financial challenge of managing daily business operations?

21. Why is it better to take money today, rather than wait until later?

22. What do financial managers try to do with cash expenditures?

23. Why do financial managers want to make credit available?

24. What is a problem with offering credit?

25. What is a way to decrease the time and expense of collecting accounts?

26. What does inventory control have to do with finance?

27. What job does a financial manager have with regard to capital expenditures?

Learning Goal 5   **Alternative Sources of Funds**

28. What is the difference between long-term and short-term financing?

29. Describe the difference between debt capital and equity capital.

Learning Goal 6   **Obtaining Short-Term Financing**

30. Why do firms need to borrow short-term funds?

31. What are six sources of short-term financing?

    a. _____   d. _____

    b. _____   e. _____

    c. _____   f. _____

32. Describe the invoice terms of 2/10 net 30.

33. When would a supplier require a promissory note?

34. What steps are recommended when borrowing from family or friends?

   a. _____

   b. _____

   c. _____

35. Why is it important for a businessperson to keep a close relationship with a banker?

36. Identify five types of bank loans.

   a. _____   d. _____

   b. _____   e. _____

   c. _____

37. What is the primary purpose of a line of credit?

38. How does factoring work?

39. How can a small business make factoring less expensive?

40. What kinds of companies sell commercial paper?

41. What are the benefits of commercial paper?

Learning Goal 7 **Obtaining Long-Term Financing**

42. What are three questions asked in setting long-term financing objectives?

    a. _____

    b. _____

    c. _____

43. What is long-term capital used for?

44. What are the two major sources of initial long-term financing?

    a. _____   b. _____

45. What is the advantage of a long-term loan?

46. What are some drawbacks to a long-term loan?

47. What is a simple explanation of a bond?

48. What does a potential investor evaluate in the purchase of a bond?

49. What are two forms of equity financing?

50. Who determines the number of shares of stock to be issued by a corporation?

51. What is unissued stock?

52. What is the most favored source of long-term capital? Why?

53. What is venture capital?

54. What are some considerations to remember when exploring venture capital?

55. What is a key job of the finance manager, or CFO?

CRITICAL THINKING EXERCISES

Learning Goals 1, 2

1. Finance is the function in a business that is responsible for acquiring the funds for the firm and for managing funds within the firm.

    Among the functions a finance manager performs are:

    a. Planning.

    b. Budgeting.

    c. Obtaining funds.

    d. Controlling funds.

    e. Collecting funds (credit management).

    f. Auditing.

    g. Managing taxes.

    h. Advising top management.

    Match the correct function to each statement below.

    a. Before Music-stor sends out quarterly financial statements, Debbie Breeze does her job, which is to ensure that no mistakes have been made, and that all transactions have been treated in accordance with established accounting rules and procedures. _____

    b. Joe Saumby determined that his firm's accounts receivable were too high, and developed a more effective collection system. _____

c. Ann Bizer decided to include money for a new bank of computers in the operating budget. _____

d. In an effort to generate capital, Gerald McMillian decided that his company should "go public" and make a stock offering. _____

e. A major automotive company developed a long-range objective of automating its production facilities, which would cost millions of dollars.
_____

f. In order to monitor expense account spending, many companies require employees to submit a receipt for any expenditure over $25.
_____

g. During a period of high inflation, the Kroger Company changed from LIFO to FIFO to determine their cost of goods sold, ultimately reducing the company's net income for tax purposes. _____

h. In a report to management, Joe Kelley outlined the effect of newly proposed pollution control requirements on the company's long range profit forecasts.
_____

Learning Goal 3

2. Outline the elements in the financial planning process.

3. There are four kinds of budgets:

   a. Operating budget.   c. Cash budget.

   b. Capital budget.   d. Master budget.

Determine which type of budget is being described in each of the following:

a. St. Louis Community College District projects that $350,000 will be spent for attendance and participation in conferences and seminars. _____

b. Kevin Nelson, the finance manager for TNG Enterprises, has just finished work on the budget that will enable him to determine how much money the firm will have to borrow for the next year. _____

c. At Whitfield School, a fund raising activity helped the school add money to the funds allocated to purchasing computer equipment for student and faculty use. _____

d. Phillip Knott is the comptroller for a major stock brokerage firm. At their annual finance meeting, he presented a summary of all the budgets for board approval. _____

Learning Goals 1, 2, 3

4. Planning is a critical element in the management process. What is the relationship between strategic planning and long-term financial planning and forecasting?

Learning Goal 4

5. Eric is upset! He has just stormed into Music-stor's finance manager's office " What's going on? I just looked at our inventory levels, and they're lower than what I think we ought to see. Don't we have the money to buy inventory? How are we going to make our orders? And what's the idea of all these credit sales? Visa? MasterCard? And another thing! Why are we always paying our bills at the last minute? Are we that short of cash? " "Hold on" said Bill Whittier, the new finance manager, " things look pretty good to me. We're actually in great shape!" "What? I don't understand!" replied Eric. "You know, I want to look into building a new plant within the next 2 years. Sales are going to continue to go way up. I need to know whether or not we're going to be able to afford it. Right now, it looks as if we are too short of cash." Explain what Bill is saying.

Learning Goals 5, 6

6. There are several sources of short-term funds:

   a. Trade credit.   d. Promissory notes.

   b. Family and friends.   e. Factoring.

   c. Commercial bank loans.   f. Commercial paper.

   Match the correct type of short-term financing to each of the following:

   A major Midwestern retailer often sells its accounts receivable for cash.
   _____

   b. Lou Fusz auto network finances its inventories, using the vehicles themselves as collateral for the loans. _____

   c. During a recent recession, Van Nuys Enterprises had some problems paying their bills on time. Afterwards, in order for them to buy with credit, Van Nuys' suppliers required them to sign a written contract. _____

   d. Echo Enterprises recently raised some "quick cash" through selling promissory notes. Echo agreed to pay the principle plus interest within 90 days of the sale. Monterrey Bay Co. bought Echo's promissory notes as an investment with their extra cash. _____

   e. Kellwood bills its retail customers on a 2/10 net 30 basis.
   _____

   f. To pay an unexpectedly high liability insurance premium, the owner of a small chemical company borrowed money from his best friend.
   _____

7. There are several kinds of bank loans:

   a. Unsecured loans.
   b. Secured loans (including pledging).
   c. Inventory financing.
   d. Line of credit.
   e. Revolving credit agreement.
   f. Commercial finance companies.

   Match each type to the following examples:

   a. Ternier Steel company is using their most recent shipment of coal as collateral for a short term loan. _____

   b. In their commodities brokerage business, Bartholomew Enterprises needs guaranteed loans without having to apply for the loan each time it is needed. They are willing to pay a fee for the guarantee. _____

   c. Rivertown Insurance is having some short-term cash problems. They have substantial accounts receivable which they intend to use as collateral for a loan. _____

   d. Danny Noble Enterprises has been in business for a fairly long time and has a great financial record. When they needed money they went to their banker and applied for the loan without needing to put up collateral. _____

   e. Because they often have a need for short term funds with short notice, Binny and Jones Manufacturing applied to their bank for a sort of "continual' unsecured loan. The bank lends Binny a given amount without Binny having to re-apply each time. While not a guaranteed loan, the funds are available if Binny's credit limit is not exceeded. _____

   f. Because they were considered a credit risk, PPI, Inc. had to pay a higher rate of interest, and pledge their inventory as collateral for the loan. They went to General Electric Capital Services, for the loan. _____

Learning Goal 7

8. There are 2 general sources of long-term funds:

   a. Debt capital—loans and bonds

   b. Equity capital—stock, retained earnings, venture capital

   Match the correct type of financing to each of the following statements:

   a. These are commonly referred to as "debentures." _____

   b. This is the least favored source of long-term financing. _____

   c. Generally the most favored source of long-term capital. _____

   d. These can be either secured or unsecured. _____

   e. For this, a business must sign a term-loan agreement because of the long repayment period. _____

   f. The key word here is "ownership." _____

   g. The number one source of funds for young, fast-growing companies. _____

   h. Using this source saves the company interest payments, dividends and any underwriting fees, and won't dilute ownership. _____

   i. The terms of agreement are called indenture terms. _____

   j. Good sources of start up capital for new companies, they often want a stake in the ownership of the business. _____

   k. With this, a company has a legal obligation to pay. _____

9. Eric and his finance manager, Joel, are in disagreement over how to finance the future growth of Music-stor. "I just want to stay out of debt if I can" says Eric, "so I think the best idea is to sell stock, go public." "Well, I understand your perspective Eric, but I'm not sure you have thought of all the consequences of selling stock. Do you like being your own boss?" asks Joel. "Yeah, sure!" replies Eric, " but what the heck does that have to do with wanting to sell stock in the company?" What does Joel mean, and what are the other arguments for and against each type of funding?

10. If leverage means raising money through debt, what do you suppose is meant by a "leveraged buyout"?

PRACTICE TEST

Multiple Choice: Circle the best answer.

1. Which of the following is not included in a list of reasons why businesses fail financially?

   a. Inadequate expense control
   b. Poor control over cash flow
   c. Undercapitalization
   d. Stock is undervalued

2. Jackie Jones is a finance manager for Pokey Poseys, a wholesale florist. As finance manager, which of the following would not be one of Jackie's responsibilities?

   a. Preparing financial statements
   b. Preparing budgets
   c. Doing cash flow analysis
   d. Planning for spending funds on long-term assets, such as plant and equipment

3. Regular internal audits are important because:

   a. the firm needs to keep a constant look out for employees who may be committing fraud.
   b. internal audits help to make accounting statements more reliable.
   c. they aid in the development of financial statements.
   d. the firm uses the audits to determine LIFO and FIFO procedures.

4. The process of analyzing short-term and long-term money flows to and from the firm is known as _____.

   a. internal auditing   c. financial planning
   b. forecasting   d. financial controls

5. Ima Midas is currently in the process of projecting how much his firm will have to spend on supplies, travel, rent, advertising, and salaries for the coming financial year. Ima is working on the _____.

   a. operating budget   c. cash budget
   b. capital budget   d. master budget

6. Which of the following is not one of the steps involved in financial planning?

   a. Forecasting short-term and long-term financial needs
   b. Developing budgets to meet those needs
   c. Establishing financial controls to keep the company focused on financial plans
   d. Developing financial statements for outside investors

7. What is the major problem with selling on credit?

   a. Too much of a firm's assets could be tied up in accounts receivable.
   b. You can't control when customers will pay their bills.
   c. It makes production scheduling more difficult.
   d. Customers who aren't allowed to buy on credit become unhappy.

8. Companies must maintain a sizable investment in inventories in order to:

   a. be able to accept credit cards.
   b. keep customers happy.
   c. increase demand for their products.
   d. reduce the need for long-term funds.

9. The time value of money means that:

   a. the value of money will fall over time.
   b. it is better to make purchases now, rather than wait until later.
   c. a monetary system will devalue its money over time.
   d. it is better to have money now, than later.

10. Which of the following is not a source of short-term funds?

    a. The sale of bonds
    b. The use of trade credit
    c. Promissory notes
    d. The use of inventory financing

11. The credit terms 2/10 net 30 means:

    a. The full amount of a bill is due within 2-10 days.
    b. Customers will receive a 10 percent discount if they pay in 30 days.
    c. A 2 percent discount will be given if customers pay within 30 days.
    d. Customers will receive a 2 percent discount if they pay within 10 days.

12. When accounts receivable or some other asset are used as collateral for a loan, the process is called

    a. a line of credit   c. trade credit
    b. a promissory note   d. pledging

13. Commercial finance companies accept more risk than banks, and the interest rates they charge are usually _____ than commercial banks.

    a. higher   c. lower
    b. about the same as   d. more variable

14. Dave Sinclair Ford usually obtains its short-term financing by offering the cars they are selling as collateral for a loan. This form of financing is called:

    a. factoring.   c. a revolving credit agreement.
    b. inventory financing. d. a line of credit.

15. Raising debt capital includes using _____ as a source of funds.

    a. the sale of bonds   c. the sale of inventory
    b. the sale of stock   d. the sale of accounts receivable

16. One of the benefits of selling bonds, over selling stock, as a source of long-term funds is that:

   a. bonds don't have to be paid back.
   b. the company isn't required to pay interest.
   c. bondholders do not have a say in running the business.
   d. interest is paid after taxes are paid.

17. The most favored source of meeting long-term capital needs is:

   a. selling stock.
   b. venture capital.
   c. selling bonds.
   d. retained earnings.

18. When starting his new software business, Bob Campbell considered using venture capital as a source of initial funding. One of the drawbacks of venture capital is that

   a. venture capitalists generally want a stake in the ownership of the business.
   b. venture capitalists charge a very high rate of interest.
   c. venture capital is very difficult to find.
   d. venture capital firms generally don't provide additional financing later on.

TRUE/FALSE

1. _____ Financial understanding is important primarily for anyone wanting to major in accounting, but not necessary for other involved in business.

2. _____ Financial managers are responsible for collecting overdue payments and making sure the company doesn't lose too much money to bad debts.

3. _____ The cash budget is often the first budget that is prepared.

4. _____ Financial control means that the actual revenues, costs, and expenses are reviewed and compared with projections.

5. _____ One way to decrease the expense of collecting accounts receivable is to accept bank credit cards.

6. _____ Equity capital is money raised primarily through the sale of bonds.

7. _____ Firms often need to borrow short-term funds to be able to pay unexpected bills.

8. _____ One benefit of borrowing from friends or family is that you don't have to draw up formal papers as you do with a bank loan.

9. _____ It is important for a businessperson to keep close relations with a banker because the banker may be able to spot cash flow problems early and point out problems.

10. _____ A line of credit guarantees a business a given amount of unsecured short-term funds.

11. _____ Long-term capital is generally used to pay for supplies, rent, and travel.

12. _____ Potential investors in bonds measure the risk involved in purchasing a bond with the return the bond promises to pay.

ANSWERS

LEARNING THE LANGUAGE

1. Commercial finance companies	18. Leverage
2. Financial control	19. Factoring
3. Long-term financing	20. Capital budget
4. Revolving credit agreement	21. Pledging
5. Term-loan agreement	22. Long-term forecast
6. Unsecured loan	23. Commercial paper
7. Budget	24. Trade credit
8. Equity capital	25. Short-term financing
9. Inventory financing	26. Master budget
10. Promissory note	27. Finance
11. Short-term forecast	28. Risk/return trade-off
12. Debt capital	29. Secured bond
13. Operating budget	30. Indenture terms
14. Secured loan	31. Cash budget
15. Cash flow forecast	32. Financial management
16. Line of credit	33. Capital expenditures
17. Unsecured bond	34. Venture capital

RETENTION CHECK

Learning Goal 1   **The Role of Finance**

1. Financial managers use the data prepared by accountants and make recommendations to top management regarding strategies for improving the health of the firm.

2.   a. Undercaptitalization—not enough funds to start with:
   b. Poor control over cash flow.
   c. Inadequate expense control.

3. Financial understanding is important to anyone who wants to start a small business, invest in stocks and bonds, or plan a retirement fund.

Learning Goal 2   **What is Finance?**

4. Financial management is the job of managing a firm's resources so it can meet its goals and objectives.

5. Most organizations will designate a manager in charge of financial operations, generally the chief financial officer, CFO. Financial management could also be in the hands of a person that serves as the company treasurer or vice president of finance.

6.
   a. Planning
   b. Budgeting
   c. Obtaining funds
   d. Controlling funds
   e. Collecting funds
   f. Auditing
   g. Managing taxes
   h. Advising top management on financial matters

7. Collection of accounts payable and overdue accounts is critical to all types of businesses. However, small businesses typically have smaller cash or credit cushions than large corporations.

8. Tax payments represent an outflow of cash from the business, and therefore fall under finance. As tax laws and tax liabilities have changed, finance specialists have become increasingly involved in tax management by analyzing the tax implications of various managerial decisions, in an attempt to minimize taxes paid by the business.

9. The internal auditor checks on the journals, ledgers, and financial statements prepared by the accounting department to make sure that all transactions have been treated in accordance with established accounting rules and procedures. Without such audits, accounting statements would be less reliable.

Learning Goal 3   **Financial Planning**

10. Financial planning involves analyzing short-term and long-term money flows to and from the firm. The overall objective of financial planning is to optimize the firm's profitability and make the best use of its money.

11. a. Forecasting both short-term and long-term financial needs
    b. Developing budgets to meet those needs
    c. Establishing financial controls

12. A short-term forecast predicts revenues, costs, and expenses for a period of one year or less. A long-term forecast predicts revenues, costs, and expenses for a period of longer than one year, sometimes as far as 5 or 10 years into the future.

13. A cash flow forecast projects the expected cash inflows and outflows in future periods. This is based on expected sales revenues and on various costs and expenses incurred and when they'll come due.

14. a. Operating budgets
    b. Capital budgets
    c. Cash budgets
    d. Master budgets

15. How much the firm will spend on supplies, travel, rent, advertising, salaries and so forth is determined in the operating budget.

16. The capital budget primarily concerns itself with the purchase of such assets as property, buildings, and equipment.

17. Cash budgets are important guidelines that assist managers in anticipating borrowing, repaying debt, cash needed for operations and expenses, and short-term investment expectations. Cash budgets assist the firm in planning for cash shortages or surpluses.

18. The cash budget is often the last budget that is prepared.

Learning Goal 4 **The Need for Operating Funds**

19. a. Funds to manage daily business operations
    b. Managing accounts receivable
    c. Obtaining inventory
    d. Major capital expenditures

20. The challenge of sound financial management is to see that funds are available to meet daily cash needs without compromising the firm's investment potential.

21. Money has a time value. If someone offered to give you money today or one year from today, you would benefit by taking the money today. You could start collecting interest or invest the money you receive today, and over time, your money would grow.

22. Financial managers often try to keep cash expenditures at a minimum, to free funds for investment in interest-bearing accounts. It is not unusual for finance managers to suggest the firm pay bills as late as possible and collect what is owed as fast as possible.

23. Financial mangers know that making credit available helps to keep current customers happy and attracts new customers. In today's highly competitive environment, many businesses would have trouble surviving without making credit available to customers.

24. The major problem with selling on credit is that as much as 25 percent or more of the business's assets could be tied up in its accounts receivable.

25. One way to decrease the time, and therefore expense, of collecting accounts receivable is to accept bank credit cards.

26. To satisfy customers, businesses must maintain inventories that often involve a sizable expenditure of funds. A carefully constructed inventory policy assists in managing the use of the firm's available funds and maximizing profitability.

27. Financial managers and analysts evaluate the appropriateness of capital purchases. It is critical that companies weigh all the possible options before committing what may be a large portion of its available resources.

Learning Goal 5 **Alternative Sources of Funds**

28. Short-term financing comes from funds used to finance current operations, which will be repaid in less that one year. Long-term financing refers to capital needed for major purchases, which will be repaid over a period longer that one year.

29. Debt capital is raised through borrowing that must be repaid. Equity capital is raised from selling stock or raised from within the company.

Learning Goal 6 **Obtaining Short-Term Financing**

30. Firms need to borrow short-term funds for purchasing additional inventory or for meeting bills that come due unexpectedly. A business sometimes needs to obtain short-term funds when the firm's money is low.

31.
    a. Trade credit
    b. Promissory note
    c. Family and friends
    d. Commercial banks
    e. Factoring
    f. Commercial paper

32. Terms of 2/10 net 30 means that the buyer can take a 2 percent discount for paying within 10 days. The total bill is due (net) in 30 days if the purchaser does not take advantage of the discount.

33. Some suppliers hesitate to give trade credit to organizations with a poor credit rating, no credit history, or a history of slow payment. In such cases, the supplier may insist that the customer sign a promissory note as a condition for obtaining credit.

34.
    a. Agree on terms at the beginning
    b. Write an agreement
    c. Pay them back the same way you would pay a bank loan

35. It is important for a businessperson to keep friendly and close relations with a banker, because the banker may spot cash flow problems early and point out danger areas. Additionally, the banker may be more willing to lend money in a crisis if the businessperson has established a strong, friendly relationship built on openness and trust.

36.
    a. Unsecured loans
    b. Secured loans
    c. Inventory financing
    d. Line of credit
    e. Revolving credit agreement

37. The primary purpose of a line of credit is to speed the borrowing process so that a firm does not have to go through the hassle of applying for a new loan every time it needs funds.

38. A firm sells many of its products on credit to consumers and businesses, creating an account receivable. Some of these buyers may be slow in paying their bills, causing the company to have a large amount of money due in accounts receivable. A factor is a market intermediary that agrees to buy the accounts receivable from the firm at a discount for cash.

39. Factoring can be less expensive if the small business selling its accounts receivable agrees to reimburse the factor for slow paying accounts. Factoring charges are even lower if the company assumes the risk of those people who don't pay at all.

40. Commercial paper is unsecured and is sold at a public sale, so only financially stable firms, mainly large corporations, are able to sell it.

41. Commercial paper is a way to get short-term funds quickly and for less than bank interest rates. It is also an investment opportunity for buyers who can afford to put up cash for short periods to earn some interest.

Learning Goal 7 **Obtaining Long-Term Financing**

42. a. What are the long-term goals and objectives of the firm?
    b. What are the financial requirements needed to achieve these goals and objectives?
    c. What sources of long-term capital are available, and which will fit our needs?

43. In business, long–term capital is used to buy fixed assets such as plant and equipment and to finance expansion of the organization.

44. a. Debt capital
    b. Equity capital

45. A major advantage of debt financing is that the interest paid on a long-term debt is tax deductible.

46. Long-term loans are often more expensive to the firm than short-term loans, because larger amounts of capital are borrowed. In addition, since the repayment period could be as long as twenty years, the lenders are not assured their capital will be repaid in full. Therefore, most long-term loans require some form of collateral.

47. To put it simply, a bond is like a company IOU with a promise to repay on a certain date. It is a binding contract through which an organization agrees to specific terms with investors, in return for investors lending money to the company.

48. Potential investors in bonds measure the risk involved in purchasing a bond with the return the bond promises to pay.

49. Two forms of equity financing are selling ownership in the firm in the form of stock, or using retained earnings the firm has reinvested in the business.

50. Generally, the organization's board of directors determines the exact number of shares of stock into which a firm will be divided.

51. Unissued stocks are shares of stock the company decides not to offer for sale.

52. Retained earnings are usually the most favored source of meeting long-term capital needs, since the company saves interest payments, dividends, and any possible underwriting fees.

53. Venture capital is money that is invested in new companies with great profit potential.

54. The venture capital firm generally wants a stake in the ownership of the business. Venture capitalists also expect a very high return on their investment. It is also important that the venture capital firm be able to come up with and be willing to provide more financing if the firm needs it.

55. A key job of the finance manager or CFO is to forecast the need for and to manage borrowed funds.

CRITICAL THINKING EXERCISES

Learning Goals 1, 2

1.
   a. Auditing
   b. Collecting funds
   c. Budgeting
   d. Obtaining funds
   e. Planning
   f. Controlling funds
   g. Managing taxes
   h. Advising top management

Learning Goal 3

2.

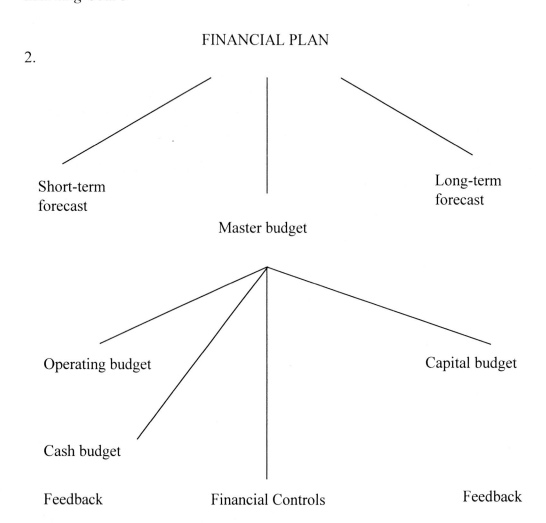

3. a. Operating budget
   b. Cash budget
   c. Capital budget
   d. Master budget

Learning Goals 1, 2, 3

4. Strategic planning helps the firm to determine what businesses it should be in within the next 5-10 years. Decisions about which direction a company should take could not be made without some knowledge of the expense of entering certain markets, as well as the profit potential of those same markets. Long-term forecasts give top management some sense of the income or profit potential with different strategic plans.

Learning Goal 4

5. Eric doesn't understand some basic ideas about financial management. Bill needs to explain the financial needs of all businesses: managing daily operations, managing accounts receivable, obtaining needed inventory (including inventory management) and major capital expenditures, and how a finance manager deals with each area.

   One of the first things a finance manager will do is to see that funds are available to meet daily cash needs, without using too much cash to take advantage of other investments. So, bills are paid at the latest date possible to allow the firm to take advantage of interest-bearing accounts. Music-stor allows for credit purchases because it helps to keep their customers happy and helps to attract new customers. With effective collection procedures, selling on credit can be a benefit to the firm. It's important to keep inventories at a level necessary to fill orders, but too high an inventory level will tie up funds that could be used elsewhere for investment. Programs like just-in-time inventory help to reduce the amount of funds a firm must tie up in inventory.

   There is no way to tell if the firm can afford to build a new plant in two years, but the finance manager will be able to evaluate the various alternatives, such as buying a facility, expanding on a current facility or building their own building.

Learning Goals 5, 6

6.   a. Factoring
   b. Bank loan (inventory financing)
   c. Promissory note
   d. Commercial paper
   e. Trade credit
   f. Family and friends

7.   a. Inventory financing
   b. Revolving credit agreement
   c. Secured loan
   d. Line of credit
   e. Line of credit
   f. Commercial credit company

Learning Goal 7

8.   a. Debt financing—bonds
   b. Equity financing—stock
   c. Equity financing—retained earnings
   d. Debt financing
   e. Debt financing—loans
   f. Equity financing—stock
   g. Equity financing—venture capital
   h. Equity financing—retained earnings
   i. Debt financing—bonds
   j. Equity financing—venture capital
   k. Debt financing—loans, bonds

9. Joel's point to Eric is that when you sell stock to the public, the common stockholders get voting rights, and management must answer to the stockholders. Creditors, such as lending institutions or bondholders generally have no say in running the business. The plus side of the equity financing is that there is no repayment obligation, as there is with debt financing, and the firm is not legally liable to pay dividends to the stockholders. Interest on debt is a legal obligation. However, the interest is tax deductible, whereas dividends are paid out of after-tax profits, and so are not deductible.

10. Leveraged buyouts occur when one firm purchases the assets of another using funds that were borrowed, either through selling bonds or obtaining loans, or a combination of both.

PRACTICE TEST

	Multiple Choice				True/False		
1.	d	10.	a	1.	F	10.	T
2.	a	11.	d	2.	T	11.	F
3.	b	12.	d	3.	F	12.	T
4.	c	13.	a	4.	T		
5.	a	14.	b	5.	T		
6.	d	15.	a	6.	F		
7.	a	16.	c	7.	T		
8.	b	17.	d	8.	F		
9.	d	18.	a	9.	T		

CHAPTER 20
SECURITIES MARKETS: FINANCING AND INVESTING

LEARNING GOALS:

After you have read and studied this chapter you should be able to:

1. Examine the functions of securities markets and investment bankers.

2. Compare the advantages and disadvantages of selling bonds and identify the classes and features of bonds.

3. Compare the advantages and disadvantages of issuing stock and outline the differences between common and preferred stock.

4. Identify the various stock exchanges and describe how to invest in securities markets and choose among different investment strategies.

5. Analyze the opportunities bonds offer as investments.

6. Explain the opportunities stock and mutual funds offer as investments and the advantage of diversifying investments.

7. Discuss the high risk involved in junk bonds, buying stock on margin, and commodities.

8. Explain securities quotations listed in the financial section of a newspaper and how the Dow Jones Averages affect the market.

LEARNING THE LANGUAGE

Listed below are important terms found in the chapter. Choose the correct term for the definition and write it in the space provided.

Blue chip stocks	Market order
Bond	Maturity date
Buying on margin	Mutual fund
Callable bond	National Association of Securities Dealers Automated Quotation System (NASDAQ)
Commodity exchange	
Common stock	Over-the-counter (OTC) market

Convertible bond	Par value
Cumulative preferred stock	Penny stocks
Debenture bond	Preemptive right
Diversification	Preferred stock
Dividends	Principal
Dow Jones Industrial Average	Program trading
Futures market	Prospectus
Growth stocks	Round lots
Income stocks	Securities and Exchange Commission (SEC)
Insider trading	Sinking fund
Institutional investor	Stock certificate
Interest	Stock exchange
Investment banker	Stock split
Junk bonds	Stockbroker
Limit order	Stocks

1. Preferred stock that accumulates unpaid dividends is _____.

2. The _____ involves the purchase and sale of goods for delivery sometime in the future.

3. Stocks called _____ offer investors a high dividend.

4. Large investors known as _____ are organizations such as pension funds, mutual funds, insurance companies, and banks that invest their own funds or the funds of others.

5. The _____ is an exchange that provides a means to trade stocks not listed on national exchanges.

6. Evidence of ownership called a _____ specifies the name of the company, the number of shares it represents, and the type of stock it is.

7. Stocks of high quality firms that pay regular dividends and generate consistent growth in the company's stock price are called _____.

8. _____ means giving instructions to computers to automatically sell if the price of stock dips to a certain price, to avoid potential losses.

9. A _____ gives common stockholders the right to purchase any new shares of common stock the firm decides to issue.

10. The most basic form of ownership of firms is _____, which includes voting rights and dividends, if the firm's board of directors offers dividends.

11. A _____ is a bond whose issuers regularly set aside funds in a reserve account so that enough capital will be accumulated by the maturity date to pay off the bond.

12. The use of knowledge or information that a person gains through their position that allows the person to benefit unfairly from fluctuations in stock prices is _____.

13. The face value of a bond is the _____.

14. The purchase of 100 shares of stock at a time is a _____.

15. A _____ is a bond that can be converted into shares of common stock in the issuing company.

16. Instructions called a _____ tell the broker to buy or sell a security immediately at the best price available.

17. A _____ is a stock that sells for less than $1.

18. High-risk, high-interest bonds are called _____.

19. A registered representative, or market intermediary known as a _____ buys and sells securities for clients.

20. A _____ gives the issuer of the bond the right to pay off the bond before its maturity date.

21. A _____ is an organization whose members can buy and sell securities for the public.

22. The exact date the issuer of a bond must pay the principal to the bondholder is known as the _____.

23. Stock called _____ gives its owners preference in the payment of dividends and an earlier claim on assets if the business is forced out of business and its assets sold.

24. _____ are specialists in assisting in the issue and selling of new securities.

25. The _____ is a dollar amount assigned to shares of stock by the corporation's charter.

26. The payment the issuer of a bond makes to the bondholders to pay for the use of borrowed money is called _____.

27. _____ are bonds that are unsecured.

28. The process of _____ is the purchase of stocks by borrowing some of the purchase cost from the brokerage firm.

29. The part of a firm's profits that are distributed to shareholders as either cash payments or additional shares of stock are called _____.

30. Stocks known as _____ are stocks of corporations whose earnings are expected to grow faster than other stocks or the overall economy.

31. A _____ is an action that gives stockholders two or more shares of stock for each one they own.

32. The technique of _____ means buying several different investment alternatives to spread the risk of investing.

33. A _____ tells a broker to buy or to sell stock at a specific price, if and when that price becomes possible.

34. Shares of ownership in a company are called _____.

35. A _____ is an organization that buys stocks and bonds and then sells shares in those securities to the public.

36. A corporate certificate called a _____ indicates that a person has loaned money to a firm.

37. The average cost of 30 selected industrial stocks called the _____ is used to give an indication of direction of the stock market over time.

38. A _____ specializes in the buying and selling of precious metals and minerals and agricultural goods.

39. The _____ is the federal government agency that has the responsibility at the federal level for regulating the various exchanges.

40. A condensed version of economic and financial information called a _____ is prepared for the SEC and must be sent to potential purchasers of the firm's stock.

41. The _____ is a nationwide electronic system that communicates over-the-counter trades to brokers.

RETENTION CHECK

Learning Goal 1   **The Function of Securities Markets**

1. What are two major functions of securities markets?

2. How do businesses benefit from the securities markets?

3. How do individuals benefit from the securities markets?

4. Explain the difference between the primary and the secondary markets.

5. What does an investment banker do for companies?

Learning Goal 2   **Debt Financing Through Selling Bonds**

6. What is the legal obligation of a company when selling bonds?

7. What is meant by the term "coupon rate" with regard to bonds?

8. What is a AAA rated bond?

9. If a $1000 bond has an interest rate of 10% and a maturity date of 2020, what does that mean to a bondholder?

10. List the advantages of raising long term capital by selling bonds.

   a. _____

   b. _____

   c. _____

11. What are the disadvantages?

   a. _____

   b. _____

   c. _____

12. Identify two classes of corporate bonds.

   a. _____

   b. _____

13. Who issues debenture bonds?

14. What are three types of secured bonds? What is their security?

   a. _____

   b. _____

   c. _____

15. Why are sinking funds attractive to firms and investors?

   a. _____

   b. _____

   c. _____

16. What is the benefit to a company of a callable bond?

17. Why would an investor convert a bond to common stock?

Learning Goal 3 **Equity Financing Through Selling Stock**

18. What is the difference between the interest on a bond and a dividend paid on a share of stock?

19. List the advantages of raising funds through the sale of stock.

   a. _____

   b. _____

   c. _____

20. What are the disadvantages?

   a. _____

   b. _____

   c. _____

21. What are two classes of stock?

   a. _____

   b. _____

22. Describe how preferred stock dividends differ from common stock dividends.

23. How is preferred stock like a bond?

24. How do preferred stock and bonds differ?

25. What are some special features of preferred stock?

26. What are two privileges of owning common stock?

Learning Goal 4   **Stock Exchanges**

27. Identify four "exchanges" where stocks are traded.

   a. _____

   b. _____

   c. _____

   d. _____

28. How are stocks traded in the NASDAQ?

29. Which stock exchange lists the largest companies? Which exchange has the largest number of listings?

30. What did the Securities Act of 1933 provide for?

31. Discuss the Securities and Exchange Act of 1934 and the responsibility of the Securities and Exchange Commission.

32. How does a stockbroker trade securities?

33. What is the difference between trading on-line and using a stockbroker?

34. List the five criteria to use when selecting an investment option.

   a. _____   d. _____

   b. _____   e. _____

   c. _____

Learning Goal 5   **Investing in Bonds**

35. What is the investment with the least possible risk? Why?

36. What are two questions first time bond investors may ask?

Learning Goal 6   **Investing in Stocks and Mutual Funds**

37. What does the market price of a stock depend upon?

38. What are "bulls and bears" in the stock market?

39. What are four different investment opportunities in stock? (in other words, four different "kinds" of stocks?)

   a. _____

   b. _____

   c. _____

   d. _____

40. What is the difference between a limit order and a market order?

41. Why would a company declare a stock split?

42. What is the benefit of a mutual fund for an investor?

43. What are some varieties of mutual funds?

44. What is the difference between a "no-load" and a "load" fund?

45. What is the difference between an open-end fund and a closed-end fund?

46. What is a portfolio strategy?

Learning Goal 7 **Investing in High Risk Investments**

47. Why are junk bonds considered "junk"?

48. What does a 50% margin rate mean?

49. What is a margin call?

50. What kinds of items are traded on a commodity exchange?

Learning Goal 8   **Understanding Information From Securities Markets**

51. How is a bond price quoted?

52. What information is included in a bond quote.

53. What information is contained in a stock quote?

   a. _____

   b. _____

   c. _____

   d. _____

   e. _____

   f. _____

   g. _____

   h. _____

54. What information is contained in a mutual fund quote?

55. What is a criticism of the Dow Jones Industrial Average?

56. What happened in October of 1987?

57. What is speculated to be the cause of the 1987 drop?

58. Why did the market drop in October of 1997?

59. What will trigger the market to halt trading?

60. What lessons can be learned from the stock market crashes in the past?

CRITICAL THINKING EXERCISES

Learning Goal 1

1. The financial manager of Music-stor has convinced the management that a bond issue is needed to raise capital for future growth. He wants to avoid the difficulty of looking for and marketing to potential investors himself, and prefers to let "experts" perform those functions. How should he go about selling this new bond issue?

Learning Goal 2

2. In discussing bonds, there are several terms with which you need to be familiar:

   a. Bond.
   b. Interest.
   c. Principal
   d. Maturity date.
   e. Unsecured bonds (debentures).
   f. Secured bonds.
   g. Sinking fund.
   h. Call provision
   i. Convertible bond.

   Match the correct term to each of the following descriptions:

   a. Gerry Hoffman will receive this on the date her bond becomes due in the year 2010.

   b. Beth Galganski will receive the principle value of her bond on this date.

c. Tom Huff is in finance with Music-stor, Inc. Each quarter he checks the amount of money the company has in this account to be sure the company can pay off their bond issue on the maturity date.

d. Because it has declared bankruptcy in the past, and the future is uncertain, TWA would probably not be able to issue this type of bond.

e. Bonnie Andersen receives $100 per year from her bond.

f. Mobil Oil issued an unsecured one at 14.4 percent due in 2004.

g. TNG Enterprises issued their debentures with this provision because they forecasted a decline in interest rates in a few years.

h. Bill Paterson bought this type of bond because he anticipated exchanging it for common stock in the firm later.

i. Caldwell Industries used real estate holdings to ensure their bonds.

3. In discussing stocks, there are several terms with which you need to be familiar:

a. Stock.
b. Stock certificate.
c. Par value.
d. Dividends.
e. Preferred stock.
f. Cumulative preferred stock.
g. Common stock.
h. Pre-emptive right.

Match the correct term to each of the following:

a. Carmen Arauz was considering buying this type of stock, but was somewhat concerned about the risk when she learned that as a stockholder of this type, if the firm closed, she would be the last to share in the firm's assets.

b. When her grandson was born, Judi Burton bought 100 shares of her favored stock. She gave his parents this, as evidence of his ownership.

c. As her grandson Burke grew, he received these periodic payments from his stock, which his parents invested for college.

d. On Burke's stock certificate, there is a dollar amount per share shown, which has no relationship to the market value, but which is used to assign the dividends that he is paid.

e. When Judi was deciding which kind of stock to purchase, she decided upon this type, because the dividends are fixed and must be paid before other dividends are paid. Further, there are no voting rights with this type of stock, which Burke really doesn't mind!

f. What Burke doesn't have is the right of the stockholder to purchase new shares when the firm makes a new issue, so that his proportionate ownership in the company is maintained.

g. One of the advantages of Burke's stock is that if the company misses his dividend, the company must pay it before it pays any other, and the missed dividends accumulate.

h. Either common or preferred, this represents ownership in a firm.

4. Why did Judi Burton decide to buy her grandson Burke preferred stock instead of common stock?

Learning Goal 4

5. What are the differences between the NYSE, the AMEX and NASDAQ?

6. How are the exchanges regulated?

7. Five criteria to use when selecting a specific investment strategy are:

    Investment risk.   Liquidity.

    Yield.   Tax consequences.

    Duration.

   Read the following situations and evaluate the criteria in terms of the needs of the potential investors.

   a. A young couple wants to invest money to begin a college tuition fund for their 5-year-old child. Since the child has no income, they are going to put the account in his name to avoid taxes.

   b. A two-career couple; both anticipate retirement within the next five years.

   c. A single person, just graduating from college; just starting a high paying job and wants to build capital. Not concerned about losing money at first.

Learning Goals 6, 7

8. There are several terms used in securities trading with which you should be familiar:

    Stockbroker.   Buying on margin.

    Growth stocks.   Stock splits.

    Income stocks.   Round lots.

    Blue chip stocks.   Margin calls.

20-21

Penny stocks.   Mutual funds.

Market order.   Diversification.

Limit order.   Bulls.

Bears.   Prospectus.

Match the correct term to each of the following:

a. In 1995 Ford Motor Company gave its stockholders one additional share of stock for every share they owned. This reduced the price from $80 per share to around $40 per share.

b. Evelyn Minervi likes to dabble in the stock market. Last year she bought a number of stocks of this type, which each sold for 45 cents per share, but which were considered fairly risky.

c. Joe Contino works for a major brokerage firm buying and selling stocks and bonds for his clients.

d. Ron Stahl recently purchased exactly 100 shares of Navistar.

e. Dexter Inholt wanted to buy 500 shares of Ford at $40, each, but he only had $12,000 to invest, so he borrowed the $8,000 he still needed from his brokerage firm.

f. The stock of Ford would be considered a _____ stock

g. Marina Vasquez called her broker and asked him to buy Pepsico stock at the best price he could get.

h. Hong Le believed the stock market was going to take a big jump after the most recent national elections, and purchased the stocks she wanted in anticipation of that.

i. Lee Kornfield, a prosperous doctor, has a lot of money invested in the market. He recently called his broker and told her to buy the stock of several firms after the price went down to a certain level.

j. When Ford's stock took a slight dip in price, Dexter Inholt got worried that his broker would ask him to come up with some money to cover the losses the stock suffered.

k. LaTonya Adams is a first time investor, unfamiliar with the market. She wants to get into the market, but diversify her risk, and invest in lots of firms. Her brother advised her to get into one of these.

l. Because he is investing money for his son's college education, Tim Martin decided to invest in several public utilities, because they offer a high dividend yield for the investment.

m. The Chesterfield Investment Club always sends for a document which discloses the financial information of the firms in which the club is interested in investing.

n. Monte McHewie sold many of the stocks he was holding after he heard some economic news that led him to believe prices in the stock market were going to decline soon.

o. Lindsey Schopp has a portfolio that consists of 10 percent high risk growth stocks, 40 percent mutual funds, 30 percent government bonds, and 20 percent commodities.

p. Casey Argetsinger bought several shares of a relatively new company, for $1.35 per share. The stock paid no dividend, but was in the biotechnology field, and was predicted to grow by 20 percent per year over the next 10 years.

9. Whereas the stock exchanges trade securities, commodities exchanges specialize in buying and selling goods such as grains, livestock, metals, natural resources and foreign currency.

Jordan Reish has a large farm in the Midwest. His primary crop is corn. Jordan usually sells the crop he will plant in the spring and harvest in the summer, in the fall before the crop is even planted. General Mills is always happy to see Jordan and others like him selling their unplanted crops, and spends a good deal of time buying these futures contracts. What are Jordan and General Mills doing, and why?

10. The financial section of *The Wall Street Journal* contains stock and bond quotes, the Dow Jones Index and mutual fund quotes. Complete the following exercises, using *The Wall Street Journal*, or your local newspaper if the information is available.

   A. Trace the stock quotes for General Motors (or for a company your instructor assigns you) for three days, using the chart given below:

52 weeks		Stock	Sym	Div	Yld %	PE	Vol 100s	Hi	Low	Close	Net Chg
Hi	Low										

   1. What was the actual price of the stock at the close of the third day?
   _____

   2. What was the net change in dollars on the third day? _____

   3. What was the highest price the stock traded for in the previous year?
   _____

   4. How many shares were traded on the second day? _____

   B. Choose a bond from the NYSE Bond section. Complete the following information:

   1. Name of company _____

   2. Interest rate _____

   3. Date of maturity _____

   4. Current yield _____

5. Close _____

6. Change _____

C. Choose a mutual fund and answer the following questions:

   1. What is the net asset value? _____

   2. Is this a "no load" fund? _____

   3. What is the change in the net asset value? _____

   4. What is the year to date return? _____

All this information was available in *The Wall Street Journal* as of May, 1998. Occasionally, the WSJ changes the type of information it provides in the quotations they publish.

D. Look at the Dow Jones Industrial Average during the time your class is studying this chapter. Answer the following questions:

   1. Have stock prices trended up or down over the last 6 months?

   2. What was the highest Dow Jones Industrial Average in the last 6 months?

   3. What was the lowest?

PRACTICE TEST

Multiple Choice: Circle the best answer.

1. The benefit of the securities market for investors is:

    a. a guaranteed high return.
    b. a convenient place to build financial future with investments.
    c. a safe alternative to putting money in a bank.
    d. a good place to look for long term sources of funds.

2. An investment-banking firm underwrites a new issue of stocks and bonds by:

    a. buying the entire bond or stock issue a company wants to sell at an agreed discount.
    b. guaranteeing a minimum price in the market for a stock or bond.
    c. selling the entire bond issue for the issuing firm.
    d. putting up collateral for long term loans, such as bonds.

3. Which of the following is not considered an advantage of selling bonds?

    a. The debt is eventually eliminated when the bonds are paid off.
    b. Interest on the bonds is not a legal obligation.
    c. Bondholders have no say in running the firm.
    d. interest is tax deductible.

4. A _____ permits a bond issuer to pay off the bond's principal prior to its maturity date.

    a. sinking fund bond   c. callable bond
    b. convertible bond   d. collateral trust bond

5. Daddy Warbucks bought his daughter Annie some stock for her birthday. The type of stock Daddy bought has a fixed dividend, and if the dividend isn't paid when it is due, the missed dividend will accumulate and be paid later. Daddy bought Annie:

    a. common stock   c. convertible stock
    b. preferred stock   d. preemptive right stock

6. Which of the following would not be included in a list of the disadvantages of equity financing through stocks?

   a. Stockholders have the right to vote and so can alter the direction of the firm.
   b. Dividends are not tax deductible.
   c. Management's decisions can be affected by the need to keep stockholders happy.
   d. There is a legal obligation to pay dividends.

7. Which stock exchange is a network of several thousand brokers who maintain contact with one another and buy and sell securities through an electronic system of communication?

   a. NASDAQ   c. AMEX
   b. NYSE   d. Chicago exchange

8. When the International Ladies Investment Club is deciding on which stock to purchase, the Club will request a _____ before making that decision.

   a. insider report   c. prospectus
   b. income statement   d. disclosure statement

9. Linda Hutton is considering investing in the stock market. Linda wants to be sure to be able to get her money back whenever she wants. Linda is concerned with:

   a. growth.   c. tax consequences.
   b. yield.   d. liquidity.

10. One of the benefits of trading on-line is that:

    a. investing on-line is quicker.
    b. when you invest on-line you are more likely to make a good decision.
    c. on-line trading services are less expensive than regular stockbroker commissions.
    d. insider trading is less likely on-line.

11. The type of bond that has the least possible risk is:

    a. a convertible bond.　　c. a discount bond.
    b. a U.S. government bond.　d. a callable bond.

12. A bond that sells for more than face value is called a:

    a. premium bond.　　　c. discount bond.
    b. U.S. government bond.　d. callable bond.

13. Maria Chadwick is interested in investing in the stock of a corporation that pays regular dividends and generates consistent growth in the price of a share. Maria is interested in purchasing:

    a. growth stocks.　c. blue chip stocks.
    b. income stocks.　d. penny stocks.

14. When the price of a share of U.S. On Line went up to $150 per share, the company declared a 3 for 1 stock split. The price of a share of U.S. On Line stock is now:

    a. $100 per share.　c. $50 per share.
    b. $75 per share.　　d. $25 per share.

15. The benefit of a mutual fund for investors is that

    a. mutual funds help investors to diversify and invest in many different companies.
    b. an investor doesn't have to do as much research.
    c. mutual funds are less expensive than most individual shares of stock.
    d. mutual funds don't charge a commission or up-front fee.

16. Ed Marino wants to invest in the stock of U.S. On Line, and is considering buying 100 shares at $50 per share. The problem is, Ed only has about $3500 in his bank. Ed can still purchase the stock through

    a. selling short.
    b. buying convertible stock which is less expensive.
    c. waiting for a stock split.
    d. buying on margin.

17. If the paper reports the bond price as 89 ½ the price an investor would have to pay is:

    a. $890.50.
    b. $8950.
    c. $895.
    d. $89.50.

18. Which of the following is not included in a stock quote from the paper?

    a. The average price over the last 52 weeks
    b. The highest price in the last 52 weeks
    c. The price to earnings ratio
    d. The net change in price from the day before

19. The Dow Jones Industrial Average

    a. identifies recessions from the last 30 years.
    b. gives an indication of the ups and downs of the stock market over time.
    c. compiles average stock prices of all stocks on the NYSE.
    d. shows the average stock price of 20 stocks for the last year.

20. After the stock market crash of 1987, the stock exchanges have made an agreement to

    a. halt trading if the Dow Jones goes up too quickly.
    b. publish the average every day.
    c. halt trading if the Dow Jones Average drops by 20 percent.
    d. continue trading as long as the Dow Jones Average doesn't change by more than 15 percent.

TRUE/FALSE

1. ____ In the securities markets, the primary markets handle the sale of new securities.

2. ____ An institutional investor is a large investor who buys the entire bond or stock issues a company wants to sell.

3. ____ A company is legally bound to pay the interest on a bond, but not the principal amount.

4. ____ A sinking fund is a provision allowing for a company to pay off a bond prior to its maturity date.

5. ____ Dividends may be distributed as cash payments or additional shares of stock.

6. ____ One of the advantages of raising capital through selling stock is that the stockholder's investment never has to be repaid.

7. ____ Common stock normally does not include voting rights.

8. ____ The NASDAQ only deals with small firms that cannot qualify for listing on the New York or American exchanges.

9. ____ A stockbroker is a registered representative who acts as an intermediary to buy and sell stocks for clients.

10. ____ A young person saving for retirement can afford to invest in higher risk stocks than a person who is nearing retirement age.

11. ____ One of the disadvantages of a corporate bond is that if you buy it, you must hold it to the maturity date.

12. ____ "Bulls" are investors who believe that stock prices are going to rise, so they buy in anticipation of the increase.

13. ____ A market order tells a broker to buy or sell a particular stock at a specific price.

14. ____ Mutual funds are probably the best way for smaller investors to get started.

15. ____ Buying on margin allows an investor to borrow money from a brokerage firm.

16. ____ The P/E ratio compares the price of a share of stock to the firm's earnings per share.

ANSWERS

LEARNING THE LANGUAGE

1. Cumulative preferred stock	23. Preferred stock
2. Futures market	24. Investment bankers
3. Income stocks	25. Par value
4. Institutional investors	26. Interest
5. Over the counter market (OTC)	27. Debenture bonds
6. Stock certificate	28. Buying on margin
7. Blue chip stocks	29. Dividends
8. Program trading	30. Growth stocks
9. Preemptive right	31. Stock split
10. Common stock	32. Diversification
11. Sinking fund bond	33. Limit order
12. Insider trading	34. Stocks
13. Principal	35. Mutual fund
14. Round lot	36. Bond
15. Convertible bond	37. Dow Jones Industrial Average
16. Market order	38. Commodity exchange
17. Penny stock	39. Securities and Exchange Commission (SEC)
18. Junk bonds	40. Prospectus
19. Stockbroker	41. National Association of Securities Dealers
20. Callable bond	Automated Quotation System (NASDAQ)
21. Stock exchange	22. Maturity date

RETENTION CHECK

Learning Goal 1 **The Function of Securities Markets**

1. Two major functions of securities markets are to help businesses find long-term funding and to give investors a place to buy and sell investments such as stocks and bonds.

2. Businesses benefit from securities markets by obtaining the capital they need to finance operations, expand their businesses, or buy goods and services.

3. Individuals benefit from the securities markets by having a convenient place to build their financial future by buying and selling stocks, bonds, mutual funds, and other investments.

4. The primary market handles the sale of new securities. After the corporation has made their money on the sale of the securities, the secondary market handles the trading of securities between investors.

5. Investment bankers are specialists who assist in the issue and sale of new securities. They underwrite new issues, by buying the entire bond or stock issue a company wants to sell at an agreed upon discount and then selling the issue to private or institutional investors at full price.

Learning Goal 2 **Debt Financing Through Selling Bonds**

6. By issuing bonds a company has legal obligation to pay regular interest payments to investors and repay the entire bond principal amount at a prescribed time, called the maturity date.

7. The interest rate paid on bonds is also called the bond's coupon rate.

8. A "AAA" rated bond is one which has a very low risk, and is issued by the best firms.

9. A 10% bond with a maturity date of 2020 means that the bondholder will receive $100 in interest per year until the year 2020, when the full principal must be repaid.

10. a. Bondholders have no vote on corporate affairs, so the management maintains control over the firm.
    b. The interest paid on bonds is tax deductible for the firm.
    c. Bonds are a temporary source of funding. They are eventually repaid, and the debt is eliminated.

11. a. Bonds are an increase in debt and could adversely affect the firm.
    b. Interest on bonds is a legal obligation.
    c. The face value of bonds must be repaid at maturity, which could cause a cash shortage.

12. a. Unsecured bonds, called debentures
    b. Secured bonds

13. Debenture bonds, or unsecured bonds, are issued only by well-respected firms with excellent credit ratings since the only security the bondholder has is the reputation and credit history of the firm.

14. a. Mortgage bonds—backed by the company's land and buildings
    b. Collateral trust bonds—backed by the stock the company owns, which is held in trust by a commercial bank
    c. Equipment trust bonds—backed by the equipment the company owns.

15. a. They provide for an orderly retirement of a bond issue.
    b. They reduce the risk of not being repaid, and so make the bond more attractive as an investment.
    c. They can support the market price of a bond because of reduced risk.

16. Callable bonds give companies some direction in long-term forecasting. The callable bond permits the bond issuer to pay off the bond's principal before its maturity date. The company can benefit if they can call in a bond issue that pays a high rate of interest, and re-issue new bonds at a lower rate of interest.

17. If the firm's common stock grew in value over time, bondholders can compare the value of the bond's interest with the possibility of a sizable profit by converting to a specified number of common shares.

Learning Goal 3 **Equity Financing Through Selling Stock**

18. Interest on bonds is a legal obligation that the company must pay. It is a tax-deductible expense for the firm. Dividends are a part of a firm's profits that *may* be distributed to shareholders. Unlike bond interest, companies are not required to pay dividends.

19. a. Because stockholders are owners, they never have to be repaid.
    b. There is no legal obligation to pay dividends.
    c. Selling stock can improve the condition of the balance sheet.

20. a. As owners, stockholders can alter the direction of the firm, by voting for the board of directors.
    b. Dividends are paid out of after-tax profits.
    c. Management decision making can be hampered by the need to keep the stockholders happy.

21. a. Preferred stock
    b. common stock

22. Preferred stock dividends differ from common stock dividends in several ways. Preferred stock is generally issued with a par value that becomes the base for the dividend the firm is willing to pay. The owner is assured that the dividends on preferred stock must be paid in full before any common stock dividends can be distributed. Common stock dividends are declared by the board of directors, and may or may not be declared in any given quarter.

23. Both preferred stock and bonds have a face (or par) value, and both have a fixed rate of return. Preferred stocks are rated by Standard & Poor's and Moody's Investment Service just like bonds.

24. As debt, companies are legally bound to pay bond interest and must repay the face value of the bond on its maturity date. Even though preferred stock dividends are generally fixed, they do not legally have to be paid, and stock never has to be repurchased. Though both bonds and stock can increase in market value, the price of stock generally increases at a higher percentage than a bond.

25. Like bonds, preferred stock can be callable. This means a company could require preferred stockholders to sell back their shares. Preferred stock can also be convertible to common stock. An important feature of preferred stock is that it is often cumulative. If one or more dividends are not paid when due, the missed dividends of cumulative preferred stock will accumulate and be paid later.

26. The privileges of common stock include the right to vote for the board of directors and important issues affecting the company and to share in the firm's profits through dividends declared by the board of directors.

Learning Goal 4 **Stock Exchanges**

27. a. New York Stock Exchange (NYSE)
    b. American Stock Exchange (AMEX)
    c. Regional exchanges
    d. Over-the-counter (NASDAQ)

28. The over the counter market provides a means to trade stocks not listed on the national securities exchanges. The OTC market is a network of several thousand brokers who maintain contact with each other and buy and sell securities through a nationwide electronic system that communicates trades through the NASDAQ.

29. The New York Stock Exchange lists the largest companies, while the NASDAQ has the largest number of listings.

30. The Securities Act of 1933 protects investors by requiring full disclosure of financial information by firms selling new stocks or bonds.

31. The Securities and Exchange Act of 1934 created the Securities and Exchange Commission, which has the responsibility at the federal level for regulating activities in the various exchanges. Companies trading on the national exchange must register with the SEC and provide annual updates. The Securities and Exchange Act of 1934 also established guidelines to prevent insiders from taking advantage of privileged information.

32. Stockbrokers place an order with a stock exchange member who goes to the place at the exchange where the bond or stock is traded and negotiates a price. When the transaction is completed, the trade is reported to your broker who notifies you to confirm your purchase.

33. On-line trading services are less expensive than regular stockbroker commissions. On-line services are targeted primarily at investors who are willing to do their own research and make their own investment decisions without the assistance of a broker.

34. a. Investment risk
    b. Yield
    c. Duration
    d. Liquidity
    e. Tax consequences

Learning Goal 5 **Investing in Bonds**

35. U.S. government bonds have the least possible risk, because they are a secure investment backed by the full faith and credit of the federal government.

36. Two questions first time bond investors have are:
    a. "If I purchase a bond, do I have to hold it to the maturity date?" (The answer is no.)
    b. "How do I know how risky a particular bond issue is as an investment?" (Standard & Poor's and Moody's Investor Service rate the level of risk of many corporate and government bonds.)

Learning Goal 6 **Investing in Stocks and Mutual Funds**

37. According to investment analysts, the market price of a common stock is dependent upon the overall performance of the corporation in meeting its business objectives. If a company reaches its stated objectives, there are opportunities for capital gains.

38. Stock investors are called bulls when they believe that stock prices are going to rise, so they buy stock in anticipation of the increase. When overall stock prices are rising, it is called a bull market. Bears are investors who expect stock prices to decline. Bears sell their stocks before they expect prices to fall. When the prices of stocks decline steadily, it is referred to as a bear market.

39. a. Growth stocks, whose earnings are expected to grow at a rate faster than other stocks:
    b. Income stocks, which offer investors a high dividend yield on their investment.
    c. Blue chip stocks that pay regular dividends and generate consistent growth in the company stock price.
    d. Penny stocks, which sells for less than $1.

40. A market order tells a broker to buy or to sell a stock immediately at the best price available. A limit order tells the broker to buy or to sell a particular stock at a specific price if that price becomes available.

41. When investors cannot afford to buy shares of stock in companies selling for a high price, the company may choose to declare a stock split; that is, they issue two or more shares for every share of stock currently outstanding.

42. The benefit of a mutual fund to an investor is they can buy shares of the mutual fund and share in the ownership of many different companies they could not afford to invest in individually. Thus mutual funds help investors diversify and provide professional investment management.

43. A variety of mutual funds is available, ranging from very conservative funds that invest only in government securities or secure corporate bonds to others that specialize in emerging high-tech firms, foreign companies, precious metals, and other investments with greater risk. Some mutual funds even invest only in socially responsible companies.

44. A no-load fund is one that charges no commission to either buy or sell its shares. A load fund would charge a commission to investors.

45. An open-end fund will accept the investment of any interested investors. Closed-end funds offer a specific number of shares for investment. Once the fund reaches its target number, no new investors are admitted into the fund.

46. A portfolio strategy involves a strategy of buying several different investment alternatives to spread the risk of investing. By diversifying investments, the investor decreases the chance of losing everything.

Learning Goal 7   **Investing in High Risk Investments**

47. Standard & Poor's Investment Advisory Service and Moody's Investor Service consider junk bonds as non-investment grade bonds because of their high-risk and high default rates. Junk bonds rely on the firm's ability to pay investors interest. If the company can't pay off the bond, the investor is left with a bond that isn't worth more than the paper it's written on.

48. If a margin rate is 50 percent, an investor may borrow 50 percent of the stock's purchase price from a broker.

49. If an investor's account goes down in market value, the broker will issue a margin call, requiring the investor to come up with more money to cover the losses the stock has suffered. If the investor is unable to make the margin call, the broker can legally sell shares of the investor's stock to reduce the broker's chance of loss.

50. Items such as coffee, wheat, pork bellies, petroleum, and other commodities that are scheduled for delivery at a given date in time are traded on the commodities market. A commodity exchange specializes in the buying and selling of precious metals and minerals, and agricultural goods. Other commodities include corn, plywood, silver, gold, U.S. Treasury bonds, potatoes, cattle, and various foreign currencies.

Learning Goal 8 **Understanding Information From Securities Markets**

51. A bond price is quoted as a percentage of the face value.

52. A bond quote in the paper contains the name of the company issuing the bond, the interest rate, the maturity date, the price of the bond, the volume and the current yield.

53. a. highest and lowest price over the past 52 weeks:
    b. company name and stock symbol
    c. last dividend per share
    d. the dividend yield
    e. the P/E ratio
    f. the number of shares traded that day
    g. the high, low and closing price for the day
    h. the net change of the stock price

54. The fund's name, the net asset value, the sale price and the net change in the NAV

55. Critics of the Dow Jones Average argue that if the purpose of the Dow is to give an indication of the direction of the broader market over time, the 30-company sample is too small to get a good statistical representation. Many investors and market analysts prefer to follow stock indexes like the Standard & Poor's 500 that tracks the performance of many more companies.

56. On October 19, 1987 the stock market suffered the largest one-day drop in its history. The Dow Jones Industrial Average fell 508 points.

57. Many analysts believe that program trading was a big cause of the stock market drop in 1987. In program trading, investors give computers instructions to automatically sell if the price of their stock dips to a certain price to avoid potential losses.

58. The Dow fell in October 1997 primarily due to fears of impending economic problems in Asian markets. Analysts believe that the market could have fallen even further had it not been for the "circuit breakers" adopted after the crash of 1987.

59. Under market rules, if the market falls 350 points, the circuit breakers kick in and halt trading for a half-hour and give investors a chance to assess the situation. Since 1997, U.S. stock exchanges have agreed to halt trading for the day if the Dow Jones Industrial average drops 20 percent.

60. Lessons to be learned are the importance of diversifying your investments and understanding the risks of investing with borrowed money that may have to be repaid quickly when prices fall. It is also wise to take a long-term perspective.

CRITICAL THINKING EXERCISES

Learning Goal 1

1. The finance manager of Music-stor has the opportunity to avoid the difficulties of a new issue by making use of specialists in the securities markets such as investment bankers. These companies will underwrite the new issue, by purchasing the entire bond issue for a discount. The investment banker will then sell the issue on the open market to either private or institutional investors, such as pension funds, mutual funds, insurance companies, or banks.

2.
   a. Principal
   b. Maturity date
   c. Sinking fund
   d. Unsecured bond (debenture)
   e. Interest
   f. Bond
   g. Call provision
   h. Convertible bond
   i. Secured bond

3. a. Common stock
    b. Stock certificate
    c. Dividends
    d. Par value
    e. Preferred stock
    f. Pre-emptive right
    g. Cumulative preferred
    h. Stock

4. While both forms of stock represent ownership, there are several differences between preferred and common stock. First, an owner of common stock has the right to vote, and so can influence corporate policy. Judi probably did not consider this to be important, as Burke was a baby, and wouldn't really be concerned about such things! Further, common stock is considered to be more risky than preferred, because if a company closes, common stockholders share in assets only <u>after</u> bondholders and preferred stockholders. Also, while preferred dividends are fixed, and sometimes accumulate, common stock dividends will only be paid after both bondholders and preferred stockholders receive their interest and dividends. If Judi was interested in starting a "college fund" for Burke, then the preferred stock was a better match for her needs.

Learning Goal 4

5. The largest exchange in the United States is the New York Stock Exchange, NYSE. The NYSE, and the American Exchange, (AMEX) are called national exchanges because they handle stocks of companies from throughout the United States. They are both located in New York City.

    NASDAQ, or the over-the-counter market, is a network of several thousand stockbrokers who maintain contact with each other and buy and sell securities through a nationwide electronic system. The stocks traded on NASDAQ are not "listed" on the national securities exchanges

    While the NYSE handles most of the largest companies, the NASDAQ handles more companies than the NYSE. Originally, the over-the-counter market dealt mostly with small firms that could not qualify for listing on a national exchange, or did not want to bother with the procedures for listing. Now, many large and well-known firms prefer their stock to be traded over-the-counter.

6. The Securities and Exchange Commission regulates the securities market. Companies listed on the national exchanges must register with the SEC and provide regular updates. All firms selling stocks or bonds must fully disclose financial information to investors.

7. a. This couple would probably want a low to moderate risk investment, which will increase over time. Tax consequences will be minimal, at least at first, as the child will have little income in the early years.
(If they opt for an interest or dividend bearing type of account, the child will be earning income, and tax consequences may become a more important consideration). They will choose an investment that will yield a high return over the long run, and liquidity isn't important for now.
b. Since this investment may be for retirement, this couple will probably want a low risk investment, with as high an after-tax yield as they can earn. It will be of short duration, since they plan to retire in five years, and they may want to keep it fairly liquid in case they retire in less than five years. A big factor will be the tax consequences, as they are a two-income family, and are probably in a high tax bracket with few deductions.
c. A young, single person will choose a higher risk investment than the others, because they probably are not concerned with long-term considerations as retirement. Since they want to build capital, the yield will be important for the short term. This individual may want to keep investments of short duration to make a large return in a few years, when they may want the money as a down payment for a house, for example. Tax consequences can be important, as there are few deductions, and they may be in a relatively high bracket.

Learning Goals 6, 7

8. a. Stock split
   b. Penny stocks
   c. Stockbroker
   d. Round lot
   e. Buying on margin
   f. Blue chip
   g. Market order
   h. Bull
   i. Limit order
   j. Margin call
   k. Mutual fund
   l. Income stock
   m. Prospectus
   n. Bear
   o. Diversification
   p. Growth stock

9. Hedging in the commodities market means buying or selling goods for delivery sometime in the future, i.e. in the futures market. This allows farmers, like Jordan, to fix a price for their crops, aids in planning. It allows buyers, like General Mills, to fix a price so that they may also plan. It prevents the risk of being caught by a price increase, and gives businesses a form of price insurance that enables them to continue business without worrying about fluctuations in commodity prices.

10. Your answers for each section will vary according to which companies you choose to study, and when you are studying this chapter. As for the Dow Jones Industrial Averages, stock prices trended upward in the mid-1990s and the average broke 9000 for the first time in early 1998. Stock prices quickly recovered from the drop in October 1997.

PRACTICE TEST

Multiple Choice				True/False			
1.	b	11.	b	1.	T	9.	T
2.	a	12.	a	2.	F	10.	T
3.	b	13.	c	3.	F	11.	F
4.	c	14.	c	4.	F	12.	T
5.	b	15.	a	5.	T	13.	F
6.	d	16.	d	6.	T	14.	T
7.	a	17.	c	7.	F	15.	T
8.	c	18.	a	8.	F	16.	T
9.	d	19.	b				
10.	c	20.	c				

CHAPTER 21
UNDERSTANDING MONEY AND FINANCIAL INSTITUTIONS

LEARNING GOALS

After you have read and studied this chapter, you should be able to:

1. Explain what money is and how its value is determined.
2. Describe how the Federal Reserve controls the money supply.
3. Trace the history of banking and the Federal Reserve System.
4. Classify the various institutions in the American banking system.
5. Explain the importance of the Federal Deposit Insurance Corporation and other organizations that guarantee funds.
6. Weigh the future of the banking system.
7. Evaluate the role and importance of international banking and the role of the World Bank and the International Monetary Fund.

LEARNING THE LANGUAGE

Listed below are important terms found in the chapter. Choose the correct term for the definition and write it in the space provided.

Automated teller machines	M-1
Banker's acceptance	M-2
Commercial and consumer finance companies	Money
Commercial bank	Money supply
Credit unions	Nonbanks
Currency	Open-market operations
Currency exchange	Pension funds
Demand deposit	Reserve requirement
Discount rate	Rising dollar
Electronic funds transfer system (EFTS)	Savings and Loan Association
Falling dollar	Savings Association Insurance Fund (SAIF)
Federal Deposit Insurance Corporation (FDIC)	Stagflation
International Monetary Fund (IMF)	Time deposit
Letter of credit	World Bank

1. Non-profit, member owned financial cooperatives called _____ offer basic services such as accepting deposits and making loans to their members.

2. With a _____ the value of the dollar changes such that the amount of goods and services you can buy with a dollar goes down.

3. The _____ is a percentage of member-bank funds checking and savings accounts that must be deposited in the Federal Reserve System.

4. Institutions called _____ offer short-term loans to businesses or individuals who either can't meet the credit requirements of regular banks or else have exceeded their credit limit and need more funds.

5. The technical name for a savings account for which the bank requires prior notice before withdrawal is called a _____.

6. A _____ is a promise that the bank will pay some specified amount at a particular time.

7. _____ is what people generally accept as payment for goods and services.

8. The interest rate the Fed charges for loans to member banks is the _____.

9. Financial organizations known as _____ accept no deposits, but offer many of the services provided by regular banks.

10. A _____ is when the value of the dollar changes such that the amount of goods and services you can buy with a dollar goes up.

11. A computerized system known as _____ electronically performs financial transactions such as making purchases, paying bills, and receiving paychecks.

12. The part of the FDIC that insures holders of accounts in savings and loan associations is called the _____.

13. All coin and paper money issued by the Federal Reserve banks and all gold coins is known as _____.

14. The _____ is the exchange of currency from one country with currency from another country.

15. A financial institution called a _____ accepts both savings and checking deposits and provides home mortgage loans.

16. The _____ is the sum of all the funds that the public has immediately available to buy goods and services.

17. A _____ is a promise by a bank that a given amount will be paid if certain conditions are met.

18. _____ are designated by corporations, nonprofit organizations, or unions to cover part of the financial needs of members when they retire.

19. A profit-making organization that receives deposits from individuals and corporations in the form of checking and savings accounts and uses some of these funds to make loans is called a _____.

20. The _____ is an independent agency of the U.S. government that insures bank deposits.

21. The buying and selling of U.S. government securities by the Fed is called _____ and has the goal of regulating the money supply.

22. _____ includes everything in M-1 plus money in savings accounts, money in money market accounts, mutual funds and certificates of deposit.

23. The technical name for a checking account is a _____, in which money can be withdrawn on demand at any time by the owner.

24. The _____ assists the smooth flow of money among nations.

25. A period of both slow growth and inflation is called _____.

26. The _____ is also known as the International Bank for Reconstruction and Development, and is primarily responsible for financing economic development.

27. Money that is quickly and easily raised, such as currency, checks, traveler's checks, is called the _____ money supply.

28. Machines called _____ give customers the convenience of 24 hour banking at a variety of outlets.

RETENTION CHECK

Learning Goal 1   **The Importance of Money**

1. What is money?

2. What is "barter?"

3. What is a problem with the barter system when compared to money?

4. What are five characteristics of "useful" money?

   a. _____   d. _____

   b. _____   e. _____

   c. _____

5. What is the difference between M-1 and M-2?

6. What is meant by "too much money chasing too few goods?"

7. What would happen if too much money were taken out of the economy?

8. What does a "falling dollar" mean for prices of Japanese goods?

9. What does a "rising dollar" mean for the prices of Japanese goods?

10. What makes our dollar "weak" or "strong"?

Learning Goal 2   **Control of the Money Supply**

11. What organization is in charge of monetary policy?

12. What are the five major parts of the Federal Reserve System?

   a. _____

   b. _____

   c. _____

   d. _____

   e. _____

13. What does the Board of Governors do?

14. Describe the Federal Open Market Committee.

15. What are some activities of the Federal Reserve?

   a. _____

   b. _____

   c. _____

   d. _____

   e. _____

   f. _____

   g. _____

16. List three ways the Federal Reserve uses to control the money supply.

   a. _____

   b. _____

   c. _____

17. Which tool is the most powerful?

18. What is the result of an increase in the reserve requirement?

19. What is the result of a decrease in the reserve requirement?

20. What is the Fed's most commonly used tool?

21. Regarding selling U.S. securities, what does the Fed do to increase or decrease the money supply?

22. Why is the Fed often called the banker's bank?

23. What is the impact of raising the discount rate?

24. What is the impact of lowering the discount rate?

Learning Goal 3 **The Development of the Federal Reserve System**

25. Why did continental currency become worthless?

26. Why were land banks established?

27. What was the first version of a federal bank?

28. Why were coins hoarded during the Civil War?

29. What happened in 1907 in the banking industry?

30. What did the Federal Reserve Act of 1913 require?

31. What led to the bank failures of the 1930's?

32. Why did the government start an insurance program?

33. Why would businesses become concerned about higher interest rates?

Learning Goal 4   The American Banking System

34. Identify three types of banking institutions.

    a. _____

    b. _____

    c. _____

35. What are two types of customers for commercial banks?

    a. _____

    b. _____

36. How does a commercial bank make a profit?

37. What are NOW and Super NOW accounts?

38. Describe a certificate of deposit.

39. Identify 12 services offered by commercial banks

a. _____   g. _____

b. _____   h. _____

c. _____   i. _____

d. _____   j. _____

e. _____   k. _____

f. _____   l. _____

40. What are two kinds of business loans offered by commercial banks?

a. _____

b. _____

41. What is a line of credit and why would a business want one?

42. What is collateral?

43. What is another name for savings and loans institutions, and why are they known as such?

44. What did the federal government allow savings and loans to do between 1979 and 1983?

   a. _____

   b. _____

   c. _____

45. What services do credit unions offer their members?

46. What are five nonbanking institutions?

   a. _____   d. _____

   b. _____   e. _____

   c. _____

47. How have brokerage firms begun to compete with regular banks?

48. Who are a finance company's primary customers?

Learning Goal 5 **How the Government Protects Your Funds**

49. List the three major sources of financial protection.

   a. _____

   b. _____

   c. _____

50. What does the FDIC do in the case of a bank failure?

51. Why were the FDIC and the FSLIC created?

52. What was the RTC?

53. What does the NCUA provide for?

Learning Goal 6 How the Government Protects Your Funds

54. What will determine the future of banks and savings and loans?

55. What are 2 major trends in banking?

56. How have the mergers in the banking industry changed banks?

57. What services are banks offering beyond regular banking?

58. What are "smart cards"?

59. What kinds of services will soon be available through on-line banking?

Learning Goal 7 **International Banking and Banking Services**

60. What three services are offered to banks to help businesses conduct business overseas?

61. How do banks make things easier for tourists?

62. What could be the international impact of the Federal Reserve System changing interest rates?

63. What has been the net result of international banking and finance?

64. What must the United States do to be a "winning player" internationally?

65. What is the World Bank responsible for?

66. What does the International Monetary fund require?

67. What does the IMF oversee?

68. Describe what happened in the late 1990s in Thailand and the impact on other Asian countries.

69. How will U.S. businesses suffer from the banking problems in Asia?

70. What is the year 2000 problem?

CRITICAL THINKING EXERCISES

Learning Goals 1, 2

1. What is the importance of the stability of money, and controlling the money supply in the international marketplace today?

2. Music-stor has made it big! Congratulations! The company has done so well here in the U.S. that management is seriously considering expanding into overseas markets. It is your job to research the idea, and you want to begin by helping other top managers understand some of the considerations of "going global." Within the context of the "value" of money, what are some of the issues you will want to bring up to your managers? What might be two "non-money" issues that would be important?

3. The Fed uses three major tools to control the money supply:

    a. Reserve requirement.

    b. Open market operations.

    c. Discount rate.

Complete the following chart illustrating how each tool is used, and its effect on the money supply and the economy:

TOOL	ACTION	EFFECT ON MONEY SUPPLY	EFFECT ON ECONOMY
Reserve requirement	Increase reserve requirement	_____	_____
	Decrease reserve requirement	_____	_____
Open market Operations	Buy government securities	_____	_____
	Sell government securities	_____	_____
Discount rate	Increase discount rate	_____	_____
	Decrease discount rate	_____	_____

Learning Goals 2, 3. 4

4. When the Fed regulates the money supply using one of the three tools just mentioned, what happens to interest rates overall? Where does stagflation fit in?

Learning Goal 4

5. The American banking system has a long history. List the major events that led up to the establishment of the Federal Reserve System, and subsequent events that have affected the American banking system.

   a. _____

   b. _____

   c. _____

d. _____

e. _____

f. _____

g. _____

h. _____

i. _____

j. _____

k. _____

l. _____

6. The American banking system consists of three types of organizations:

   a. Commercial banks.

   b. Savings and loans associations.

   c. Credit unions.

   Match each of the following descriptions to the correct type of institution:

   a. Offers interest-bearing checking accounts called share draft accounts at relatively high rates. _____

   b. Also known as thrift institutions. _____

   c. Offer a wide variety of services, to depositors and borrowers, including ATMs, credit cards, short and long term loans, financial counseling and tax deferred individual retirement accounts. _____

d. Have been able to offer NOW and Super NOW accounts since 1981. _____

e. As a result of changes in the banking industry, these have become similar to commercial banks, but are governed by different rules. _____

f. Since they are member owned and non-profit, they are exempt from federal income taxes. _____

7   a. What is the difference between demand deposit and a time deposit?

    b. What are three kinds of checking accounts, and what is the difference between them?

       1.

       2.

       3.

    c. What are two kinds of savings accounts offered by commercial banks, and how are they different?

       1.

       2.

8. What changes in the banking industry have made savings and loans more like commercial banks and why were the changes necessary? What happened in the 1980s to savings and loans?

9. How are credit unions different from commercial banks and S&Ls?

10. Describe how nonbanks are becoming an important financial force, and how they compete with traditional banking institutions.

Learning Goal 5

11. A. How does the FDIC protect your money?

   B. What is the difference between the FSLIC and SAIF, and why was SAIF created?

Learning Goal 6

12. Compare what you have learned in earlier chapters about the trends in businesses to become more efficient and competitive to the trends in the U.S. banking industry. Why are these changes necessary?

13. In previous chapters, we have discussed the global nature of the marketplace, and the need for U.S. businesses to become and stay more competitive. How does what we have learned in those chapters about U.S. business relate to international banking and the U.S. banking industry?

14. How does the state of Asian banks today parallel the failure of savings and loans in the United States during the 1980? How does that affect the United States?

PRACTICE TEST

Multiple Choice: Circle the best answer.

1. When eggs are used to buy admission to a movie, and sausages used to pay for electric power, a _____ system is being used.

    a. barter
    b. direct marketing
    c. monetary policy
    d. inflation

2. Which of the following would not be included in a list of characteristics of money?

    a. Portability
    b. Divisibility
    c. Stability
    d. Usability

3. When the price of a European coffee maker becomes less expensive to buy here in the United States, you could say that we are experiencing a:

    a. falling dollar.
    b. inflated dollar.
    c. rising dollar.
    d. stable dollar.

4. Which of the following is not one of the functions of the Federal Reserve?

    a. Buying and selling foreign currency
    b. Supervising banks
    c. Lending money to member banks
    d. Setting inflation rates

5. When the Fed increases the reserve requirement:

    a. interest rates will go down.
    b. banks will have more money to lend.
    c. inflation could go up.
    d. banks have less money to lend.

6. The discount rate is the rate:

   a. banks charge their best customers.
   b. the Fed charges for loans to member banks.
   c. the Fed charges for selling bonds.
   d. the amount of money member banks must keep on hand at the Fed.

7. The bank failures of 1907 and the resulting cash shortage problems led to the creation of:

   a. the Federal Reserve System.
   b. the gold standard.
   c. monetary policy.
   d. the money supply.

8. After the stock market crash of 1929, and the resulting bank failures of that time, Congress passed legislation creating:

   a. laws which prevented banks from failing.
   b. the Federal Reserve System.
   c. federal deposit insurance.
   d. nonbanks.

9. The technical name for a checking account is a:

   a. demand deposit.
   b. time deposit.
   c. certificate of deposit.
   d. deposit insurance.

10. The difference between a NOW account and a savings account is that:

    a. a NOW account doesn't pay interest, and a savings account does.
    b. a NOW account has a maturity date, but a savings account does not.
    c. you can't withdraw money from a NOW account until the maturity date, but you can withdraw from a savings account any time.
    d. you can write checks on a NOW account, but not on a savings account.

11. Competition between banks and nonbanks, such as insurance companies and pension funds, has:

    a. decreased with the deregulation of the banking industry.
    b. not changed in 50 years, since the creation of the Federal Reserve System.
    c. increased significantly as nonbanks offer many of the services provided by regular banks.
    d. stabilized with the bull stock market of the late 1990s.

12. The Federal Deposit Insurance Corporation insures accounts up to:

    a. $10,000.
    b. $50,000.
    c. $100,000.
    d. $500,000.

13. Funds in savings and loan institutions are protected by the:

    a. Federal Deposit Insurance Corporation (FDIC).
    b. National Credit Union Association (NCUA).
    c. Resolution Trust Corporation (RTC).
    d. Savings Association Insurance Fund (SAIF).

14. Recent banking trends include all but which of the following?

    a. Closures and foreclosures
    b. Offering insurance
    c. Mergers and acquisitions between all size banks
    d. Offering the sale of stocks and bonds

15. Smart cards:

    a. are a new credit card offered by nonbanks.
    b. allow you to buy airplane tickets at the gate simply by using a special reading device.
    c. allow customers to buy goods and services on-line.
    d. allow for electronic banking.

16. Which of the following is not a way banks help businesses conduct business overseas?

    a. Guarantee a certain exchange rate.
    b. Offer letters of credit.
    c. Banker's acceptance.
    d. Currency exchange.

17. The organization which is responsible for financing economic development is the:

    a. Federal Reserve Bank.
    b. International Monetary Fund.
    c. World Bank.
    d. Bank of the Americas.

18. The net result of the banking problems in Asia include all of the following except:

    a. U.S producers could have trouble selling their goods in Asia.
    b. Some U.S. banks could suffer.
    c. Asian countries will sell their goods to the U.S. at reduced prices.
    d. U.S. banks will be able to expand into the Asian market.

TRUE/FALSE

1. _____ The banking system is expected to become more complex as the flow of money from one country to another becomes freer.

2. _____ The definition of M-2 money supply includes currency, money that is available for writing checks and money that is held in travelers' checks.

3. _____ If there is too much money in the economy, prices would go up because people would bid up the prices of goods and services.

4. _____ An increase in the discount rate would encourage businesses to borrow money and thus stimulate the economy.

5. _____ The most commonly used tool by the Fed is open market operations.

6. _____ Continental currency, the first paper money printed in the United States, became very valuable over the years as the first form of money used in the U.S.

7. _____ Stagflation is a situation of slow economic growth combined with inflation.

8. _____ Commercial banks have two types of customers—borrowers and lenders.

9. _____ Unlike a NOW account, a certificate of deposit has a maturity date, and that is when interest is paid.

10. _____ Commercial banks are offering a wider variety of services, such as brokerage services, financial counseling, automatic payment of bills and IRAs.

11. _____ The only type of institution in which funds are protected by the U.S. government is a commercial bank.

12. _____ The U.S. financial community and the U.S. economy appear to be in the best shape in years.

13. _____ Most banks are resisting going to banking on-line.

14. _____ The latest technology makes it safer to do electronic banking than giving your credit card to a retailer.

15. _____ The result of international banking has been to link the economies of the world into one interrelated system with no regulatory control.

ANSWERS

LEARNING THE LANGUAGE

1. Credit unions	15. Savings and Loan Association
2. Falling dollar	16. Money supply
3. Reserve requirement	17. Letter of credit
4. Commercial/consumer finance companies	18. Pension funds
5. Time deposit	19. Commercial bank
6. Banker's acceptance	20. Federal Deposit Insurance Corporation (FDIC)
7. Money	21. Open-market operations
8. Discount rate	22. M-2
9. Nonbanks	23. Demand deposit
10. Rising dollar	24. International Monetary Fund (IMF)
11. Electronic Funds Transfer System (EFTS)	25. Stagflation
12. Savings Association Insurance Fund (SAIF)	26. World Bank
13. Currency	27. M-1
14. Currency exchange	28. Automatic Teller Machines

RETENTION CHECK

Learning Goal 1   **The Importance of Money**

1. Money is anything that people generally accept as payment for goods and services. Objects as diverse as salt, feathers, stones, rare shells, tea and horses have been used as money.

2. Barter is the trading of goods and services for other goods and services directly.

3. The problem with barter is that the goods used may be difficult to carry around. People need an object that's more portable, divisible, durable and stable so that they can trade goods and services without actually carrying the goods around with them.

4.
   a. Portability
   b. Divisibility
   c. Stability
   d. Durability
   e. Difficult to counterfeit

5. M-1 includes coins and paper bills, money that is available by writing checks and money that is held in traveler's checks, or, money that is easily available to pay for goods and services. M-2 includes all of that, but adds in money held in savings accounts and other forms of savings that is not as readily available.

6. "Too much money chasing too few goods" means that more people try to buy goods and services with their money and bid up the price to get what they want. That is called inflation.

7. If too much money were taken out of the economy prices would go down because there would be an oversupply of goods and services compared to the money available to buy them.

8. A falling dollar means that the amount of goods and service you can buy with a dollar goes down. When the dollar is falling, the price of a Japanese good will go up, because it takes more dollars to buy that good compared to the Japanese yen.

9. A rising dollar means that the amount of goods and services you can buy with a dollar goes up. Thus the price you pay for a Japanese good today is lower than a few years ago because of the rising dollar relative to the Japanese yen.

10. What makes a dollar weak or strong (falling or rising dollar) is the position of the U.S. economy relative to other economies. When the economy is strong, people want to buy dollars and the value of the dollar rises. When the economy is perceived as weakening, people no longer want dollars and the value of the dollar falls. The value of a dollar depends upon a strong economy.

Learning Goal 2   **Control of the Money Supply**

11. The Federal Reserve System (the Fed) is in charge of monetary policy. The head of the Fed (Alan Greenspan in 1998) is one of the most influential people in the world because he controls the money that much of the world depends on for trade.

12. The Federal Reserve System consists of:
    a. The board of governors.
    b. The Federal Open Market Operations.
    c. 12 Federal Reserve Banks.
    d. Three advisory councils.
    e. The member banks of the system.

13. The board of governors administers and supervises the 12 Federal Reserve System banks. Seven members are appointed by the President and confirmed by the Senate.

14. The Federal Open Market Committee has 12 voting members and is the policy-making body. The committee is made up of the seven board of governors plus the president of the New York Reserve Bank. Four others rotate in from the other Reserve Banks. The advisory councils offer suggestions to the board and the FOMC. The councils represent the various banking districts, consumers, and member institutions, including banks, S&Ls and credit unions.

15. The Federal Reserve:
    a. buys and sells foreign currencies.
    b. regulates various types of credit.
    c. supervises banks.
    d. collects data on the money supply and other economic activities.
    e. lends money to member banks.
    f. sets the rate charged for such loans.
    g. buys and sells government securities.

16. a. Reserve requirements
    b. Open-market operations
    c. The discount rate

17. The most powerful tool the Fed has to regulate the money supply is the reserve requirement.

18. When the Fed increases the reserve requirement, banks have less money to loan, and money becomes scarce. In the long run, this tends to reduce inflation. It is so powerful because of the amount of money affected when the reserve is changed.

19. A decrease in the reserve requirement increases the funds available to banks for loans, so banks make more loans, and money becomes more readily available. An increase in the money supply stimulates the economy to achieve higher growth rates but can also create inflationary pressures.

20. Open market operations are the Fed's most commonly used tool.

21. To decrease the money supply, the federal government sells U.S. government securities to the public. The money it gets as payment is taken out of circulation, decreasing the money supply. If the Fed wants to increase the money supply, it buys government securities from individuals, corporations, or organizations that are willing to sell.

22. One reason the Fed is called the banker's bank is that member banks can borrow money from the Fed and then pass it on to their customers as loans. The discount rate is the interest rate that the Fed charges for loans to member banks.

23. An increase in the discount rate by the Fed discourages banks from borrowing and consequently reduces the number of available loans, resulting in a decrease in the money supply.

24. Lowering the discount rate encourages member bank borrowing and increases the funds available for loans, which increases the money supply.

Learning Goal 3 **The Development of the Federal Reserve System**

25. Continental currency became worthless after a few years because people didn't trust its value.

26. Land banks were established to lend money to farmers.

27. In 1781, Alexander Hamilton persuaded Congress to form a central bank. It was the first version of a federal bank, but closed in 1811. It was replaced in 1816 because state chartered banks couldn't support the War of 1812.

28. During the Civil War, coins were hoarded because they were worth more as gold and silver than as coins.

29. Many banks failed in 1907. People got nervous about their money and went to the bank to withdraw their funds. Shortly after, the cash ran out and some banks had to refuse money to depositors. The cash shortage problems of 1907 led to the formation of an organization that could lend money to banks – the Federal Reserve System.

30. Under the Federal Reserve Act of 1913, all federally chartered banks had to join the Federal Reserve. State banks could also join.

31. The stock market crash of 1929 led to bank failures in the early 1930s. The stock market began tumbling, and people ran to the bank to get their money out. In spite of the Federal Reserve, banks ran out of money, and states were forced to close banks.

32. In 1933 and 1935 Congress passed legislation to strengthen the banking system, to further protect us from bank failures.

33. Businesses are concerned with higher interest rates because higher rates mean a higher cost of borrowing money. If businesses stop borrowing, then business growth slows, people are fired, and the whole economy stagnates. It is possible to have both slow growth and inflation. That situation is called stagflation.

Learning Goal 4 **The American Banking System**

34. a. Commercial banks
     b. Savings and loan associations
     c. Credit unions

35. a. Depositors
    b. Borrowers

36. A commercial bank uses customer deposits as inputs, on which it pays interest, and invests that money in interest-bearing loans to other customers, mostly businesses. Commercial banks make a profit if the revenue generated by loans exceeds the interest paid to depositors plus all other operating expenses.

37. A NOW account typically pays an annual interest rate but usually requires depositors always to maintain a certain minimum balance in the account. A Super NOW account pays a higher interest to attract larger deposits. However Super NOW accounts require a larger minimum balance. They sometimes offer free, unlimited check-writing privileges.

38. A certificate of deposit is a time deposit, or savings account that earns interest delivered at the end of the certificate's maturity date. The depositor agrees not to withdraw any of the funds in the account until the end of the specified period.

39. a. Checking accounts   g. Automatic bill paying
    b. Savings accounts   h. Safe deposit boxes
    c. ATMs   i. IRAs
    d. Credit cards   j. Traveler's checks
    e. Brokerage services   k. Overdraft protection
    f. Financial counseling l. Loans

40. a. Short-term loans, to be repaid within one year.
    b. Long-term loans, which are payable for a period greater than one year, typically 2 to 5 years. They can be extended for as long as 20 years.

41. Many businesses borrow on a short-term basis to get urgently needed cash for items such as seasonal inventory. Businesses find it useful to establish a line of credit before they actually need money. This involves getting approval for a specified loan amount beforehand, so the firm can immediately borrow the money whenever it's needed.

42. Collateral is some object of value, such as a home or stock, that may be sold if the loan is not paid any other way.

43. S&L's are often known as thrift institutions since their original purpose was to promote consumer thrift, or saving, and home ownership.

44. Between 1979 and 1983 many savings and loan institutions failed. Faced with this, the government permitted S&Ls:
    a. to offer NOW and Super NOW accounts.
    b. to allocate up to 10 percent of their funds to commercial loans.
    c. to offer mortgage loans with adjustable interest rates based on market conditions.

45. Credit unions offer their members interest-bearing checking accounts at relatively high rates, short-term loans at relatively low rates, financial counseling, life insurance and a limited number of home mortgage loans.

46. a. Life insurance companies
    b. Pension funds
    c. Brokerage firms
    d. Commercial finance companies
    e. Corporate financial services

47. Brokerage houses have made inroads into regular banking business by offering high-yield combination savings and checking accounts. In addition, brokerage firms offer checking privileges on accounts. In addition, investors can get loans from their broker, using their securities as collateral.

48. The primary customers of commercial and consumer finance companies are new businesses and individuals with no credit history. College students often turn to finance companies for loans to pay for their education.

Learning Goal 5 **How the Government Protects Your Funds**

49. a. Federal Deposit Insurance Corporation (FDIC)
    b. Savings Association Insurance Fund (SAIF)
    c. National Credit Union Administration (NCUA)

50. If a bank were to fail, the FDIC would arrange to have its accounts transferred to another bank or pay off depositors up to a certain amount. If one of the top ten banks in the United States would fail, the FDIC has a contingency plan to nationalize the bank so that it wouldn't fail.

51. The FDIC and the FSLIC were started during the Great Depression. Many banks and thrifts failed during those years, and people were losing confidence in them. The FDIC and FSLIC were designed to create more confidence in banking institutions.

52. The Resolution Trust Corporation was created by the government to sell the real estate of failed savings and loan institutions. The money from these sales went to pay back the money the government lost from the S&L crisis.

53. The NCUA provides up to $100,000 coverage per individual depositor per institution. The coverage includes all accounts, and additional protection can be obtained by holding accounts jointly or in trust.

Learning Goal 6 **How the Government Protects Your Funds**

54. The future of banks and savings and loans lies in decisions made by the Federal Reserve through monetary policy, and in the overall strength of the U.S. and world economies.

55. Two major trends in banking are interstate banking and expansion of services.

56. Mergers in the banking industry may strengthen banks, as they become more efficient. However there is a counter trend toward the opening of community banks that are more user friendly and convenient than the megabanks currently being created through mergers.

57. In some states, banks can engage in brokerage and underwriting, insurance, securities and real estate.

58. Smart cards may be the currency of the future. They are an advanced version of the cards used in electronic transfer system. With such cards you can buy airline tickets right at the gate, rent a car the same way, pay for a hotel and more.

59. With on-line banking, you will be able to obtain information on every aspect of your personal finances. You can pay bills on line as well as use other services.

Learning Goal 7 **International Banking and Banking Services**

60. Banks help businesses conduct business overseas by providing letters of credit, banker's acceptances, and currency exchange.

61. Banks are making it easier for tourists to buy goods and services through automatic teller machines offering foreign currencies. You can often get a better exchange rate with an ATM than from your hotel.

62. If the Federal Reserve decides to lower interest rates, foreign investors can withdraw their money from the United States in minutes and put it in countries with higher rates.

63. The net result of international banking and finance has been to link the economies of the world into one interrelated system with no regulatory control. American firms must compete for funds with firms all over the world.

64. A world economy has evolved, financed by international banks. The United States is one player in the game. To be a winning player, America must stay financially secure and its businesses must stay competitive in world markets.

65. The World Bank is primarily responsible for financing economic development.

66. The International Monetary fund was established to assist the smooth flow of money among nations. It requires members to allow their currency to be exchanged for foreign currencies freely, to keep the IMF informed about changes in monetary policy, and to modify those policies on the advice of the IMF to accommodate the needs of the entire membership.

67. The IMF is an overseer of member countries' monetary and exchange rate policies. The IMF's goal is to maintain a global monetary system that works best for all nations.

68. The Thai economy began to slow in 1997, and people began to sell the baht. The Thai central bank spent all of its reserves trying to keep the value of the baht up. It didn't succeed and Thailand soon owed other countries billions of dollars. Its currency was worth less than half what it was earlier and the stock market fell over 35 percent by the end of 1997.

    The situation spread across Asia, and the value of currencies in other countries dropped as well, along with the Asian stock markets.

69. Asian countries are desperate for U.S. dollars, and intend to sell their products to the U.S. at greatly reduced prices. This is good for consumers, but not so good for companies that compete against Asian companies. In addition, U.S. producers will have trouble selling goods and services in Asia because the people have less money to buy.

70. The year 2000 problem is a computer problem that will occur when the decade changes to the year 2000. The computers will read 1900, and may simply be unable to work. This includes all computers of the Federal Reserve. Further, the computers may miscalculate numbers, mortgage payments and stock prices.

CRITICAL THINKING EXERCISES

1. The stability of the value of money in the global marketplace is important because if the value is not stable, other countries will not accept that money in trade. In other words, if the marketplace believes your money will not be valuable to use, the market will not accept your money as payment for what you want to buy.

    The money supply needs to be controlled in order to control prices, and in part, the American economy. If there is too much money in the economy, prices of goods and services will increase, because demand will be greater than supply. If there is less money, people will not be spending at the same rate, demand correspondingly goes down, and prices will go down. That could result in an oversupply of goods and services, and possibly a recession. What makes a dollar weak or strong is the position of the U.S. economy relative to other economies. When the economy is strong, people want to buy dollars and the value of the dollar rises. The value of the dollar depends on a strong economy.

2. Some of the "money" issues Music-stor will need to research relate to how strong the American dollar is compared to the currency of the countries in which Music-stor is interested. If our dollar is weak in comparison to the British pound, the Japanese yen, or others, Music-stor could be very affordable for their target market. If our dollar is strong, the price of Music-stor could be too high for some. Further, we would want to know what the forecast might be for the future of the U.S. economy. Is our economy expected to be strong? What are the forecasts for recession, inflation, and income growth, both here and in our target countries?

Some of the "non-money" issues revolve around: the target market, whether or not it is common to listen to tapes and c.d.'s in the car in other countries, how many cars are equipped with tape and c.d. players, whether or not our product is adaptable to the interior design of other models, how big the car market is, growth projections for the car market, etc.

3.

Tool	Action	Effect on Money supply	Effect on Economy
Reserve Requirement	Increase	Decrease	Slows down
	Decrease	Increase	Stimulated
Open market operations	Buy securities	Increase	Stimulated
	Sell securities	Decrease	Slows down
Discount rate	Increase	Decrease	Slows down
	Decrease	Increase	Stimulated

Learning Goals 2, 3, 4

4. When the Fed takes action to increase the money supply (either by decreasing the reserve rate, decreasing the discount rate or buying government bonds), interest rates will go down. Think of <u>interest</u> as the <u>price</u> of money. When the supply goes up, the price will generally go down. Correspondingly, if interest rates have declined, demand for goods and services could go up, the economy begins to grow, and inflation may begin to heat up. The opposite effect occurs when the Fed reduces the money supply. Interest rates will rise, which will slow demand for goods and services, which slows economic growth. Inflation will also then slow down, as supply begins to equal or exceed demand, and prices will stabilize.

Stagflation occurs when economic growth has slowed, but there is a high rate of inflation.

Learning Goal 4

5.   a. Paper money established in 1690.
        b. Land banks established to lend money to farmers.
        c. Central bank established in 1781.
        d. Central bank closed in 1811.
        e. Second central bank established in 1816 to support War of 1812.
        f. Division between state banks and central bank.
        g. Central bank closed in 1836.
        h. Civil War - banks issuing their own currency.
        i. Cash shortage problems in 1907; banks began to fail.
        j. Federal Reserve System established in 1913 to lend money to banks.
        k. Stock market crash of 1929 and subsequent bank failures in 1930s.
        l. Legislation passed to strengthen banking system, establishing federal deposit insurance in 1933 and 1935.

6.   a. Credit unions
        b. Savings and loan association
        c. Commercial banks
        d. Savings and loan association
        e. Savings and loan association
        f. Credit union

7.   a. Demand deposits are the technical name for checking accounts. They have this name because the money is available upon demand from the depositor. Time deposits are the technical name for savings accounts, so called because the bank can require a prior notice before withdrawal of funds from the account.
        b. 1. Non-interest bearing checking accounts
           2. NOW accounts, which pay an annual interest rate and require depositors to maintain a minimum balance at all times. The number of checks that can be written is restricted.
           3. A Super NOW account pays higher interest than a NOW account. They require a larger minimum balance than regular NOW accounts, and typically offer free and unlimited check-writing privileges.
        c. 1. Passbook savings accounts, with which the depositor has no checking privileges, and can withdraw money at any time.
           2. Certificates of deposit earn an interest rate that's delivered at the end of the certificate's maturity date. Funds may not be withdrawn without penalties, and the maturity dates vary from three months to five years. Interest rates vary depending upon the time to maturity.

8. Between 1979 and 1983 about 20 percent of the nation's S&Ls failed. To help alleviate this situation, the federal government permitted S&Ls to offer NOW and Super NOW accounts, to allocate up to 10 percent of their funds to commercial loans, and to offer mortgage loans with adjustable interest rates based on market conditions. In addition, S&Ls were permitted to offer a variety of other banking services, such as financial counseling to small businesses and credit cards. As a result, S&Ls have become more like commercial banks.

9. Credit unions offer services similar to banks and S&Ls, but differ in their ownership structure. Credit unions are financial cooperatives, owned by members, while banks and savings and loans are often publicly held corporations. Credit unions are also not for profit institutions, while banks and credit unions are profit-making organizations.

10. Nonbanks are financial institutions that accept no deposits but offer many of the services offered by regular banks. Nonbanks include life insurance companies, pension funds, brokerage firms, commercial finance companies, and corporate financial services. The diversity of financial services and investment alternatives offered by nonbanks have caused banks to expand the services they offer. For example, life insurance companies invest the funds they receive from policyholders in corporate and government bonds. In recent years, more insurance companies have begun to provide long-term financing for real estate development projects. In fact, banks today are merging with brokerage firms to offer full service financial assistance. Pension funds typically invest in corporate stocks and bonds, and government securities. Some large pension funds lend money directly to corporations. Brokerage houses have made serious inroads into regular banks' domain by offering high-yield combination savings and checking accounts. In addition, investors can get loans from their broker. In fact, banks today are merging with brokerage firms to offer full-service financial assistance.

Learning Goal 5

11. A. In the case of a bank failure, the FDIC would arrange to have your accounts at that bank transferred to another bank, or pay you off up to $100,000.
B. The FSLIC was established in 1934 to protect the deposits of savings and loan customers, and to create more confidence in the banking industry at a time when many institutions were failing. (Remember, this was during the Great Depression, and hundreds of banks were failing.) As we have studied, in the 1980s S&Ls again began to fail. The government was again responsible for making sure that depositors would get their money back. When the FSLIC began to have financial troubles, the government created the Resolution Trust Corporation, the RTC, to sell the real estate of the failed institutions. To get more control over the banking system, the government placed the FSLIC under the FDIC and gave it the name of The Savings Association Insurance Fund, SAIF.

Learning Goal 6

12. U.S. businesses, through mergers and acquisitions, became much larger and diversified in the 1980s. One company no longer relied on a single product or small variety of products to provide most of its revenue. At the same time, major U.S. firms were creating smaller, more manageable units which are more adaptable to meeting changing customer needs, and these individual units have more freedom to be responsive to the market.

    The same trend is occurring in the banking industry. State banks are offering insurance, engaging in securities sales, and selling real estate. Federal banks will likely enter the same markets, thus reducing their dependence upon deposits and loans for their revenue. Further, as banks diversify, they are changing in size, and mergers are creating huge banks.

13. The U.S. banking system is directly tied to the success of banking and businesses throughout the world. American firms must compete for funds with firms all over the world. If a firm in another country is more efficient than one here in the United States, the more efficient firm will have better access to international funds. Therefore, U.S. businesses must compete not only in the marketplace, but in the financial arena as well.

    Further, today's money markets form a global system, and international bankers will not be nationalistic in their dealings. They will send money to those countries where they can get the best return on their money with an acceptable risk. When the Federal Reserve System makes a move to lower interest rates in the U.S., foreign investors may withdraw their money from the U.S. and put it in countries with higher rates. To be an effective player in the international marketplace and financial worlds, the U.S. must stay financially secure and businesses must stay competitive in world markets.

14. The same practices that led to the financial failure of the S&Ls in the United States are leading to problems in the banking industry in Asia. Countries such as Indonesia, Thailand, and Japan were growing rapidly. Real estate prices skyrocketed. Banks were eager to lend money to real estate investors and other investors. Money poured into those countries from all over the world. Banks became a little careless with their lending practices and took big risks, similar to what happened in the United States.

The problems began in Thailand with the Thai central bank, and spread to other countries in Asia. The value of currencies in many countries dropped, and stock market values fell. While the Asian countries received help from the IMF, the problem is that the people who benefited from those IMF dollars were bankers from around the world who had lent the money to the Asian countries in the first place. They took high risks, but were not forced to suffer the consequences. The policies of the IMF are being challenged. Furthermore, Asian countries are desperate for U.S. dollars and intend to sell their products to the U.S. at greatly reduced prices. This could affect U.S. businesses. In addition, U.S. producers will have trouble selling goods and services in Asia because the people have less money to buy.

PRACTICE TEST

Multiple Choice				True/False			
1.	a	10.	d	1.	T	9.	T
2.	d	11.	c	2.	F	10.	T
3.	c	12.	c	3.	T	11.	F
4.	d	13.	d	4.	F	12.	T
5.	d	14.	a	5.	T	13.	F
6.	b	15.	b	6.	F	14.	T
7.	a	16.	a	7.	T	15.	T
8.	c	17.	c	8.	F	16.	
9.	a	18.	d				

CHAPTER 22
MANAGING PERSONAL FINANCES: THE ROAD TO ENTREPRENEURSHIP

LEARNING GOALS

After you have read and studied this chapter, you should be able to:

1. Describe the six steps one should take to generate capital
2. Explain the best way to preserve capital and begin investing.
3. Compare and contrast various types of life, health, and other insurance alternatives.
4. Outline a strategy for retiring with enough money to last a lifetime.

LEARNING THE LANGUAGE

Listed below are important terms found in this chapter. Choose the correct term for the definition and write it in the space provided.

IRA	Term insurance
Social security	

1. Pure insurance protection for a given number of years is _____.

2. A(n) _____ is a tax-deferred investment plan that enables you and your spouse to save part of your income for retirement.

3. The term _____ is used to describe the Old-Age, Survivors, and Disability Insurance Program established in 1935.

RETENTION CHECK

Learning Goal 1   **The Need for Personal Financial Planning**

1. What are the chances of moving up in management today?

2. How can we start thinking and acting like an entrepreneur?

3. What are six steps you can take today to get control of your finances?

   a. _____

   b. _____

   c. _____

   d. _____

   e. _____

   f. _____

4. What will your personal assets include?

5. What's the best way to keep track of expenses?

6. What should you do to plan for large expenditures?

7. How is running a household's finances like running a small business?

8. Why should you pay off debts as soon as possible?

9. What is the best way to save money?

10. What segment of the population is the fastest growing group of entrepreneurs?

Learning Goal 2 **Building Your Capital Account**

11. How can you accumulate capital?

12. List the steps to take to build a capital account.

   a. _____

   b. _____

   c. _____

13. What are the advantages of investing in real estate (such as a home)?

   a. _____

   b. _____

   c. _____

   d. _____

14. What is the benefit of home ownership with regard to taxes?

15. What is the key element to getting an optimum return on a home?

16. What is one of the worst places to keep long-term investments?

17. What over time has been one of the best places to invest?

Learning Goal 3 **Learning to Manage Credit and Insurance**

18. What are three reasons why credit cards are an important element in a personal financial investment plan?

    a. _____

    b. _____

    c. _____

19. Identify the problems with owning a credit card.

   a. _____

   b. _____

20. What are some reasons for buying life insurance?

   a. _____

   b. _____

   c. _____

   d. _____

21. When do insurance needs decline?

   a. _____

   b. _____

   c. _____

   d. _____

22. What is the danger of not having health and disability insurance?

Learning Goal 4   **Planning Your Retirement**

23. Identify four types of retirement plans

   a. _____

   b. _____

   c. _____

   d. _____

24. What are the problems facing the Social Security system?

25. What could be the result of the problems in the Social Security system?

26. What does a traditional IRA allow for?

27. What is a Roth IRA?

28. What are some sources for IRAs?

29. Why is a traditional IRA a good deal for a young investor without a company sponsored retirement plan?

30. What is the penalty for withdrawing the money from an IRA before the age of 59 and a half?

31. What are the benefits of 401(k) plans?

   a. _____

   b. _____

   c. _____

32. Describe the characteristics of 401(k) plans.

33. Who is a Keogh plan for?

34. What is the advantage of a Keogh plan?

35. What are three ways a Keogh plan is like an IRA?

36. What is a financial planner?

37. What is a financial supermarket?

38. What are some of the areas a financial planner will cover?

CRITICAL THINKING EXERCISES

Learning Goal 1

1. What is the only way to accumulate enough money to start your own business, or to make investments?

2. The six steps to get control of your finances are:

    a. Take an inventory of you financial assets.

    b. Keep track of all of your expenses.

    c. Prepare a budget.

    d. Pay off your debts.

    e. Start a savings plan.

    f. Only borrow money to buy assets that have the potential to increase in value.

    We only have a short period of time, but in at least a week, do as many of these steps as possible:

    Inventory of assets: Do you own a car? house? appliances? stocks? savings account? checking account? collectibles?

Expenses: What do you spend in a day on food? newspapers? travel? supplies?

What do you spend in a month on food? housing? car payments? utilities?

Are you spending more than you are earning? Keep a small notebook handy to record all your spending for one day for a week.

Budget: Listing all your sources of revenue, determine how much you can spend in a month. Set up accounts for money you are going to pay to yourself, for savings, and for major purchases you will want to make sometime in the future as well as for items which may not be paid every month, but will come due eventually, like car or life insurance. Can you spend less than you are making?

Pay off your debts: Can you pay off your credit cards, if you have them? Are there any other debts that can be paid off now?

Start a savings plan: In your budget, did you pay yourself first?

Identify those loans that were for articles which will depreciate in value (educational loans don't count! Your education will help you accumulate capital in the long run!)

It's not easy, is it?

Learning Goal 1, 2

3. "The principle is simple: To accumulate capital, you have to earn more than you spend."

   A. Take a few minutes to think about the way you spend money (beyond money for tuition, books and other school related items.) Using your text for suggestions, list some ways in which you could begin to accumulate capital for the future:

   1. _____

   2. _____

   3. _____

   4. _____

B. Investigate the real estate market in your area. Determine the amount by which home prices in your area have appreciated (or depreciated) in the last 5 years. You can probably find a source for this information in your campus library or on the Internet.

C. Interest on mortgage payments is tax deductible. A typical house payment in the 1990s will range from $800 to $1500 per month, with most of that going toward interest in the early years of the mortgage. Assume that after graduation you are in the 28% tax bracket. If your payments are $1200 per month, what is your real cost?

Learning Goal 2

4. There was talk in the mid 1990s of revising the tax structure in the U.S., and of eliminating the home mortgage interest deduction. What effect could that have on the housing industry? On the price of home you may choose to buy? On the house payment you may be willing to take on?

5. "Plastic!" Credit cards are a helpful tool to the financially careful buyer. If you have credit cards, you are probably aware of the advantages:

Useful for identification

Helpful to keep track of purchases

Convenient, in place of cash

You may also be aware of the disadvantages, primarily high interest rates and the convenience of purchasing something you cannot afford.

A. If you have credit cards, figure the amount you spent last month using each card, and for what purchases. What is the interest rate on your cards? Did you make purchases you would not have made without the card?

B. Look at the budget you developed earlier. Do you have an account for credit card payments? Did you budget to pay the entire amount, or only a portion of the bill?

C. How much did you pay in interest on credit card accounts over the last six months? The last year? You could have increased your capital account by that amount.

Learning Goal 3

6. Why should young couples invest in life insurance? What other kinds of insurance should you have?

Learning Goal 4

7. Compare and contrast a Keogh, 401(K) and an IRA.

PRACTICE TEST

Multiple Choice: Circle the best answer.

1. The chances of finding an excellent job and moving up through management today are:

    a. the best they have ever been.
    b. better than they were in the last 10 years, but not as good as it will be.
    c. less today than in the past.
    d. virtually nonexistent.

2. The first step in taking control of your finances should be:

    a. Keep track of all your expenses.
    b. Prepare a budget.
    c. Pay off your debts.
    d. Take an inventory of your assets.

3. Jerry and Jane are having a discussion about their finances. They are wondering what to do about the amount of money they are spending, how to control their financial situation as well, and how to reach their financial goals. One technique to help them would be to:

    a. prepare a budget.
    b. do an asset inventory.
    c. develop an income statement.
    d. quit spending money on anything but the bare basics.

4. When planning for the future, an investment in a college education will:

    a. provide you with a new ideas.
    b. give you a chance to learn about different ways of life.
    c. improve your earning potential.
    d. all of the above.

5. To accumulate capital you have to:

   a. get the highest paying job you can find.
   b. earn more than you spend.
   c. borrow money and invest.
   d. buy assets which appreciate in value.

6. Historically, one of the better investments a person can make is in:

   a. a home.
   b. cars.
   c. credit cards.
   d. an apartment.

7. From a financial standpoint, it is best to buy:

   a. the largest home you can find in an neighborhood where homes are less expensive.
   b. the smallest home in the best neighborhood.
   c. the smallest home in the least expensive neighborhood.
   d. the largest home in the most expensive neighborhood you can find.

8. One of the dangers of a credit card is that:

   a. it is difficult to keep track of purchases.
   b. it can be an inconvenience carrying too many credit cards around.
   c. merchants won't accept credit cards as a form of identification.
   d. consumers may buy goods they wouldn't normally buy if they had to pay cash.

9. Today, the preferred form of life insurance is called:

   a. Universal life insurance
   b. Term life insurance
   c. Variable life insurance
   d. Whole life insurance

10. Which of the following is not likely to happen with the Social Security system in the future?

    a. Serious cuts in benefits
    b. Reduced cost of living adjustments
    c. Later retirement age to collect
    d. Lower social security taxes

11. A tax-deferred retirement plan that can be used as a supplement to a company sponsored plan is

    a. a traditional IRA.
    b. 401(k) plan.
    c. a Keogh plan.
    d. a traditional savings account.

12. The funds and earnings in a traditional IRA account

    a. are taxed as you go along.
    b. are not taxed.
    c. are subject to double taxation.
    d. are not taxed until they are withdrawn.

TRUE/FALSE

1. ____ In developing an income statement for yourself, your pay check would be considered as revenue.

2. ____ One of the best ways to keep track of your expenses is to carry a notepad with you everywhere you go and record what you spend as you go through the day.

3. ____ The first thing you should do with any extra money you have is buy an asset which will appreciate in value.

4. ____ Statistics indicate that a majority of the population in the U.S. has accumulated enough money by retirement to live comfortably.

5. ____ The first steps to accumulating capital are finding employment and living frugally.

6. ____ One of the investment benefits of owning a home is that it is a way of forced savings.

7. ____ Home ownership generally provides few tax advantages.

8. ____ For young investors, one of the best places to keep your long-term investments is in a bank or savings and loan.

9. ____ Credit card limits prevent people from spending too much with a credit card.

10. ____ Other than life insurance, you should also carry health, disability, and auto insurance policies.

11. ____ Significant changes are expected to occur in the Social Security system as the number of people retiring and living longer is increasing.

12. ____ One of the benefits of a 401(k) plan is that employers often match part of your deposit.

ANSWERS

LEARNING THE LANGUAGE

1. Term insurance	3. Social Security
2. IRA	

RETENTION CHECK

Learning Goal 1   **The Need for Personal Financial Planning**

1. The chance for finding an excellent job and then moving up through management is much less today than it was in the past. Many middle management jobs have been eliminated so there are many people competing for fewer and fewer management jobs.

2. To start thinking and acting like an entrepreneur, we can learn to manage our own careers and finances by planning, budgeting, controlling, and being self-disciplined.

3.   a. Take an inventory of your financial assets.
   b. Keep track of all your expenses.
   c. Prepare a budget.
   d. Pay off your debts.
   e. Start a savings plan.
   f. If you have to borrow money, only borrow it to buy assets that have the potential to increase in value.

4. Personal assets include such items as a TV, VCR, computer, bicycle, car, jewelry and clothes, as well as savings.

5. You won't believe how much you "fritter away" on miscellaneous items unless you keep a detailed record The best way to keep track of expenses is to carry a notepad with you wherever you go and record what you spend as you go through the day. At the end of the week, record your journal entries into a record book. Develop certain categories to make the task easier and more informative.

6. For large expenditures, it is a good idea to save a certain amount each month in a separate account. When it comes time to make that purchase, you have the cash so you won't have to pay any finance charges.

7. It takes the same careful record keeping, the same budgeting process and forecasting, the same control procedures and the same need to periodically borrow funds to run a household's finances as it does to run a small business.

8. Debts often carry high interest rates. Credit card debt may be costing you 16 percent or more a year. It's better to pay off the debt at 16 percent than to put the money in the bank earning only 5 percent or so.

9. The best way to save money is to pay yourself first. That is, take your paycheck, take out money for savings, and then plan what to do with the rest.

10. Generation Xers, people in their twenties and early thirties, represent the fastest-growing segment of the American population starting their own companies.

Learning Goal 2 **Building Your Capital Account**

11. To accumulate capital, you have to earn more than you spend.

12. a. Find a job.
    b. Live frugally
    c. Invest in a home when you have accumulated the money.

13. a. A home is an investment you can live in.
    b. Payments are relatively fixed.
    c. It is a good way to force yourself to save.
    d. Interest on home mortgages is tax deductible.

14. Interest on mortgage payments and real estate taxes are tax deductible. During the first few years, almost all the mortgage payments go for interest on the loan so almost all the early payments are tax deductible.

15. The key element to getting the optimum return on a home is a good location.

16. One of the worst places for young people to keep long-term investments is in a bank or savings and loan.

17. One of the best places to invest over time has been the stock market.

Learning Goal 3   **Learning to Manage Credit and Insurance**

18.
   a. Credit cards are needed as a form of identification.
   b. They are a way to keep track of purchases.
   c. Credit cards are convenient.

19.
   a. Consumers are tempted to make purchases they would not make if they had to pay cash or write a check, and pile up debt as a result.
   b. High rates of interest

20.
   a. Children are young and need money for education.
   b. Mortgage is high relative to income.
   c. Often there are auto payments and other bills survivors have to pay.
   d. Loss of income would be disastrous.

21.
   a. Children are grown.
   b. Mortgage is low or completely paid off.
   c. Insurance needs are few.
   d. Retirement income is needed.

22. Hospital costs are too high to risk financial ruin by going uninsured. It is a good idea to supplement health insurance policies with disability insurance that pays part of the cost of a long-term sickness or an accident.

Learning Goal 4   **Planning Your Retirement**

23.   a. Social Security
       b. IRAs
       c. 401(K) plans
       d. Keogh plans

24. The problem with the Social Security system is that the number of workers paying into Social Security is declining, but the number of people retiring and living longer is increasing dramatically.

25. The result of problems in the Social Security system is likely to be serious cuts in benefits, a much later retirement age, reduced cost of living adjustments and/or much higher Social Security taxes.

26. A traditional IRA allows people who qualify to deduct the money they put into an IRA account from their reported income.

27. A Roth IRA is the newest kind of IRA. People who invest in this kind of IRA don't get up-front deductions on their taxes, but withdrawals are tax-free.

28. Some choices for IRAs included a local bank, savings and loan or credit union. Insurance companies also offer IRAs. You can also put funds into stocks, bonds, mutual funds, or precious metals.

29. A traditional IRA is a good deal for a young investor because the invested money is not taxed. That means fast good returns, tax free.

30. If you take the money out of an IRA before you are 59 and a half years you will pay a 10 percent penalty and pay taxes on the income.

31. The benefits of 401(k) plans are:

    a. The money you put in reduces your present taxable income.
    b. Tax is deferred on the earnings.
    c. Employers often match part of your deposit.

32. Normally you can't withdraw funds from this account until you are 59, but often you can borrow from the account. You can usually select how the money in the plan is invested: stocks, bonds, and in some cases real estate.

33. A Keogh plan is for small business people who don't have the benefit of a corporate retirement system.

34. The advantage of Keogh plans is that the maximum that can be invested is more than $30,000 per year.

35. A Keogh plan is like an IRA because funds and returns aren't taxed until they are withdrawn. As with an IRA account, there is a 10 percent penalty for early withdrawal. Also, funds may be withdrawn in a lump sum or spread out over the years like an IRA.

36. A financial planner assists in developing a comprehensive program that covers investments, taxes, insurance, and other financial matters.

37. A financial supermarket provides a wide variety of financial services ranging from banking services to mutual funds, insurance, tax assistance, stocks, bonds, and real estate.

38. Most financial planners begin with life insurance, and explore health and disability insurance. Financial planning covers all aspects of investing all the way to retirement and death. A financial planner can steer you into the proper mix of IRA investments, stocks, bonds, precious metals, real estate and so on.

CRITICAL THINKING EXERCISES

Learning Goal 1

1. The only way to accumulate enough money to start your own business or to make investments is to make more than you spend. There are six steps to get control of your finances and build a capital account, including: taking an inventory of your assets, keeping track of all your expenses, preparing a budget, paying off your debts, starting a savings plan, and only borrowing money to buy assets which will increase in value.

2. Obviously, everyone will have different answers. This is primarily to get you started on the road to good personal financial planning!

Learning Goals 1, 2

3. A. This is another section where each individual will have varied answers. Some suggestions may include: living at home while going to school, buying used books, keep clothing allowances to a minimum, walking or riding a bike when you can, eating at home, or if you are in a house or apartment, making meals at home. For students returning to school after being out for a while, the methods of accumulating capital will be different—and you may already have discovered ways of your own!
B. Prices in different parts of the country vary widely. Some areas that have been hit by unemployment may have seen a decline in the price of homes. Other areas may have seen above average increases.
C. Your real cost will be $864 with an interest deduction.

Learning Goal 2

4. The housing industry could be negatively affected by a change in the tax laws, if we assume that the interest deduction is a major factor in the decision to buy a house. People will probably still be interested in owning a home for its advantages of fixed payments and living convenience as well as the appreciation factor. The price of home an individual may choose to buy might change, and probably, the house payment people are willing to take on will go down if there is no mortgage interest deduction incentive.

5. Your answers will vary. If you have no credit cards yet, use this information to make good decisions about whether to apply for a credit card, and how to use it.

Learning Goal 3

6. Because so many couples today are two career families, the loss of the income of one spouse can have a devastating financial effect. It is for that reason that young couples need to invest in some kind of life insurance plan. Health insurance is necessary because of the high cost of medical care. Disability insurance is needed to make up for lost income in the event one spouse is injured and can 't work for an extended period, or at all.

Learning Goal 7

7. The money invested in an IRA is not taxed. Earnings are not taxed until you take them out when you retire, presumably when you are at a lower tax rate. The money cannot be taken out until the age of 59 without paying a penalty. An IRA is for workers to use as a supplement to a company-sponsored retirement plan and Social Security. It is not connected with your employer. A 401(K) plan is offered by employers, who will often match your contribution. Further, you can borrow the funds from a 401(K), whereas that isn't an option in an IRA.

The Keogh plan is for small business people who do not have the benefit of a corporate retirement system, whereas the 401(K) is a company sponsored program. The benefit over an IRA is that the maximum amount that can be invested is much greater.

A Keogh is like an IRA and the 401(K) in that the funds are not taxed, nor are the earnings, and there is a penalty for early withdrawal. All these plans are designed to protect people from the decline in the value of the Social Security system.

PRACTICE TEST

Multiple Choice				True/False			
1.	c	7.	b	1.	T	7.	F
2.	d	8.	d	2.	T	8.	F
3.	a	9.	b	3.	F	9.	F
4.	d	10.	d	4.	F	10.	T
5.	b	11.	a	5.	T	11.	T
6.	a	12.	d	6.	T	12.	T

APPENDIX
MANAGING RISK

LEARNING THE LANGUAGE

Listed here are important terms found in this appendix. Choose the correct term for each definition below and write it in the space provided.

Health maintenance organizations (HMOs)	Pure risk
Insurable interest	Risk
Insurable risk	Rule of indemnity
Insurance policy	Self-insurance
Law of large numbers	Speculative risk
Mutual insurance company	Stock insurance company
Preferred provider organization (PPOs)	Uninsurable risk
Premium	

1. A _____ is a type of insurance company owned by stockholders.

2. A written contract known as a(n) _____ is between the insured and an insurance company that promises to pay for all or part of a loss.

3. The _____ says that an insured person or organization cannot collect more than the actual loss from an insurable risk.

4. The threat of loss with no chance of profit is called _____.

5. The _____ is a principle that if a large number of people are exposed to the same risk, a predictable number of losses will occur during a given period.

6. A chance of either profit or loss is called _____.

7. The chance of loss, the degree of probability of loss, and the amount of possible loss is called _____.

8. A _____ is a type of insurance company owned by its policyholders.

9. Health care organizations known as _____ require members to choose from a restricted list of doctors.

10. The fee charged by an insurance company for an insurance policy is a _____.

11. An _____ is one that no insurance company will cover.

12. The practice of setting aside money to cover routine claims and buying only "catastrophe" policies to cover big losses is called _____.

13. An _____ is a risk that the typical insurance company will cover.

14. Health care organizations, which allow members to choose their own physicians for a fee, are called _____.

15. The possibility of the policyholder to suffer a loss is called _____.

RETENTION CHECK

Learning Goal 1 **Managing Risk**

1. What are two kinds of risk?

    a. _____

    b. _____

2. What is the difference between the two?

3. Which kind of risk is of most concern to business people?

4. List four methods businesses use to manage pure risk.

   a. _____   c. _____

   b. _____   d. _____

5. What is the best way to reduce risk?

6. How do some companies avoid risk?

7. Why are some firms turning to self-insurance?

8. When is self-insurance most appropriate?

Learning Goal 2 **Buying Insurance to Cover Risk**

9. What are four kinds of uninsurable risk?

   a. _____

   b. _____

   c. _____

   d. _____

10. Identify the guidelines used to evaluate whether or not a risk is insurable.

   a. _____

   b. _____

   c. _____

   d. _____

   e. _____

11. How are the premiums for an insurance policy determined?

12. What is the difference between a stock insurance company and a mutual insurance company?

Learning Goal 3   **Types of Insurance**

13. What are six types of insurance to cover losses?

   a. _____   d. _____

   b. _____   e. _____

   c. _____   f. _____

14. What are three major options for health insurance?

15. What are some features of an HMO?

16. What are some complaints about HMOs?

17. What are some characteristics of a PPO?

18. Why do most businesses and individuals choose to join an HMO or a PPO?

19. Describe disability insurance.

20. Who provides worker's compensation and what does it guarantee?

21. Who does professional liability insurance cover?

22. What is product liability insurance?

23. Name four kinds of property and liability insurance.

    a. _____

    b. _____

    c. _____

    d. _____

24. Identify three kinds of health insurance.

    a. _____

    b. _____

    c. _____

25. What are four kinds of life insurance?

    a. _____

    b. _____

    c. _____

    d. _____

Learning Goal 4 **The Risk of Damaging the Environment**

26. What are some environmental risks we are facing?

CRITICAL THINKING EXERCISES

1. Businesses have four options to avoid losses stemming from pure risk situations.

    a. Reduce the risk.　　　　c. Buy insurance to cover the risk.

    b. Avoid the risk.　　　　d. Self-insure against the risk.

    Read the following situations, and determine which option the firm is choosing in each case.

    a. The president of an asbestos removal firm in Merriam, Kansas, closed his firm for four months.

    b. A group of 27 accounting firms formed its own insurance company to insure themselves.

    c. Workers and visitors on construction sites are required to wear hard hats.

    d. Senoret Chemical Company experienced a 1600% increase in its liability coverage premium.

2. Many variables determine which risks are insurable. Using your text, determine which of the following situations would constitute an insurable risk.

    a. TNG Enterprises would like to buy insurance to cover loss of computer equipment from power surges and possible spills.

    b. Gilmores, Inc., a retail store in Kalamazoo, would like to insure against losses occurring when a competitor, Steketees, implements an aggressive marketing campaign.

    c. Chrysler wants to buy insurance to cover losses created by a breakdown with their robotic and computer driven manufacturing systems.

    d. PPI, a small manufacturing firm, wants to insure themselves against losses created by damage from a fire set accidentally.

e. Residents in Morgan City, Louisiana, East Lansing, Michigan, and Valley Park, Missouri, want to buy flood insurance.

f. Residents of Morgan City, Louisiana, however, face a high risk of flooding, because the Mississippi river is cutting a new tributary through that city, and floods regularly.

g. Boeing has extensive contracts with the government to build fighter planes. The company wants insurance to cover losses that may occur if Congress cuts the defense budget by over 20%.

3. What are the areas covered by public liability insurance?

4. Distinguish between HMOs and PPOs.

PRACTICE TEST

Multiple Choice: Circle the best answer.

1. When Macy's orders inventory for the Christmas season, the company has to predict what their customers will want to buy that season. The kind of risk being described is:

    a. speculative risk.
    b. pure risk.
    c. insurable risk.
    d. self-insurance.

2. Which of the following is not one of the options a firm has available to manage risk?

    a. Reduce the risk.
    b. Avoid the risk.
    c. Buy insurance against the risk.
    d. Find another company to take the risk.

3. It is when a company has several widely distributed facilities that _____ is the most appropriate.

    a. Reducing the risk.
    b. Avoiding the risk.
    c. Self-insurance.
    d. Finding another company to take the risk.

4. An insurable risk is one in which:

    a. the loss is measurable.
    b. the loss is not accidental.
    c. the risk is dispersed.
    d. the policyholder has no insurable interest.

5. The idea that an insured person or organization cannot collect more than the actual loss from an insurable risk is called the:

    a. law of large numbers.
    b. rule of indemnity.
    c. disability insurance.
    d. insurable interest.

6. A type of insurance that requires members to choose from a restricted list of doctors is called a:

   a. health maintenance organization.
   b. preferred provider organization.
   c. disability insurance.
   d. professional liability insurance.

7. Disability insurance:

   a. replaces all your income if you become disabled.
   b. starts immediately after your disability.
   c. is required from employers.
   d. replaces a portion of your income.

8. Which of the following is not a type of property and liability insurance?

   a. Professional liability
   b. Credit life insurance
   c. Business interruption insurance
   d. Computer coverage

9. If a person is injured when using a product and sues the manufacturer, the company is covered by:

   a. workers compensation.
   b. disability insurance.
   c. product liability insurance.
   d. business interruption insurance.

10. Which of the following is not an environmental risk faced by businesses?

    a. Tornadoes
    b. Global warming
    c. Nuclear issues
    d. Damage to the ozone

TRUE/FALSE

1. _____ A firm can reduce risk by establishing loss prevention programs such as fire drills, health education and accident prevention programs.

2. _____ One type of risk that cannot be covered is loss from accidental injury.

3. _____ The rule of indemnity is the principle that if a large number of people are exposed to the same risk, a predictable number of losses will occur during a given period.

4. _____ One of the complaints about an HMO is that members can't choose their own doctors.

5. _____ To save money, HMOs generally must approve treatment before it is given.

6. _____ PPOs are less expensive than HMOs because you can choose your own doctor.

7. _____ Employers are required to provide worker's compensation insurance.

8. _____ Many professionals other than doctors and lawyers are buying malpractice insurance.

ANSWERS

LEARNING THE LANGUAGE

1. Stock insurance company	9. Health maintenance organization (HMO)
2. Insurance policy	10. Premium
3. Rule of indemnity	11. Uninsurable risk
4. Pure risk	12 Self-insurance
5. Law of large numbers	13. Insurable risk
6. Speculative risk	14. Preferred provider organization (PPO)
7. Risk	15. Insurable interest
8. Mutual insurance company	

RETENTION CHECK

Managing Risk

1.   a. speculative risk
      b. pure risk

2.   Speculative risk involves a chance of either profit or loss. It includes the chance the firm takes to make extra money by buying new machinery, acquiring more inventory and making other decisions in which the probability of loss may be relatively low and the amount of loss is known. An entrepreneur takes speculative risk on the chance of making a profit.

     Pure risk is the threat of loss with no chance for profit. It involves the threat of fire, accident or loss. If such events occur, a company loses money, but if the events do not occur, the company gains nothing.

3.   The risk that is of most concern to businesspeople is pure risk.

4.   Firms can manage risk by:
     a. reducing the risk.
     b. avoiding the risk.
     c. self-insuring against the risk.
     d. buying insurance against the risk.

5.   A firm can reduce risk by establishing loss-prevention programs such as fire drills, health education, safety inspections, equipment maintenance, and accident prevention programs.

Retail stores use mirrors, video cameras, and other devices to prevent shoplifting for example.

6. Companies avoid risk by not accepting hazardous jobs and by outsourcing shipping and other functions. For example, the threat of lawsuits has driven away some drug companies from manufacturing vaccines, and some consulting engineers refuse to work on hazardous sites.

7. Many companies and municipalities have turned to self-insurance because they either can't find or can't afford conventional policies. Such firms set aside money to cover routine claims and buy only "catastrophe" policies to cover big losses. Self-insurance lowers the cost of insurance by allowing companies to take out insurance only for large losses.

8. Self insurance is most appropriate when a firm has several widely distributed facilities.

Buying Insurance to Cover Risk

9.
   a. Market risks (from price changes, style changes, new products).
   b. Political risks (from war or government restrictions)
   c. Personal risks (from loss of job)
   d. Risks of operation (strikes or inefficient machinery)

10. An insurable risk is evaluated using the following criteria:
    a. The policyholder must have an insurable interest.
    b. The loss should be measurable.
    c. The chance of loss should be measurable.
    d. The loss should be accidental.
    e. The risk should be dispersed.

11. Premiums for insurance policies are determined by using the law of large numbers. This states that if a large number of people or organizations are exposed to the same risk, a predictable number of losses will occur. The higher the risk the higher the potential cost to the company, and the higher the premium. Today, however, higher premiums are being charged to cover higher anticipated court costs and damage awards.

12. Stock insurance companies are owned by stockholders, like any other investor-owned company. Mutual insurance companies are owned by their policyholders. A mutual insurance company does not earn profits for its owners. It is a nonprofit organization, and any excess funds go to the policyholders/investors in the form of dividends or premium reductions.

Types of Insurance

13. a. health insurance
     b. liability insurance
     c. disability insurance
     d. worker's compensation
     e. life insurance
     f. "other"

14. Three major options for health insurance are health care providers, such as Blue Cross/Blue Shield, health maintenance organizations (HMOs) and preferred provider organizations (PPOs).

15. HMOs offer a full range of health care benefits. Emphasis is on helping members stay healthy instead of on treating illnesses. Members do not receive bills and do not have to fill out claim forms for routine service. HMOs employ or contract with doctors, hospitals and other systems of health care and members must use those providers. HMOs are less expensive than comprehensive health insurance providers.

16. Members complain about not being able to choose doctors or getting the care they want or need. Some physicians complain that they lose some freedom to do what is needed to make people well and they often receive less compensation than they feel is appropriate for the services they provide.

17. Preferred provider organizations contract with hospitals and doctors, but do not require members to choose only from those physicians. Members have to pay more if they don't use a doctor on the preferred list. Also members have to pay a deductible before the PPO will pay any bills. When the plan does pay, members usually have to pay part of the bill. This payment is called co-insurance.

18. Most individuals and businesses choose to join a PPO or an HMO because they can cost as much as 80 percent less than comprehensive individual health insurance policies.

19. Disability insurance replaces part of your income if you become disabled and unable to work. Usually, before you can begin collecting there is a period of time you must be disabled. Many employers provide this type of insurance, but some do not.

20. Worker's compensation insurance guarantees payment of wages, medical care, and rehabilitation services for employees who are injured on the job. Employers in all 50 states are required to provide this type of insurance.

21. Professional liability insurance covers people who are found liable for professional negligence, such as lawyers, doctors, dentists, mortgage brokers, and real estate appraisers.

22. Product liability insurance provides coverage against liability arising out of products sold.

23. a. fire
    b. automobile
    c. computer coverage
    d. professional liability

24. a. basic health insurance
    b. major medical
    c. hospitalization

25. a. group life insurance
    b. owner or key executive insurance
    c. term life insurance
    d. credit life insurance

26. Some environmental threats included global warming and resulting damage to the ozone level, chemical gas leaks, and nuclear issues.

CRITICAL THINKING EXERCISES

1. a. Avoid risk
   b. Self-insure against the risk
   c. Reduce the risk
   d. Buy insurance to cover the risk.

2. a. Yes, companies can buy insurance against the loss of computer equipment.
   b. No, this would be an uninsurable risk.
   c. No, a company cannot insure against inefficient machinery or machinery that breaks down or doesn't work.
   d. Yes fire damage can be insured against.
   e. Yes, probably, unless the occurrence of loss has been too high.
   f. No, most likely because the probability of flooding in Morgan City is too high.
   g. No this would be a "political risk" and is uninsurable.

3. Some state and federal agencies provide insurance protection, which is known as public insurance. Some forms of public insurance are unemployment compensation, for unemployed workers, Social Security which provides retirement, health and disability insurance, the FHA, Federal Housing Administration, which provides mortgage insurance, and National Flood Insurance. Other types of insurance are provided to property owners in high-crime areas, compensation for damaged crops and insurance against pension loss if a company declares bankruptcy.

4. Health maintenance organizations and PPOs have a number of similarities. Both contract with hospitals and doctors. However, while HMOs require members to use the doctors in the plan, preferred provider organizations allow members to choose from other doctors, at a cost. HMOs are less expensive than PPOs for that reason, and because they generally do not require a co-insurance payment, as PPOs require.

PRACTICE TEST

Multiple Choice				True/False			
1.	a	6.	a	1.	T	5.	T
2.	d	7.	d	2.	F	6.	F
3.	c	8.	c	3.	F	7.	T
4.	c	9.	c	4.	T	8.	T
5.	b	10.	a				